BIRDS
of the
GREAT PLAINS

Bob Jennings
Ted T. Cable
Roger Burrows

with contributions from
Chris Fisher & Andy Bezener

LONE
PINE

Lone Pine Publishing International

The Distributor: Lone Pine Publishing
1808 B Street NW, Suite 140
Auburn, WA, USA 98001

Website: www.lonepinepublishing.com

Library and Archives Canada Cataloguing in Publication

Jennings, Bob
        Birds of the Great Plains / Bob Jennings, Ted T. Cable, Roger Burrows.

Includes bibliographical references and index.
ISBN-13 978-1-55105-369-1.—ISBN-10 1-55105-369-1

        1. Birds—Great Plains—Identification. I. Cable, Ted T.
II. Burrows, Roger, 1942– III. Title.

QL683.G68J45 2005   598'.0978   C2004-905302-7

Cover Illustration: Gary Ross
Illustrations: Gary Ross, Ted Nordhagen, Eva Pluciennik
Scanning & Digital Film: Elite Lithographers Co.

PC: P1

CONTENTS

ACKNOWLEDGMENTS

"The geese pass swiftly, but the song does not. I sit in the growing dusk and remember the gift sent down. I cannot fly and I cannot match their song, but I can, for a moment, find their freedom within myself. It is enough."
—*From the Stump,* Bob Jennings

Bob Jennings passed away in the fall of 2004 and was unable to see this book in its final stages. His wife requested that Ted T. Cable be consulted for the remainder of the project, and Ted's support has been invaluable. We hope that any changes made in the later stages of this project reflect Bob's intentions for the book, and we trust that he would be proud of this book in its final form. We feel blessed to have been touched by his enthusiasm for the natural world and by his humor, and we are pleased that some of his personality and knowledge live on within the pages of this book.
—Editorial staff at Lone Pine Publishing

Thanks are extended to the growing family of ornithologists and dedicated birders who have offered their inspiration and expertise to help build Lone Pine's expanding library of field guides. Thanks also go to John Acorn, Chris Fisher, Andy Bezener and Eloise Pulos for their contributions to previous books in this series. In addition, thank you to Gary Ross, Ted Nordhagen and Ewa Pluciennik, whose skilled illustrations have brought each page to life.

Greater White-fronted Goose
size 30 in • p. 35

Snow Goose
size 31 in • p. 36

Ross's Goose
size 24 in • p. 37

Canada Goose
size 35 in • p. 38

Trumpeter Swan
size 66 in • p. 39

Tundra Swan
size 54 in • p. 40

Wood Duck
size 17 in • p. 41

Gadwall
size 20 in • p. 42

American Wigeon
size 20 in • p. 43

Mallard
size 24 in • p. 44

Blue-winged Teal
size 15 in • p. 45

Cinnamon Teal
size 16 in • p. 46

Northern Shoveler
size 19 in • p. 47

Northern Pintail
size 23 in • p. 48

Green-winged Teal
size 14 in • p. 49

Canvasback
size 20 in • p. 50

Redhead
size 20 in • p. 51

Ring-necked Duck
size 16 in • p. 52

Lesser Scaup
size 16 in • p. 53

Surf Scoter
size 18 in • p. 54

White-winged Scoter
size 21 in • p. 55

Black Scoter
size 18 in • p. 56

Long-tailed Duck
size 18 in • p. 57

Bufflehead
size 14 in • p. 58

Common Goldeneye
size 18 in • p. 59

Hooded Merganser
size 17 in • p. 60

WATERFOWL

Common Merganser
size 25 in • p. 61

Red-breasted Merganser
size 23 in • p. 62

Ruddy Duck
size 15 in • p. 63

GROUSE & ALLIES

Gray Partridge
size 12 in • p. 64

Ring-necked Pheasant
size 33 in • p. 65

Ruffed Grouse
size 17 in • p. 66

Sharp-tailed Grouse
size 17 in • p. 67

Greater Prairie-Chicken
size 17 in • p. 68

Lesser Prairie-Chicken
size 16 in • p. 69

Wild Turkey
size 3 ft • p. 70

Scaled Quail
size 11 in • p. 71

Northern Bobwhite
size 10 in • p. 72

DIVING BIRDS

Common Loon
size 32 in • p. 73

Pied-billed Grebe
size 13 in • p. 74

Horned Grebe
size 13 in • p. 75

Red-necked Grebe
size 19 in • p. 76

Eared Grebe
size 13 in • p. 77

Western Grebe
size 25 in • p. 78

American White Pelican
size 65 in • p. 79

Double-crested Cormorant
size 29 in • p. 80

HERONLIKE BIRDS

American Bittern
size 25 in • p. 81

Least Bittern
size 12 in • p. 82

Great Blue Heron
size 51 in • p. 83

Great Egret
size 39 in • p. 84

Snowy Egret
size 24 in • p. 85

Little Blue Heron
size 24 in • p. 86

Cattle Egret
size 20 in • p. 87

Green Heron
size 18 in • p. 88

Black-crowned Night-Heron
size 24 in • p. 89

Yellow-crowned Night-Heron
size 24 in • p. 90

White-faced Ibis
size 25 in • p. 91

Turkey Vulture
size 28 in • p. 92

Osprey
size 23 in • p. 93

Mississippi Kite
size 14 in • p. 94

Bald Eagle
size 37 in • p. 95

Northern Harrier
size 20 in • p. 96

Sharp-shinned Hawk
size 11 in • p. 97

Cooper's Hawk
size 16 in • p. 98

Northern Goshawk
size 23 • p. 99

Red-shouldered Hawk
size 19 in • p. 100

Broad-winged Hawk
size 16 in • p. 101

Swainson's Hawk
size 20 in • p. 102

Red-tailed Hawk
size 20 in • p. 103

Ferruginous Hawk
size 23 in • p. 104

Rough-legged Hawk
size 21 in • p. 105

Golden Eagle
size 35 in • p. 106

American Kestrel
size 8 in • p. 107

Merlin
size 11 in • p. 108

Peregrine Falcon
size 16 in • p. 109

Prairie Falcon
size 16 in • p. 110

Yellow Rail
size 7 in • p. 111

Black Rail
size 6 in • p. 112

RAILS, COOTS & CRANES

King Rail
size 15 in • p. 113

Virginia Rail
size 10 in • p. 114

Sora
size 9 in • p. 115

Common Moorhen
size 13 in • p. 116

American Coot
size 14 in • p. 117

Sandhill Crane
size 4 ft • p. 118

SHOREBIRDS

Black-bellied Plover
size 12 in • p. 119

American Golden-Plover
size 10 in • p. 120

Snowy Plover
size 7 in • p. 121

Semipalmated Plover
size 7 in • p. 122

Piping Plover
size 7 in • p. 123

Killdeer
size 10 in • p. 124

Mountain Plover
size 9 in • p. 125

Black-necked Stilt
size 14 in • p. 126

American Avocet
size 17 in • p. 127

Greater Yellowlegs
size 14 in • p. 128

Lesser Yellowlegs
size 10 in • p. 129

Solitary Sandpiper
size 8 in • p. 130

Willet
size 15 in • p. 131

Spotted Sandpiper
size 7 in • p. 132

Upland Sandpiper
size 11 in • p. 133

Whimbrel
size 18 in • p. 134

Long-billed Curlew
size 23 in • p. 135

Hudsonian Godwit
size 14 in • p. 136

Marbled Godwit
size 18 in • p. 137

Semipalmated Sandpiper
size 6 in • p. 138

Western Sandpiper
size 6 in • p. 139

Least Sandpiper
size 6 in • p. 140

White-rumped Sandpiper
size 7 in • p. 141

Baird's Sandpiper
size 7 in • p. 142

Pectoral Sandpiper
size 9 in • p. 143

Dunlin
size 8 in • p. 144

Stilt Sandpiper
size 8 in • p. 145

Buff-breasted Sandpiper
size 8 in • p. 146

Short-billed Dowitcher
size 11 in • p. 147

Long-billed Dowitcher
size 12 in • p. 148

Wilson's Snipe
size 11 in • p. 149

American Woodcock
size 11 in • p. 150

Wilson's Phalarope
size 9 in • p. 151

Red-necked Phalarope
size 7 in • p. 152

Franklin's Gull
size 14 in • p. 153

Bonaparte's Gull
size 13 in • p. 154

Ring-billed Gull
size 19 in • p. 155

California Gull
size 19 in • p. 156

Herring Gull
size 24 in • p. 157

Common Tern
size 15 in • p. 158

Forster's Tern
size 15 in • p. 159

Least Tern
size 9 in • p. 160

Black Tern
size 9 in • p. 161

Rock Pigeon
size 12 in • p. 162

Mourning Dove
size 12 in • p. 163

DOVES, CUCKOOS & ROADRUNNERS

Black-billed Cuckoo
size 12 in • p. 164

Yellow-billed Cuckoo
size 12 in • p. 165

Greater Roadrunner
size 23 in • p. 166

OWLS

Barn Owl
size 15 in • p. 167

Eastern Screech-Owl
size 8 in • p. 168

Great Horned Owl
size 22 in • p. 169

Snowy Owl
size 24 in • p. 170

Burrowing Owl
size 8 in • p. 171

Barred Owl
size 20 in • p. 172

Long-eared Owl
size 14 in • p. 173

Short-eared Owl
size 15 in • p. 174

Northern Saw-whet Owl
size 8 in • p. 175

NIGHTJARS, SWIFTS & HUMMINGBIRDS

Common Nighthawk
size 9 in • p. 176

Common Poorwill
size 8 in • p. 177

Chuck-will's-widow
size 12 in • p. 178

Whip-poor-will
size 9 in • p. 179

Chimney Swift
size 5 in • p. 180

White-throated Swift
size 6 in • p. 181

Ruby-throated Hummingbird
size 4 in • p. 182

Belted Kingfisher
size 12 in • p. 183

WOODPECKERS

Lewis's Woodpecker
size 11 in • p. 184

Red-headed Woodpecker
size 9 in • p. 185

Red-bellied Woodpecker
size 10 in • p. 186

Yellow-bellied Sapsucker
size 8 in • p. 187

Ladder-backed Woodpecker
size 7 in • p. 188

Downy Woodpecker
size 6 in • p. 189

Hairy Woodpecker
size 9 in • p. 190

Northern Flicker
size 13 in • p. 191

Pileated Woodpecker
size 17 in • p. 192

Olive-sided Flycatcher
size 7 in • p. 194

Western Wood-Pewee
size 6 in • p. 195

Eastern Wood-Pewee
size 6 in • p. 196

Yellow-bellied Flycatcher
size 5 in • p. 197

Acadian Flycatcher
size 6 in • p. 198

Alder Flycatcher
size 6 in • p. 199

Willow Flycatcher
size 6 in • p. 200

Least Flycatcher
size 5 in • p. 201

Eastern Phoebe
size 7 in • p. 202

Say's Phoebe
size 7 in • p. 203

Ash-throated Flycatcher
size 7 in • p. 204

Great Crested Flycatcher
size 8 in • p. 205

Western Kingbird
size 8 in • p. 206

Eastern Kingbird
size 8 in • p. 207

Scissor-tailed Flycatcher
size 13 in • p. 208

Loggerhead Shrike
size 9 in • p. 209

Northern Shrike
size 10 in • p. 210

White-eyed Vireo
size 5 in • p. 211

Bell's Vireo
size 5 in • p. 212

Yellow-throated Vireo
size 5 in • p. 213

Blue-headed Vireo
size 5 in • p. 214

Warbling Vireo
size 5 in • p. 215

Philadelphia Vireo
size 5 in • p. 216

Red-eyed Vireo
size 6 in • p. 217

Blue Jay
size 12 in • p. 218

Western Scrub-Jay
size 12 in • p. 219

JAYS & CROWS

Pinyon Jay
size 10 in • p. 220

Black-billed Magpie
size 20 in • p. 221

American Crow
size 19 in • p. 222

Chihuahuan Raven
size 19 in • p. 223

LARKS & SWALLOWS

Horned Lark
size 7 in • p. 224

Purple Martin
size 8 in • p. 225

Tree Swallow
size 5 in • p. 226

Violet-green Swallow
size 5 in • p. 227

Northern Rough-winged Swallow
size 5 in • p. 228

Bank Swallow
size 5 in • p. 229

Cliff Swallow
size 5 in • p. 230

Barn Swallow
size 7 in • p. 231

CHICKADEES, NUTHATCHES & WRENS

Carolina Chickadee
size 5 in • p. 232

Black-capped Chickadee
size 5 in • p. 233

Tufted Titmouse
size 6 in • p. 234

Red-breasted Nuthatch
size 4 in • p. 235

White-breasted Nuthatch
size 6 in • p. 236

Brown Creeper
size 5 in • p. 237

Rock Wren
size 6 in • p. 238

Canyon Wren
size 6 in • p. 239

Carolina Wren
size 5 in • p. 240

Bewick's Wren
size 5 in • p. 241

House Wren
size 5 in • p. 242

Winter Wren
size 4 in • p. 243

Sedge Wren
size 4 in • p. 244

Marsh Wren
size 5 in • p. 245

Golden-crowned Kinglet
size 4 in • p. 246

Ruby-crowned Kinglet
size 4 in • p. 247

Blue-gray Gnatcatcher
size 4 in • p. 248

Eastern Bluebird
size 7 in • p. 249

Western Bluebird
size 7 in • p. 250

Mountain Bluebird
size 7 in • p. 251

Townsend's Solitaire
size 8 in • p. 252

Veery
size 7 in • p. 253

Gray-cheeked Thrush
size 7 in • p. 254

Swainson's Thrush
size 7 in • p. 255

Hermit Thrush
size 7 in • p. 256

Wood Thrush
size 8 in • p. 257

American Robin
size 10 in • p. 258

Gray Catbird
size 9 in • p. 259

Northern Mockingbird
size 10 in • p. 260

Sage Thrasher
size 8 in • p. 261

Brown Thrasher
size 11 in • p. 262

Curve-billed Thrasher
size 10 in • p. 263

European Starling
size 8 in • p. 264

American Pipit
size 6 in • p. 265

Sprague's Pipit
size 6 in • p. 266

Bohemian Waxwing
size 8 in • p. 267

Cedar Waxwing
size 7 in • p. 268

Tennessee Warbler
size 5 in • p. 269

Orange-crowned Warbler
size 5 in • p. 270

Nashville Warbler
size 5 in • p. 271

Northern Parula
size 4 in • p. 272

Yellow Warbler
size 5 in • p. 273

Chestnut-sided Warbler
size 5 in • p. 274

WOOD-WARBLERS & TANAGERS

Magnolia Warbler
size 5 in • p. 275

Yellow-rumped Warbler
size 5 in • p. 276

Black-throated Green Warbler
size 5 in • p. 277

Blackburnian Warbler
size 5 in • p. 278

Yellow-throated Warbler
size 5 in • p. 279

Pine Warbler
size 5 in • p. 280

Prairie Warbler
size 5 in • p. 281

Palm Warbler
size 5 in • p. 282

Bay-breasted Warbler
size 5 in • p. 283

Blackpoll Warbler
size 5 in • p. 284

Black-and-white Warbler
size 5 in • p. 285

American Redstart
size 5 in • p. 286

Prothonotary Warbler
size 5 in • p. 287

Ovenbird
size 6 in • p. 288

Northern Waterthrush
size 5 in • p. 289

Louisiana Waterthrush
size 6 in • p. 290

Kentucky Warbler
size 5 in • p. 291

Mourning Warbler
size 5 in • p. 292

Common Yellowthroat
size 5 in • p. 293

Wilson's Warbler
size 5 in • p. 294

Canada Warbler
size 5 in • p. 295

Yellow-breasted Chat
size 7 in • p. 296

Summer Tanager
size 7 in • p. 297

Scarlet Tanager
size 7 in • p. 298

Western Tanager
size 7 in • p. 299

SPARROWS, GROSBEAKS & BUNTINGS

Spotted Towhee
size 8 in • p. 300

Eastern Towhee
size 8 in • p. 301

Cassin's Sparrow
size 6 in • p. 302

Rufous-crowned Sparrow
size 6 in • p. 303

American Tree Sparrow
size 6 in • p. 304

Chipping Sparrow
size 5 in • p. 305

Clay-colored Sparrow
size 5 in • p. 306

Brewer's Sparrow
size 5 in • p. 307

Field Sparrow
size 5 in • p. 308

Vesper Sparrow
size 6 in • p. 309

Lark Sparrow
size 6 in • p. 310

Lark Bunting
size 7 in • p. 311

Savannah Sparrow
size 5 in • p. 312

Grasshopper Sparrow
size 5 in • p. 313

Baird's Sparrow
size 5 in • p. 314

Henslow's Sparrow
size 5 in • p. 315

Le Conte's Sparrow
size 5 in • p. 316

Nelson's Sharp-tailed Sparrow
size 5 in • p. 317

Fox Sparrow
size 7 in • p. 318

Song Sparrow
size 6 in • p. 319

Lincoln's Sparrow
size 5 in • p. 320

Swamp Sparrow
size 5 in • p. 321

White-throated Sparrow
size 7 in • p. 322

Harris's Sparrow
size 7 in • p. 323

White-crowned Sparrow
size 7 in • p. 324

Dark-eyed Junco
size 6 in • p. 325

McCown's Longspur
size 6 in • p. 326

Lapland Longspur
size 6 in • p. 327

Smith's Longspur
size 6 in • p. 328

Chestnut-collared Longspur
size 6 in • p. 329

Snow Bunting
size 6 in • p. 330

Northern Cardinal
size 8 in • p. 331

SPARROWS, GROSBEAKS & BUNTINGS

Rose-breasted Grosbeak
size 8 in • p. 332

Black-headed Grosbeak
size 8 in • p. 333

Blue Grosbeak
size 6 in • p. 334

Lazuli Bunting
size 6 in • p. 335

Indigo Bunting
size 5 in • p. 336

Painted Bunting
size 5 in • p. 337

Dickcissel
size 6 in • p. 338

Bobolink
size 7 in • p. 339

BLACKBIRDS & ALLIES

Red-winged Blackbird
size 8 in • p. 340

Eastern Meadowlark
size 9 in • p. 341

Western Meadowlark
size 9 in • p. 342

Yellow-headed Blackbird
size 9 in • p. 343

Rusty Blackbird
size 9 in • p. 344

Brewer's Blackbird
size 9 in • p. 345

Common Grackle
size 12 in • p. 346

Great-tailed Grackle
size 16 in • p. 347

Brown-headed Cowbird
size 7 in • p. 348

Orchard Oriole
size 7 in • p. 349

Baltimore Oriole
size 8 in • p. 350

Bullock's Oriole
size 8 in • p. 351

FINCHLIKE BIRDS

Purple Finch
size 6 in • p. 352

House Finch
size 6 in • p. 353

Red Crossbill
size 6 in • p. 354

Common Redpoll
size 5 in • p. 355

Pine Siskin
size 5 in • p. 356

American Goldfinch
size 5 in • p. 357

Evening Grosbeak
size 8 in • p. 358

House Sparrow
size 6 in • p. 359

INTRODUCTION

BIRDING IN THE GREAT PLAINS

In recent decades, birding in North America has evolved from an eccentric pursuit practiced by a few dedicated individuals to a continent-wide activity that boasts millions of professional and amateur participants. Birding has become popular for numerous good reasons. Many people find it simple and relaxing, and others enjoy the outdoor exercise that it affords. Some see it as a rewarding learning experience, an opportunity to socialize with like-minded people and a way to monitor the health of the local environment. Still others watch birds to reconnect with nature. These days, a visit to any of the Great Plains' premier birding locations would doubtless uncover still more reasons why people watch birds.

When we mention "Great Plains" in this book, we are referring to the states of North Dakota, South Dakota, Nebraska, Kansas and Oklahoma, as well as adjoining portions of Montana, Wyoming, Colorado, New Mexico, Texas, Minnesota, Iowa and Missouri. (Many of these states are or will be dealt with in their entirety in other Lone Pine books. The Canadian section of the Great Plains is covered in Lone Pine's Canadian provincial guides.)

We are truly blessed by the geographical and biological diversity of this region, especially with respect to its grasslands, which include some of the most threatened prairie habitats in North America. In addition to supporting a wide range of breeding birds, some of which are very rare elsewhere, the Great Plains region welcomes a large number of spring and fall migrants moving between breeding and wintering grounds and many winter residents. In all, over 500 bird species have been seen and recorded in the Great Plains, and by some estimates, more than 380 species make annual appearances. Similar climate conditions and habitats recur across the Great Plains, resulting in many bird species being found throughout the region. Therefore, it makes sense to discuss them in a single book.

The Great Plains also has a long tradition of friendly birding. In general, Great Plains birders and bird clubs are willing to help beginners and involve novices in their projects. Christmas bird counts, breeding bird surveys, field trips, bluebird and swallow nest box programs, and birding lectures and workshops all provide a chance for novice, intermediate and expert birders to interact and share the splendor of birds. So, whatever your level, there is ample opportunity for you to get involved!

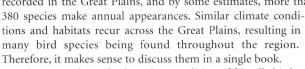

Greater Roadrunner

BIRDING BY HABITAT

The Great Plains can be separated into five biophysical regions or "bioregions": Short-grass Prairie, Tall-grass Prairie, Black Hills, Tall-grass Savanna and Oak-pine Woodland. Each bioregion is composed of a number of different habitats, including freshwater wetlands, grasslands, agricultural lands, riparian woodlands, oak and other deciduous woodlands and urban areas. Each habitat is a community of plants and animals supported by the infrastructure of water and soil and regulated by the constraints of topography, climate and elevation.

Simply put, a bird's habitat is the place in which it normally lives. Some birds prefer the open water, some birds are found in cattail marshes, others like mature conifer forest, and still others prefer abandoned agricultural fields overgrown with tall grass and shrubs. Knowledge of a bird's habitat increases the chances of identifying the bird correctly or of finding a sought-after species. Habitats are just like neighborhoods: if you associate friends with the suburb in which they live, you can easily learn to associate specific birds with their preferred habitats. Most birds leave their usual habitats only in migration, particularly during inclement weather.

BIRD LISTING

Many birders keep lists of the species they have seen during excursions or at home. It is up to you to decide what kind of list—systematic or casual—you will keep, and you may choose not to make lists at all. However, lists may prove rewarding in unexpected ways, and after you visit a new area, your list becomes a souvenir of your experiences there. By reviewing it, you can recall memories and details that may otherwise be forgotten. Keeping regular, accurate lists of birds in your neighborhood can also be useful for researchers. It can be interesting to compare the arrival dates and last sightings of hummingbirds and other seasonal visitors or to note the first sighting of a new visitor to your area. These records also help track species increases and declines, such as might result from local changes to habitat or food supply.

Although computer software for listing birds is now readily available, many naturalists simply keep records in field notebooks. Many birders prefer to use a pocket audio recorder in the field and to transcribe their observations into a dry notebook at home. If you want to go a step further, you can now keep your bird sighting records in a free Internet database at http://www.eBird.org/.

BIRDING ACTIVITIES

Birding Groups

Activities such as Christmas bird counts, breeding bird surveys, birding festivals and the meetings of your local birding or natural history club offer opportunities to meet other people with similar interests. These encounters can make birding even more pleasurable, and there is always something to be learned when birders of all levels gather. If you are interested in bird conservation and environmental issues, natural history groups and conscientious birding stores can keep you informed about the situation in your area and what you can do to help. Phone-in rare-bird hotlines were once common in the Great Plains, but they are steadily being replaced by birding-dedicated listservs on the Internet. Either can provide up-to-date information on the sightings of rarities, which are often easier to locate than you might think. Here is a brief list of contacts that will help you get involved:

Organizations

American Birding Association
P.O. Box 6599
Colorado Springs, CO 80934
(719) 578-9703 or (800) 850-2473
http://www.americanbirding.org/

Denver Field Ornithologists
Zoology Department
Denver Museum of Natural History
2001 Colorado Boulevard
Denver, CO 80205
http://www.dfobirders.org/

Iowa Ornithologists' Union
http://www.iowabirds.org/iou/

Kansas Ornithological Society
http://www.ksbirds.org/kos/

Minnesota Ornithologists' Union
J.F. Bell Museum of Natural History
University of Minnesota
10 Church Street SE
Minneapolis, MN 55455-0104
http://www.cbs.umn.edu/~mou/

National Audubon Society
700 Broadway
New York, NY 10003
(212) 979-3000
http://www.audubon.org/
(follow the links to find the chapter
nearest you)

Nebraska Ornithologists' Union
3745 Garfield
Lincoln, NE 68506
http://rip.physics.unk.edu/NOU/

New Mexico Ornithological Society
P.O. Box 3068
Albuquerque, NM 87190-3068
http://www.nmosbirds.org/

Oklahoma Ornithological Society
P.O. Box 2931
Claremore, OK 74018
http://www.okbirds.org/

South Dakota Ornithologists' Union
http://www.homepages.dsu.edu/palmerj/
SDOU/SDOU.html

Bird Hotlines
Colorado (303) 659-8750
Iowa (712) 364-2863
Kansas—*no longer in operation*
Minnesota (763) 780-8890 or
(800) 657-3700
Missouri—*no longer in operation*
Montana (406) 721-9799
Nebraska—*no longer in operation*
New Mexico (505) 884-3269
North Dakota (701) 250-4481
Oklahoma—*no longer in operation*
South Dakota (605) 773-6460
Texas (713) 369-9673
Wyoming (307) 265-2473

Bird Conservation
The Great Plains region is a great place to watch birds. After all, there are still large areas of protected grasslands and wetlands here, including national and state parks, national wildlife refuges and management areas, national forests, national grasslands, state wildlife areas and local nature centers. We hope that more people will learn to appreciate nature in the form of birding, and that those people will do their best to protect the nature that remains. Many bird enthusiasts support groups such as Ducks Unlimited, which helps waterbirds by buying and managing tracts of good habitat, and the Nature Conservancy, which often manages habitats valuable to birds and other wildlife.

Landscaping your own property to provide native plant cover and natural foods for birds is an immediate way to ensure the conservation of bird habitat. The cumulative effects of such urban nature-scaping can be significant. If your yard is to become a bird sanctuary, you may want to keep the neighborhood cats out—every year cats kill millions of birds. Check with the local Humane Society for methods of protecting both your feline friends and wild birds. Ultimately, cats are best kept indoors.

Bird Feeding

Many people set up backyard bird feeders to attract birds to their yards, especially in winter. By choosing the right kinds of food, you can attract specific birds. If you have a feeder, keep it stocked through late spring. The weather may be balmy, but birds have a hard time finding food before flowers bloom, seeds develop and insects hatch. In summer, hummingbirds can be attracted to your yard with a special feeder filled with artificial nectar (a simple sugar solution of 1 part white sugar and 3 to 4 parts water). Be sure to follow the feeder's cleaning instructions.

Birdbaths will also bring birds to your yard, and heated birdbaths are particularly effective in winter. Avoid birdbaths that have exposed metal parts, because wet birds can accidentally freeze to them. In general, feeding birds is good, especially if you provide food by growing native berry- or seed-producing plants in your backyard. Contrary to popular opinion, birds do not become dependent on feeders, nor do they subsequently forget to forage naturally. For more information, read some of the many good books about feeding birds and landscaping your yard to provide natural foods and nest sites.

Nest Boxes

Another popular way to attract birds is to set out nest boxes, especially for wrens, bluebirds and swallows. Not all birds will use nest boxes—only species that normally use cavities in trees are comfortable in such confined spaces. Large nest boxes can attract kestrels, owls and cavity-nesting ducks.

Cleaning Feeders and Nest Boxes

Nest boxes and feeding stations must be kept clean to prevent birds from becoming ill or spreading disease. Old nest material may harbor parasites and their eggs. Once the birds have left for the season, remove the old nest material and wash and scrub the nest box with detergent or a 10 percent bleach solution (1 part bleach to 9 parts water). You can also scald the nest box with boiling water. Rinse it well and let it dry thoroughly before you remount it.

Mountain Bluebird

Feeding stations should be cleaned monthly. Feeders can become moldy, and any seed, fruit or suet that is moldy or spoiled must be removed. Unclean bird feeders can also be contaminated with salmonella and possibly other infectious agents. Clean and disinfect feeding stations with a 10 percent bleach solution, scrubbing thoroughly. Rinse the feeder well and allow it to dry completely before refilling it. Discarded seed and feces on the ground under the feeding station should also be removed.

We advise that you wear rubber gloves and a mask when cleaning nest boxes or feeders.

West Nile Virus

Since the West Nile Virus first surfaced in North America in 1999, it has caused fear and misunderstanding—some people have become afraid of contracting the disease from birds, and health departments in some communities have advised residents to eliminate feeding stations and birdbaths. To date, the disease affects at least 138 species of birds. Because of their size, corvids (crows, jays and ravens) and raptors have been the most obvious victims, but the disease also affects smaller species. The virus is transmitted to birds and to humans (as well as some other mammals) by mosquitoes that have bitten infected birds. Humans cannot contract the disease from casual contact with infected birds, and birds do not get the disease from other birds. As well, not all mosquito species can carry the disease. According to the Centers for Disease Control and Prevention (CDC), only about 20 percent of people who are bitten and become infected will develop any symptoms at all, and fewer than 1 percent will become severely ill. You can check for the latest developments at http://www.cdc.gov/ncidod/dvbid/westnile/.

Because mosquitoes breed in standing water, birdbaths have the potential to become mosquito breeding grounds. Birdbaths should be emptied and the water changed at least weekly. Drippers, circulating pumps, fountains or waterfalls that keep water moving will prevent mosquitoes from laying their eggs in the water. As well, bird-friendly products are available to treat water in birdbaths. You can contact your local nature store or garden center, or do some research on-line, for more information on these products.

Black-billed Magpie

Top Birding Sites in the Great Plains

Montana
1. Bowdoin NWR
2. Comertown Pothole Prairie Preserve
3. Medicine Lake NWR
4. Charles M. Russell NWR
5. Four Dances Natural Area

North Dakota
6. Theodore Roosevelt National Park
7. J. Clark Salyer NWR
8. Wakopa WMA
9. Icelandic SP
10. Turtle River SP
11. Kellys Slough NWR
12. Oak Grove Park
13. Sheyenne National Grassland
14. Arrowwood NWR
15. Long Lake NWR

South Dakota
16. Grand River National Grassland
17. Ordway Prairie
18. Sand Lake NWR
19. Sica Hollow SP
20. Waubay NWR
21. Black Hills area
22. Badlands NP
23. Lacreek NWR
24. Farm Island Recreation Area
25. Newton Hills SP

Minnesota
26. Agassiz NWR
27. Buffalo River SP
28. Rothsay WMA
29. Big Stone NWR
30. Salt Lake WMA
31. Blue Mounds SP

Wyoming
32. Devils Tower National Monument

33. Thunder Basin National Grassland
34. Keyhole SP
35. Glendo Reservoir
36. Table Mountain WHMA

Nebraska
37. Chadron SP
38. Valentine NWR
39. Crescent Lake NWR
40. Crane Meadows Nature Center
41. Platte River Valley
42. Fontanelle Forest Nature Center
43. Burchard Lake WMA
44. Indian Cave SP

Iowa
45. Lost Island Nature Center
46. Buena Vista County Conservation Park
47. Stone SP
48. DeSoto NWR
49. Forney Lake Wildlife Area

Colorado
50. Northern Colorado Environmental Learning Center
51. Pawnee National Grassland
52. Prewitt Reservoir
53. Muir Springs Park
54. Bonny Lake SP
55. Barr Lake SP
56. Fountain Creek Regional Park
57. Comanche National Grassland

Kansas
58. Clinton Reservoir
59. Scott SP
60. Wilson Reservoir
61. Cheyenne Bottoms Wildlife Area

62. Konza Prairie
63. Cimarron National Grassland
64. Quivira NWR
65. Milford Reservoir
66. Flint Hills NWR
67. Marais des Cygnes WMA & NWR

Missouri
68. Squaw Creek NWR
69. Schell-Osage Wildlife Area
70. Prairie SP

New Mexico
71. Chapulin Mountain National Monument
72. Clayton Lake SP
73. Kiowa National Grassland
74. Bitter Lake NWR

Texas
75. Rita Blanca National Grassland
76. Lake Rita Blanca
77. Lake Meredith National Recreation Area
78. Buffalo Lake NWR
79. Palo Duro Canyon SP
80. Caprock Canyons SP
81. Muleshoe NWR

Oklahoma
82. Black Mesa SP
83. Salt Plains NWR
84. Tallgrass Prairie National Preserve
85. Lake Keystone
86. Oxley Nature Center & Mohawk Park
87. Sequoyah NWR
88. Wichita Mountains NWR
89. Martin Park Nature Center
90. Hackberry Flats
91. Beaver's Bend SP

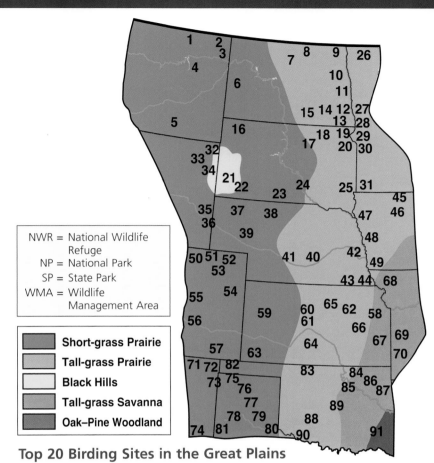

NWR = National Wildlife Refuge
NP = National Park
SP = State Park
WMA = Wildlife Management Area

Short-grass Prairie
Tall-grass Prairie
Black Hills
Tall-grass Savanna
Oak–Pine Woodland

Top 20 Birding Sites in the Great Plains

Charles M. Russell National Wildlife Refuge, Montana

This huge refuge of over one million acres stretches along 125 miles of the Missouri River in north-central Montana. The Fort Peck Reservoir, at over 245,000 acres, is a good spot to look for waterfowl. California and Ring-billed gulls nest on the refuge, and many unusual gull species have been reported. Geese and ducks are abundant, both in migration and as breeding species. Shorebirds to watch for are Piping and Mountain plovers, and Upland and Spotted sandpipers. Ospreys nest here, as do Northern Harriers, Red-tailed and Ferruginous hawks, Prairie Falcons and Merlins. Away from the lakes, there is prairie grassland, deep-cut "breaks" or ravines and wooded bottomland. Prairie is the place to try for both Sage-Grouse and Sharp-tailed Grouse. In autumn, the "breaks" may shelter thousands of Mourning Doves and a variety of owl species. Other prizes include the Pinyon Jay, Sage Thrasher and Mountain Bluebird. The UL Bend National Wildlife Refuge section includes a 24,000-acre wilderness with no vehicular access, but ample room to walk and watch birds. To help plan your trip, look for information on War Horse National Wildlife Refuge, Lake Mason National Wildlife Refuge, Hailstone National Wildlife Refuge and Halfbreed National Wildlife Refuge, all elements of the Charles M. Russell complex.

Long Lake National Wildlife Refuge, North Dakota

This refuge consists primarily of a shallow, 18-mile-long, saline lake. The wetlands here comprise 16,000 acres within the 22,000-acre refuge, the remainder of which is mixed-grass prairie and some cropland. This is a major stopover and staging area for many species and has been designated as a globally important shorebird reserve. Thousands of Sandhill Cranes pass through here, and there is a fair chance of finding Whooping Cranes during their migration. Many species of geese and ducks also use the area. Breeding birds you might expect here include the Western Grebe, Black-crowned Night-Heron, American Avocet, Marbled Godwit and White-faced Ibis. Piping Plovers nest here, as do Forster's Terns and Franklin's Gulls. Sedge Wrens and Marsh Wrens like the marshy areas. Observation blinds are provided near Sharp-tailed Grouse leks, and you may even find Greater Prairie-Chickens. Most of the typical grassland sparrows occur here in spring and summer, but uncommon species such as Baird's, Henslow's and Le Conte's sparrows are possible with some luck. Winter visits might afford you a look at Snow Buntings, House Wrens, Purple Finches and an occasional Snowy Owl.

Theodore Roosevelt National Park, North Dakota

Theodore Roosevelt National Park consists of three separate sections—the North Unit, the Elkhorn Ranch Unit and the South Unit—spread along a 50-mile stretch within the larger Little Missouri National Grassland. There is good birding in all three units. The biggest problem is tearing your eyes away from the spectacular scenery long enough to look at the birds. This is the Badlands, a place where erosion has transformed the landscape into strange and uncanny shapes, monuments to the power of nature and time. There is a range of interesting habitats to explore. The river bottom is forested with a mix of bur oak, elm, cottonwood and ash-leaved maple. The rolling grassland hills are covered with mixed-grass prairie, sage, rabbitbrush and juniper. In the woods, you may find Northern Flickers, Red-headed Woodpeckers, Orchard Orioles and Red-eyed Vireos. The forested waterways are the best place to look for warblers in spring; Yellow, Yellow-rumped and Black-and-white warblers, Ovenbirds and American Redstarts are all possible. In more open areas, Sharp-tailed Grouse, Lazuli Buntings and Sprague's Pipits may be found. Sparrow species here include the Field, Chipping, Clay-colored, Vesper, Lark and Grasshopper. Rock and House wrens nest here, as do Golden Eagles and Prairie Falcons. Common Poorwills are found in some years, but Common Nighthawks are regular.

Common Nighthawk

Black Hills area, South Dakota

Rising out of the rolling grasslands of western South Dakota, the forested Black Hills provide an outpost for birds usually seen farther west. Harney Peak, at over 7200 feet, is the highest point in North America east of the Rocky Mountains. The higher elevation allows for more annual rainfall, and there are thick forests of ponderosa pine and Black Hills spruce. These provide habitat for many species that are not seen anywhere else in the Great Plains. Deciduous forest in the broad valley floors will have Dusky Flycatchers, Gray Catbirds, Warbling Vireos and perhaps Lewis's Woodpeckers. Aspen groves higher in the hills are home to Ruffed Grouse and Red-naped Sapsuckers. Areas with more spruce cover provide habitat for Ruby-crowned and Golden-crowned kinglets, and the fortunate will locate a Black-backed or American Three-toed woodpecker. Streams provide habitat for the American Dipper. Other species found here include the Northern Saw-whet Owl, Violet-green Swallow, White-throated Swift, Townsend's Solitaire, Gray Jay, Clark's Nutcracker and Cordilleran Flycatcher. Pinyon Jays and Northern Goshawks are uncommon but permanent residents.

Snow Goose

Sand Lake National Wildlife Refuge, South Dakota

The Sand Lake refuge, located in northeastern South Dakota, is composed of 21,498 acres of wetlands and prairie. Marsh habitat comprises 11,000 acres of the refuge, with about 7500 acres of grassland, 2500 acres of cropland for wildlife food and a sparse 300 acres of woodland. This is the largest Franklin's Gull nesting area in the world, with several hundred thousand of these gulls breeding here each year. The marshes also provide nesting habitat for pelicans, cormorants, grebes, egrets, White-faced Ibises and Forster's Terns. Yellow-headed and Red-winged blackbirds are also abundant. The grassy uplands are habitat for Upland Sandpipers, Marbled Godwits, Ring-necked Pheasants and Gray Partridges. A summer visit might also provide glimpses of Bobolinks, Dickcissels, Lark Buntings and a variety of grassland sparrows. If you visit during spring migration, you may experience a truly amazing spectacle: Snow Geese pass through the refuge in numbers that have reached over one million birds in some years. Combine that with abundant Canada and Greater White-fronted geese, a variety of duck species and a few hundred Tundra Swans, and a sunrise visit to Sand Lake will not soon be forgotten. There is a short hiking trail at the Columbia Day Use Area, along with picnic and restroom facilities and interpretive panels. From April through mid-September, a 15-mile driving tour is available, which will guide you to a variety of the refuge's habitats.

Blue Mounds State Park, Minnesota

Located in the southwestern corner of Minnesota, Blue Mounds State Park is in a region known as Coteau des Prairies, meaning "highland or upland prairie." The park contains one of the remaining fragments of tall-grass prairie in Minnesota. Over 230 species of birds have been recorded in this 1800-acre park, with a potential 81 nesting species. This is a great spot during migration, with 29 species of warblers and vireos, 10 species of flycatchers and 17 species of sparrows documented. It is the only reliable place in Minnesota for the Blue Grosbeak, and the only spot where Brewer's Sparrow has been recorded. The Northern Mockingbird nests here, and there are two small ponds in the park that attract waterfowl. The park's extensive unplowed prairie is attractive to grassland birds such as Western and Eastern meadowlarks, Bobolinks and Upland Sandpipers. Sparrow species include the Grasshopper, Clay-colored, Chipping, Lark and Song. Watch for raptors such as Red-tailed, Swainson's and Ferruginous hawks and American Kestrels.

Devils Tower National Monument, Wyoming

Devils Tower was the first National Monument established in the National Park system and was created by Theodore Roosevelt in 1906. The 1400-acre park lies on the extreme northwestern edge of the Black Hills ecosystem and provides a chance to see species not commonly encountered elsewhere in the Great Plains. Habitat types include ponderosa pine forests with occasional aspen groves, a small amount of grassland and some deciduous woodland. The Tower itself, the remnants of an ancient volcanic core, is steep and barren, but does provide nesting sites for White-throated Swifts, Rock Wrens and an occasional Prairie Falcon. The wooded areas are good for a variety of woodpeckers. Gray and Pinyon jays occur here, as does the Northern Goshawk. Other possibilities include the Western Tanager, Pine Siskin, Townsend's Solitaire, Mountain Bluebird, Brewer's Blackbird and Common Grackle. Winter is quiet, but birders may still find Bald Eagles, Golden Eagles, Cassin's Finches and Red Crossbills.

Crescent Lake National Wildlife Refuge, Nebraska

The Crescent Lake refuge is located in the Nebraska panhandle, a land where trees are few and far between. The 46,000 acres of this refuge are grassy, rolling sandhills interspersed with potholes, marshes and lakes. Usually the only thing taller than the grass and yucca is the mix of cattails and rushes at the water's edge. A few groves of trees occur where there is sufficient moisture, and these areas are always worth checking. Sharp-tailed Grouse use numerous leks at the refuge in spring. Check at the headquarters to see if blinds are available. You may need to make a reservation for a blind, and be sure to understand the rules of its use. Other breeding birds here include Western and Pied-billed Grebes, American Avocets, Wilson's Phalaropes, Upland Sandpipers and Wilson's Snipes. American Coots nest here, as do Redheads, Canvasbacks and Ruddy Ducks. Check marshy areas for Marsh Wrens and Yellow-headed Blackbirds. Migrants through the area include American White Pelicans, Snow Geese, Sandhill Cranes and both yellowlegs species. Watch for the Swainson's Thrush, Least Flycatcher, Yellow-rumped Warbler and Common Yellowthroat. Winter is a quiet time here, but you might see Canada Geese, Rough-legged Hawks, Horned Larks and even Northern Shrikes.

Fontanelle Forest Nature Center, Nebraska

Located in the Omaha area, this complex of properties borders the Missouri River and provides an extensive system of trails through wetlands, prairie and oak savanna. An interesting feature of the property is the steep ravines through "loess" bluffs—wind-deposited soil with many interesting plant associations. Stop at the Katherine and Fred Buffett Forest Learning Center in Bellevue to pay your admission and get information about birding opportunities. There is a one-mile, barrier-free boardwalk as part of the trail complex. Birds here reflect the proximity of the deciduous forest, and breeding species include the Green Heron, Virginia Rail, Wood Duck, Red-Shouldered Hawk and Scarlet Tanager. Red-bellied and Red-headed woodpeckers are both resident. Migration brings a multitude of warblers, several of which remain to nest. In winter, watch for Brown Creepers, Dark-eyed Juncos and Song, Fox, White-crowned and Harris's sparrows. Check the river for wintering waterfowl and Bald Eagles.

Stone State Park and vicinity, Iowa

Stone State Park, Sioux City Prairie and Five Ridge Prairie Preserve are among the few remnants of native prairie and loess hills left in Iowa. Stone State Park includes the Dorothy Pecaut Nature Center, while Five Ridge Prairie is about 6 miles north of the state park, and the Sioux City Prairie is south of the park. There are prairie expanses on the hillsides and the tops of the ridges. Streams making their way to the Big Sioux River provide areas of bottomland hardwood forest. In winter, check for Snow Geese, Canada Geese, Common Goldeneyes, Common Mergansers, Bald Eagles, Sharp-shinned Hawks, Cooper's Hawks, Winter Wrens, Harris's Sparrows and Swamp Sparrows. Breeding birds in the area include the Great Blue Heron, Great Egret, Wood Duck, Mallard, Red-tailed Hawk, Eastern Screech-Owl, Whip-poor-will and Chimney Swift. In migration, watch for American White Pelicans, Franklin's Gulls, Black Terns, Marsh Wrens and several warbler species passing through the woodlands.

Barr Lake State Park, Colorado

Barr Lake State Park is composed of a large lake and 700 surrounding acres of grassland. There is a 9-mile loop trail around the lake, but the park provides a motorized tram that tours the loop. The lake itself attracts many water-loving birds, such as grebes, Northern Pintails, all three teal species, Canvasbacks, Redheads and Common Goldeneyes. Among the resident birds are Northern Harriers, Ring-necked Pheasants, Horned Larks, Black-billed Magpies, Downy Woodpeckers and Hairy Woodpeckers. During migration there are Olive-sided, Willow, Least, Hammond's and Cordilleran flycatchers. In summer, you may find Tree, Barn, and Cliff swallows, Blue Grosbeaks and Western Wood-Pewees. This is a good place to find California Gulls, Forster's Terns and Black Terns. The trees around the lake attract migrating warblers in spring, among them Yellow, Townsend's and Wilson's warblers, American Redstarts and Ovenbirds. In winter, look for Mountain Bluebirds, the Harlan's form of the Red-tailed Hawk, Brown Creepers, Dark-eyed Juncos and Pine Siskins. Barr Lake State Park is also home to the Rocky Mountain Bird Observatory.

Pawnee National Grassland, Colorado

To most people, Colorado represents mountains, but birders know that the plains and prairies are rich with bird life. This tour starts in Fort Collins, where you will take State 14 east through Ault and then another 30 miles or so to Briggsdale. At Briggsdale, head north through the short-grass prairie. Stop at the Crow Valley Recreation Area, one of the few spots with trees in this vast expanse of grass. Look here for Eastern and Western kingbirds, and Orchard and Bullock's orioles. Leave Crow Valley to drive the prairie, where the main attractions are breeding populations of the Mountain Plover, Chestnut-collared Longspur and McCown's Longspur. You may also find Brewer's, Lark, Grasshopper and Vesper sparrows. Anywhere there are trees, such as the windbreaks at the Central Plains Experimental Range complex, look carefully for such species as the Northern Mockingbird, Brown Thrasher and American Robin. Plumbeous Vireos, Cliff Swallows and Black-headed Grosbeaks are fairly common in the right season. If you wind your way far enough east, you'll come to the Pawnee Buttes, rising 500 feet above the prairie. This is a good spot to look for Peregrine Falcons, Swainson's Hawks, Ferruginous Hawks and even Golden Eagles.

Cheyenne Bottoms Wildlife Area, Kansas

If it's spring and if you are looking for shorebirds, Cheyenne Bottoms is the place to be. This 41,000-acre natural depression is located on the Central Flyway and is a major stopping place for shorebirds during spring migration. For some species, such as the White-rumped, Baird's and Stilt sandpipers, Long-billed Dowitcher and Wilson's Phalarope, the majority of their entire population may pass through on the way north. Grebes, cormorants, egrets, herons, bitterns and White-faced Ibises all breed here in season. Other nesting species include Virginia, King and even rarely Black rails. Add Northern Harriers, Bell's Vireos and Yellow-headed Blackbirds, and a trip to "The Bottoms" becomes a real pleasure. This is also a good place to try your luck for Whooping Cranes in spring and fall. During migration, watch for Peregrine Falcons, Prairie Falcons and an occasional Bald Eagle. Since your attention will be focused on the birds, be aware that the small Massasauga rattlesnake likes the damp, grassy fields as well. This area is heavily hunted so before visiting it you might want to check with Kansas Wildlife and Parks for the dates of hunting season.

Virginia Rail

Cimarron National Grassland, Kansas

Start your visit to this area of short-grass prairie and sandsage by stopping by the Forest Service office in Elkhart to pick up a free copy of "Birds of the Cimarron National Grassland." If you visit in spring, you'll want to ask about viewing sites for the Lesser Prairie-Chicken. The Cimarron River Picnic Area is another spot to visit, as the biggest trees to be found locally are near watercourses. Look for Great Horned Owls, Red-headed Woodpeckers, Ladder-backed Woodpeckers and several species of fly-catchers. Winter raptors of the grassland include Ferruginous and Rough-legged hawks, Prairie Falcons and Merlins. Drive to Point of Rocks, a high spot that was a landmark on the Santa Fe Trail, to look for Greater Roadrunners, Rock Wrens and both Green-tailed and Canyon towhees. In spring, brushy areas are worth checking for migrant warblers, including the MacGillivray's. Driving the grasslands might produce the Long-billed Curlew, Mountain Plover, Burrowing Owl and Scaled Quail. In winter, check the flocks of longspurs. Lapland Longspurs will be the most common, but McCown's and Chestnut-collared longspurs are possible. This corner of Kansas has produced many unusual state records. The Elkhurst Cemetery and sewage ponds can provide excellent birding during migration.

Squaw Creek National Wildlife Refuge, Missouri

The Missouri River valley in the northwestern corner of Missouri is home to the 7000-acre Squaw Creek National Wildlife Refuge. Most of the refuge was historically natural marsh, and about half the area has been dredged to provide a series of management ponds, although there are still natural marshes and some riparian woodlands. The refuge always has something of interest, but most people come in December to see the spectacular Snow Goose congregations, which sometimes number 300,000 to 400,000 birds. Other goose species to watch for include the Ross's, Canada and Greater White-fronted. Mid-morning is the best time to experience the spectacle, when the birds return from their dawn feeding in nearby agricultural fields. The large concentrations of waterfowl also attract many Bald Eagles and even a few Golden Eagles. Watch for Short-eared Owls, and check the cedars near the headquarters for possible Northern Saw-whet Owl appearances. In spring, look to the marshy areas for nesting Least Bitterns, Soras, King Rails, Virginia Rails and Marsh Wrens. Mixed in with the Red-winged Blackbird hordes, be alert for the Yellow-headed Blackbird, which also nests here. Most of the refuge tour is by a 10-mile loop road, with few places to get out and walk.

Short-eared Owl

Bitter Lake National Wildlife Refuge, New Mexico

This 24,000-acre refuge is located approximately 10 miles northeast of Roswell, New Mexico, where the plains give way to the Chihuahuan Desert of the Southwest. Habitats range from dry desert scrub and grasslands to scattered ponds and wet-season lakes and marshes. Winter is best for Sandhill Cranes and waterfowl such as Snow Geese, Ross's Geese, Northern Shovelers and Gadwalls. Watch for Great Blue Herons, Snowy Egrets and Black-crowned Night-Herons as well. You should see Swainson's, Red-tailed and Ferruginous hawks, and Harris's Hawk is possible in some years. A summer visit might turn up nesting American Avocets, Black-necked Stilts and Snowy Plovers. Bitter Lake is the only spot in New Mexico where Interior Least Terns are known to nest. Drier portions of the refuge can reveal Vermilion and Ash-throated flycatchers and perhaps the Crissal Thrasher and Western Tanager. Spend some time seeking the Black-chinned Hummingbird, Sedge Wren, Marsh Wren, Black Phoebe and Say's Phoebe. Large black birds overhead will be either Turkey Vultures or Chihuahuan Ravens. Stop by the headquarters in the Middle Tract for information and to start the 8-mile auto loop. The South Tract is closed to the public, and the North Tract contains the Salt Creek Wilderness, a day-use area accessible only by foot or on horseback.

Muleshoe National Wildlife Refuge, Texas

This is the oldest National Wildlife Refuge in Texas and was established to provide a winter sanctuary for Sandhill Cranes, as well as other waterfowl. The cranes are present from early October through February. They leave the refuge early in the day to feed on harvested agricultural fields in the area and return in the evenings. The refuge contains 5809 acres of short-grass prairie and "playas," or sinkhole lakes. If the year has been dry, the playas will contain little water, but in wet years there can be 600 acres of lake. Other than the cranes, there may be an abundance of waterfowl wintering here, including Eared Grebes, Green-winged Teals, Cinnamon Teals, Northern Pintails and Ruddy Ducks. Watch for raptors such as Swainson's, Rough-legged and Ferruginous hawks. Be alert for Golden Eagles as well. Burrowing Owls favor the prairie dog towns and Scaled Quail should be easy to find. Snowy Plovers are present in spring and summer. Other birds to watch for include Horned Larks, Curve-billed Thrashers and Lark Buntings.

Palo Duro Canyon State Park, Texas

Palo Duro Canyon is often called the "Grand Canyon of Texas." The canyon is 120 miles long and provides an oasis for birds and other wildlife. Habitats to explore include mesquite grassland, juniper woodland and wooded stream-sides. In winter, the canyon provides a sheltered environment that may support Mountain Bluebirds, Townsend's Solitaires, Inca Doves, Spotted Towhees and even Northern Shrikes. Possible, but less common, are Sage Thrashers and both Red-naped and Yellow-bellied sapsuckers. In summer, this is a good place to search for the Painted Bunting, Ash-throated Flycatcher, Carolina Chickadee, Black-crested Titmouse and Western Scrub-Jay. The Bushtit is a possibility, as are the Say's Phoebe, Greater Roadrunner and Scaled Quail. Don't leave the canyon without spending some time learning about the human history of this special place. People have lived here for more than 12,000 years!

Oxley Nature Center and Mohawk Park, Oklahoma

Located in Mohawk Park, on the north side of Tulsa, Oxley Nature Center and the surrounding areas are always productive. This 800-acre natural area contains a variety of habitats for birders to explore, and the center's extensive trail system leads through deciduous forest, along creeks, across a marsh boardwalk and through a small prairie. Spring is the time for migrants, with over 25 warbler species recorded. Other breeding species include the Red-shouldered Hawk, Barred Owl, Indigo Bunting, Eastern Bluebird, Carolina Wren, Carolina Chickadee and Ruby-throated Hummingbird. Pileated Woodpeckers are resident but require patience to find. In winter, sparrows are abundant in open areas. Lake Yahola, a municipal reservoir on the west border of the nature center, should be checked as well, especially in winter months. Ring-billed and Herring gulls are regular, but rarities such as Thayer's, Glaucous and Sabine's gulls have been found. The North Woods Unit of the nature center, adjacent to Lake Yahola, is worth checking in any season.

Wichita Mountains National Wildlife Refuge, Oklahoma

This huge refuge of almost 60,000 acres in southwestern Oklahoma was established for the protection of bison, elk and longhorn cattle, but has much to attract the birder. Approximately two-thirds of the refuge is forested with a mix of blackjack oak, post oak, ash and pecan. There are scattered lakes and ponds, and the wooded streams offer shelter for Carolina Chickadees, Western Wood-pewees, Eastern Phoebes and Painted Buntings. Mississippi Kites can be found here in spring and summer. Drive to the top of Mount Scott for an outstanding view of the surrounding prairie and granite ridges. This is a wonderful area for Canyon Wrens, Rock Wrens and Rufous-crowned Sparrows. In winter, Lake Elmer Thomas will host good numbers of waterfowl, including American Wigeons, Green-winged and Blue-winged teals and Wood Ducks. Bluestem prairies cover the other third of the refuge. Look here for Western Kingbirds, both Eastern and Western meadowlarks and Dickcissels. You may even find a Greater Roadrunner, and this is the best place in Oklahoma to search for the endangered Black-capped Vireo. Check at the new visitor center for information on the best spots. In winter, Chestnut-collared Longspurs are possible, and there may occasionally be Lapland Longspurs.

Carolina Chickadee

ABOUT THE SPECIES ACCOUNTS

This book gives detailed accounts of 324 species of birds that occur regularly on the Great Plains and can be expected on an annual basis. A further 50 occasional species and species of special note are briefly mentioned in an illustrated appendix. The order of the birds and their common and scientific names follow the American Ornithologists' Union's *Check-list of North American Birds* (7th edition, July 1998, revised to include the *Forty-fifth Supplement*, 2004).

As well as discussing the identifying features of a bird, each species account also attempts to bring the bird to life by describing its various character traits. Personifying a bird helps us to relate to it on a personal level, though the characterizations should not be mistaken for scientific propositions. Nonetheless, we hope that a lively, engaging text will communicate our scientific knowledge as smoothly and effectively as possible.

One of the challenges of birding is that many species look different in spring and summer than they do in fall and winter, as they switch between breeding and nonbreeding plumages, and immature birds often look different from their parents. This book does not try to describe or illustrate all the different plumages of a species; instead, it focuses on the forms that are most likely to be seen in our area.

ID: It is difficult to describe the features of a bird without being able to visualize it, so this section is best used in combination with the illustrations. Where appropriate, the description is subdivided to highlight the differences between male and female adult birds, breeding and nonbreeding birds and immatures. The descriptions use as few technical terms as possible, favoring easily understood language. Birds may not have "jaw lines," "eyebrows" or "chins," but these and other scientifically inaccurate terms are easily understood by all readers. Some of the most common features of birds are pointed out in the Glossary illustration (p. 370).

Size: The size measurement, the average length of the bird's body from bill to tail, is an approximate measurement of the bird as it is seen in nature. The size of larger birds is often given as a range because of variation among individuals. Please note that birds with long tails often have large measurements that do not necessarily reflect "body" size. In addition, wingspan (from wing tip to wing tip) is given.

Habitat: The habitats we have listed describe where each species is most commonly found. In most cases it is a generalized description, but if a bird is restricted to a specific habitat, the habitat is described precisely. Because of the freedom flight gives them, birds can turn up almost anywhere. However, they will usually be found in environments that provide the specific food, water, cover or nesting habitat they require.

Nesting: The reproductive strategies used by different bird species vary: in each species account, nest location and structure, clutch size, incubation period and parental duties are discussed. Remember that birding ethics discourage the disturbance of active bird nests. If you disturb a nest, you may drive off the parents during a critical period or expose defenseless young to predators. The nesting behavior of birds not known to nest in our region is not described.

Feeding: Birds spend a great deal of time foraging for food. If you know what a bird eats and where the food is found, you will have a good chance of finding the bird you are looking for.

Voice: You will hear many birds, particularly songbirds, that may remain hidden from view. Memorable paraphrases of distinctive sounds will aid you in identifying a species. These paraphrases often only loosely resemble the call, song or sound produced by the bird. Should one of our paraphrases not work for you, feel free to make up your own—the creative exercise will reinforce your memory of the bird's vocalizations.

Similar Species: To the extent practicable, similar species and their distinguishing features are briefly discussed. If you concentrate on the most relevant field marks, the subtle differences between species can be reduced to easily identifiable traits. You might find it useful to consult this section when finalizing your identification; knowing the most relevant field marks will speed up the identification process. Even experienced birders can mistake one species for another.

Range Maps: The range map for each species represents the overall range of the species in an average year. Most birds will confine their annual movements to this range, although each year some birds wander beyond their traditional boundaries. These maps do not show differences in abundance within the range—areas of a range with good habitat will support a denser population than areas with poorer habitat. These maps also cannot show small pockets within the range where the species may actually be absent, or how the range may change from year to year.

Unlike most other field guides, we have attempted to show migratory pathways—areas of the region where birds may appear while en route to nesting or winter habitat. Many of these migratory routes are "best guesses" that will no doubt be refined as new discoveries are made. The representations of these pathways do not distinguish high-use migration corridors from areas that are seldom used.

Range Map Symbols

summer

possible breeding area

migration

winter

year-round

Nonpasserine birds represent 17 of the 18 orders of birds found in the Great Plains, about 53 percent of the species in our region. They are grouped together and called "nonpasserines" because, with few exceptions, they are easily distinguished from the "passerines," or "perching birds," which make up the 18th order. Being from 17 different orders, however, means that nonpasserines vary considerably in their appearance and habits—they include everything from the 5-foot-tall Great Blue Heron to the 4-inch-long Ruby-throated Hummingbird.

Generally speaking, nonpasserines do not "sing." Instead, their vocalizations are referred to as "calls." There are also other morphological differences. For example, the muscles and tendons in the legs of passerines are adapted to grip a perch, and the toes of passerines are never webbed. Many nonpasserines are large, so they are among our most notable birds. Waterfowl, raptors, gulls, shorebirds and woodpeckers are easily identified by most people. Some of the smaller nonpasserines, such as doves, swifts and hummingbirds, are frequently thought of as passerines by novice birders and can cause those beginners some identification problems. With a little practice, however, they will become recognizable as nonpasserines. By learning to separate the nonpasserines from the passerines at a glance, birders effectively reduce by half the number of possible species for an unidentified bird.

Waterfowl

Diving Birds

Heronlike Birds

Birds of Prey

Rails, Coots & Cranes

Shorebirds

Gulls & Terns

Doves, Cuckoos & Roadrunners

Owls

Nightjars, Swifts & Hummingbirds

Woodpeckers

GREATER WHITE-FRONTED GOOSE

Anser albifrons

The Greater White-fronted Goose is probably most familiar to hunters, who know it as "Speckle Belly." It has an almost circumpolar arctic distribution, and it is the only North American representative of the five species of gray geese found in Eurasia. Like most geese, the White-front is normally a long-lived bird that mates for life, with both parents caring for the young. • Greater White-fronted Geese breed on the arctic tundra and winter in the southern U.S. and Mexico. They can be seen in our region, especially during spring migration, when they stop to refuel on aquatic plants in shallow ponds and marshes or on freshly sprouted grains in fields and pastures. They often travel among flocks of Canada Geese. The slightly smaller Greater White-fronted Geese can best be distinguished by their bright orange feet, which shine like beacons as the birds stand on frozen spring wetlands and fields.

ID: brown overall; black speckling on belly; white around pinkish bill and on forehead; white hindquarters; black band on upper tail; orange legs and feet.
Size: *L* 27–33 in; *W* 4½–5 ft.

Habitat: croplands, fields, open areas and shallow marshes.

Nesting: does not nest in the Great Plains.
Feeding: dabbles in water and gleans the ground for grass shoots, sprouting and waste grain and occasionally aquatic invertebrates.
Voice: high-pitched "laugh."
Similar Species: *Canada Goose* (p. 38): white "chin strap"; black neck; unspeckled pale belly. *Snow Goose* (p. 36): white head and upper neck; blue morph has all-dark breast and belly.

SNOW GOOSE

Chen caerulescens

The Great Plains does not receive the staggering numbers of migrating Snow Geese found in some other areas, but these birds are still sure to come in spring and fall. Landing in farmers' fields, these cackling geese fuel up on waste grain from the previous year's crops. In recent years, North American Snow Goose populations have increased dramatically, as the birds take advantage of human-induced changes in the landscape and the food supply. • Snow Geese grub for their food, often targeting the underground parts of plants. Their strong, serrated bills are well designed for pulling up the root stalks of marsh plants and gripping slippery grasses. Because of their large numbers, there is concern that they may be degrading the sensitive tundra environment that they use for nesting. • Unlike Canada Geese, which fly in orderly V-formations, migrating Snow Geese usually form oscillating, wavy lines. • Until 1983, the two color morphs, white and blue, were considered different species. The scientific name *caerulescens*, which means "bluish" in Latin, was coined to describe the rarer blue morph.

blue morph

ID: white overall (occasionally stained rusty by iron in the water); black wing tips; pink bill with dark "grinning patch"; pink legs and feet. *Blue morph:* dark, bluish gray body; white head and upper neck. *In flight:* flock often forms a scattered "V."
Size: *L* 28–33 in; *W* 4½–5 ft.
Habitat: shallow wetlands, lakes and fields.

Nesting: does not nest in the Great Plains.
Feeding: grazes on waste grain and new sprouts; also eats aquatic vegetation, grasses, sedges and roots.
Voice: loud, nasal, constant *houk-houk* in flight.
Similar Species: *Ross's Goose* (p. 37): smaller; shorter neck; no black "grinning patch." *Tundra* (p. 40), *Trumpeter* (p. 39) and *Mute swans:* larger; white wing tips. *American White Pelican* (p. 79): much larger bill and body.

ROSS'S GOOSE

Chen rossii

Ross's Geese are rarely seen away from their favored staging sites, but single birds and small flocks may join large flocks of Snow Geese in areas outside their normal routes. To see more than just a few of North America's smallest geese among the milling masses of larger Snow Geese, travel to the eastern Great Plains. National wildlife refuges and wildlife management areas attract migrants from the Canadian Arctic that arrive in late October and leave for Mexico by late November. Spring migration tends to be more leisurely, with flocks returning in late March and remaining until mid-May before heading north. The size and composition of migrating flocks vary—unlike most geese, which form family flocks for migration and overwintering, young Ross's Geese regularly gather in crèches. • The particularly handsome but very rare dark-morph (blue) Ross's Goose may have originated from occasional hybridization between white-morph Ross's Geese and dark-morph Snow Geese.

ID: white overall; black wing tips; small, triangular, deep pink bill with greenish "warts" at base; pink legs and feet. *Dark morph:* white head; bluish gray body plumage.
Size: *L* 21–26 in; *W* 4–4¼ ft.

Habitat: ponds, lakes, reservoirs, shallow wetlands and grain fields.
Nesting: does not nest in the Great Plains.
Feeding: eats most parts of waste crops, grasses and sedges on land; swims or wades in shallows to eat aquatic plants;

smaller bill allows it to eat shorter grasses than the Snow Goose; often digs for roots.
Voice: flight call is a high-pitched *kug, kek* or *ke-gak.*
Similar Species: *Snow Goose* (p. 36): larger; prominent black "grinning patch" on sides of more angular, rounder-based bill; slightly longer neck; head may be stained orange or rusty; dark-morph birds are darker on the head and body; noisier, with slower, less squeaky flock calls.
Emperor Goose: extremely rare; slightly larger; silvery gray overall; white head, nape and tail; small, pinkish bill; orange legs and feet.

CANADA GOOSE

Branta canadensis

Canada Geese are among the most recognizable birds in our region, but they are also among the least valued. Few people realize that at one time these birds were hunted almost to extinction. Populations have since been reestablished, and, in recent decades, these large, bold geese have inundated urban waterfronts, picnic sites, golf courses and city parks. • Many geese overwinter in sheltered locations where food is available year-round. Several small, migratory races pass through the Great Plains in spring and fall, with some overwintering in the region's southern states. It should be noted that in 2004, the Canada Goose, which comprises 11 subspecies, was split into two species. The smaller races, including the former *B.c. hutchinsii,* have been elevated to full species rank and are now known as Cackling Geese *(B. hutchinsii).* • Canada Goose pairs mate for life, and unlike most birds, the parents do not sever bonds with their young until the beginning of the next year's nesting, almost a year after the young are born, thus increasing the young birds' chances for survival.

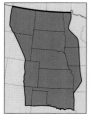

ID: dark brown upperparts; light brown underparts; long, black neck; white "chin strap"; white undertail coverts; short, black tail.
Size: *L* 21–48 in; *W* 3½–5 ft.
Habitat: lakeshores, riverbanks, ponds, farmland and city parks.
Nesting: on an island or shoreline; usually on the ground but may use a heron rookery; female builds a nest of plant materials lined with down; female incubates 3–8 white eggs for 25–28 days while the male stands guard.
Feeding: grazes on new sprouts, aquatic vegetation, grass and roots; tips up for aquatic roots and tubers.
Voice: loud, familiar *ah-honk,* often answered by other Canada Geese.
Similar Species: *Greater White-fronted Goose* (p. 35): all-brown neck and head except for white around base of bill; dark speckling on belly; orange legs. *Brant:* less common; black head, neck and upper breast with white "necklace." *Snow Goose* (p. 36): blue morph has white head and upper neck.

TRUMPETER SWAN
Cygnus buccinator

The Trumpeter Swan is the world's largest species of waterfowl. It was hunted nearly to extinction for its meat and feathers in the early 20th century. Attempts to reintroduce the Trumpeter Swan to former parts of its breeding range are meeting with success in Nebraska and South Dakota. By respecting the sensitivity of Trumpeter Swan nest sites and protecting this species' habitat across our region, we may once again hear the resonant notes of this magnificent bird throughout the Great Plains. • The neck of the Trumpeter Swan is twice the length of its body. Both "trumpeter" and *buccinator* refer to this bird's loud, bugling voice, which is produced when air is forced through the long windpipe that runs through the keel of the bird's breastbone.

ID: all-white plumage; large, solid black bill; black skin extends from bill to eyes; black legs and feet; neck is kinked at base when standing or swimming. *Immature:* usually tinged pale grayish brown overall; bill can be mostly pinkish orange with black base; dusky yellow legs and feet.

Size: *L* 5–6 ft; *W* 6–7 ft.

Habitat: lakes and large wetlands; extremely local.

Nesting: always close to water; on shore, on a small island or on a muskrat lodge or beaver lodge; male gathers marsh plants such as cattails, bulrushes, sedges and grass; female constructs a nest mound and lines it with down; mostly the female incubates 4–6 creamy white to dull white eggs for 32–37 days.

Feeding: tips up, surface gleans and occasionally grazes for vegetation; primarily eats pondweeds, duckweed, aquatic tubers and roots.

Voice: loud, resonant, buglelike *koh-hoh.*

Similar Species: *Tundra Swan* (p. 40): more common; smaller; often shows yellow lores; rounder neck and head; softer, more nasal voice. *Snow Goose* (p. 36): smaller; black wing tips; shorter neck; pinkish bill.

TUNDRA SWAN
Cygnus columbianus

The long neck and powerful bill of the Tundra Swan indicate an adaptation to life in and about extensive, shallow wetlands, where it grazes grass and gleans from the land like a goose, skims the water's surface for food or tips up like a dabbling duck. Exceptional underwater reach and bill strength suitable for grasping and rooting out bottom-growing tubers and shoots enable the Tundra Swan to exploit resources unavailable to geese and ducks. • A rare migrant in the Great Plains, the Tundra Swan sometimes winters here. • Distinguishing among swan species often comes down to the bill. Although the bright orange bill of the Mute Swan is hard to mistake, the subtle difference in slope between the bills of the Tundra Swan and the Trumpeter Swan, and the yellow at the base of the Tundra's bill, can be more difficult to discern. • In the early 19th century, members of the Lewis and Clark expedition found this bird near the Columbia River, thus its scientific name *columbianus*.

ID: white plumage; neck (held straight up) and head show rounded, slightly curving profile; large, black bill; often shows yellow lores; black legs and feet. *Immature:* tinged pale grayish brown overall; mostly pinkish orange bill with black tip; dark gray legs and feet.
Size: *L* 4–5 ft; *W* 6–7 ft.
Habitat: shallow areas of lakes and wetlands, agricultural fields and flooded pastures.
Nesting: does not nest in the Great Plains.

Feeding: tips up, dabbles and surface gleans for aquatic vegetation and aquatic invertebrates; grazes for tubers, roots and waste grain.
Voice: migrating flocks constantly repeat a high-pitched, quivering *oo-oo-whoo*.
Similar Species: *Trumpeter Swan* (p. 39): extremely rare; larger; black lores; neck and head show more angular profile; loud, buglelike voice. *Mute Swan:* downpointed, orange bill with black knob on top at base; neck usually held in S-shape; reddish orange bill adjoins black area on face; wings often held in arch over back while swimming. *Snow Goose* (p. 36): smaller; black wing tips; shorter neck; pinkish bill.

WOOD DUCK

Aix sponsa

The male Wood Duck is one of the most colorful waterbirds in North America, and books, magazines, postcards and calendars routinely celebrate its beauty. • Truly birds of the forest, Wood Ducks will sometimes nest in trees that are over a mile from the nearest body of water. Forced into the adventures of life at an early age, newly hatched ducklings often jump 20 feet or more out of their nest cavity in a tree to follow their mother to the nearest body of water. The little bundles of down are not exactly feather light, but they bounce fairly well and seldom sustain injury. • Landowners with a small, tree-lined pond or other suitable wetland may attract a family of Wood Ducks by building a suitably sized nest box with a predator guard and lining it with sawdust. The nest box should be erected close to the wetland shoreline at a reasonable height, usually at least 5 feet from the ground.

ID: *Male*: white spots on purplish chestnut breast; black-and-white shoulder slash; golden sides; dark back and hindquarters; glossy, green head with some white streaks; crest is slicked back from crown; white "chin" and throat; mostly orange bill. *Female*: white-streaked, mottled brown breast; grayish brown upperparts; white belly; white, teardrop-shaped eye patch; dark bill.
Size: *L* 15–20 in; *W* 30 in.
Habitat: swamps, ponds, marshes and lakeshores with wooded edges.

Nesting: in a hollow, tree cavity or nest box, usually near water and up to 30 ft above the ground; cavity is lined with down; female incubates 9–14 white to buff eggs for 25–35 days.
Feeding: gleans the water's surface and tips up for aquatic vegetation, especially duckweed, aquatic sedges and grasses; eats more fruits and nuts than other ducks.
Voice: *Male:* ascending *ter-wee-wee*. *Female:* squeaky *woo-e-e-k*.
Similar Species: *Hooded Merganser* (p. 60): male has black-and-white breast, black head with white crest patch and slim, black bill. *Harlequin Duck:* very rare; male is bluish gray overall with chestnut sides and patches of black and white.

GADWALL

Anas strepera

Male Gadwalls lack the striking plumage of most other male ducks, but they nevertheless have a dignified appearance and a subtle beauty. Once you learn their field marks—a black rump and white wing patches—male Gadwalls are surprisingly easy to identify. • Ducks in the genus *Anas*, the dabbling ducks, are typically observed tipping up their hindquarters and submerging their heads to feed, but the Gadwall dives more often than others of this group. It feeds equally during the day and night, a strategy that reduces the risk of predation by making the sleeping and feeding periods shorter. • These birds have expanded their range throughout North America, and numbers in this area have greatly increased since the 1950s. The majority of Gadwalls overwinter on the Gulf Coast of the United States and Mexico, although increasing numbers overwinter on inland lakes across the country.

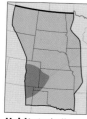

ID: white belly. *Male:* mostly gray; black hindquarters; dark bill (partly orange in late summer). *Female:* mottled brown; brown bill with orange sides. *In flight:* white speculum. **Size:** *L* 18–22 in; *W* 33 in.

Habitat: shallow wetlands, lake borders and beaver ponds.

Nesting: in tall vegetation, sometimes far from water; nest is well concealed in a scraped-out hollow, often with grass arching overhead; nest of grass and other dry vegetation is lined with down; female incubates 8–11 white eggs for 24–27 days.

Feeding: dabbles and tips up for aquatic plants; also eats aquatic invertebrates, tadpoles and small fish; grazes on grass and waste grain during migration; one of the few dabblers to routinely dive for food.

Voice: *Male:* simple, single quack; often whistles harshly. *Female:* high *kaak kaaak kak-kak-kak* series, oscillating in volume.

Similar Species: *American Wigeon* (p. 43): green speculum; breeding male has white forehead and green swipe trailing from each eye; female and nonbreeding male have brown-and-white hindquarters. *Mallard* (p. 44), *Northern Pintail* (p. 48) and *other dabbling ducks* (pp. 41–49): in general, speculum not white, hindquarters not wholly black and bill not orange-sided.

AMERICAN WIGEON

Anas americana

The male American Wigeon's characteristic three-syllable, piping whistle sets it apart from the wetland orchestra's usual buzzes, quacks and ticks. Listen carefully, however, and you'll realize where toy makers got the sound for rubber duckies. • Although this bird frequently dabbles for food, nothing seems to please a wigeon more than the succulent stems and leaves of pond-bottom plants. These plants grow far too deep for dabbling ducks, so wigeons often pirate food from accomplished divers, such as American Coots, Canvasbacks, Redheads and scaups. In contrast to other ducks, though, the American Wigeon is a good walker and is commonly observed grazing on shore. • The American Wigeon nests farther north than any other dabbling duck with the exception of the Northern Pintail. Pair bonds are strong and last well into incubation. • Because of the male's bright white crown and forehead, some people call this bird "Baldpate."

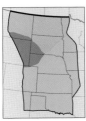

ID: cinnamon breast and sides; white belly; black-tipped, bluish gray bill; grayish brown legs and feet. *Breeding male:* white face with brown speckles; white forehead and crown; green swipe extends back from eye; black hindquarters. *Female:* grayish head; brown underparts. *In flight:* large, white upperwing patch; green speculum; white "wing pits."
Size: *L* 18–23 in; *W* 32 in.
Habitat: shallow wetlands, lake edges and ponds.
Nesting: always on dry ground, often far from water; well concealed in tall vegetation; nest is built with grass, leaves and down; female incubates 8–11 white eggs for 23–25 days.
Feeding: dabbles and tips up for the leaves and stems of pondweeds and other aquatic plants; also grazes and uproots young shoots in fields; may eat some invertebrates; occasionally pirates food from other birds.
Voice: *Male:* nasal, frequently repeated whistle: *whee WHEE wheew. Female:* soft, seldom heard quack.
Similar Species: *Gadwall* (p. 42): brown wings with white speculum; yellowish orange legs and feet; breeding male has all-brown head and dark bill; nonbreeding male and female have orange-sided bills. *Eurasian Wigeon:* rare; gray "wing pits"; breeding male has rufous head without green eye swipe, rosy breast and gray sides; female usually has browner head.

43

MALLARD

Anas platyrhynchos

The male Mallard in breeding plumage, with his iridescent, green head and chestnut brown breast, is the classic wild duck. After breeding, the extravagant plumage is replaced by an "eclipse" plumage that camouflages the male during the flightless period. By early fall, he will usually have molted back into breeding colors. • Mallards can be seen almost any day of the year, often in flocks and always near open water. These confident ducks have even been known to take up residence in local swimming pools. • Wild Mallards will freely hybridize with domestic ducks, which were originally derived from Mallards in Europe. The resulting offspring, often seen in city parks, are a confusing blend of both parents. • Most people think of the Mallard's quack as the classic duck call; indeed, the Mallard is the only duck that really "quacks." • The body heat of a brooding hen is enough to increase the growth rate of nearby grass, which she manipulates to further conceal her precious nest. • *Platyrhynchos* is Greek for "broad, flat bill."

ID: orange feet and legs. *Breeding male:* light gray body plumage; chestnut brown breast; white "necklace"; glossy, green head; yellow bill; black tail feathers curl upward. *Female:* mottled brown overall; black-marked, orange bill. *In flight:* dark blue speculum bordered by white.
Size: *L* 20–28 in; *W* 35 in.
Habitat: lakes, wetlands, rivers, city parks, agricultural areas and sewage lagoons.
Nesting: in tall vegetation or under a bush, often near water; nest of grass and other plant material is lined with down; female incubates 7–10 light green to white eggs for 26–30 days.
Feeding: tips up and dabbles in shallows for the seeds of sedges, willows and pondweeds; also eats insects, aquatic invertebrates, larval amphibians and fish eggs.
Voice: *Male:* deep, quiet quacks. *Female:* loud quacks; very vocal.
Similar Species: *Northern Shoveler* (p. 47): much larger, darker bill; male has white breast and chestnut brown flanks. *American Black Duck* (p. 360): rare; darker than female Mallard; purple speculum without white border. *Common Merganser* (p. 61): male has blood red bill and white neck and underparts.

BLUE-WINGED TEAL

Anas discors

The small, speedy Blue-winged Teal is renowned for its aviation skills. It can be identified in flight by its small size and by its precise execution of sharp twists and turns. • Despite the similarity in names, the Green-winged Teal is not the Blue-winged Teal's closest relative. The Blue-winged Teal is more closely related to the Northern Shoveler and the Cinnamon Teal. These birds all have broad, flat bills, pale blue forewings and green speculums. Female Cinnamon Teals and Blue-winged Teals are so similar in appearance that even expert birders and ornithologists can have difficulty distinguishing them in the field. • Blue-winged Teals migrate farther than most ducks, summering as far north as the Canadian tundra and overwintering mainly in Central and South America. • The scientific name *discors* is Latin for "without harmony," which might refer to this bird's call as it takes flight—or to its contrasting plumage.

ID: *Breeding male:* black-spotted, buff breast and sides; bluish gray head; vertical, white crescent ahead of eye; dark gray bill. *Female:* mottled brown overall; white throat; broken white eye ring; gray bill. *In flight:* light blue forewing patch; green speculum.
Size: *L* 14–16 in; *W* 23 in.
Habitat: shallow lake edges and wetlands; prefers areas of short but dense emergent vegetation.

Nesting: in grass along a shoreline or in a meadow; nest is built with grass and considerable amounts of down; female incubates 8–13 white, sometimes olive-tinged, eggs for 23–27 days.
Feeding: gleans the water's surface for sedge and grass seeds, pondweeds, duckweed and aquatic invertebrates.
Voice: *Male:* soft *keck-keck-keck. Female:* soft quacks.
Similar Species: *Cinnamon Teal* (p. 46): female is richer brown overall, with less distinct facial markings. *Green-winged Teal* (p. 49): female has black-and-green speculum, gray forewing, darker face and smaller bill. *Northern Shoveler* (p. 47): larger; female has much larger, orangy bill with paler base.

CINNAMON TEAL
Anas cyanoptera

When the morning sun strikes a wetland in spring, the male Cinnamon Teal glows upon the water like an ember. The intense reddish brown plumage, accented by ruby red eyes, makes this bird worth admiring at any time of day. • Teals push northward each spring from southern wintering grounds to dot the reed-fringed pothole ponds and marshes of the western Great Plains. Their presence in the eastern part of the region, however, is more sporadic. • Female ducks of most species are abandoned by their mates during nesting, but female Cinnamon Teals may be accompanied by their partners throughout the nesting cycle. Males have sometimes even been seen accompanying their mates and young. • The scientific name—from *cyano*, "blue," and *pteron*, "wing"—refers to this bird's blue forewing patch, which is easily seen when the bird is in flight. It also reflects the similarity of this species to the Blue-winged Teal, with which it may occasionally interbreed.

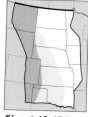

ID: long, broad, gray bill. *Breeding male:* intensely cinnamon red underparts, neck and head; red eyes. *Female:* mottled warm brown overall; orangy areas on bill; dark eyes. *In flight:* blue forewing patch; green speculum.
Size: *L* 15–17 in; *W* 22 in.
Habitat: shallow wetlands with extensive emergent vegetation and sedge beds.
Nesting: in a shallow depression hidden in tall grass or weeds near water; nest is lined with down and grass; female incubates 8–12 nearly white eggs for 21–25 days.

Feeding: dabbles in shallow water for grass and sedge seeds, pondweeds, duckweed and aquatic invertebrates; occasionally tips up.
Voice: *Male:* whistled *peep*. *Female:* rough *karr, karr, karr.*
Similar Species: *Blue-winged Teal* (p. 45): female is generally more gray and less brown with stronger facial markings and smaller bill. *Green-winged Teal* (p. 49): non-breeding male and female are generally darker overall with gray forewings and smaller bills. *Ruddy Duck* (p. 63): breeding male has black crown, white "cheek," blue bill and stiff, upward-angled tail.

NORTHERN SHOVELER

Anas clypeata

The initial reaction upon meeting the Northern Shoveler for the first time is often, "Wow, look at the big honker on that Mallard!" A closer look, however, reveals an altogether different bird. The extra large, spoonlike bill allows this handsome duck to strain small invertebrates from the water and from the bottoms of ponds. The Northern Shoveler eats much smaller organisms than do most other waterfowl, and its intestines are elongated to prolong the digestion of these hard-bodied invertebrates. The shoveler's specialized feeding strategy means that it is rarely seen tipping up—it is more often found in the shallows of ponds and marshes where the mucky bottom is easiest to access. • The scientific name *clypeata*, Latin for "furnished with a shield," possibly refers to the chestnut patches on the flanks of the male. This species was once placed in its own genus, *Spatula*, the meaning of which needs no explanation.

ID: large, spatulate bill. *Breeding male:* chestnut brown flanks; white breast; green head; yellow eyes; dark gray bill. *Female:* mottled brown overall; brown eyes; gray-smudged, orangy bill. *In flight:* blue forewing patch; green speculum with adjoining white bar.

Size: *L* 18–20 in; *W* 30 in.

Habitat: shallow marshes, bogs and lakes with muddy bottoms and emergent vegetation, usually in open and semi-open areas.

Nesting: in a shallow hollow on dry ground, usually within 150 ft of water;

female builds a nest of dry grass and down and incubates 10–12 pale, greenish buff eggs for 21–28 days.

Feeding: dabbles in shallow and often muddy water; strains out plant and animal matter, especially aquatic crustaceans, insect larvae and seeds; rarely tips up.

Voice: generally quiet; occasional raspy chuckle or quack; most often heard during spring courtship.

Similar Species: *Mallard* (p. 44): larger; white-bordered, dark blue speculum; brownish gray forewing; smaller bill; breeding male has chestnut brown breast, white flanks and yellow bill; female is generally darker, with dark eye line. *Blue-winged Teal* (p. 45): smaller overall; female has much smaller, gray bill with white at base and yellow legs.

NORTHERN PINTAIL

Anas acuta

The trademark long, tapering tail feathers of the elegant and graceful male Northern Pintail, which are easily seen in flight and point skyward when the bird dabbles, give this species its name. In the Great Plains, only the male Long-tailed Duck shares this feature. • Pintails breed earlier than most waterfowl, with nesting in the U.S. beginning in mid-April. Migrating pintails are often seen in flocks of 20 to 40 birds, but some early spring flocks in flooded agricultural fields have been known to consist of nearly 10,000 individuals. • This widespread duck appears to be in an overall decline across its range in central and western North America. Most pintails migrating through the Great Plains are heading to and from breeding sites in northern Canada. Many birds nest in the pothole region of the northern Great Plains, some remain year-round in the southern Great Plains, and a few flocks overwinter in eastern Kansas and Oklahoma.

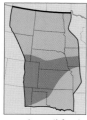

ID: long, slender neck; dark, glossy bill. *Breeding male:* dusty gray body plumage; black-and-white hindquarters; white of breast extends up sides of neck; medium brown head (pale on non-breeding birds); long, tapering tail feathers. *Female:* mottled light brown overall. *In flight:* slender body; speculum (greenish on male and brownish on female) has white trailing edge.
Size: *L* 21–25 in; *W* 34 in.
Habitat: shallow wetlands, fields and lake edges.
Nesting: in a small depression in low vege-tation; nest of grass, leaves and moss is lined with down; female incubates 6–12 greenish buff eggs for 22–25 days.
Feeding: tips up and dabbles in shallows for seeds of sedges, willows and pond-weeds; also eats aquatic invertebrates and larval amphibians; eats waste grain in agri-cultural areas during migration; more var-ied diet than other dabbling ducks.
Voice: *Male:* soft, whistling call. *Female:* rough quack.
Similar Species: male is distinctive. *Mallard* (p. 44) and *Gadwall* (p. 42): females are chunkier, with white under-wing coverts, shorter necks and tails and dark-and-orange bills. *Blue-winged Teal* (p. 45): smaller; female is grayer overall, with green speculum, blue forewing patch and dark eye line. *Long-tailed Duck* (p. 57): chunkier; all-dark wings; dark and light areas on head.

GREEN-WINGED TEAL

Anas crecca

The Green-winged Teal is one of the speediest and most maneuverable of waterfowl. When intruders cause these small ducks to rocket up from a wetland's surface, the birds circle quickly overhead in small, tight-flying flocks, returning to the water only when the threat has departed. A predator's only chance of catching a healthy Green-winged Teal is to snatch it from the water or from a nest. Although the females go to great lengths to conceal their nests within the protective cover of grass and brush, some nests may still be discovered by hungry predators. • Green-winged Teals often undertake a partial migration before molting into their post-breeding flightless "eclipse" plumage, which leaves them without a full set of flight feathers. • The name "teal" possibly originated from the medieval English word *tele* or the old Dutch word *teling*, both of which mean "small," in reference to the Green-winged Teal's Eurasian variant, the Common Teal.

ID: small bill; dusky legs and feet. *Breeding male:* pale gray overall; black-spotted, rufous-tinged, creamy breast; white shoulder slash; chestnut brown head; green swipe extends back from eye. *Female:* mottled brown overall; pale belly. *In flight:* green-and-black speculum.

Size: *L* 12–16 in; *W* 23 in.

Habitat: shallow lakes, wetlands, beaver ponds and meandering rivers.

Nesting: in tall vegetation; well-concealed nest of grass and leaves is lined with down; female incubates 6–14 cream to pale buff eggs for 20–24 days.

Feeding: dabbles in shallows, particularly on mudflats, for aquatic invertebrates, larval amphibians, marsh plant seeds and pondweeds.

Voice: *Male:* crisp whistle. *Female:* soft quack.

Similar Species: *American Wigeon* (p. 43): breeding male is generally rufous brown, with white-speckled face and white forehead and crown. *Blue-winged Teal* (p. 45) and *Cinnamon Teal* (p. 46): females have blue forewing patches, larger bills and yellowish legs and feet.

CANVASBACK

Aythya valisineria

Most male ducks sport richly decorated backs, but the breeding male Canvasback has a bright, clean-looking back that, appropriately, appears to be wrapped in white canvas. In profile, a Canvasback of either gender casts a noble image—the long bill meets the forecrown with no apparent break in angle, allowing the bird to be recognized at long range. The white back and unique profile are unmistakable field marks. • Canvasbacks are diving ducks that are typically found on large areas of open water. Because these birds prefer large lakes and bays and the deepest areas of wetlands, birders often need binoculars to admire the male's wild red eyes and mahogany head. Canvasbacks are most likely to be seen during spring and fall migration, when flocks composed of more than 10,000 individuals occasionally converge on a suitable wetland. • *Valisineria* is a variation on the name of one of the Canvasback's favorite foods, American wild celery (*Vallisneria americana*).

ID: consistent, relaxed upward slope from bill to forehead. *Male:* canvas white back and sides; chestnut brown head; black breast and hindquarters; red eyes. *Female:* light gray back and sides; paler brown head and neck; black eyes.

Size: *L* 19–22 in; *W* 29 in.

Habitat: marshes, ponds, shallow lakes and other wetlands; large lakes in migration.

Nesting: suspended above shallow water in a dense stand of cattails and bulrushes (occasionally on dry ground); basket nest of reeds and grass is lined with down;

female incubates 7–9 olive green eggs for up to 29 days.

Feeding: dives to depths of up to 30 ft (averages 10–15 ft); feeds on roots, tubers and basal stems of plants (including pondweeds and wild celery) and bulrush seeds; occasionally eats aquatic invertebrates.

Voice: generally quiet. *Male:* occasional coos and "growls" during courtship. *Female:* low, soft, "purring" quack or *kuck;* also "growls."

Similar Species: *Redhead* (p. 51): rounded rather than sloped forehead; breeding male has gray back, brighter head color, yellow eyes and black-tipped, bluish bill; female is generally browner, with white ring and black tip on bill.

REDHEAD

Aythya americana

Officially a diving duck, the Redhead will occasionally feed on the surface of a wetland like a dabbler. • During the breeding season, pairs of Redheads scatter across the marshes, lake edges and wetlands of central and western North America. They prefer large marshes, where they can easily blend into the busy goings-on of woodland summer life. Female Redheads usually incubate their own eggs and brood their young as other ducks do, but they occasionally lay their eggs in the nests of other ducks. Where the ranges of the Blue-winged Teal and the Ring-necked Duck overlap with the Redhead's, egg dumping (also known as "brood parasitism") may occur. • To distinguish a Redhead from a Canvasback, most birders will tell you to contrast the birds' profiles. However, the most obvious difference between them is the color of their backs: the male Redhead's back is gray, whereas the Canvasback's is white; their mates have, respectively, brown and light gray backs.

ID: black-tipped, bluish gray bill. *Male:* black breast and hindquarters; gray back and sides; rounded, reddish brown head; yellow eyes. *Female:* dark brown overall with lighter "chin" and "cheek" patches; brown eyes.

Size: *L* 18–22 in; *W* 29 in.

Habitat: large wetlands, ponds, lakes, bays and rivers.

Nesting: suspended over shallow water at the base of emergent vegetation (sometimes on dry ground); deep basket nest of reeds and grass is lined with fine white down; female incubates 9–14 greenish eggs for 23–29 days; female may lay eggs in other ducks' nests.

Feeding: dives to depths of 10 ft; eats primarily aquatic vegetation, especially pondweeds, duckweed and the leaves and stems of plants; occasionally eats aquatic invertebrates.

Voice: generally quiet. *Male:* catlike *meow* in courtship. *Female:* rolling *kurr-kurr-kurr;* *squak* when alarmed.

Similar Species: *Canvasback* (p. 50): bill slopes onto forehead; male has different back, head, eye and bill colors; female is mostly light gray. *Ring-necked Duck* (p. 52): female has noticeably darker upperparts, peaked head, more prominent white eye ring and bill ring. *Lesser Scaup* (p. 53) and *Greater Scaup* (p. 360): males have dark heads and whiter sides; females are darker brown and have more white at base of bill.

51

RING-NECKED DUCK

Aythya collaris

After seeing the Ring-necked Duck in the wild, you may wonder why it was not named the "Ring-billed Duck," and you would not be the first birder to ponder this perplexing puzzle. The official name relates to the indistinct cinnamon "collar" (hence *collaris*) that an ornithologist noted on a museum specimen. The distinctive white bill markings and angular head, however, are field marks that immediately strike a birder looking at a live duck through binoculars. • Ring-necks are diving ducks, but they prefer to feed in shallow shoreline waters, frequently tipping up for food like dabblers. They ride high on the water and tend to carry their tails clear of the water's surface. • The Ring-necked Duck nests in the northern Great Plains, and it can nest even in boggy areas where a more picky eater would find it hard to eke out a living. Small, shy, nonbreeding groups are often seen floating on sedge-meadow wetlands and tree-edged beaver ponds farther south during summer.

ID: *Male:* black back, hindquarters and breast; gray sides; white shoulder slash; angular, dark purple head; bluish gray bill with white band next to black tip and thin, white border at base. *Female:* dark brown upperparts; medium brown sides; pale belly; white eye ring; pale crescent at front of face; dark bill with white band next to black tip.
Size: *L* 14–18 in; *W* 25 in.
Habitat: wooded ponds, swamps, marshes and sloughs with emergent vegetation; small lakes.

Nesting: on a hummock or shoreline; frequently over water; bulky nest of grass and moss is lined with down; female incubates 8–10 olive tan eggs for 25–29 days.
Feeding: dives underwater for aquatic vegetation, including seeds, tubers and pondweed leaves; also eats aquatic invertebrates and mollusks.
Voice: seldom heard. *Male:* low-pitched, hissing whistle. *Female:* growling *churr*.
Similar Species: *Lesser Scaup* (p. 53) and *Greater Scaup* (p. 360): no white ring near tip of bill; male has speckled, grayish back without shoulder slash; female has broad, distinct white border around base of bill. *Redhead* (p. 51): female has less contrast between back and sides, rounded rather than peaked head and less white on front of face.

LESSER SCAUP

Aythya affinis

The male Lesser Scaup and its close relative the male Greater Scaup mirror the color pattern of an Oreo cookie: they are black at both ends and light in the middle. Although the two species may occur together on large lakes during migration, they tend not to mingle. The Lesser Scaup is most at home among the lakes of forested areas, but it can also be found nesting in marshes. • This diving duck leaps up neatly before diving underwater, where it propels itself with powerful strokes of its feet. • The scientific name *affinis* is Latin for "adjacent" or "allied"—a reference to this scaup's close association to other diving ducks. "Scaup" might refer to a preferred winter food of this duck—shellfish beds are called "scalps" in Scotland—or it might be a phonetic imitation of one of its calls. • Both the Lesser Scaup and the Greater Scaup are known by the nickname "Bluebill."

ID: yellow eyes; black-tipped, bluish gray bill. *Male:* glossy, often purplish black head; black breast and hindquarters; dusty white sides (whitest in breeding plumage); grayish back. *Female:* dark brown overall; well-defined white patch at base of bill.
Size: *L* 15–18 in; *W* 25 in.
Habitat: *Breeding:* woodland ponds, wetlands and lake edges with grassy margins. *In migration:* lakes, large marshes and rivers.
Nesting: in tall, concealing vegetation, generally close to water and possibly on an island; nest hollow built of grass is lined with down; female incubates 8–14 olive buff eggs for about 21–27 days.
Feeding: dives underwater for aquatic invertebrates, mostly mollusks, crustaceous and insect larvae; occasionally eats aquatic vegetation.
Voice: deep *scaup* alarm call. *Male:* soft *whee-oooh* in courtship. *Female:* purring *kwah*.
Similar Species: *Greater Scaup* (p. 360): less common; migrant only; slightly larger; more prominent white wing-flash; more rounded head; slightly larger bill; male's head is usually greenish black. *Ring-necked Duck* (p. 52): white-ringed bill; male has white shoulder slash and black back; female has brown eye with white ring. *Redhead* (p. 51): female is warmer brown overall, with less white at base of bill and brown eye with white ring.

53

SURF SCOTER

Melanitta perspicillata

Like all scoters, the Surf Scoter breeds to the north of the lower 48 states, but it is the only scoter that breeds and winters exclusively in North America. Most scoters spend their winters just beyond the breaking surf on both the Atlantic and Pacific coasts, but a few birds migrate to the Gulf Coast, sometimes appearing on large reservoirs within the Great Plains. • Like other far northern breeders, Surf Scoters pair up before arriving on their summer breeding grounds to take advantage of the precious little summer available to them. • The Surf Scoter has the unfortunate distinction of being one of the least-studied waterbirds in North America. Much of what is known of its behavior and distribution was documented for the first time only in the latter part of the 20th century. • *Melanitta* means "black duck," and *perspicillata* is Latin for "spectacular," referring to the male's colorful, bulbous bill.

ID: stocky body; large, bulbous bill; sloping forehead. *Male:* black overall; white forehead and nape; mostly orange bill with black spot outlined in white; pale eyes; orangy feet and legs. *Female:* brown overall; whitish patches at nape, behind "cheek" and at base of dark gray bill. *In flight:* all-black wings.

Size: *L* 16–20 in; *W* 30 in.

Habitat: large, deep lakes and large rivers.

Nesting: does not nest in the Great Plains.

Feeding: dives to depths of 30 ft; eats mostly mollusks; also takes aquatic insect larvae, crustaceans and some aquatic vegetation.

Voice: generally quiet; infrequent low, harsh croaks. *Male:* occasional low, clear whistle. *Female:* guttural *krraak krraak*.

Similar Species: *White-winged Scoter* (p. 55): white wing patches; male has white patch below eye and less showy, orange-tipped bill; female has all-dark nape and smaller white area at base of bill. *Black Scoter* (p. 56): entirely black male has dark eyes and yellow bulge on upper bill; female has well-defined, light "cheek" patch and thinner bill.

WHITE-WINGED SCOTER
Melanitta fusca

The White-winged Scoter is the largest and most abundant of the three species of scoters in North America, but just a few migrate through the Great Plains between their breeding grounds and the Gulf Coast. • Scoters have small wings relative to the weight of their bodies, so they require long stretches of water for takeoff. As White-winged Scoters race across our lakes, their flapping wings reveal a key identifying feature—the white trailing-edge wing patches strike a sharp contrast to the bird's otherwise black plumage. • The White-winged Scoter often eats hard-shelled clams and shellfish whole. It relies upon its remarkably powerful gizzard to crush shells that we would use a hammer to open. • Scoters may be named for the way they "scoot" across the water's surface to travel quickly from one foraging site to another. The name "coot" has been incorrectly applied to all three species of scoter because of a superficial resemblance between these totally unrelated species.

ID: stocky body; sloping forehead; large, bulbous bill with fully feathered base. *Male:* black overall; white patch below pale eye; bill with dark base has orange area extending back from tip. *Female:* brown overall; grayish brown bill; whitish patches behind "cheek" and on lores. *In flight:* white wing patches.
Size: *L* 18–24 in; *W* 34 in.
Habitat: large, deep lakes and large rivers.
Nesting: does not nest in the Great Plains.

Feeding: deep underwater dives last up to 1 minute; eats mostly mollusks; may also take crustaceans, aquatic insects and some small fish.
Voice: courting pair produces harsh, guttural noises, between a *crook* and a quack.
Similar Species: *Surf Scoter* (p. 54): white nape patch; all-black wings; male has white forehead and more bulbous orange bill with white-bordered black spot. *Black Scoter* (p. 56): all-dark wings; male has all-dark head, yellow bulge on upper bill and dark eyes; female has large, light "cheek" patch. *American Coot* (p. 117): all-dark plumage except for white forehead "shield"; dark-ringed, white bill; red eyes; large, lobed toes.

BLACK SCOTER

Melanitta nigra

Migration is a lengthy and tiring journey, especially after a rigorous breeding season, so many Black Scoters make rest stops on large bodies of water as they travel southward. Like the other scoters, most of these birds overwinter on the Atlantic and Pacific coasts, but a few move to the Gulf of Mexico, crossing the Great Plains and giving us a chance to catch a glimpse of one or two. • The male is the only North American duck with uniformly black plumage. Also, unlike other scoters, which generally look downward while floating on the water, the Black Scoter tends to hold its head high. The most vocal of the scoters, it often reveals its presence with plaintive, mellow whistling calls from far out on open water. • Of the three species of scoters in the region, the Black Scoter is the least common. This rarity belies its earlier designation of "Common Scoter," the name still given to the Eurasian *nigra* subspecies.

ID: *Male:* black overall; large, yellow bulge on upper bill; dark eyes. *Female:* brown overall; dark head with light "cheek" patch; dark gray bill. *In flight:* all-dark wings.
Size: *L* 17–20 in; *W* 28 in.

Habitat: large, deep lakes, large rivers and sewage lagoons.
Nesting: does not nest in the Great Plains.
Feeding: dives underwater; eats mostly mollusks and aquatic insect larvae; occasionally eats aquatic vegetation and small fish.

Voice: generally quiet; infrequently gives an unusual *cour-loo;* wings whistle in flight.
Similar Species: *White-winged Scoter* (p. 55): white wing patches; bill is fully feathered at base; male has white patch below pale eye and orange bill tip; female has 2 whitish areas on side of head. *Surf Scoter* (p. 54): white nape patch; male has white forehead and white-bordered black spot on bill; female has 2 whitish patches on side of head. *American Coot* (p. 117): white forehead "shield"; dark ring on white bill; red eyes; large, lobed toes.

LONG-TAILED DUCK

Clangula hyemalis

Long-tailed Ducks are tundra nesters that move to open water in winter. Most of these birds go west to the Pacific, but a few head south. Some of them go to the Gulf Coast, but a few turn up on large lakes and reservoirs in the Great Plains, where they are often the highlight of a Christmas bird count. They are among the noisiest breeders on the arctic tundra, but during migration and over winter they remain relatively silent. • The breeding and nonbreeding plumages of the male are almost like photo negatives of each other: the spring breeding plumage is mostly dark with white highlights, whereas the winter plumage is mostly white with dark patches. • Long-tailed Ducks are among the world's deepest diving waterfowl—they make regular dives to depths of more than 200 feet. • Until recently, this duck was officially called "Oldsquaw," a name that many people still use.

nonbreeding

nonbreeding

ID: *Breeding male:* dark neck and upperparts; white belly; dark head with white "eye patch"; dark bill with orangy band; long, dark, central tail feathers. *Breeding female:* dark crown, throat patch, wings and back; white underparts; gray bill; short tail. *Nonbreeding male:* long white patches on black back; dark breast; white belly; pale head with gray "eye patch"; white neck with dark brown patch. *Nonbreeding*

female: similar to breeding female, but with more white on head and sides.
Size: *L* 17–20 in; *W* 28 in.
Habitat: large, deep lakes and wetlands.
Nesting: does not nest in the Great Plains.
Feeding: dives for mollusks, crustaceans and aquatic insects; occasionally eats roots and young shoots; may also take some small fish.
Voice: courtship call of *owl-owl-owlet* is rarely heard outside breeding range.
Similar Species: *Northern Pintail* (p. 48): male has gray sides, thin, white line extending up side of neck, brown head and gray bill.

BUFFLEHEAD

Bucephala albeola

Buffleheads are frequently among the first diving ducks identified by people with a growing awareness of wild waterfowl. Their abundance on park ponds, urban reservoirs and similar expanses of open water causes them to be widely noticed, particularly the simply and boldly patterned male. In his striking, black-and-white breeding plumage, which features a large white patch on the rear of the head, he resembles few other species. Somber but appealing, the female has a sooty head ornamented with a pretty white "cheek" spot. • Winter imposes many limiting factors on birds, so food and suitable habitat may be scarce at times. Fortunately for the tiny Bufflehead, it is right at home on lakes amid its larger relatives. If you are lucky, you may even see a whole flock dive at the same time. • *Bucephala*, meaning "ox-headed" in Greek, refers to the shape of the head; *albeola*, Latin for "white," refers to the male's plumage.

ID: small, rounded body; short neck; dark eyes; short, gray bill. *Breeding male:* dark back; white underparts and neck; head appears black or iridescent, dark green or purple except for white wedge at back. *Female:* dark upperparts; light brown sides; white belly; dark brown head; white, oval "ear" patch. *In flight:* white speculum; male has large, white band on upperwing.

Size: *L* 13–15 in; *W* 21 in.

Habitat: open water of lakes, large ponds and rivers.

Nesting: natural tree cavity or nest box, usually near water, is lined with down;

female incubates 6–12 ivory-colored eggs for 28–33 days.

Feeding: dives for aquatic invertebrates; takes water boatmen and mayfly and damselfly larvae in summer; favors mollusks, particularly snails, and crustaceans in migration and in winter; also eats some small fish and pondweeds.

Voice: *Male:* growling call. *Female:* harsh quack.

Similar Species: *Hooded Merganser* (p. 60): male has rusty sides, white crest outlined in black and black bill. *Harlequin Duck:* rare; female and nonbreeding male have browner sides, white on front of face and no white in wings. *Common Goldeneye* (p. 59): larger; male has iridescent, dark head with white patch between eye and blackish bill. *Other diving ducks* (pp. 50–63): much larger.

COMMON GOLDENEYE
Bucephala clangula

The courtship display of the male Common Goldeneye, surely a serious matter to the bird itself, looks to us like an avian slapstick routine. Beginning in winter, he performs a number of odd postures and vocalizations, often in front of apparently disinterested females. In one common routine, he arches his puffy, iridescent head backward until his forehead seems to touch his back. Next, he catapults his neck forward like a coiled spring while producing a seemingly painful *peent* sound. • Common Goldeneyes nest in northern forests around the world, frequently near lakes rich in aquatic invertebrates but without fish. The females often lay their eggs in the nests of other goldeneyes and other cavity-nesting ducks. After hatching, the ducklings remain in the nest for one to three days before jumping out of the tree cavity, often falling a long distance to the ground below. • Because of the sound from the wings in flight, the Common Goldeneye is frequently called "Whistler."

ID: black wings with large, white patches; steep forehead with peaked crown; golden eyes. *Male:* dark back; white sides and belly; dark, iridescent, often greenish head; round, white "cheek" patch; dark bill. *Female:* medium brown head; grayish brown body plumage; lighter breast and belly; dark bill tipped with yellow in spring and summer.
Size: *L* 16–20 in; *W* 26 in.
Habitat: *Breeding:* marshes, ponds, lakes and rivers. *In migration* and *winter:* open water of lakes, large ponds and rivers.

Nesting: in a tree cavity or nest box lined with wood chips and down; often close to water (occasionally quite far from it); female incubates 6–10 bluish green eggs for 28–32 days; 2 females may each lay a clutch in the same nest if cavities are scarce.
Feeding: dives for crustaceans, mollusks and aquatic insect larvae; also eats tubers, leeches, frogs and small fish.
Voice: *Male:* nasal *peent* and hoarse *kraaagh* in courtship; whistling from wings. *Female:* harsh croak.
Similar Species: *Barrow's Goldeneye:* more steeply sloped forehead; shorter bill; male has crescent-shaped "cheek" patch; female usually has yellower bill.

59

HOODED MERGANSER
Lophodytes cucullatus

Extremely attractive and exceptionally shy, the Hooded Merganser is among many a birder's most sought-after ducks—especially the handsome male. The drake normally holds his brilliant crest flat, but in moments of arousal or agitation, he quickly unfolds it to attract a mate or to signal approaching danger. He displays his full range of colors and athletic abilities in elaborate late-winter courtship displays and chases. • Although their breeding range extends into the Great Plains, Hoodies attain their greatest summer density in the Great Lakes region, wherever woodlands occur near waterways. • All mergansers have thin bills with small, toothlike serrations to help the birds keep a firm grasp on slippery prey. The smallest of the mergansers, Hoodies have a more diverse diet than their larger relatives. They add crustaceans, insects and even acorns to the usual diet of fish. • Unusually, female Hooded Mergansers have been known to share the incubation of eggs with female Wood Ducks and goldeneyes.

ID: slim body; thin, pointed, dark bill. *Breeding male:* black back; rusty sides; white breast with 2 black slashes; black head; bold, white crest outlined in black; yellow eyes. *Female:* dusky brown body; shaggy, brown crest; reddish eyes. *In flight:* small, white wing patches.

Size: *L* 16–18 in; *W* 24 in.

Habitat: forest-edged ponds, wetlands, lakes and rivers.

Nesting: usually in a tree cavity or nest box 15–40 ft above the ground, lined with leaves, grass and down; female incubates

10–12 spherical, white eggs for 29–33 days; some females lay their eggs in other birds' nests, including those of other species.

Feeding: very diverse diet; typically dives for small fish, caddisfly and dragonfly larvae, snails, amphibians and crayfish.

Voice: low grunts and croaks. *Male:* froglike *crrrrooo* in courtship display. *Female:* generally quiet; occasional harsh *gak* or croaking *croo-croo-crook*.

Similar Species: *Bufflehead* (p. 58): smaller; male has white underparts, dark eyes, paler bill and no crest. *Red-breasted Merganser* (p. 62) and *Common Merganser* (p. 61): larger; females have longer, orange bills. *Other diving ducks* (pp. 50–63): females lack crest.

COMMON MERGANSER

Mergus merganser

Straining like a jumbo jet in takeoff, the Common Merganser runs along the surface of the water, beating its wings until it gains sufficient speed to become airborne. Once up and away, this great duck flies arrow-straight, low over the water, making broad, sweeping turns to follow meandering rivers and lake shorelines. • Highly social, Common Mergansers often gather in large groups during migration and in winter, when any open water with a fish-filled shoal might support good numbers of these skilled divers. • Common Mergansers breed among forest-edged waterways wherever there are cool, clear and unpolluted lakes and rivers. They prefer to nest in cavities but will sometimes make do with ground nests if necessary in areas with good fishing. • North America's most widespread and abundant merganser, the Common Merganser also occurs in Europe and Asia; in some places it is known as "Goosander."

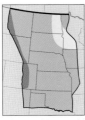

ID: large, elongated body. *Breeding male:* white body with dark back stripe; glossy, uncrested, green head; dark eyes; blood red bill and feet. *Female and nonbreeding male:* gray body; rusty neck and crested head; white "chin" and breast; orangy brown eyes; orange bill and feet. *In flight:* shallow wingbeats; compressed, arrowlike body.
Size: *L* 22–27 in; *W* 34 in.
Habitat: large rivers and deep lakes.
Nesting: often in a tree cavity 15–20 ft above the ground; occasionally on the ground, under a bush or log, on a cliff ledge or in a large nest box; usually near water; cavity is lined with wood chips and down; female incubates 8–11 pale buff eggs for 30–35 days.
Feeding: dives to depths of 30 ft for small fish, usually whitefish, trout, perch and minnows; juvenile eats aquatic invertebrates.
Voice: *Male:* harsh *uig-a,* like a guitar twang. *Female:* harsh *karr karr.*
Similar Species: *Red-breasted Merganser* (p. 62): shaggy crest; red eyes; thinner bill; breeding male has gray sides and rusty breast; female and nonbreeding male have indistinct pale "chin" and breast. *Mallard* (p. 44): breeding male has chestnut breast and yellow bill. *Common Goldeneye* (p. 59): smaller; male has white "cheek," golden eyes and stubby, dark bill. *Common Loon* (p. 73): much heavier; breeding bird has white-checkered back.

RED-BREASTED MERGANSER

Mergus serrator

Its glossy, slicked-back crest and wild red eyes give the breeding male Red-breasted Merganser the disheveled, wave-bashed look of an adrenalized wind-surfer. This species was formerly called "Sawbill" and "Sea-Robin," and it's a good thing that bird names are now standardized—who knows what we would be calling this punk-haired bird today. • Most Red-breasted Mergansers overwinter on salt water, but a few move southward through the Great Plains and turn up on lakes and reservoirs, especially favoring the Kansas salt marshes at Cheyenne Bottoms Wildlife Area and Quivira NWR. • This species breeds farther north than the other two mergansers—outside our region and as far north as the Arctic—and usually on the ground instead of in a cavity. • Red-breasts will sometimes fish cooperatively, funneling fish for easier capture.

ID: large, elongated body; red eyes; thin, serrated, orange bill; shaggy, slicked-back head crest. *Breeding male:* gray sides; black-and-white shoulders; light rusty breast spotted with black; white "collar"; green head. *Female* and *nonbreeding male:* grayish brown overall; reddish brown head; white "chin," foreneck and breast. *In flight:* male has large, white wing patch and speculum crossed by 2 narrow, black bars; female has 1 dark bar separating white speculum from smaller white upperwing patch.

Size: *L* 19–26 in; *W* 30 in.
Habitat: lakes and large rivers, especially those with rocky shorelines and islands.
Nesting: does not nest in the Great Plains.
Feeding: dives underwater for small fish; also eats aquatic invertebrates, fish eggs and crustaceans.
Voice: generally quiet. *Male:* catlike *yeow* during courtship and feeding. *Female:* harsh *kho-kha*.
Similar Species: *Common Merganser* (p. 61): thicker bill; breeding male has white body and breast, blood red bill and no crest; clear contrast between rusty foreneck and white "chin" and breast on female and nonbreeding male.

RUDDY DUCK
Oxyura jamaicensis

The clown of the wetlands, the small male Ruddy Duck displays energetic courtship behavior with comedic enthusiasm. He vigorously pumps his bright blue bill, almost touching his breast. The *plap, plap, plap-plap-plap* of the display increases in speed to its hilarious climax: a spasmodic jerk and sputter. • Female Ruddies commonly lay up to 10 eggs at a time—a remarkable feat considering that their eggs are bigger than those of a Mallard and that a Mallard is significantly larger than a Ruddy Duck. Females often take part in the unusual practice of dumping eggs in a communal "dummy" nest that may finally accumulate as many as 60 eggs that will receive no motherly care. • Some people might imagine birding paradise as a deep, lush green forest or a dense, marshy wetland, but birders searching for Ruddy Ducks might find a local sewage lagoon a desirable place to visit.

breeding

breeding

ID: short neck; large head; long, stiff tail feathers (often held upward). *Breeding male:* chestnut red body; black crown; white "cheek"; large, blue bill; black tail. *Female:* brown overall; whitish "cheek" with fuzzy brown stripe; darker crown and back; large, gray bill. *Nonbreeding male:* similar to female but with unstriped "cheek."
Size: *L* 15–16 in; *W* 18½ in.
Habitat: *Breeding:* shallow marshes with dense emergent vegetation such as cattails or bulrushes and muddy bottoms. *In migration* and *winter:* sewage lagoons and lakes with open, shallow water.

Nesting: in cattails, bulrushes or other emergent vegetation; female typically suspends a woven platform nest of grass and rushes, lined with down, over water (may use abandoned duck or coot nest, muskrat lodge or exposed log); female incubates 5–10 rough, whitish eggs for 23–26 days; occasional brood parasite.
Feeding: dives to the bottom of wetlands for seeds of pondweeds, sedges and bulrushes and for the leafy parts of aquatic plants; also eats a few aquatic invertebrates.
Voice: *Male: chuck-chuck-chuck-chur-r-r-r* during courtship display. *Female:* generally silent.
Similar Species: *Cinnamon Teal* (p. 46): breeding male has cinnamon red "cheeks" and gray bill. *Other diving ducks* (pp. 50–62): females have shorter, less stiff tails and no facial stripe.

GRAY PARTRIDGE
Perdix perdix

Introduced decades ago for hunting, the Gray Partridge is now well established in suitable habitat in the northern Great Plains. • Throughout much of the year, Gray Partridges are probably best seen "graveling up" along quiet country roads. Like other seed-eating birds, this species regularly swallows bits of gravel that it keeps in its gizzard, a muscular grinding pouch of its stomach, to help crush the hard seeds it feeds on. • During cold weather, Gray Partridges huddle together in a circle with each bird facing outward, ready to burst into flight at the first sign of danger. Although they are relatively hardy birds, many perish in harsh weather, and some birds become trapped under layers of hardened snow when taking refuge from the cold.

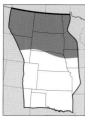

ID: small, rounded, body; mottled brown back; grayish underparts with chestnut barring on flanks; gray breast; orangy brown throat and face; short tail with chestnut outer feathers; bare, yellowish legs. *Male:* white-bordered, dark chestnut brown patch on belly. *Female:* paler face and throat.
Size: *L* 12–13 in; *W* 19–20 in.
Habitat: grassy ditches, weedy fields and agricultural croplands, often near hedgerows, farmsteads or other cover.

Nesting: on the ground; in hay fields, pastures and overgrown fence lines and field margins; a scratched-out depression is lined with grass; female incubates 15–20 olive-colored eggs for about 24 days.
Feeding: probes fields for waste grain and seeds; may also eat leaves, buds and large insects; often feeds among livestock manure piles in winter; forages at dawn and dusk in summer.
Voice: *kuta-kut-kut-kut* call when excited; also utters a loud *kar-wit kar-wit. Male: kee-uck,* like a rusty gate hinge, primarily at dawn and dusk; also a *scirl.*
Similar Species: *Ruffed Grouse* (p. 66): larger; dark barring on flanks; less striking facial coloration; dark tail bands.

RING-NECKED PHEASANT

Phasianus colchicus

Anative of Asia, the spectacular Ring-necked Pheasant was introduced to North America in the late 1800s as a game bird for hunters, but cold, snowy winters are a problem for this bird. Unlike our native grouse, the Ring-necked Pheasant does not have insulating feathers on its legs and feet, and it cannot survive on native plants alone. The availability of grain and corn crops, as well as hedgerows and sheltering woodlots, has helped this pheasant to survive in our area. • Birders hear this bird more often than they see it—the male's loud *ka-squawk* call is recognizable near farms, woodlots and brushy suburban parks. • Ring-necked Pheasants are not very strong long-distance fliers, but they are swift runners and can fly in explosive bursts to cross small open areas and escape predators.

ID: large body; unfeathered, grayish legs; long, sharp, dark-barred tail. *Male:* green head; naked, red face patch; white "collar"; bronze underparts. *Female:* mottled brown overall; light underparts.

Size: *Male: L* 30–36 in; *W* 31 in. *Female: L* 20–26 in; *W* 31 in.

Habitat: *Breeding:* grasslands, grassy ditches, hay fields and grassy or weedy fields, fence lines, crop margins and woodlot edges. *Fall:* grain and corn fields. *Winter:* woodlots, cattail marshes and shrubby areas close to soybean fields or corn fields.

Nesting: on the ground, among grass or sparse vegetation or next to a log or other natural debris; in a slight depression lined with grass and leaves; female incubates 10–12 olive buff eggs for 23–28 days; male abstains from parental duties.

Feeding: *Summer:* gleans the ground and vegetation for weed seeds, grains and insects. *Winter:* eats mostly seeds, corn kernels and buds.

Voice: *Male:* loud, raspy, roosterlike crowing: *ka-squawk;* whirring of wings, mostly just before sunrise.

Similar Species: male is distinctive. *Ruffed Grouse* (p. 66): smaller; dark barring on flanks; small crest; short tail with 1 broad, dark band.

65

RUFFED GROUSE

Bonasa umbellus

It always seems to happen without warning: a mysterious beat echoes through the forest and your body reverberates as if you've been caught in the shockwave of a mild earthquake. Actually, what you are feeling are the sounds of a "drumming" Ruffed Grouse. Every spring, and occasionally in fall, the male Ruffed Grouse proclaims his territory. He struts along a fallen log with his tail fanned and his neck feathers ruffed, periodically beating the air with accelerating wingstrokes. • Common and widespread in North America, the Ruffed Grouse inhabits a wide variety of woodland habitats ranging from small hardwood woodlots and suburban riparian woodlands to vast expanses of mixedwood and boreal forest. • Populations of Ruffed Grouse seem to fluctuate over a 10-year cycle. Many predators rely on this bird for food and show matching population fluctuations. • During winter, scales grow out along the sides of this bird's feet, giving the Ruffed Grouse temporary "snowshoes."

♂

gray morph

ID: mottled, grayish (sometimes reddish) brown overall; black feathers on sides of lower neck (most visible when fluffed out in male's courtship displays); small head crest; gray- or reddish-barred tail has broad, dark, subterminal band (incomplete on female) and white tip.
Size: *L* 15–19 in; *W* 22 in.
Habitat: hardwood and mixed forests and riparian woodlands; in many areas favors young, second-growth stands with birch and poplar.

Nesting: in a shallow depression among leaf litter and similar materials; often beside boulders, under a log or at the base of a tree; female incubates 9–12 buff-colored eggs for 23–25 days.
Feeding: gleans from the ground and vegetation; omnivorous diet includes seeds, buds, flowers, berries, catkins, leaves, insects, spiders and snails; may take small frogs.
Voice: *Male:* produces hollow, drumming sound of accelerating, deep booms using wings in courtship. *Female:* clucks and "hisses" around her chicks.
Similar Species: *Spruce Grouse* (p. 360): rare; darker overall, especially male; no head crest; white-marked, dark tail; male has red eye combs. *Sharp-tailed Grouse* (p. 67): tawnier overall; no black "ruff"; yellow eye combs; pointed tail.

SHARP-TAILED GROUSE
Tympanuchus phasianellus

I n spring, male Sharp-tailed Grouse gather at traditional dancing grounds (leks) to perform their mating rituals (which have been emulated in the traditional dance of many native cultures on the prairies). With wings drooping at their sides, tails pointing skyward and purple air sacs inflated, the males furiously pummel the ground with their feet, vigorously cooing and cackling for a crowd of prospective mates. Each male has a small stage within the circular lek that he defends against rival males with kicks and warning calls. • The Sharp-tailed Grouse is a common, permanent resident in the northern part of the region, where it is most abundant in lightly grazed to ungrazed pastures with patches of snowberry and wild rose. The few records that exist in the north suggest that it is widespread but uncommon in recent burns and dry bogs. • As with other grouse, Sharp-tail numbers rise and fall dramatically over time. In years of high abundance, large numbers of Sharp-tails move great distances, often colonizing new areas of suitable habitat.

ID: white-mottled, brown-and-black upperparts, neck and breast; dark "V"s on white belly; small head crest; yellow eye combs; white throat; white undertail coverts and outer tail feathers; long, dark-marked, central tail feathers; feathered legs. *Male:* inflates purplish pink air sacs on neck in courtship displays.
Size: *L* 17 in; *W* 25–26 in.
Habitat: grasslands and lightly grazed pastures with patches of snowberry and wild rose, open bogs, fens and forest clearings.

Nesting: on the ground; usually under cover near the lek; in a depression lined with grass and feathers; female incubates 10–13 light brown eggs dotted with reddish brown for about 24 days.
Feeding: eats buds, seeds, flowers, green shoots and berries; also eats insects.
Voice: *Male:* mournful *coo-oo* call and a cackling *cac-cac-cac-cac* during courtship.
Similar Species: *Ruffed Grouse* (p. 66): broad, fan-shaped tail with broad, dark, subterminal band; black neck "ruff." *Spruce Grouse* (p. 360): rare; darker overall; fan-shaped, black tail; male has black throat and red eye combs. *Ring-necked Pheasant* (p. 65): larger; unfeathered legs; female has paler markings on underparts and longer tail.

GREATER PRAIRIE-CHICKEN

Tympanuchus cupido

The sights and sounds of male Greater Prairie-Chickens dancing and boom-ing on their leks are impressive, especially to the females that gather to decide which male has best intimidated his rivals while demonstrating his dancing prowess. • The Greater Prairie-Chicken is a bird of the wetter tallgrass prairies in the north-central and eastern Great Plains, so its range does not overlap that of the Lesser Prairie-Chicken. It does, however, often come into contact with the Sharp-tailed Grouse. In general, the Greater Prairie-Chicken prefers more open habitats than the Sharp-tailed Grouse, which often chooses patches of open prairie with trees or glades in aspen parklands. • The loss of its native grassland habitat to agriculture and urban development has severely reduced the range and abundance of this once common bird.

ID: fairly robust; gener-ally pale with dark-edged, warm brown barring overall except on forehead, throat and "chin"; pale neck feathers; dark eye line. *Male:* cinnamon and buff neck crest raised in display; yellowish orange combs and large air sacs. *In flight:* small, fan-shaped tail.
Size: *L* 17 in; *W* 27–29 in.
Habitat: tallgrass prairies, taller grassy areas in prairies, farmland and grain fields; prairie openings in oak woodlands, oak savannas and riparian oak thickets.
Nesting: female forms a bowl-shaped depression on the ground amidst tall grass, lines it with feathers, dried grass, leaves or small twigs and incubates 8–13 dark-speckled, tawny olive eggs for 23–25 days;

nestlings are brooded for 7 days and then follow female.
Feeding: picks leaves, seeds, buds, grains and insects off the ground and low vegeta-tion, rarely off trees; in North Dakota, 90 percent of winter food is grain (much lower elsewhere).
Voice: *Male:* low-frequency booming *whhooo-doo-dooohh* on lek accompanied by foot stamping, wing shaking and tail clicking. *Female:* low *kuk, kwerr* and *brirrb* calls.
Similar Species: *Lesser Prairie-Chicken* (p. 69): different range; grayer; less distinct barring, especially on belly; male has smaller, redder air sacs. *Sharp-tailed Grouse* (p. 67): grayer overall; white-mottled upperparts; pale below with dark "V"s; sharp, dark-tipped tail; male has purplish air sacs and no raised neck crest. *Ruffed Grouse* (p. 66): broader tail with dark band; coarser barring; black neck "ruff"; inhabits wooded areas.

LESSER PRAIRIE-CHICKEN

Tympanuchus pallidicinctus

Spring dawns and early evenings are highlighted by the impressive mating dances of male Lesser Prairie-Chickens. Fanning their tails as they begin to stomp, they inflate their air sacs and lift their head feathers in an attempt to woo observing females. Up to 40 males have been observed vying for mates in the same lek, resulting in some aggressive jumping and cackling. However, the dancing is in vain for males new to the lek: only the few dominant males will win mates. • The Lesser Prairie-Chicken inhabits the shortgrass prairie in the south of our region, nesting among shinnery oak and sand sagebrush. Although it resembles its northern counterpart, the Greater Prairie-Chicken, confusion is unnecessary because the ranges of the two birds do not overlap. • The loss of native prairie and overgrazing have reduced this historically popular game species to isolated populations that cover less than 10 percent of its original range. It is currently a candidate for threatened status under the U.S. Endangered Species Act.

ID: stocky body; overall grayish brown barring, lighter on belly; short tail; dark eye stripe. *Male:* yellow eye combs; reddish air sacs and raised black-and-white head feathers in display.
Size: *L* 16 in; *W* 25 in.

Habitat: shortgrass prairie; uses shinnery oak and sagebrush for cover.

Nesting: surrounded by grass or shrubs; female scrapes out a small depression in the sand and lines it with grass; female incubates 11–13 dark-speckled, whitish eggs for 22–24 days.

Feeding: on ground or in a small bush; eats seeds, acorns, buds and insects.

Voice: normally utters a high cluck; gives sharp, descending cackles in defensive or aggressive situations. *Male:* uses air sacs to emit a booming *whup whup whu-dup* on the lek.

Similar Species: *Greater Prairie-Chicken* (p. 68): different range; larger; darker, browner streaking on underparts; male has yellowish orange air sacs. *Sharp-tailed Grouse* (p. 67): different range; white-mottled upperparts; pale below with dark "V"s; sharp tail; male has purplish air sacs and no raised neck crest.

WILD TURKEY
Meleagris gallopavo

The Wild Turkey was once very common throughout most of eastern North America, but habitat loss and overhunting during the 20th century took a toll on this bird. Today, efforts at restoration have reestablished the Wild Turkey across much of its former range. • Although turkeys prefer to feed on the ground and travel by foot—they can run faster than 19 miles per hour—they are able to fly short distances, and they roost in trees at night. • This charismatic bird is North America's only widely domesticated native animal. The wild ancestors of most other domestic animals came from Europe. • The wary Wild Turkey has acute senses and a highly developed social system. Early in life, both male and female turkeys gobble, but the females eventually outgrow this practice, leaving males to gobble competitively for the honor of mating. • If Congress had taken Benjamin Franklin's advice in 1782, our national emblem would be the Wild Turkey instead of the majestic Bald Eagle.

ID: hefty body; dark, glossy, colorful, iridescent body plumage; largely unfeathered legs; barred, copper-colored tail. *Male:* long central breast tassel; naked, blue-and-red head; red wattles. *Female:* slimmer and less iridescent than male; naked, bluish gray head.
Size: *Male: L* 3–3½ ft; *W* 5½ ft. *Female: L* 3 ft; *W* 4 ft.
Habitat: hardwood, mixed and riparian woodlands; occasionally eats waste grain and corn in late fall and winter.
Nesting: in a woodland or at a field edge; in a depression on the ground under thick cover; nest is lined with grass and leaves; female incubates 10–12 brown-speckled, pale buff eggs for up to 28 days.
Feeding: in fields near protective woods; forages on the ground for seeds, fruits, bulbs and sedges; also eats insects, especially beetles and grasshoppers; may take small amphibians.
Voice: wide array of sounds; loud *pert* in alarm; gathering call is a cluck; contact call is a loud *keouk-keouk-keouk. Male:* gobbles loudly in courtship.
Similar Species: other grouse and grouse-like birds are much smaller. *Ring-necked Pheasant* (p. 65): tawnier overall; plumage not iridescent; feathered head and neck; long, narrow tail.

SCALED QUAIL

Calliopepla squamata

A favorite of both hunters and birdwatchers, the quirky little Scaled Quail can be found hiding underneath farm equipment or mesquite bushes in arid scrubland habitat. Winter coveys break into breeding pairs around March or April, giving the male cause to show off his plumage atop a fence post, calling to proclaim his breeding territory. • Breeding depends on summer precipitation—under good conditions, females will lay more than one clutch per season. Despite the females' egg-laying efforts, the population of the Scaled Quail is decreasing as a result of habitat loss. Overgrazing removes the quail's much-loved greenery, and fire suppression allows shrubbery to encroach, bringing with it the better adapted Gambel's Quail *(C. gambellii).* • Also called "Blue Quail" because of its color, this bird gets its "scaly" appearance from black edging along its feathers, and the showy head "plume" has earned it the charming nickname of "Cottontop." • As a unique adaptation for winter survival, the digestive tract of this quail can change to collect more energy from lower quality foods, such as tumbleweed seeds.

ID: stocky body; generally pale bluish gray and brown; white, horizontal stripes along sides; 1 white wing bar; "scaly" neck and underparts; white tuft on head (largest on male); gray-tipped tail.

Size: *L* 10–12 in; *W* 14 in.
Habitat: arid scrub- and grasslands; may be found in coveys around log piles or farm equipment; usually within 1–2 mi of water.

Nesting: on the ground, under thick vegetation, in a grass- and leaf-lined small depression; female incubates 12–14 white eggs with brown speckling for 22–23 days as male defends nest territory.
Feeding: feeds in groups at dawn and dusk; eats seeds, insects and vegetation.
Voice: various clicks and trills; throaty *chip-chuk!* when a covey is separated. *Male:* loud *sheesh!*
Similar Species: *Gambel's Quail:* female has white-streaked, chestnut sides, buffy chest and thin, black head plume.

71

NORTHERN BOBWHITE

Colinus virginianus

Throughout fall and winter, Northern Bobwhites typically travel in coveys (large family groups), collectively seeking out sources of food and huddling together during cold nights. When they huddle, members of the covey all face outward, enabling the group to detect danger from any direction. With the arrival of summer, breeding pairs break away from their coveys to perform elaborate courtship rituals in preparation for another nesting season. • The male's characteristic, whistled *bob-white* call, usually issued in spring, is often the only evidence of this bird's presence among the dense, tangled vegetation of its rural woodland home. • Bobwhites benefit from habitat disturbance, using the early successional habitats created by fire, agriculture and forestry. • The Northern Bobwhite is the only quail native to eastern North America.

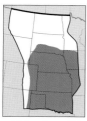

ID: mottled brown, buff and black upperparts; white crescents and spots edged in black on chestnut brown sides and upper breast; short tail. *Male:* white throat; broad, white "eyebrow." *Female:* buff throat and "eyebrow." *Immature:* smaller and duller overall; no black on underparts.
Size: *L* 10 in; *W* 13 in.
Habitat: farmland, open woodlands, woodland edges, grassy fence lines, roadside ditches and brushy, open country.

Nesting: on the ground, in a shallow depression lined with grass and leaves and often concealed by surrounding vegetation or a woven partial dome; pair incubates 12–16 white to pale buff eggs for 22–24 days.
Feeding: eats seasonally available seeds, berries, leaves, roots and nuts; also takes insects and other invertebrates.
Voice: whistled *hoy* is given year-round. *Male:* a whistled, rising *bob-white* in spring and summer.
Similar Species: *Ruffed Grouse* (p. 66): much larger; coarsely dark-barred underparts; black "ruff"; plainer face; larger, fan-shaped tail with broad, dark band.

COMMON LOON

Gavia immer

A classic symbol of northern lakes, the Common Loon is mainly a migrant in the Great Plains. • Loons float very low on the water, disappearing behind swells, then reappearing like ethereal guardians of the water. • With nearly solid bones that make them less buoyant (most birds have hollow bones) and feet placed well back on their bodies for efficient underwater propulsion, Common Loons are well adapted to their aquatic lifestyle. Small bass, perch, sunfish, pike and whitefish are all fair game for these excellent underwater hunters. On land, however, their rear-placed legs make walking seem difficult, and with their heavy bodies and small wing size, takeoff requires a lengthy sprint across the water. • "Loon" may be derived from the Scandinavian word *lom*, meaning "clumsy person," in reference to the awkwardness of these birds on land.

nonbreeding

ID: *Breeding:* black-and-white "checkerboard" upperparts; white breast and underparts; black-lined, white "necklace"; green-tinged, black head; stout, thick, black bill; red eyes. *Nonbreeding:* much duller plumage; sandy brown back; whitish throat area; gray bill; reddish brown eyes. *In flight:* long wings beat constantly; hunchbacked appearance; legs trail behind tail.

Size: *L* 28–35 in; *W* 4–5 ft.

Habitat: *Breeding:* large lakes, often with islands that provide undisturbed shorelines for nesting. *Winter:* lakes with open water.

Nesting: on a muskrat lodge, small island or projecting shoreline; always very near water; pair builds nest mound of aquatic vegetation; pair incubates 1–3 dark-spotted, olive eggs for 24–31 days; pair rears the young.

Feeding: pursues small fish underwater to depths of 180 ft; occasionally eats large aquatic invertebrates and larval and adult amphibians.

Voice: alarm call is a quavering tremolo, often called "loon laughter"; contact call is a long but simple, wailing *where aaare you?*; breeding notes are soft, short hoots. *Male:* territorial call is an undulating, complex yodel.

Similar Species: *Red-throated Loon* (p. 360): slimmer; shorter wings; slender bill; gray head and neck with red throat in breeding plumage; nonbreeding plumage shows white face, throat and foreneck, gray crown and nape and white-dotted back.

73

PIED-BILLED GREBE
Podilymbus podiceps

The odd, exuberant chortle of the Pied-billed Grebe fits right in with the boisterous cacophony of the prairie's wetland communities. Heard more frequently than seen, the Pied-billed Grebe is the smallest, shyest and least colorful of our grebes. This extremely wary bird tends to swim inconspicuously in the shallow waters of quiet bays and rivers, only occasionally voicing its strange chuckle or whinny, but it is far more common than encounters would lead you to believe. • So that approaching predators can be readily seen, a pair will build its floating nest among sparse vegetation. When frightened by an intruder, these birds cover their eggs, leaving a nest that looks like nothing more than a mat of debris, and slowly slide underwater, with just the nostrils and eyes exposed. • The scientific name *podiceps*, which means "rump foot," refers to the location of the feet, which is toward the back of this bird's body.

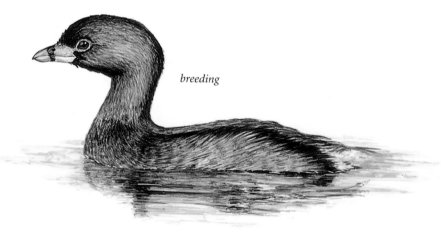

breeding

ID: brown overall, darkest above; laterally compressed "chicken bill"; black eyes; very short tail. *Breeding:* pale belly; white undertail coverts; black throat; black ring on pale bill; whitish eye ring. *Nonbreeding:* white "chin" and throat; yellowish eye ring; all-yellowish bill.
Size: *L* 12–15 in; *W* 16 in.
Habitat: ponds, marshes and backwaters with sparse emergent vegetation.
Nesting: among sparse vegetation in sheltered bays, ponds and marshes; floating platform nest of wet and decaying plants is anchored to or placed among emergent vegetation; pair incubates 4–5 white to buff eggs for about 23 days and raises the young together.
Feeding: makes shallow dives and gleans the water's surface for aquatic invertebrates, small fish and adult and larval amphibians; occasionally eats aquatic plants.
Voice: loud, whooping call begins quickly, then slows down: *kuk-kuk-kuk cow cow cow cowp cowp cowp.*
Similar Species: *Eared Grebe* (p. 77) and *Horned Grebe* (p. 75): head is black above and white below in nonbreeding plumage; red eyes; much slimmer bills. *American Coot* (p. 117): all-dark body; pale bill extends onto forehead; bigger feet.

HORNED GREBE

Podiceps auritus

Riding high in the water, the compact little Horned Grebe has a rounded head outline with slightly puffed "cheeks." The neck is somewhat curved or thrust forward when this bird swims. • The Horned Grebe flies more readily than most grebes, with a strong, direct, loonlike flight. • A grebe catches its food in long dives that start with a pronounced upward and forward leap. These dives may last up to three minutes, and the bird might travel as far as 400 feet underwater, propelling itself solely with its feet. Unlike most swimming birds, which have fully webbed feet, a grebe has each of its forward-pointing toes individually webbed or "lobed." • The name *auritus* ("eared"), refers to the golden feather tufts, or "horns," of the breeding plumage. Residents of the southern Great Plains have a chance to see Horned Grebes in their dazzling breeding finery during their spring migration, whereas birders in the northern Great Plains might see them on their nesting lakes and ponds.

nonbreeding

ID: black back; white underparts; red eyes. *Breeding:* rufous flanks and neck; black head; flat crown; dense golden "ear" tufts; dark bill with white tip. *Nonbreeding:* gray flanks and hindneck; white foreneck and "cheek"; black "hood"; paler bill.
Size: *L* 12–15 in; *W* 18 in.
Habitat: wetlands and large lakes.
Nesting: usually singly or in groups of 2–3 pairs; in thick vegetation along the edges of lakes, ponds, marshes and reservoirs; pair incubates 4–7 white eggs for 22–25 days and raises the young together.

Feeding: makes shallow dives and gleans the water's surface for aquatic insects, crustaceans, mollusks, small fish and adult and larval amphibians.
Voice: normally quiet; loud series of croaks and shrieking notes and a sharp *keark keark* during courtship; shrill *kowee* alarm call.
Similar Species: *Eared Grebe* (p. 77): finer bill; all-black neck and fanned-out tufts in breeding plumage; black "cheek" and dark neck in nonbreeding plumage. *Pied-billed Grebe* (p. 74): mostly brown body; thicker, stubbier bill; dark eyes. *Red-necked Grebe* (p. 76): larger; longer, yellowish bill; dark eyes; white "cheek" and no "ear" tufts in breeding plumage.

RED-NECKED GREBE

Podiceps grisegena

Red-necked Grebes are not as vocally refined as loons, but few loons can match the verbal vigor of a pair of Red-necks romancing the passions of spring. Although their whinnylike calls are a raucous part of springtime evenings in their breeding territory—the wild laughter typically lasts throughout the night in late May—Red-necks are otherwise usually quiet and retiring. • In the northern Great Plains, breeding-plumaged birds arrive from their coastal wintering grounds in their best finery. But Red-necked Grebes are also rare winter visitors to most of the southern Great Plains, where the drab, winter-plumaged birds are sometimes mistaken for mergansers. • All grebes feed, sleep and court on water, and they even carry their newly hatched young on their backs. The striped young are able to stay aboard even when the parents dive underwater. • The Red-necked Grebe is one of North America's largest grebes. The scientific name *grisegena* means "gray cheek"—a distinctive field mark of this bird in nonbreeding plumage.

breeding

ID: black to brownish upperparts; light underparts; dark eyes. *Breeding:* rusty neck; small black "hood"; large whitish "cheek" patch; straight, heavy bill is dark above and yellow below. *Nonbreeding:* pale, grayish brown foreneck, "chin" and "cheek"; duskier bill.
Size: *L* 17–22 in; *W* 24 in.
Habitat: open, deep lakes.
Nesting: floating platform nest of aquatic vegetation is anchored to submerged plants; pair incubates 4–5 white

eggs, often stained by wet vegetation, for 20–23 days.
Feeding: dives and gleans the water's surface for small fish, aquatic invertebrates and amphibians.
Voice: silent in migration; raucous, whinnylike "laughter" in courtship.
Similar Species: *Horned Grebe* (p. 75): smaller; shorter, pale-tipped bill; red eyes; all-dark head, except lores and golden "horns," in breeding plumage; bright white "cheek" in nonbreeding plumage. *Eared Grebe* (p. 77): nonbreeding is smaller with red eyes and smaller bill. *Pied-billed Grebe* (p. 74): smaller; mostly brown body; thicker, stubbier bill. *Mergansers* (pp. 60–62): larger; shorter necks; head crests; hook-tipped bills.

EARED GREBE

Podiceps nigricollis

The most abundant grebe not only in North America but also the world, the Eared Grebe also inhabits parts of Europe, Asia, Central Africa and South America. • Eared Grebes undergo cyclical periods of atrophy and hypertrophy, meaning that their internal organs and pectoral muscles shrink or swell depending on when the birds need to migrate. This strategy leaves Eared Grebes flightless for a longer period—nine to ten months per year—than any other flying bird in the world. • Like other grebes, the Eared Grebe eats feathers. The feathers often pack the digestive tract, and it is thought that they protect the stomach lining and intestines from sharp fish bones or parasites, or perhaps they slow the passage of food and allow more time for complete digestion. • The scientific name *nigricollis* means "black neck," a characteristic of this bird's breeding plumage.

breeding

ID: dark upperparts; white underparts; slightly raised crown; red eyes; thin, straight bill. *Breeding:* red flanks; black neck, head and bill; fanned-out, golden "ear" tufts. *Nonbreeding:* smudgy gray flanks, upper forehead neck and lower face; black "hood"; gray bill.

Size: *L* 11½–14 in; *W* 16 in.

Habitat: wetlands, large lakes, sewage disposal ponds.

Nesting: usually colonial; in thick vegetation on lake edges, ponds and marshes; shallow, flimsy, floating platform nest of wet and decaying plants is anchored to or placed among emergent vegetation; pair incubates 3–5 white eggs for around 21 days and raises the young together.

Feeding: makes shallow dives and gleans the water's surface for aquatic insects, crustaceans, mollusks, small fish and larval and adult amphibians.

Voice: mellow *poo-eee-chk* during breeding season; otherwise usually quiet.

Similar Species: *Horned Grebe* (p. 75): thicker, white-tipped bill; rufous neck and denser tufts in breeding plumage; large, crisp, white "cheek" patch in nonbreeding plumage. *Pied-billed Grebe* (p. 74): mostly brown body; black eyes; thicker, stubbier bill. *Red-necked Grebe* (p. 76): larger; dark eyes; longer, yellowish bill; red neck, large, crisp, whitish "cheek" patch and no tufts in breeding plumage; dusky white "cheek" and whitish partial "collar" in nonbreeding plumage.

WESTERN GREBE

Aechmophorus occidentalis

Western Grebe courtship displays are among the most elaborate and beautiful rituals in the bird world. During the "weed dance," the male and female swim with their torsos and heads held high, caressing each other with aquatic vegetation held in their bills. Better known is the "rushing" display, which involves two or more individuals exploding into a paddling sprint side by side across the water's surface. The grebes stand high, feet paddling furiously, with their wings stretched back and heads and necks held rigid, until the race ends with the birds making a graceful, headfirst dive. • As with most grebes, Western Grebe eggs hatch at regular intervals. Parental duties are often divided, with each parent feeding half the fledged young. • Many lakes that once supported nesting colonies have been turned into vacation resorts. Unlike its Red-necked relative, the Western Grebe seems unable to adjust to the disturbances created by cottagers and recreationalists and abandons the site.

ID: black upperparts from base of bill to tail; white underparts from "chin" to belly; long, slender neck; long, thin, yellow bill; white "cheek"; black on face extends below red eyes.

Size: *L* 25 in; *W* 24 in.

Habitat: large, deep lakes with emergent vegetation for nesting.

Nesting: usually in colonies; floating nest of fresh and decaying vegetation is anchored or placed among emergent vegetation; pair incubates 2–7 bluish green to buffy eggs (becoming stained brown) for about 23 days.

Feeding: gleans the water's surface and dives for small fish, some amphibians and aquatic invertebrates.

Voice: high-pitched, double-note *crreeet-crreeet* call series sounds like a squeaky wheel.

Similar Species: *Clark's Grebe* (p. 361): white on face extends above eyes; orangy yellow bill; single-note call. *Red-necked Grebe* (p. 76): shorter; nonbreeding bird has darker sides and shorter, stockier neck, shorter bill and dark eyes.

AMERICAN WHITE PELICAN

Pelecanus erythrorhynchos

The American White Pelican is a majestic wetland presence. Its wingspan is only a foot shy of the height of a basketball hoop, but it is best known for its porous, bucketlike bill, which is dramatically adapted for feeding. As a pelican lifts its bill from the water, fish are held within a flexible pouch while the water drains out. In a single scoop, a pelican can hold over 3 gallons of water and fish, which is about two to three times as much as its stomach can hold. This impressive feat inspired Dixon Lanier Merritt to quip, "A wonderful bird is the pelican, his bill will hold more than his belican!" American White Pelicans eat about 4 pounds of fish per day, but because they prefer nongame fish they do not pose a threat to the potential catches of anglers. • All other large, white birds with black wing tips fly with their necks extended—the American White Pelican is the only one to fly with its neck pulled back toward its wings.

nonbreeding

ID: very large, stocky body; long, orange bill; orange throat pouch and skin patch around eye; short tail. *Breeding:* small, keeled plate on upper mandible; crest on back of head. *Immature:* brown-tinged white plumage. *In flight:* white wing has black trailing edge and tip.
Size: *L* 4½–6 ft; *W* 9 ft.
Habitat: large lakes and rivers.

Nesting: colonial; on a bare, low-lying island; nest scrape is lined with pebbles and debris or is completely unlined; pair incubates 2 dull white eggs for 29–36 days; second hatchling often dies; young are fed by regurgitation.
Feeding: surface-dips for small fish and amphibians; small groups of pelicans often feed cooperatively by herding fish into large concentrations.
Voice: generally quiet; rarely issues piglike grunts.
Similar Species: no other large, white bird has a long bill with a pouch.

DOUBLE-CRESTED CORMORANT

Phalacrocorax auritus

Slick-feathered and often appearing disheveled, the Double-crested Cormorant has a beauty that can take longer to appreciate than that of other birds, especially when extra-close encounters reveal the foul stench of fish oil. Nevertheless, this bird's mastery of the aquatic environment is virtually unsurpassed. Its long, rudderlike tail, excellent underwater vision and sealed nostrils contribute to the success of its aquatic lifestyle, and its underwater diving is further aided by a lack of buoyancy—unlike most birds, cormorants do not have oil glands to supply waterproofing. Therefore, instead of floating on the water after a bout of diving, a Double-crested Cormorant will often perch in a tree with its wings partially spread in an attempt to dry its feathers. • Once believed to compete with anglers, cormorants are now known to take mostly fish that are of little value to humans.

breeding

ID: all-black body; long, crooked neck; amber "chin" and lores; blue eyes; thin, hook-tipped bill. *Breeding:* intensely orangy yellow throat pouch; fine, black plumes trail from "eyebrows." *Immature:* brown upperparts; buff throat and breast. *In flight:* rapid wingbeats; kinked neck.
Size: *L* 26–32 in; *W* 4½ ft.
Habitat: large lakes and large, meandering rivers; small treed islands.
Nesting: colonial; on the ground on a low-lying island, often with terns and gulls, or precariously high in a tree; nest platform is made of sticks, aquatic vegetation and guano; pair incubates 3–6 bluish white eggs for 25–33 days; young are fed by regurgitation.
Feeding: long underwater dives to depths of 30 ft or more when after small schooling fish or, rarely, amphibians and invertebrates; grasps prey with bill to bring it to the surface.
Voice: generally quiet; may issue piglike grunts or croaks, especially near nesting colonies.
Similar Species: *Neotropic Cormorant:* mostly in southern region; smaller; longer tail; breeding adult has white border to yellow throat patch. *Anhinga:* mostly in extreme southeast of region; white-streaked back and upperwings; longer, broader tail; longer, sharp bill.

AMERICAN BITTERN

Botaurus lentiginosus

Even though it is common around productive marsh habitat, the secretive American Bittern is uncommonly or even rarely seen, but late mornings and early afternoons are the best times to try to catch a glimpse. At the approach of an intruder, a bittern's first reaction is to freeze with its bill pointed skyward—its vertically streaked, brown plumage blends perfectly with its wetland surroundings. An American Bittern will always face an intruder, moving ever so slowly to keep its camouflaged breast toward danger. In most cases, intruders simply pass by without ever noticing the bird. This defensive reaction can sometimes result in an unfortunate comical turn for the bittern—it will try to mimic reeds even in an entirely open field. • Although the American Bittern's camouflage often fools potential predators, the cryptic plumage is most likely an adaptation to reduce the bird's visibility to prey while hunting. The camouflage is at its most effective in the dim light situations of dawn and dusk, this bird's preferred hunting times.

ID: brown upperparts; brown streaking from "chin" through breast; black streak from bill down neck to shoulder; straight, stout, blackish yellow bill; greenish yellow legs and feet; short tail. *In flight:* black outer wings.

Size: *L* 23–27 in; *W* 3½ ft.

Habitat: marshes, wetlands and lake edges with tall, dense grass, sedges, bulrushes and cattails.

Nesting: singly; above the waterline in dense vegetation; nest platform is made of grass, sedges and dead reeds; nest often has separate entrance and exit paths; female incubates 3–5 pale olive or buff eggs for 24–28 days.

Feeding: patient stand-and-wait predator; strikes at small fish, crayfish, amphibians, reptiles, mammals and insects.

Voice: deep, slow, resonant, repetitive *pomp-er-lunk* or *onk-a-BLONK;* most often heard in the evening and at night.

Similar Species: *Least Bittern* (p. 82): immature is tawnier overall with no black neck streak. *Green Heron* (p. 88): immature is browner overall with no black neck streak. *Black-crowned Night-Heron* (p. 89) and *Yellow-crowned Night-Heron* (p. 90): immatures are more grayish brown with white-flecked upperparts, red eyes and no black neck streak.

LEAST BITTERN

Ixobrychus exilis

Least Bittern sightings tend to be rare, in part because of this bird's secretive behavior and solitary lifestyle. The smallest of the herons and one of North America's most reclusive marsh birds, it lives among tall, impenetrable stands of cattails that conceal most of its movements as its slender body passes freely and unnoticed through dense marshland habitat. When seen, this expert climber is often 3 feet or more above water, hopping about from reed to reed and clinging to vertical stems. In this way, it can forage even over fairly deep water without getting its feet wet. • *Ixobrychus* is Greek for "reed-howler" and refers to the sound this bird makes, which has been likened to that of blowing through the stem of a reed, and the species name, *exilis*, is Latin for "slender."

ID: rich buff flanks and sides; white underparts; brown-streaked foreneck; mostly pale bill; yellowish legs; short tail. *Male:* black back and crown. *Female:* dark brown back and head. *Immature:* similar to female, but with darker streaking on breast and back. *In flight:* large, buffy orange shoulder patches; dark trailing edge and tip on upperwing.
Size: *L* 11–14½ in; *W* 17 in.
Habitat: freshwater marshes with cattails and other dense emergent vegetation.
Nesting: usually well concealed within dense vegetation; mostly the male constructs a platform of dry plant stalks on top of bent marsh vegetation; pair incubates 4–5 pale green or blue eggs for 17–20 days; pair feeds the young by regurgitation.
Feeding: stabs prey with bill; eats mostly small fish; also takes large insects, tadpoles, frogs, small snakes, leeches and crayfish; may build a hunting platform.
Voice: *tut-tut* call; *koh* alarm call. *Male:* guttural *uh-uh-uh-oo-oo-oo-ooah. Female:* ticking sound.
Similar Species: *American Bittern* (p. 81): much larger; browner overall; bolder streaking on underparts; black streak from bill to shoulder. *Black-crowned Night-Heron* (p. 89) and *Yellow-crowned Night-Heron* (p. 90): immatures have white-flecked, grayish brown upperparts. *Green Heron* (p. 88): immature has dark brown upperparts and less tidy streaking on neck.

GREAT BLUE HERON

Ardea herodias

The sight of a majestic Great Blue Heron is always memorable, whether you are observing its stealthy, often motionless, hunting strategy or tracking its graceful wingbeats. However, its large nest colonies (rookeries), which are usually in high trees, are sensitive to human disturbance, so it is best to observe nesting birds from a distance. • Great Blues winter farther north than other herons and are thus vulnerable to prolonged cold weather. In many places, spotting one would highlight your local Christmas bird count. • This heron is often mistaken for a crane, but, unlike a crane, which holds its neck outstretched in flight, the Great Blue folds its neck back over its shoulders in an S-shape. • Mostly a fish eater, this bird may also be found stalking fields and meadows in search of rodents.

breeding

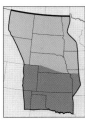

ID: large body; bluish gray overall; long, curving neck; straight, yellow bill; chestnut brown thighs; long, pinkish to dark gray legs. *Breeding:* richer colors; dark plumes streak from crown and lighter ones from lower throat. *In flight:* slow, steady wingbeats; neck folds back over shoulders; legs trail behind body.

Size: *L* 4–4½ ft; *W* 6 ft.

Habitat: forages along the edges of rivers, lakes, marshes, fields and wet meadows.

Nesting: colonial; usually in a tree but occasionally on the ground; flimsy to elaborate stick-and-twig platform to 4 ft in diameter is added onto annually; pair incubates 4–7 pale blue eggs for about 28 days.

Feeding: patient stand-and-wait predator or stalks slowly; strikes at small fish, amphibians, small mammals, aquatic invertebrates and reptiles; rarely scavenges.

Voice: usually quiet away from the nest; occasionally gives a deep, harsh *frahnk frahnk frahnk,* usually during takeoff.

Similar Species: *Yellow-crowned Night-Heron* (p. 90): much smaller; shorter legs and bill; mostly black head with white crown and "cheek." *Egrets* (pp. 84–87): smaller; predominately white. *Sandhill Crane* (p. 118): gray overall with rusty areas; red "cap"; flies with neck outstretched. *Little Blue Heron* (p. 86): much smaller; dark overall; purplish head; dark-tipped, light gray bill.

GREAT EGRET

Ardea alba

E grets are a group of herons marked by impressive breeding plumes, referred to as "aigrettes." In the early 20th century, the plumes of the Great Egret and Snowy Egret were widely used to decorate hats. An ounce of egret feathers could cost as much as $32—more than an ounce of gold at that time—and, as a result, egret populations began to disappear. • Some of the first conservation legislation in North America was enacted to outlaw the hunting of the Great Egret. This bird became the symbol for the National Audubon Society, one of our country's oldest conservation organizations. The Great Egret is now recovering and expanding its range, probably to where it formerly nested, so future nesting may occur throughout the wetlands of the Great Plains.

nonbreeding

breeding

ID: all-white plumage; yellow bill; black legs and feet. *Breeding:* white plumes trail from throat and rump; skin patch between eyes and base of bill becomes greenish. *In flight:* neck folds back over shoulders; legs extend backward.
Size: *L* 3–3½ ft; *W* 4 ft.
Habitat: marshes, open riverbanks, irrigation canals and lakeshores.
Nesting: colonial, but may nest in isolated pairs; in a tree or tall shrub; pair builds a

platform of sticks and incubates 3–5 pale bluish green eggs for 23–26 days.
Feeding: patient stand-and-wait predator; occasionally stalks slowly, stabbing at frogs, lizards, snakes and small mammals.
Voice: very low, dry croaks.
Similar Species: *Snowy Egret* (p. 85): smaller; shorter neck; black bill; yellow feet; breeding bird has head plumes. *Cattle Egret* (p. 87): nonbreeding bird is smaller and stockier with shorter neck and bill. *Little Blue Heron* (p. 86): smaller; immature develops gray smudges by first spring, has sharper, dark-tipped, pale bill and paler legs and feet.

SNOWY EGRET

Egretta thula

Already distinguished by a spotless white plumage and bright yellow feet, the Snowy Egret stands out even more with the striking black legs of breeding season. • Although softer, more delicate plumes and greater abundance and range led to the Snowy Egret being more strongly affected by plume hunters than the Great Egret, it is being seen increasingly often in our region. Mainly a wanderer in inland areas, it does breed in several southern Great Plains states. Its propensity for far-ranging post-breeding dispersal is much like that of the Great Egret, and frequent spring sightings suggest future range extension into the central Great Plains if suitable habitat is provided. • The Snowy Egret uses a greater variety of feeding techniques than most other herons. By poking its feet in shallow wetland muck, it spooks potential prey out of hiding. Even more deviously, this bird is known to create shade by extending its wings over open water. Any fish succumbing to the attraction of the cool shade are promptly seized. Some paleontologists have suggested that this use was one of the original functions of bird wings.

breeding

nonbreeding

ID: white plumage; yellow feet. *Breeding:* long plumes on throat and rump; head plumes; orange lores; black bill and legs. *Nonbreeding:* black-and-yellow bill and legs. *Immature:* more yellow on legs.

Size: *L* 22–26 in; *W* 3½ ft.

Habitat: open edges of rivers, lakes and marshes.

Nesting: colonial, often with Great Blue Herons and Double-crested Cormorants, but may nest in isolated pairs; in a tree or tall shrub; pair builds a platform of sticks and incubates 3–5 pale bluish green eggs for 23–26 days.

Feeding: stirs wetland muck with its feet; stands and waits with wings held open; occasionally hovers and stabs; eats small fish, amphibians and invertebrates.

Voice: raspy, hoarse, nasal croaks.

Similar Species: *Great Egret* (p. 84): larger; longer neck; longer, yellow bill; black feet. *Cattle Egret* (p. 87): stockier; breeding bird has orange-tinged plumes and orange bill, legs and feet; nonbreeding bird has yellow bill and black legs and feet. *Little Blue Heron* (p. 86): immature develops gray smudges by first spring, has sharper, dark-tipped, pale bill and paler legs and feet.

LITTLE BLUE HERON

Egretta caerulea

Because of its dark adult plumage and absence of aigrette plumes, the Little Blue Heron was only occasionally taken by the plume hunters of a century ago and did not suffer the same population decimation as its showier relatives. Although adults of the species are quite distinctive, immature Little Blues are white, like Snowy Egrets and Cattle Egrets, making identification confusing. It takes two years for Little Blue Herons to develop the completely dark plumage of adult birds. • In the Great Plains, this medium-sized heron breeds in Oklahoma, Kansas and Missouri. • Feeding behavior is often the best way to distinguish herons. Larger herons seem graceful even while lunging for a fish, whereas the Little Blue Heron often seems tentative and stiff in its hunting maneuvers as it awkwardly jabs at prey.

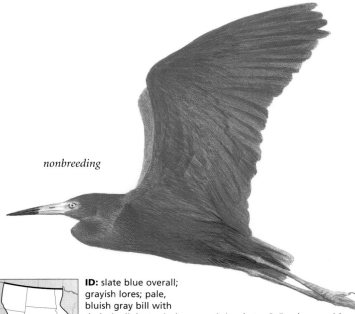

nonbreeding

ID: slate blue overall; grayish lores; pale, bluish gray bill with dark tip; light to dusky green legs and feet. *Breeding:* shaggy, maroon-colored head and neck. *Nonbreeding:* smooth, purplish head and neck. *Immature:* white overall with gray wing tips, developing smudgy grayish blue areas when molting to adult plumage; yellowish olive legs.
Size: *L* 24 in; *W* 3½ ft.
Habitat: marshes, ponds, lakes, streams and meadows.
Nesting: nests in a shrub or tree above water; pair builds a large nest of sticks;

pair incubates 3–5 pale greenish blue eggs for 22–24 days.
Feeding: patient stand-and-wait predator; sometimes wades slowly to stalk prey; eats mostly fish and crayfish; also takes grasshoppers and other insects, frogs, lizards, snakes and turtles.
Voice: generally silent.
Similar Species: *Snowy Egret* (p. 85): all-white wings; yellow lores; black bill; blackish legs; yellow feet; juvenile has yellowish legs and may have dark-tipped, pale bill. *Cattle Egret* (p. 87): shorter, yellow to orangy bill; yellow to purplish orange lores; black-and-yellow to orange legs and feet; immature has darker bill, legs and feet.

CATTLE EGRET

Bubulcus ibis

Over the last century—and without help from humans—the Cattle Egret has dispersed from Africa to inhabit every continent except Antarctica. Like most herons, the Cattle Egret is a natural wanderer. It spread from Africa to Brazil, through the Caribbean and, by 1950, to Florida, then across the U.S. • The Cattle Egret gets its name from its habit of following grazing animals. Unlike other egrets, it has a diet that consists of terrestrial invertebrates, and it usually feeds on the insects and other small creatures found around ungulates. When foraging, the Cattle Egret sometimes uses a "leapfrog" feeding strategy in which birds leapfrog over one another, stirring up insects for the birds that follow. • This bird's scientific name *Bubulcus* means "belonging to or concerning cattle."

breeding

nonbreeding

ID: mostly white. *Breeding:* buff orange throat, rump and crown; long plumes on throat and rump; reddish orange legs and bill; yellow to purplish orange lores. *Nonbreeding:* dusky legs and feet. *Immature:* dark bill.
Size: *L* 19–21 in; *W* 35–37 in.
Habitat: agricultural fields, ranchlands and marshes.
Nesting: colonial; often among other herons; in a tree or tall shrub; male

supplies sticks for female to build a platform or shallow bowl; pair incubates 3–4 pale blue eggs for 21–26 days.
Feeding: picks grasshoppers, other insects, worms, small vertebrates and spiders from fields; often associated with livestock.
Voice: generally silent.
Similar Species: *Great Egret* (p. 84): much larger; longer neck; longer bill; black legs and feet. *Snowy Egret* (p. 85): black-and-yellow bill and legs; yellow feet. *Little Blue Heron* (p. 86): immature has bluish gray bill with dark tip and yellowish olive legs. *Gulls* (pp. 153–57): typically gray mantle; stout, stubby bill; short legs; webbed feet; less erect stance.

GREEN HERON

Butorides virescens

I f the light is just right, you may be fortunate enough to see the glimmer of green on the back and outer wings of this crow-sized bird—the source of its common name and the scientific name *virescens*, which is Latin for "becoming green." Most of the time, however, this magical shine is not apparent, especially when the Green Heron stands frozen under the shade of dense marshland vegetation. • The Green Heron prefers to hunt for frogs and small fish in shallow, weedy wetlands, where it often perches just above the water's surface. While hunting, it will sometimes drop small pieces of debris, including twigs, vegetation and feathers, onto the water's surface as bait to attract fish within striking range. • Unlike most herons, Green Herons nest singly rather than communally, although they sometimes form loose colonies.

ID: stocky body; bluish gray back and wings mixed with iridescent green; chestnut upper breast, neck and face; grayish brown belly; greenish black crown; amber eyes; grayish lores; dusky bill; relatively short, amber to orange legs; short tail. *Immature:* dark brown upperparts; heavy brown-and-white streaking on neck and underparts; yellow lores; yellow lower mandible; yellowish green legs.
Size: *L* 15–22 in; *W* 26 in.
Habitat: marshes, lakes and streams with dense shoreline or emergent vegetation.
Nesting: nests singly or in small, loose groups; in a tree or shrub, usually very close to water; male begins and female completes a stick platform; pair incubates 3–5 pale bluish green to green eggs for 19–21 days; young are fed by regurgitation.
Feeding: slowly stalks or stands and waits; stabs mostly small fish with bill; also takes a wide variety of other small aquatic and terrestrial creatures.
Voice: generally silent; loud *kowp, kyow* or *skow* in alarm or flight; harsh *raah* in aggression.
Similar Species: *Black-crowned Night-Heron* (p. 89): immature is bulkier, with streaked face, gray lores, heavier bill and orangy red eyes. *Least Bittern* (p. 82): buffy yellow shoulder patches; tidier neck streaks; yellow bill; lives among reeds. *American Bittern* (p. 81): larger; black streak from bill to shoulder. *Little Blue Heron* (p. 86): slate blue overall.

BLACK-CROWNED NIGHT-HERON
Nycticorax nycticorax

When the setting sun has sent most wetland waders to their nightly roosts, Black-crowned Night-Herons arrive to hunt the marshy waters and to voice the hoarse squawks that gave them the scientific name *Nycticorax*, which means "night raven." Using their large, light-sensitive eyes, they patrol the shallows for prey. Remaining alongside water until morning, they then flap off to their treetop roosts. • When Black-crowned Night-Herons hunt by day, a popular strategy is to sit motionless atop a few bent-over cattails. Anything passing below the perch becomes fair game—even ducklings, small shorebirds or young muskrats. • Young night-herons are commonly seen around large cattail marshes in fall. Because of their heavily streaked underparts, they are easily confused with American Bitterns and other immature herons. • The Black-crowned Night-Heron is the most abundant heron in the world, occurring virtually worldwide.

breeding

ID: black "cap" and back; gray neck and wings; white underparts, foreneck, "cheek" and forehead; large, red eyes; stout, black bill; dull yellow legs. *Breeding:* 2 white plumes trail down from crown. *Immature:* grayish brown upperparts flecked with white; fuzzily streaked, brown-and-white underparts; orangy red eyes; gray-and-yellow bill.
Size: *L* 23–26 in; *W* 3½ ft.
Habitat: shallow cattail and bulrush marshes, lakeshores and along slow rivers.
Nesting: colonial; in a tree or shrub; male gathers materials for female to build a loose twig-and-stick nest platform lined with finer materials; pair incubates 3–4 pale green eggs for 21–26 days.
Feeding: often at dusk; patient stand-and-wait predator; stabs for small fish, amphibians, aquatic invertebrates, reptiles, young birds and small mammals.
Voice: deep, guttural *quark* or *wok,* often given when taking flight.
Similar Species: *Yellow-crowned Night-Heron* (p. 90): slimmer; gray overall; black head with pale yellow crown and white "cheek" patch; generally darker immature has crisper streaking and dark bill. *Green Heron* (p. 88): immature has heavily brown-streaked underparts, neck and "cheek" and thinner bill. *American Bittern* (p. 81): lighter tan overall; black streak from bill to shoulder; blackish yellow bill. *Great Blue Heron* (p. 83): much larger and rangier.

YELLOW-CROWNED NIGHT-HERON

Nyctanassa violacea

Night-herons are named for their habit of hunting from dusk until dawn, yet the Yellow-crowned member of the family quite commonly hunts throughout the daylight hours as well, particularly when there are hungry mouths to feed. Its secretive habits, choice of dense, concealing habitats and slow, nearly imperceptible hunting movements combine to make this bird a challenge to locate and observe. • The adult Yellow-crowned Night-Heron rarely exhibits its striking head pattern away from its nesting colony. Much more likely to be seen is the cryptically patterned juvenile with its disruptive coloration, long, yellowish-green legs and thick, dark bill. • The red eyes of both the Yellow-crowned Night-Heron and the Black-crowned Night-Heron may be an adaptation to their nocturnal foraging. • *Nyctanassa* is from Greek words meaning "night" and "a lady." The origins of *violacea*, Latin for "violet-colored," are lost in obscurity.

breeding

Nesting: loosely colonial, often nesting singly near water; crude platform of dead sticks is built in a tree overhanging water; pair incubates typically 3–5 pale bluish green eggs for 24–25 days and feeds the young until they fledge.

Feeding: mostly in early morning or evening; stand-and-wait forager; eats mainly crustaceans; will also take amphibians, fish, insects and mollusks.

Voice: usual call is a crowlike squawk.

Similar Species: *Black-crowned Night-Heron* (p. 89): stockier; black back; paler wings, underparts and face; black crown and white throat; warmer brown immature has coarser, fuzzier streaks on underparts and partly yellow bill. *Great Blue Heron* (p. 83): much larger and rangier.

ID: bluish gray overall; long neck, often held hunched over shoulders; pale yellow forehead, crown and head plumes; bold, black face with white "cheek"; bright, red eyes; dark bill; yellowish legs and feet. *Immature:* brownish gray upperparts flecked with white; crisply streaked, brown-and-white underparts; orangy red eyes.

Size: *L* 24 in; *W* 42 in.

Habitat: *Breeding:* riparian areas; lakes and marshes.

WHITE-FACED IBIS

Plegadis chihi

Revered in many parts of the world, ibises are slender, long-legged, highly social wading birds. The White-faced Ibis breeds mainly in the large wetlands of western North America, occupying the same kinds of habitats as the Glossy Ibis of eastern North America, with a preference for flooded croplands and the expansive reedbeds and muddy shallows of federal wildlife refuges. It is an uncommon breeder in the Great Plains, and nesting is restricted to a few suitable areas in Kansas, Colorado, Nebraska and South Dakota. • Ibises require high-quality marshes for nesting, and, if necessary, they will abandon and relocate breeding sites to ensure optimal conditions. Flying rapidly, they easily traverse the miles between their secluded nesting colonies and outlying feeding locations, where their long legs, slender toes and remarkable downcurved bill all contribute to their success in extracting prey from soft or semi-fluid soil.

breeding

nonbreeding

ID: dark red eyes; long, downcurved, gray bill; long legs. *Breeding:* maroon body with iridescent, greenish lower back and wing coverts; V-shaped patch of red skin from eye to base of bill, with white border; rich red legs. *Nonbreeding* and *immature:* generally brown, with less distinct greenish gloss; dusky pinkish facial skin between eye and bill; dark red legs.
Size: *L* 19–26 in; *W* 36 in.
Habitat: large wetlands and marshes, flooded fields, wet meadows and marshy shorelines of lakes.

Nesting: colonial; in bulrushes or other emergent vegetation; deep cup nest of coarse materials is lined with fine plant matter; pair incubates 3–4 bluish green eggs for about 22 days; young forage with adults well into fall.
Feeding: probes and gleans soil and shallow water for aquatic invertebrates, amphibians and other small vertebrates.
Voice: generally quiet; occasionally gives a series of low, ducklike quacks.
Similar Species: *Egrets* and *other herons* (pp. 81–90): mostly very different plumage colors; shorter, straight bills. *Long-billed Curlew* (p. 135): brown upperparts; buffy underparts; cinnamon underwing linings; more uniformly thin, longer bill. *Double-crested Cormorant* (p. 80): much shorter bill and legs; looks heavier in flight and flies more directly.

91

TURKEY VULTURE

Cathartes aura

Unmatched at using updrafts and thermals, Turkey Vultures can tease lift from the slightest pocket of rising air to patrol the skies when other soaring birds are grounded. • The bill and feet of the Turkey Vulture, which eats carrion almost exclusively, are not nearly as powerful as those of eagles, hawks and falcons, which kill live prey. Indeed, recent studies have shown that American vultures are more closely related to storks. DNA similarities with storks, and the shared tendency to defecate on their own legs to cool down, strongly support this taxonomic reclassification. The Turkey Vulture's red, featherless head may appear grotesque, but this adaptation allows it to remain relatively clean while feeding on messy carcasses. • Vultures seem to have mastered the art of regurgitation. This ability allows parents to transport food over long distances to their young and also enables engorged birds to repulse an attacker or "lighten up" for an emergency takeoff.

ID: brownish black overall; bare, red head; short, stout, mostly whitish bill. *Immature:* gray head. *In flight:* small-looking head; silvery gray flight feathers; black wing linings; holds wings in shallow "V"; side-to-side rocking when soaring.
Size: L 26–32 in; W 5½–6 ft.
Habitat: usually seen flying over open country, shorelines and roads; rarely seen over forested areas or woods with sizeable open areas.
Nesting: in a cave crevice or among boulders; sometimes in a hollow stump or log,

without added nest material; pair incubates 2 dull white eggs, spotted and blotched with reddish brown, for up to 41 days; young are fed by regurgitation.
Feeding: eats carrion (mostly mammalian) almost exclusively, occasionally supplemented by insects and near-dead fish; not commonly seen at roadkills.
Voice: generally silent; occasionally produces a hiss or grunt if threatened.
Similar Species: *Black Vulture* (p. 361): mostly a rare visitor; blacker; wrinkly, gray head and upper neck; large silvery tips on black wings. *Golden Eagle* (p. 106) and *Bald Eagle* (p. 95): in flight, wings are held flat, head is more prominent and color patterns of underwings and tail are different; do not rock when soaring.

OSPREY

Pandion haliaetus

The Osprey eats almost nothing but fish. A dark eye line across its white face blocks glare, helping it to spot a slow-moving shadow or a flash of silver near the water's surface as it surveys waterways from the air. Meanwhile, its white belly makes it hard for fish to see it hovering far above. Folding its wings, the Osprey hurls itself into a headfirst dive toward its target. An instant before striking the water, the bird rights itself and thrusts its feet forward to grasp its slippery prey, often striking the water with a tremendous splash. Using its specialized feet, with two sharp-spined toes facing forward and two facing backward, the Osprey can clamp tightly onto the slipperiest of fish to prevent a squirmy escape. • The only species in its family, the Osprey is one of the world's most widely distributed birds, inhabiting every continent except Antarctica.

ID: dark brown upperparts; white underparts; fine, dark "necklace," generally most prominent on female; light crown; white face; dark eye line; yellow eyes; gray legs and feet. *In flight:* long wings, held in shallow "M," show dark "wrist" patches, white coverts and mostly dark flight feathers below and dark above; banded, brown-and-white tail.

Size: L 22–25 in; W 4½–6 ft.

Habitat: lakes and slowly flowing rivers and streams.

Nesting: on a treetop, usually near water, or on a specially made platform, utility pole or tower up to 100 ft high; massive stick nest is reused over many years; pair incubates 2–4 yellowish eggs, spotted and blotched with reddish brown, for about 38 days; pair feeds the young, with the male hunting most.

Feeding: dramatic, feet-first dives into the water; small fish make up almost the entire diet.

Voice: series of melodious ascending whistles: *chewk-chewk-chewk;* also an often-heard *kip-kip-kip.*

Similar Species: *Bald Eagle* (p. 95): immature has all-brown or white-mottled underparts, larger bill with yellow base and yellow legs and feet; wings held straighter while soaring. *Rough-legged Hawk* (p. 105): smaller; light morph has dark-marked underparts and wing linings and dark-tipped, white tail and flight feathers; hovers with wings in open "V."

MISSISSIPPI KITE

Ictinia mississippiensis

Constantly fanning and twisting its long tail, using it as a rudder to swiftly adjust its position among the airy heights, the Mississippi Kite deftly pursues flying insects such as dragonflies, cicadas, beetles and grasshoppers. These prey items, mostly caught on the wing or hawked out of the air, are often held in the bird's claws and eaten while it continues to astound observers with its lissome flight. Occasionally, a blazing acrobatic aerial pursuit results in the capture of a bat, swallow or swift. • This gregarious inhabitant of riparian woodlands and swamps relies on the protection of tall trees for nesting and social nighttime roosting but also needs adjacent open country to provide ample hunting opportunities. The planting of shelterbelts and urban trees appears to have allowed expansion of its breeding range westward and northward from the southeastern U.S. into the southern Great Plains, and sightings are annually reported as far north as southern New England. The Mississippi Kite overwinters in southern South America.

ID: gray overall, darkest at tail, paler below and on head; black area around reddish brown eye. *Immature:* darkly brownish upperparts; brown-streaked underparts; pale translucent bands in dark tail. *In flight:* long, narrow, dark wings with pale secondaries seen from above; never hovers.
Size: *L* 14½ in; *W* 35 in.
Habitat: riparian woodlands, swamps, woodlot groves and shelterbelts near open country, including brush-, scrub- and grasslands.
Nesting: nests in small, loose colonies; pair constructs a flimsy, leaf-lined stick platform in a relatively tall tree or shrub near the edge of a wooded area; pair incubates 1–2 white eggs for about 30 days.
Feeding: catches prey largely on the wing or in swooping flight; large flying insects form the bulk of the diet; small birds and bats are also taken, plus small terrestrial mammals, amphibians and reptiles; occasionally scavenges roadkill.
Voice: generally silent; *kee kew, kee kew* alarm call.
Similar Species: *Northern Harrier* (p. 96): male has white underparts, brown flecks on breast, dark wing tips and white rump patch. *Peregrine Falcon* (p. 109): mostly a migrant; finely dark-barred white underparts; dark "helmet."

BALD EAGLE

Haliaeetus leucocephalus

The Bald Eagle can be a source of inspiration and wonder for any birder. As of the writing of this book, it is considered a threatened species. Although it cannot compete with the Golden Eagle in strength of talon and character, legends persist that endow this bird with a mystical quality that is difficult to dispute. • The Bald Eagle feeds mostly on fish and scavenged carrion. Sometimes an eagle will steal food from an Osprey, resulting in a spectacu-lar aerial chase. • Pairs perform dramatic aerial displays—the most impressive display involves the two birds flying to a great height, locking talons and then tumbling perilously toward the earth, breaking off just when a crash seems certain. Bald Eagles generally mate for life, and pairs annually renew their bonds by adding new sticks and branches to their massive nests, the largest of any North American bird. • Only in its fourth or fifth year does a Bald Eagle develop the characteristic white head and tail plumage.

immature

ID: dark brown overall; white head and tail; pale yellow eyes; yellow bill and feet. *1st-year:* dark overall; dark bill; some white in underwings; dark eyes. *2nd-year:* white belly and dark "bib"; more white in underwings; yellowish eyes. *3rd-year:* mostly white plumage; significant yellow at base of bill; yellow eyes. *4th-year:* light head with dark facial streak; variable pale and dark plumage; yellow bill; paler eyes. *In flight:* broad wings held flat.
Size: *L* 30–43 in; *W* 5½–8 ft.
Habitat: large lakes and rivers.

Nesting: usually in a tree bordering a lake or large river, but may be far from water; huge stick nest, up to 15 ft across, is often reused for many years; pair incubates 1–3 white eggs for 34–36 days; pair feeds the young.
Feeding: eats waterbirds, small mammals and fish captured at the water's surface; frequently feeds on carrion.
Voice: thin, weak squeal or gull-like cackle: *kleek-kik-kik-kik* or *kah-kah-kah.*
Similar Species: adult is distinctive. *Golden Eagle* (p. 106): dark overall, except for golden nape and possible faint tail band; paler bill; immature has prominent white patch on wings and at base of tail. *Osprey* (p. 93): all-white underparts; dark bill; dark "wrist" patches; M-shaped wings in flight.

NORTHERN HARRIER

Circus cyaneus

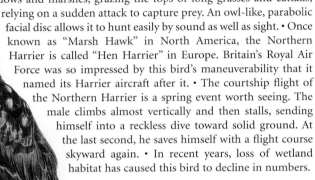

Possibly the easiest raptor to identify in flight, the Northern Harrier routinely flies closer to the ground than any other midsized bird. It cruises low over fields, meadows and marshes, grazing the tops of long grasses and cattails, relying on a sudden attack to capture prey. An owl-like, parabolic facial disc allows it to hunt easily by sound as well as sight. • Once known as "Marsh Hawk" in North America, the Northern Harrier is called "Hen Harrier" in Europe. Britain's Royal Air Force was so impressed by this bird's maneuverability that it named its Harrier aircraft after it. • The courtship flight of the Northern Harrier is a spring event worth seeing. The male climbs almost vertically and then stalls, sending himself into a reckless dive toward solid ground. At the last second, he saves himself with a flight course skyward again. • In recent years, loss of wetland habitat has caused this bird to decline in numbers.

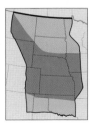

ID: *Male:* bluish to silvery gray upperparts; largely white underparts; brown-flecked breast. *Female:* dark brown upperparts; streaked, brown-and-buff underparts. *Immature:* brown upperparts; weakly streaked, orangy brown underparts. *In flight:* white rump; long wings and tail; male's black-tipped wings are white below and gray above; female has barred, dark-and-white underwings; indistinct tail bands with darker subterminal band.
Size: *L* 16–24 in; *W* 3½–4 ft.
Habitat: open country, including fields, wet meadows, cattail marshes, bogs and croplands.

Nesting: on the ground, often on a slightly raised mound; usually in grass, cattails or tall vegetation; shallow depression or platform nest is lined with grass, sticks and cattails; female incubates 4–6 bluish white eggs for 30–32 days.
Feeding: hunts in low, rising-and-falling flights, often skimming the vegetation; eats small mammals, birds, amphibians, reptiles and some invertebrates.
Voice: generally quiet; most vocal near the nest, with a high-pitched *ke-ke-ke-ke-ke-ke,* and during courtship.
Similar Species: *Rough-legged Hawk* (p. 105): generally dark except for broad, white bands on underside of flight feathers and at base of tail; broader wings; dark "wrist" patches; plainer face. *Red-tailed Hawk* (p. 103): bulkier; dark rump; shorter tail, red except on Harlan's subspecies.

SHARP-SHINNED HAWK

Accipiter striatus

The small Sharp-shinned Hawk preys almost exclusively on small birds. After a successful high-speed chase, it usually perches on a favorite "plucking post" to dine, grasping its meal in its razor-sharp talons. • Most people never see a Sharpie nest, because the birds are very tight sitters. Disturb one, however, and you will feel the occupants' wrath. These birds are feisty defenders of their nest and young. • When delivering food to his nestlings, a male Sharp-shinned Hawk is cautious around his mate—she is typically one-third larger than he is and notoriously short-tempered. • The accipiters (named for their genus) are a group of woodland hawks with three species in North America. Their short, rounded wings, long, rudderlike tails and flap-and-glide flight pattern give them the maneuverability necessary to negotiate a maze of forest foliage at high speed.

ID: bluish gray back; rufous, horizontal bars on white underparts; red eyes; long, straight, heavily barred, square-tipped tail. *Immature:* brown upperparts; vertical, brown streaks on white breast and belly; yellow eyes. *In flight:* dark barring on pale underwings; flap-and-glide flier; very agile in wooded areas.
Size: *Male: L* 10–12 in; *W* 20–24 in. *Female: L* 12–14 in; *W* 24–28 in.
Habitat: dense to semi-open forests and large woodlots; occasionally along rivers and in urban areas; favors bogs and dense, moist, coniferous forests for nesting.
Nesting: in a conifer; usually builds a new stick nest each year; may remodel an abandoned crow nest; female incubates 4–5 brown-blotched, bluish white eggs for 34–35 days; male feeds the female during incubation.
Feeding: pursues small birds through forests; rarely takes small mammals, amphibians and insects.
Voice: generally silent; intense, much repeated *kik-kik-kik-kik* during breeding season.
Similar Species: *Cooper's Hawk* (p. 98): crown is darker than nape and back; larger; broader, more rounded tail has broader terminal band. *Northern Goshawk* (p. 99): much larger; grayish brown breast; white "eyebrow"; more tail bands. *Merlin* (p. 108): vertical, brown streaking on underparts; dark "tear streak"; dark eyes; pointed wings; rapid wingbeats.

COOPER'S HAWK

Accipiter cooperii

Gliding silently along forest clearings, the Cooper's Hawk uses surprise and speed to snatch its prey in midair. Females can seize and decapitate birds as large as Ruffed Grouse, which they sometimes pursue on the ground like overweight roadrunners. • As a result of legal protection and the banning of DDT use throughout North America, the Cooper's Hawk is increasing in numbers and slowly recolonizing former habitats in our region. • Distinguishing the Cooper's Hawk from the Sharp-shinned Hawk is challenging. The dark crown and the larger, more rounded tail of the larger, heavier Cooper's are good clues. In flight, the Cooper's has a shallower, stiffer-winged flight, whereas the Sharpie has deeper wing-beats with more wing bending. As well, the Cooper's Hawk typically perches on fence posts, poles and tree branches, but the Sharp-shin uses almost exclusively tree branches.

immature

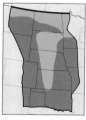

ID: bluish gray back; rufous, horizontal barring on underparts; dark barring on pale undertail and underwings; squarish head; red eyes; long, straight, heavily barred, rounded tail with white terminal band. *Immature:* brown overall; vertical, brown streaks on breast and belly; yellow eyes. *In flight:* flap-and-glide flier.
Size: *Male: L* 15–17 in; *W* 27–32 in. *Female: L* 17–19 in; *W* 32–37 in.
Habitat: mixed woodlands, riparian woodlands and urban woodlots.

Nesting: nest of sticks and twigs in a tree crotch 20–65 ft above the ground, often near a stream or pond; might reuse an abandoned crow nest; female incubates 3–5 bluish white eggs for 34–36 days; male feeds the female during incubation.
Feeding: pursues prey in flights through forest; eats mostly songbirds but occasionally takes squirrels and chipmunks; uses a "plucking post" or nest for eating.
Voice: fast *cac-cac-cac-cac*.
Similar Species: *Sharp-shinned Hawk* (p. 97): less distinct crown; smaller; less rounded tail tip; thinner, terminal tail band. *Northern Goshawk* (p. 99): larger; grayish brown breast; white "eyebrow"; more tail bands. *Merlin* (p. 108): smaller; vertical, brown streaking on underparts; dark "tear streak"; dark eyes; pointed wings; rapid wingbeats.

NORTHERN GOSHAWK

Accipiter gentilis

The Northern Goshawk is an agile and powerful predator that will prey on any animal it can overtake. Capable of negotiating lightning-fast turns through dense forest cover, it dispatches its catches with powerful talons. This raptor has even been known to chase elusive quarry on foot through dense thickets. • Equally ferocious when defending their nest sites, Northern Goshawks—especially the females—are devoted parents. Unfortunate souls who wander too close to a goshawk nest may be assaulted by an almost deafening, squawking dive-bomb attack. • All three accipiter species were once subjected to scorn and disapproval for their "blood-thirsty" habit of hunting songbirds. This type of thinking resulted in unwarranted persecution that, thankfully, has largely been abandoned.

ID: bluish gray back; fine, vertical, gray streaking on pale breast and belly; mostly indistinct gray barring on pale under-tail and underwings; dark crown; white "eyebrow"; red eyes; long, faintly banded tail. *Immature:* brown upperparts; vertical, brown streaking on whitish breast and belly; brown barring on pale undertail and underwings; yellow eyes.
Size: *Male:* L 21–23 in; W 3–3½ ft. *Female:* L 23–25 in; W 3½–4 ft.
Habitat: *Breeding:* mature woodlands. *Nonbreeding:* forest edges, semi-open parklands and farmland.
Nesting: in deep woods; male builds a large, bulky stick platform in a tree crotch,

usually 25–80 ft above the ground; nest is often reused for several years; female incu-bates 2–4 bluish white eggs for 35–36 days; male feeds the female during incubation.
Feeding: low foraging flights through the forest; feeds primarily on grouse, rabbits and squirrels.
Voice: generally silent; loud, fast, shrill *kak-kak-kak-kak* during breeding season.
Similar Species: *Cooper's Hawk* (p. 98) and *Sharp-shinned Hawk* (p. 97): smaller; reddish breast barring; no white "eye-brow"; immatures have no or less promi-nent "eyebrow" and narrower tail with fewer bars. *Buteos* (pp. 100–05): chunkier; different plumage patterns; shorter tails; broader wings; gray or brown eyes. *Gyrfalcon:* rare; gray morph has stronger barring, plainer face and dark eyes; pointier wings in flight.

99

RED-SHOULDERED HAWK

Buteo lineatus

As spring approaches and pair bonds form, the normally quiet Red-shouldered Hawk utters loud, shrieking *key-ah* calls. However, be forewarned that Blue Jays have mastered an impressive impersonation of these vocalizations. • In summer, the dense cover of this buteo's forested breeding habitat allows few viewing opportunities. Fortunately for birders, this hawk's spring and fall use of telephone poles and fence posts for hunting gives a better glimpse into its otherwise private life. • The Red-shouldered Hawk favors wetter habitats than the closely related Broad-winged Hawk and Red-tailed Hawk. It nests in mature trees, usually around river bottoms and in lowland tracts of woods alongside creeks. If left undisturbed, a pair will remain faithful to a productive nesting site, returning yearly. After the parents die, one of the young will carry on the family nesting tradition.

Habitat: mature hardwood and mixed forests and large woodlots, wooded riparian areas, swampy woodlands.

Nesting: in the crotch of a hardwood (prefers mature maple, ash and beech), usually 15–80 ft above the ground; pair assembles a bulky nest of sticks and twigs; nest is often reused; female incubates 2–4 darkly blotched, bluish white eggs for about 33 days; both adults raise the young.

Feeding: prey is usually detected from a fence post, tree or telephone pole and caught in a swooping attack; may catch prey flushed by low flight; eats small mammals, birds, reptiles and amphibians.

Voice: repeated series of high *key-ah* notes.

Similar Species: *Light-morph Broad-winged Hawk* (p. 101): light morph has brown upperparts, coarser barring on underparts, mostly white underwings (dark at trailing edge and tips) and wider, white tail bands. *Red-tailed Hawk* (p. 103): uniformly colored upperwings; broader tail is reddish, white or more finely barred.

ID: white-mottled, dark brown upperparts; dark rufous shoulders; orange-barred breast and belly with paler undertail coverts; narrow, white bars on dark tail. *Immature:* large, brown, "teardrop" streaks on white underparts. *In flight:* light-and-dark barring below on flight feathers; elongated whitish markings near wing tips; light orange underwing linings.

Size: *L* 19 in; *W* 3½ ft.

BROAD-WINGED HAWK

Buteo platypterus

Each fall, the mass exodus of Broad-wings in migration to Central and South America offers birders in the eastern Great Plains a chance to enjoy an unforgettable experience. In good flight years, when cool weather, moderate northwest winds and sunny skies prevail, many Broad-wings can be observed. The action begins at the end of the nesting season, when large groups of buteos and other hawks spiral up from their forest retreats, testing thermals. Broad-winged Hawks are often the most numerous species in these flocks. At other times, the generally shy and secretive Broad-winged Hawk shuns the open fields and forest clearings favored by other buteos, such as the Red-tailed Hawk, to seclude itself in dense, often wet forests, where its short, broad wings and highly flexible tail help it to maneuver. • Most hunting is done from a high perch with a good view. If flushed from its perch, a Broad-wing will return and resume its vigilant search for a meal.

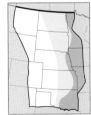

ID: dark brown upperparts; white breast heavily barred in rufous brown; broadly banded, black-and-white tail; dark eyes. *Dark morph:* rare; brown underparts and wing linings. *Immature:* dark brown, "teardrop" streaks on white breast, belly and sides; fainter, finer, buff-and-dark-brown tail bands. *In flight:* broad wings with pointed tips; pale underwings outlined with dark brown.

Size: *L* 14–19 in; *W* 32–39 in.

Habitat: *Breeding:* dense mixed and hardwood forests and woodlots. *In migration:* escarpments and shorelines; also uses riparian and hardwood forests and woodland edges.

Nesting: usually in a crotch of a hardwood, 20–40 ft above the ground, often near water; usually builds a new bulky stick nest each year; mostly the female incubates 2–4 brown-spotted, whitish eggs for 28–31 days; both adults raise the young.

Feeding: swoops from a perch for small mammals, amphibians, insects and young birds; often seen hunting from roadside telephone poles in northern areas.

Voice: high-pitched, whistled *peeeo-wee-ee;* generally silent in migration.

Similar Species: *Other buteos* (pp. 100–05): underwings less strikingly dark-outlined; narrower white tail bands or different pattern. *Accipiters* (pp. 97–99): red eyes (pale yellow on immature); longer, narrower tails with less distinct banding.

SWAINSON'S HAWK

Buteo swainsoni

The Red-tailed Hawk may dominate most of North America's skies, but the Swainson's Hawk takes center stage in the open country of the Great Plains, especially where ground squirrels and gophers are abundant. • Twice a year, Swainson's Hawks undertake long migratory journeys that may lead them as far south as the southern tip of South America and as far north as Alaska. Traveling up to 12,500 miles in a single year, Swainson's Hawks are second only to Peregrine Falcons for long-distance travel among birds of prey. The massive "kettles" of Swainson's Hawks migrating through Central America have been likened to the legendary flocks of Passenger Pigeons *(Ectopistes migratorius)* that once blackened the sky. Unfortunately, many Swainson's Hawks are killed by the incautious use of insecticides in Argentina, reminding us that the conservation of migratory species requires international cooperation. • This hawk is named for Englishman William Swainson, an early 19th-century illustrator of natural history.

light morph

dark morph

Habitat: open fields, grasslands, sagebrush and agricultural areas.

Nesting: in a tree or shrub adjacent to open habitat, rarely on cliffs; nest of sticks, twigs and forbs is lined with bark and fresh leaves; pair incubates 2–4 brown-spotted, whitish eggs for 28–35 days.

Feeding: dives for voles, mice, ground squirrels and similar mammals; also eats snakes, small birds and large insects, such as grasshoppers and crickets.

Voice: typical hawk call: *keeeaar.*

Similar Species: *Red-tailed Hawk* (p. 103): underparts are often streaked; face is never white; tail is often red and seldom banded; heftier, rounder wings, held flatter in flight; from below, only tips of flight feathers are dark; lower-pitched call. *Other buteos* (pp. 100–05): flight feathers are generally paler than wing lining. *Golden Eagle* (p. 106): much larger; golden nape; massive bill.

ID: dark brown upperparts. *Dark morph:* largely dark underparts; brown-flecked, whitish undertail coverts. *Light morph:* mostly white underparts and face; brown "bib." *Immature:* dark-and-white mottling overall. *In flight:* narrowly banded tail; holds long, pointed wings in shallow "V" when soaring; brown wing linings blend with dark flight feathers on dark morph; white wing linings contrast with dark flight feathers on light morph.

Size: *L* 19–22 in; *W* 4½ ft.

RED-TAILED HAWK

Buteo jamaicensis

Conspicuous year-round, particularly near agricultural lands, the Red-tailed Hawk is the most commonly seen hawk in many areas of North America. An afternoon drive through the countryside will typically reveal resident Red-tails perching on exposed tree limbs, fence posts or utility poles overlooking open fields and roadsides. • During their spring courtship, excited Red-tailed Hawks dive at each other, sometimes locking talons and tumbling through the air together, breaking off to avoid crashing to the ground. • The Red-tailed Hawk's impressive, piercing call is often misleadingly paired with the image of an eagle in TV commercials and movies. • The Harlan's subspecies overwinters in the southeast of our region but may be seen elsewhere in migration to and from its Alaskan breeding grounds.

Harlan's

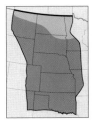

ID: dark brown upperparts with white highlights; whitish underparts with belly band of dark brown streaks or all-brown underparts; red tail. *Harlan's:* blacker dark areas; dark-and-white breast; whitish tail, sometimes banded. *Immature:* variable; generally darker; brown-and-light tail. *In flight:* underwings show whitish to brown linings with dark leading edge and light flight feathers; fan-shaped tail.
Size: *Male: L* 18–23 in; *W* 4–5 ft. *Female: L* 20–25 in; *W* 4–5 ft.
Habitat: open country with some trees; also roadsides, fields, woodlots, hedgerows, mixed forests and moist woodlands.
Nesting: in woodlands adjoining open habitat; usually in a hardwood, rarely on a cliff or in a conifer; bulky stick nest is usually added to annually; pair incubates 2–4 brown-blotched, whitish eggs for 28–35 days; male brings food to the female and young.
Feeding: scans for food while perched or soaring; drops to capture prey; rarely stalks prey on foot; eats voles, mice, rabbits, chipmunks, birds, amphibians, reptiles and (rarely) large insects.
Voice: powerful, descending scream: *keeearrrr.*
Similar Species: *Rough-legged Hawk* (p. 105): feathered legs; large underwing "wrist" patches; white tail underside with dark band near tip. *Broad-winged Hawk* (p. 101): mostly migratory; smaller; horizontal belly streaks or all-brown underparts; crisper wing border; broadly banded tail. *Red-shouldered Hawk* (p. 100): reddish shoulders and underparts. *Swainson's Hawk* (p. 102): all-dark upperparts; narrower wings with dark flight feathers and pale to brown linings.

FERRUGINOUS HAWK

Buteo regalis

Often seen cruising low over the prairies or circling high above the badlands, the Ferruginous Hawk is our largest buteo and is a bird of noble splendor well deserving of the scientific name *regalis*. Its size, rich color and relative rarity make it the favorite buteo of many birders in the region. • Lately, conservationists have been concerned about this species' population. The loss of pristine grasslands to agriculture and rodent control campaigns have localized and reduced numbers of Ferruginous Hawks. These birds suffered from human intervention in the past also—the bones and wool of wandering bison served as nest material until the herds were eliminated. • Ferruginous Hawks typically nest in trees, and, on the prairies, each and every lone cottonwood may have either a pair of Swainson's or a pair of Ferruginous Hawks in its crown. Artificial nesting platforms erected by conscientious land stewards help improve their housing situation.

light morph

light morph

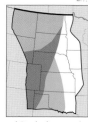

ID: fully feathered legs. *Light morph:* rusty shoulders and back; light underparts and head; rusty on sides and legs; white tail is tipped with rust above. *Dark morph:* dark brown overall with rusty tinges; tail is white below and gray above. *Immature:* very light underparts and underwing flight feathers and sometimes wing linings and legs. *In flight:* dark wing linings and light flight feathers below; white on upperwings near tips.
Size: *L* 23 in; *W* 56 in.

Habitat: open grasslands, badlands and croplands.
Nesting: usually in a solitary tree, on a cliff or on the ground; large, compact nest of sticks, weeds and cow dung is lined with finer materials; female incubates 2–4 eggs for 32–33 days; male provides food.
Feeding: dives from high, soaring flights; primarily eats ground squirrels, rabbits and hares; also takes snakes and small birds.
Voice: typical, hawk-style *kreeah,* dropping at the end.
Similar Species: *Red-tailed Hawk* (p. 103): generally darker underparts; dark leading edge on wing lining; usually has red tail. *Swainson's Hawk* (p. 102): dark flight feathers; usually light wing linings. *Rough-legged Hawk* (p. 105): no rust in plumage; smaller bill and feet; dark "wrist" patches.

ROUGH-LEGGED HAWK

Buteo lagopus

When lemming and vole numbers are high in their arctic breeding grounds, Rough-legged Hawks can produce up to seven young, resulting in many sightings during the winter months. In lean years, a pair is fortunate to raise a single chick, and sightings here are subsequently more rare. • While hunting, the Rough-legged Hawk often "wind-hovers" to scan the ground below, flapping to maintain a stationary position while facing upwind; this hunting technique serves as an excellent long-distance identification tool for birders. Hovering is often necessary because of a lack of high perches in open-country habitat, but this bird will use available poles and fence posts. • Rough-legged Hawks show great variety in coloration, ranging from a whitish light morph with dark patterning to almost entirely dark dark-morph birds that have distinctive whitish areas. • The name *lagopus*, meaning "hare's foot," refers to this bird's distinctive feathered legs, which are an adaptation for survival in cold climates.

light morph

light morph

ID: fully feathered legs. *Light morph:* white mottling on dark brown upperparts; white underparts with wide, dark abdominal "belt"; dark streaks on breast and head. *Dark morph:* generally dark brown overall. *Immature:* lighter streaking on breast; bold belly band; pale leg feathers. *In flight:* underwings show light flight feathers and dark edges, tips and large "wrist" patches, with all-dark linings on dark-morph bird; tail is white below with 1 wide, dark subterminal band and dark on top, with white base on light-morph bird; frequently hovers.

Size: *L* 19–24 in; *W* 4–4½ ft.
Habitat: fields, meadows, open bogs and agricultural croplands.
Nesting: does not nest in the Great Plains.
Feeding: soars and hovers while searching for prey; primarily eats small rodents; occasionally eats birds, amphibians and large insects.
Voice: alarm call is a catlike *kee-eer,* usually dropping at the end.
Similar Species: *Other buteos* (pp. 100–04): rarely hover; smaller or no "wrist" patches; different tail color patterns. *Northern Harrier* (p. 96): facial disc; female has more uniform streaking on underparts, white rump, longer, thinner, weakly banded tail and no "wrist" patches.

GOLDEN EAGLE

Aquila chrysaetos

The Golden Eagle embodies the wonder and wildness of the North American landscape and is unforgettable when seen soaring overhead—its wingspan usually exceeds 6 feet! Yet with the advent of widespread human development and intensive agricultural practices, this noble bird became the victim of a lengthy persecution. Perceived as a threat to livestock, it was subject to bounties encouraging its shooting and poisoning, but it is now protected under the Migratory Bird Act and the Bald and Golden Eagle Protection Act. • More closely related to the buteos than to the Bald Eagle, this active and impressive predator takes prey as large as foxes, cranes and geese. It can soar high above mountain passes for hours, sometimes stooping at great speeds—150 to 200 miles per hour—for prey or for fun. • Associated mostly with mountainous areas of the West, this regal eagle is a rare treat for more easterly birders. Its migration route along the Rocky Mountains was unknown until 1992.

ID: very large; brown overall; gold-tinted neck and head; brown eyes; dark bill; mostly feathered legs; brown tail has grayish white bands. *Immature:* often has large white patch on wing; tail is white at base. *In flight:* relatively short neck; long, large, roughly rectangular wings; long tail.
Size: *L* 30–40 in; *W* 6½–7½ ft.
Habitat: *Breeding:* largely open areas with suitable nest sites. *In migration:* along escarpments and lake shorelines. *Winter:* semi-open woodlands and fields.
Nesting: on a bluff or sometimes a tall tree; large basket of sticks is lined with grass, forbs and leaves; new material is added annually for years; pair incubates 1–3 brown-marked, buffy or whitish eggs for 40–45 days.
Feeding: swoops on prey from a soaring flight; eats largely hares, grouse, rodents, foxes and occasionally young ungulates; also eats carrion.
Voice: generally quiet; rarely a short bark.
Similar Species: *Bald Eagle* (p. 95): immature has longer neck, shorter tail and different patterns of white on wings and tail. *Turkey Vulture* (p. 92): smaller; smaller, bare, red head; weaker bill; pale flight feathers; dark wing linings. *Rough-legged Hawk* (p. 105): smaller; smaller bill; dark morph has large white areas underneath in flight.

AMERICAN KESTREL

Falco sparverius

The American Kestrel is the smallest and most common of our falcons. It is frequently seen hovering above open areas as it hunts small rodents, and a kestrel perched on a telephone wire or fence post along an open field is a familiar sight year-round in much of our area. Even when viewed from afar, a repeated lifting of the tail while perched to scout below for prey helps identify the American Kestrel. • Studies have shown that the Eurasian Kestrel *(F. tinnunculus)* can detect ultraviolet reflections from rodent urine on the ground, and perhaps its American cousin has the same ability. • The American Kestrel's diminutive size allows it to nest in tree cavities, which helps protect defenseless young kestrels from hungry predators. • Old field guides and old-time birders refer to the American Kestrel as "Sparrow Hawk," and the scientific name *sparverius* means "pertaining to a sparrow."

ID: rusty back; bluish gray crown with rusty center; 2 distinctive, vertical facial stripes. *Male:* bluish gray wings; black-spotted, orangy buff-and-white underparts; black-tipped tail. *Female:* rusty wings; rust-streaked, white underparts. *In flight:* long, rusty tail; buoyant, indirect flight; frequently hovers.

Size: *L* 7½–8 in; *W* 20–24 in.

Habitat: open fields, riparian woodlands, woodlots, forest edges, bogs, roadside ditches, grassy highway medians, grasslands and croplands.

Nesting: in a tree cavity (usually an abandoned woodpecker or flicker cavity) or a nest box; mostly the female incubates 4–6 white to pale brown eggs, spotted with brown and gray, for 29–30 days; pair raises the young.

Feeding: swoops from a perch or from hovering flight; eats mostly insects and some small rodents, birds, reptiles and amphibians.

Voice: loud, often repeated, shrill *killy-killy-killy* when excited; female's voice is lower pitched.

Similar Species: *Merlin* (p. 108): grayer overall; plainer face; multi-banded tail; does not hover; more powerful, direct flight. *Sharp-shinned Hawk* (p. 97): gray back; dense, horizontal, rufous barring on underparts; rounder wings; narrower tail; flap-and-glide flight. *Mississippi Kite* (p. 94): juvenile is gray overall with brown-streaked underparts, brown wing linings and white-banded, dark tail; does not hover.

MERLIN

Falco columbarius

As with all falcons, the Merlin's main weapons are speed, surprise and sharp, daggerlike talons. This small falcon's sleek body, long, narrow tail and pointed wings increase its aerodynamic efficiency for high-speed songbird pursuits. Horned Larks and Cedar Waxwings are famous for trying to outfly the Merlin, which results in prey and pursuer circling to great heights. • Most Merlins migrate to Central and South America each fall, but a few overwinter in North America to capitalize on the abundance of Cedar Waxwings, European Starlings and House Sparrows. • Medieval falconers termed the Merlin "the lady's hawk," and Catherine the Great and Mary, Queen of Scots, were among the enthusiasts who would pitch Merlins and Sky Larks *(Alauda arvensis)* into matches of aerial prowess. • The Merlin was formerly known as "Pigeon Hawk," and *columbarius* comes from Latin for "pigeon," a bird that it somewhat resembles in flight.

Nesting: in a tree; usually reuses an abandoned raptor, crow, jay or squirrel nest; mostly the female incubates 4–5 whitish eggs, marked with reddish brown, for 28–32 days; male feeds the female away from the nest; pair raises the young.

Feeding: overtakes smaller birds in flight; also eats rodents and large insects, such as grasshoppers and dragonflies; may also take bats.

Voice: calls in flight or while perched, often around the nest; loud, noisy, cackling cry: *kek-kek-kek-kek-kek* or *ki-ki-ki-ki.*

Similar Species: *American Kestrel* (p. 107): more colorful; 2 facial stripes; less direct flight; often hovers. *Prairie Falcon* (p. 110) and *Peregrine Falcon* (p. 109): immatures are larger with stronger facial markings and more finely barred tails. *Sharp-shinned Hawk* (p. 97) and *Cooper's Hawk* (p. 98): rounded wings; reddish, horizontal barring on breast and belly. *Rock Pigeon* (p. 162): broader wings and tail.

ID: heavily brown-streaked, pale underparts; 1 indistinct, vertical facial stripe; dark eye line. *Male:* bluish gray back and crown. *Female:* brownish gray back and crown. *In flight:* long, narrow wings and banded tail; very rapid, shallow wingbeats.

Size: *L* 10–12 in; *W* 23–26 in.

Habitat: *Breeding:* open and second-growth, mixed and coniferous forests and plantations adjacent to open hunting grounds. *In migration:* open fields and lakeshores.

PEREGRINE FALCON

Falco peregrinus

No bird elicits more admiration than a hunting Peregrine Falcon in full flight, and nothing causes more panic in a tightly packed flock of ducks or shorebirds. Every twist and turn the flock makes is matched by the falcon until it finds a weaker or less-experienced bird. Diving at speeds of up to 220 miles per hour, the Peregrine clenches its feet and then strikes its prey with a lethal blow that often sends both falcon and prey tumbling. • The Peregrine Falcon's awesome speed and hunting skills were no defense against the pesticide DDT. Contaminated birds laid eggs with thin shells that broke during incubation. The species was completely eradicated east of the Mississippi River by 1964. Following the 1972 North American banning of DDT, the Eastern Peregrine Recovery Program, begun in 1975, successfully reintroduced the Peregrine Falcon in the eastern U.S. Now it nests on ledges of tall buildings and feeds on pigeons.

ID: bluish gray back, "helmet" and vertical "mustache"; light underparts with dark, fine spotting and barring. *Immature:* dark areas are brown; heavy, vertical streaking on underparts; grayer (rather than yellow) feet and cere. *In flight:* pointed wings; dark-banded tail.

Size: *Male: L* 15–17 in; *W* 3–3½ ft. *Female: L* 17–19 in; *W* 3½–4 ft.

Habitat: lakeshores, river valleys, river mouths, urban areas and open fields.

Nesting: in cities where it was reintroduced; usually on a skyscraper ledge; no material is added, but the nest is littered with prey remains, leaves and grass; mostly the female incubates 3–4 creamy to buff eggs, heavily blotched with reddish brown, for 32–34 days.

Feeding: high-speed, diving stoops; strikes birds with clenched feet in midair; takes primarily pigeons, waterfowl, shorebirds, flickers and large songbirds; rarely eats small mammals or carrion; consumes prey on a nearby perch.

Voice: loud, harsh, continuous *cack-cack-cack-cack-cack* near the nest.

Similar Species: *Gyrfalcon:* rare and only in winter; larger; more uniform head coloration; longer tail. *Merlin* (p. 108): smaller; more uniform head coloration; vertically streaked breast and belly; stronger tail barring.

109

PRAIRIE FALCON
Falco mexicanus

Rocketing overhead like super-charged fighter jets, Prairie Falcons often seem to appear out of nowhere. At other times, they soar for long periods on updrafts or along ridgelines. • During spring and summer, Prairie Falcons usually concentrate their hunting efforts over ground squirrel colonies, readily swooping over expanses of windswept grass to pick off naïve young-sters. As summer fades to fall, large flocks of migrating songbirds often capture the attention of these pallid "ghosts of the plains." • Like any human pilot learning to fly a plane, freshly fledged falcons only get to keep their wings if they survive flight training. Inexperienced and over-eager falcons can easily misjudge their flight speed or their ability to pull out of a dive and risk serious injury or death when pushing their limits in early hunting forays.

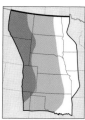

ID: brown upperparts; pale face with dark, brown "ear" patch and vertical "mustache" stripe; brown-spotted, white underparts. *Immature:* streaked underparts. *In flight:* dark band beginning at "wing pit"; long, narrow, finely banded tail; quick wingbeats and direct flight.

Size: *Male: L* 14–15 in; *W* 37–39 in. *Female: L* 17–18 in; *W* 41–43 in.

Habitat: *Breeding:* river canyons, cliffs, rimrocks or rocky promontories in arid, open lowlands or high, intermontane valleys. *In migration* and *winter:* open, treeless country, such as fields, pastures, grasslands and sagebrush flats.

Nesting: on a cliff ledge, in a crevice or on a rocky promontory; rarely in an abandoned nest of another raptor or crow; usually without nest material; mostly the female incubates 3–5 whitish eggs, spotted with brown, for about 30 days; male brings food to the female and young.

Feeding: high-speed strike-and-kill by diving swoops, low flights or chases on the wing; eats ground squirrels, small birds and small vertebrates; also takes some lizards and large insects; females consume more mammalian prey than do males.

Voice: generally silent; rapid, shrill *kik-kik-kik-kik* alarm call near the nest.

Similar Species: *Peregrine Falcon* (p. 109): darker facial markings; underparts are mostly horizontally barred; uniform underwing coloration. *Merlin* (p. 108): much smaller; plainer face and underwings. *American Kestrel* (p. 107): much smaller; more colorful; often hovers.

YELLOW RAIL
Coturnicops noveboracensis

The Yellow Rail might be the most challenging of our breeding birds to find. Not only is it quite rare and cryptic, but it is most active at night, when the majority of naturalists are dreaming of birds behind closed eyelids. Under a blanket of darkness, this secretive bird slips quietly through tall sedges, grasses and cattails, more like a small mammal than a bird, picking food from the ground and searching for snails and earthworms. By day, the shy Yellow Rail hides behind a cover of dense, marshy vegetation. Only in spring does the Yellow Rail reveal its presence by issuing its distinctive, repetitive "ticking" calls. • With their laterally compressed bodies, rails are masters at slipping through tightly packed stands of marsh vegetation. Their large feet, which distribute the birds' weight to help them rest atop thin mats of floating plant material, add to their strange appearance.

ID: mostly tawny; black stripes with fine, white barring on upperparts and flanks; white throat and belly; black crown; broad, dark line through eye; short, yellow bill. *Immature:* darker overall; white speckles on head and neck; duskier bill. *In flight:* tawny-and-gray upperwing has white trailing edge near body.
Size: *L* 6½–7½ in; *W* 11 in.
Habitat: sedge marshes and wet sedge meadows.

Nesting: on the ground or low over water, hidden by overhanging plants; shallow cup nest of grass or sedges; female incubates 8–10 buff-colored eggs, speckled with reddish brown, for up to 18 days.
Feeding: picks food from the ground and aquatic vegetation; eats mostly snails, aquatic insects, spiders and possibly earthworms; occasionally eats seeds.
Voice: clicking sounds: *tik, tik, tik-tik-tik.*
Similar Species: *Sora* (p. 115): mottled, browner back; breeding birds have black face and throat; brown-and-gray upperwing with all-gray trailing edge; distinctly different call. *Virginia Rail* (p. 114): immature has mottled, brown upperparts, black-marked, pale underparts and longer, grayish bill.

111

BLACK RAIL
Laterallus jamaicensis

The sparrow-sized Black Rail is one of North America's most elusive and seldom-seen marshland birds. Its diminutive size and secretive, partly nocturnal habits leave many a birdwatcher wondering if this creature really exists. Its calls are often the only clue to its presence. • Because the Black Rail is rarely seen and is practically impossible to observe for any extended period of time, much remains to be learned about its natural history and population dynamics. Furthermore, many of its preferred marshland habitats have been drained to increase croplands or add yet another golf course or subdivision to the mix, so any remaining pairs are clinging precariously to diminishing habitats in wildlife refuges and management areas where waterfowl and upland game birds are the main beneficiaries. A few pairs persist in such areas in southern Kansas and southeastern Colorado, but elsewhere our smallest rail is merely an occasional visitor.

ID: small, stocky body; brown-mottled, blackish upperparts with white flecking; chestnut nape; blackish gray underparts with white barring on flanks; short, black bill; red eyes; large feet. *Immature:* little or no brown on back; duller, brownish eyes. *In flight:* mostly dark gray.
Size: *L* 6 in; *W* 9 in.
Habitat: *Breeding:* wet meadows and overgrown marshes.

Nesting: among dense vegetation above water or the ground; cup-shaped nest of vegetation with a woven, domed canopy and a ramp of dead vegetation to the ground or to the water's surface; pair incubates 6–8 whitish eggs with fine, brown dots for 17–20 days.
Feeding: eats mostly insects, small crustaceans and seeds.
Voice: *Male:* repeated *ki-kee-der* call note. *Female:* deeper *who-whoo* call note.
Similar Species: *Virginia Rail* (p. 114): larger; much rustier overall; longer bill; immature has no white flecks on upperparts. *Sora* (p. 115): larger; much lighter coloration; black "mask"; yellow bill; greenish legs.

KING RAIL

Rallus elegans

At roughly the size of a farmyard chicken, the King Rail is the largest rail in North America. Unlike some of the more secretive rails, it is often seen wading through shallow water along the edge of a freshwater marsh, stalking its prey within full view of eager onlookers. Crayfish, small fish, spiders, beetles, snails, frogs and a whole host of aquatic insects keep this formidable hunter occupied and well fed. • King Rail nests, which are commonly built above shallow water, often include a protective dome of woven vegetation and a well-engineered entrance ramp. Despite these deluxe features, young rails and their attending parents desert the nest mere hours after the eggs hatch. • As with a number of other marsh-dwelling species, a loss of habitat to agriculture and urban uses has caused a drop in numbers from historic levels.

ID: black back feathers with buffy or tawny edges; cinnamon shoulders and underparts; strongly barred, black-and-white flanks; grayish brown "cheeks"; long, slightly down-curved, gray-and-orange bill. *Immature:* somewhat drabber upperparts; mottled, black-and-white underparts and neck. *In flight:* broad wing tips.

Size: *L* 15 in; *W* 20 in.

Habitat: freshwater marshes, shrubby swamps, marshy riparian shorelines and flooded fields with shrubby margins.

Nesting: among clumps of grass or sedge, just above water or the ground; male builds most of the platform nest, with a canopy and entrance ramp, using marsh vegetation; pair incubates 10–12 pale buff eggs, lightly spotted with brown, for about 21–23 days.

Feeding: aquatic insects, crustaceans and occasionally seeds; small fish and amphibians are caught by foraging in shallow water, often in or near dense plant cover.

Voice: up to 10 evenly spaced *kek* notes form a chattering call.

Similar Species: *Virginia Rail* (p. 114): much smaller; more gray on face; redder bill, legs and feet. *Least Bittern* (p. 82): solid black or dark brown back feathers; buffy orange face and shoulder patches; thicker bill; usually perched on reeds.

113

VIRGINIA RAIL
Rallus limicola

The best way to meet a Virginia Rail is to sit alongside a wetland in spring, clap your hands three or four times to imitate this bird's *ki-dick* calls and wait patiently. If you are lucky, a Virginia Rail will reveal itself for a brief instant, but usually you will only hear this elusive bird call in response. • When pursued by an intruder or predator, rails will almost always attempt to scurry away through dense, concealing vegetation rather than risk exposure in a getaway flight. With their modified feather tips and flexible vertebrae, these very narrow birds can easily squeeze through the tight confines of their marshy homes. • The Virginia Rail and its relative the Sora often inhabit the same marshes. The secret of their successful coexistence is their different microhabitat preferences and diets. The Virginia Rail typically favors the dry shores of marshes and feeds on invertebrates, whereas the Sora prefers waterfront property and eats plants and seeds.

ID: chestnut brown upperparts with black stripes; rusty breast; barred, white-and-black flanks; mostly gray face; long, down-curved, reddish bill, legs and feet. *Immature:* much darker overall; mostly black underparts with some white; dusky bill. *In flight:* rusty upperwing with blackish flight feathers; broad wing tips.

Size: *L* 9–11 in; *W* 13 in.

Habitat: wetlands, especially cattail and bulrush marshes.

Nesting: in emergent vegetation, usually suspended just above water; concealed, loose, basket nest is made of coarse grass,

cattail stems or sedges; pair incubates 5–13 brown-spotted, pale buff eggs for up to 20 days.

Feeding: probes into soft substrates and gleans vegetation for invertebrates such as beetles, snails, spiders, earthworms, insect larvae and nymphs; also eats some pondweeds and seeds.

Voice: usual call is an often-repeated, telegraph-like *kidick, kidick*; also "oinks" and croaks.

Similar Species: *King Rail* (p. 113): much larger; gray face; drabber bill and legs. *Sora* (p. 115): browner and grayer overall; more black on face; shorter, yellow bill; greenish yellow legs and feet. *Yellow Rail* (p. 111): black-and-tawny stripes on back; short, yellowish bill; pointier wings; tawny-and-gray upperwing has white trailing edge near body.

SORA

Porzana carolina

Two ascending whistles followed by a strange, descending whinny abruptly announce the presence of the often undetectable Sora. The Sora is the most common and widespread rail in North America and, like most rails, is seldom seen by birders; its elusive habits and preference for dense marshlands force most would-be observers to settle for a quick look. On occasion, however, this small bird has been known to parade around, unconcerned with onlookers, while it searches the shallows for food. • Even though its feet are not webbed or lobed, the Sora swims quite well over short distances. It may appear to be a weak and reluctant flyer, but the Sora migrates hundreds of miles each year between its breeding and wintering wetlands.

ID: black-mottled, brown upperparts with white streaks; black-and-white barring on belly; gray neck and breast; black "mask" from front of face to foreneck (less extensive on non-breeding bird); short, yellow bill; greenish yellow legs and feet. *Immature:* buffier with paler underparts; buffy brown face with little black; duskier bill. *In flight:* relatively long, pointed wings; brown-and-gray upperwing with all-gray trailing edge.
Size: *L* 8–10 in; *W* 14 in.
Habitat: wetlands with abundant emergent cattails, bulrushes, sedges and grasses.

Nesting: usually over water, but occasionally in a wet meadow under concealing vegetation; well-built basket nest is made of grass and aquatic vegetation; pair incubates 10–12 buff or olive buff, darkly speckled eggs for 18–20 days.
Feeding: gleans and probes mud for seeds, plants, aquatic insects and mollusks.
Voice: usual call is a clear, 2-note *coo-wee;* sharp *keek* alarm call; courtship song begins *or-AH or-AH*, descending quickly in a series of maniacal *weee-weee-weee* notes.
Similar Species: *Virginia Rail* (p. 114) and *King Rail* (p. 113): more rusty or cinnamon, especially on breast; long, downcurved bill. *Yellow Rail* (p. 111): black-striped, tawny upperparts and flanks; tawny breast; white trailing edge near body on tawny-and-gray upperwing.

115

COMMON MOORHEN

Gallinula chloropus

A curious-looking creature that appears to have been assembled from bits and pieces left over from other birds, the Common Moorhen has the bill of a chicken, the body of a duck and the long legs and large feet of a small heron. As it strolls around a wetland, its head bobs back and forth in synchrony with its legs, producing a comical, chugging stride. • Unlike most other members of the rail family, the Common Moorhen is quite comfortable feeding in open areas. • For moorhens, the responsibilities of parenthood do not end when their eggs have hatched—parents feed and shelter their young for several weeks, until they are capable of feeding themselves and flying on their own. • Although the Common Moorhen resembles its close relative the American Coot, its delicate manner and elusive tendencies easily distinguish it from the loud and gregarious coot. • The scientific name *chloropus* is Greek for "green foot."

ID: grayish overall; brownish back; horizontal, white streak on flanks and on undertail coverts; dark gray head; reddish forehead shield and yellow-tipped bill; long, greenish yellow legs and large feet.
Breeding: brighter bill and forehead shield.
Immature: duller plumage, especially on head; whitish throat; brownish forehead and bill. *In flight:* brown-and-gray wing has white leading edge near body.
Size: *L* 12–15 in; *W* 21 in.
Habitat: freshwater marshes, ponds, lakes and sewage lagoons.

Nesting: in shallow water or along a shoreline; pair builds a platform nest or a wide, shallow cup of bulrushes, cattails and reeds, often with a ramp leading to the water; pair incubates 8–11 buff-colored eggs with brown spotting or blotching for 19–22 days.
Feeding: eats mostly aquatic vegetation, berries and other fruits, tadpoles, insects, snails, worms and spiders; sometimes takes carrion and bird eggs.
Voice: various sounds include chickenlike clucks, screams, squeaks and a loud *cup*.
Male: harsh *ticket-ticket-ticket* in courting.
Similar Species: *American Coot* (p. 117): all-dark flanks; white bill and forehead shield; lobed toes; white trailing edge on wing near body.

AMERICAN COOT
Fulica americana

The American Coot is truly an all-terrain bird: in its quest for food it dives and dabbles like a duck, grazes confidently on land and swims about skilfully with its lobed feet. • American Coots squabble constantly during the breeding season, not just among themselves, but also with any waterbird that has the audacity to intrude upon their waterfront property. These odd birds can often be seen scooting across the surface of the water, charging rivals with flailing, splashing wings in an attempt to intimidate. Outside the breeding season, coots gather amicably together in large groups. During spring and fall, thousands congregate at a few select staging sites in our region. These numerous waterfowl are easy to spot because of their pendulous head movements while swimming. • The American Coot is colloquially known as "Mud Hen," and many people mistakenly believe that the American Coot is a species of duck.

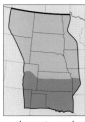

ID: grayish black overall; reddish spot on white forehead shield; red eyes; white, chicken-like bill with dark ring near tip; long, greenish yellow legs and feet with large, lobed toes. *Immature:* browner overall; lighter underparts, neck and head; grayish brown crown and forehead; grayish bill. *In flight:* white trailing edge on wing near body.
Size: *L* 13–16 in; *W* 24 in.
Habitat: shallow marshes, ponds and wetlands with open water and emergent vegetation; also sewage lagoons.
Nesting: in emergent vegetation; pair builds a floating nest of cattails and grass;

pair incubates 6–11 brown-spotted, buffy white eggs for 21–25 days.
Feeding: gleans the water's surface; sometimes dives, tips up or even grazes on land; eats aquatic vegetation, insects, snails, crayfish, worms, tadpoles and fish; may steal food from ducks.
Voice: calls frequently in summer, day and night: *kuk-kuk-kuk-kuk-kuk;* also grunts.
Similar Species: *Common Moorhen* (p. 116): white streak on flanks; reddish forehead shield and yellow- tipped bill; white leading edge on wing. *Ducks* (pp. 41–63): different plumage patterns or colors; broader, flatter bills; webbed feet. *Grebes* (pp. 74–78): much more white in plumage; no white forehead shield; bills mostly finer.

SANDHILL CRANE

Grus canadensis

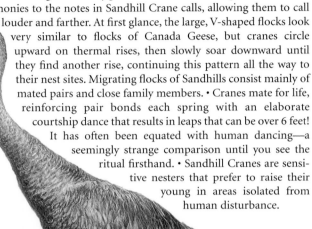

Deep, resonant, rattling calls announce the approach of a flock of migrating Sandhill Cranes long before they pass overhead. The coiling of their trachea adds harmonies to the notes in Sandhill Crane calls, allowing them to call louder and farther. At first glance, the large, V-shaped flocks look very similar to flocks of Canada Geese, but cranes circle upward on thermal rises, then slowly soar downward until they find another rise, continuing this pattern all the way to their nest sites. Migrating flocks of Sandhills consist mainly of mated pairs and close family members. • Cranes mate for life, reinforcing pair bonds each spring with an elaborate courtship dance that results in leaps that can be over 6 feet! It has often been equated with human dancing—a seemingly strange comparison until you see the ritual firsthand. • Sandhill Cranes are sensitive nesters that prefer to raise their young in areas isolated from human disturbance.

ID: very large, gray body, often stained rusty red by iron oxides in the water; long neck; naked, red crown; long, straight, dusky bill; long, dark legs. *Immature:* brown-tinged upperparts; brownish gray crown; paler bill. *In flight:* extends neck and legs; often glides, soars and circles.

Size: *L* 3½–4 ft; *W* 6–7 ft.

Habitat: *Breeding:* isolated, open marshes, fens and bogs surrounded by forests or shrubs. *In migration:* agricultural fields and shorelines.

Nesting: on a large mound of aquatic vegetation in water or along a shoreline; pair incubates 2 brown-splotched, olive buff eggs for 29–32 days (staggered hatching); young fly at about 50 days.

Feeding: probes and gleans the ground for insects, soft-bodied invertebrates, waste grain, shoots and tubers; frequently eats small vertebrates.

Voice: loud, resonant, rattling *gu-rrroo gu-rrroo gurrroo*.

Similar Species: *Great Blue Heron* (p. 83): slimmer; white crown (dark on immature); black "eyebrow"; neck is folded back over shoulders in flight. *Whooping Crane* (p. 361): all-white plumage; red or blackish patch extends from bill to "cheeks"; black flight feathers at wing tips.

BLACK-BELLIED PLOVER
Pluvialis squatarola

During the last days of May, small flocks of Black-bellied Plovers bring their haunting, whistled flight calls to springtime for a brief period, when they stand out against the drab soil of plowed fields in their black-and-white breeding plumage. When they tarry longer, at the end of the fall passage, is the best time to see these arctic breeders. The adults in their worn-out breeding plumage appear first, followed by the plain, gray, immature birds. From time to time, large flocks of hundreds of birds can be seen, but such occurrences are considered rare. • Black-bellied Plovers forage for small invertebrates with a robinlike run-and-stop technique, frequently pausing to lift their heads for a reassuring scan of their surroundings. • Most plovers have three toes, but the Black-belly, the largest North American plover, has a fourth toe higher on its leg, like most sandpipers.

nonbreeding

nonbreeding

ID: short, black bill; long, black legs. *Breeding:* mottled, black-and-white back; white undertail coverts; black belly, flanks, breast and face; curved, white stripe from forehead down neck and sides of breast. *Nonbreeding:* mottled, grayish brown upperparts; lightly streaked, pale underparts; faint, pale "eyebrow." *In flight:* black "wing pits"; white wing linings; whitish rump.
Size: *L* 10½–13 in; *W* 29 in.

Habitat: plowed fields, sod farms, meadows, lakeshores and mudflats along the edges of reservoirs, marshes and sewage lagoons.
Nesting: does not nest in the Great Plains.
Feeding: run-and-stop foraging technique; eats insects, mollusks and crustaceans.
Voice: rich, plaintive, 3-syllable whistle: *pee-oo-ee.*
Similar Species: *American Golden-Plover* (p. 120): gold-mottled upperparts; black undertail coverts in breeding plumage; gray "wing pits." *Mountain Plover* (p. 125): plain, grayish brown above and white below; smudgy breast band; pale legs; dark area on top of tail; low, rapid flight; usually solitary.

119

AMERICAN GOLDEN-PLOVER

Pluvialis dominica

A mere 150 years ago, the American Golden-Plover population was among the largest of any bird in the world. Then, in the late 1800s, market gunners mercilessly culled the great flocks in both spring and fall, with a single day's shooting often yielding tens of thousands of birds. Populations have recovered somewhat, but they will likely never return to their former numbers. • Although this bird is boldly marked in breeding plumage, the white stripe down its side disrupts the image seen by a predator, confusing the hunter as to where the head and tail are. The cryptic coloration of speckles on the top of the body blends well with the golden, mottled earth of this bird's arctic breeding grounds. • Between the Canadian Arctic and its South American wintering grounds, the American Golden-Plover was once accompanied by large numbers of the Whimbrel-like Eskimo Curlew (*Numenius borealis*). Decimated by overhunting, it was last recorded in 1963. If it still exists, it will likely be found traveling alongside the American Golden-Plover.

breeding

ID: straight, black bill; long, black legs. *Breeding:* dark upperparts speckled with gold and white; black underparts, including undertail coverts, and face; curved, white stripe from forehead down to shoulders. *Nonbreeding:* much less gold and black on upperparts; brown streaking on pale neck and underparts; broad, pale "eyebrow." *In flight:* gray "wing pits." **Size:** *L* 10–11 in; *W* 26 in.

Habitat: cultivated fields, sod farms, meadows, lakeshores and mudflats along the edges of reservoirs, marshes and sewage lagoons.
Nesting: does not nest in the Great Plains.
Feeding: run-and-stop foraging technique; snatches insects, mollusks and crustaceans; also takes seeds and berries.
Voice: soft, melodious whistle: *quee, quee-dle.*
Similar Species: *Black-bellied Plover* (p. 119): no gold speckling on upperparts; white undertail coverts year-round; paler crown; conspicuous black "wing pits" in flight.

SNOWY PLOVER

Charadrius alexandrinus

The Snowy Plover comes to the Great Plains as a summer breeder along the barren shorelines of interior alkali lakes. The species was at one time more widely distributed than it currently is, but human development now restricts this threatened species to a few undisturbed protected areas. • In our region, searching for Snowy Plovers is likely to disrupt nesting activities. Well-intentioned birders can inadvertently keep the parents away from their nests for prolonged periods, and the nests themselves are notoriously difficult to spot and might easily be crushed under a carelessly placed foot. Unfortunately for Great Plains birders, finding Snowies in the nonbreeding season, when human disturbances are minimized, requires a trip to the coast of the Gulf of Mexico or the Pacific Coast, where this bird blends unseen into its surrounding environment, moving like a ghost over isolated coastal dunes and open sandy beaches.

breeding

ID: light brown upperparts; white underparts; thin, black bill; slate gray legs. *Breeding:* variable dark patches on shoulder, forehead and ear area. *In flight:* large gray area on underwing near tip.

Size: *L* 6–7 in; *W* 17 in.

Habitat: shorelines of alkaline lakes.

Nesting: on bare ground, sometimes near a grass clump or piece of driftwood (probably as a landmark); lines a shallow scrape with pebbles, shells, grass and other debris; pair incubates 3 pale buff eggs dotted with black for 26–32 days; young leave the nest within hours of hatching.

Feeding: uses run-and-stop foraging technique to catch mostly insects here.

Voice: soft, whistled *ku-wheat* or *chu-wee* flight call; also gives a low *krut*.

Similar Species: *Semipalmated Plover* (p. 122): strictly a migrant; darker back; full, black "collar" year-round; thicker, orange-and-black bill; orangy legs; more white on underwing near tip. *Killdeer* (p. 124): much larger; darker back; 2 black breast bands; rusty tail.

SEMIPALMATED PLOVER

Charadrius semipalmatus

On the way to their arctic breeding grounds, small flocks of Semipalmated Plovers commonly touch down on our mudflats and marshes. Watch for them in late May and early June, but keep your eyes peeled because they are around for a short time only. If these birds seem to be in a hurry, they are! These long-distance migrants are under tremendous pressure to begin breeding before the end of the short northern summer. After nesting, the adults will leave the breeding grounds as early as July to enjoy a prolonged, leisurely migration to the coastlines of the southern U.S., Central America or South America. The young begin their journey as soon as they are strong enough to fly. • The scientific name *semipalmatus*, meaning "half-webbed," refers to the slight webbing between the toes of this plover. The webbing is thought to give the bird's feet more surface area when it is walking on soft substrates.

ID: dark brown back; white underparts; horizontal, black band on breast; brown head; white throat, "collar" and small "eyebrow"; black band across forehead and past eye; white patch above stubby, black-tipped bill with orange base; long, orangy yellow legs. *Immature:* dark areas are brown, not black; drabber legs and bill. *In flight:* thin, grayish edge along much of white underwing.
Size: *L* 7 in; *W* 19 in.
Habitat: sandy beaches, lakeshores, river edges and mudflats.

Nesting: does not nest in the Great Plains.
Feeding: run-and-stop foraging technique, usually on shorelines and beaches; eats crustaceans, worms and insects.
Voice: crisp, high-pitched, 2-part, rising whistle: *tu-wee*.
Similar Species: *Killdeer* (p. 124): larger; 2 black bands across breast; rusty rump. *Piping Plover* (p. 123): much lighter, grayer upperparts; narrower breast band is incomplete in females and most males; no dark band past eye. *Snowy Plover* (p. 121): slightly smaller; lighter, grayer upperparts; incomplete breast band; thinner, all-dark bill; grayish legs; more gray at tip of underwing.

PIPING PLOVER

Charadrius melodus

A master of illusion, the Piping Plover is hardly noticeable when it settles on shorelines and beaches. Its pale plumage is the perfect camouflage against a sandy beach. As well, the dark bands across its forehead and neckline resemble scattered pebbles or strips of washed-up vegetation. This plover's cryptic plumage, however, has done little to protect it from wetland drainage, increased predation and disturbance by humans. The recreational use of beaches during summer—along with an increase in human-tolerant predators such as gulls, raccoons and skunks—has impaired this plover's ability to reproduce successfully. Formerly more common, the Piping Plover is now an endangered species. • On beaches with wave action, these birds often employ a foot-trembling strategy to entice invertebrates to the surface. • If threatened, Piping Plover chicks typically take to the water and swim away, whereas adults rarely swim at all.

ID: pale, sandy upperparts; white underparts; orangy yellow legs. *Breeding:* black forehead band; black "necklace" (sometimes incomplete, especially on females); black-tipped bill with orange base. *Nonbreeding:* gray breast and forehead bands; all-black bill. *In flight:* thin, grayish edge along much of white underwing.

Size: *L* 7 in; *W* 19 in.

Habitat: sandy beaches and open lakeshores.

Nesting: on bare sand along an open shoreline; in a shallow scrape sometimes lined with pebbles and tiny shells; pair incubates 4 pale buff eggs, blotched with dark brown and black, for 26–28 days.

Feeding: run-and-stop foraging technique; eats worms and insects; takes almost all its food from the ground.

Voice: clear, whistled melody: *peep peep peep-lo.*

Similar Species: *Semipalmated Plover* (p. 122): much darker, browner upperparts; dark band extends past eye. *Killdeer* (p. 124): larger; much darker upperparts; rusty rump; 2 black breast bands.

123

KILLDEER

Charadrius vociferus

The ubiquitous Killdeer is often the first shorebird a birder learns to identify. Its boisterous calls rarely fail to catch the attention of people passing through its wide variety of nesting environments. The Killdeer's preference for open fields, gravel driveways, beach edges, golf courses and abandoned industrial areas has allowed it to thrive throughout our rural and suburban landscapes. • If you happen to wander too close to a Killdeer nest, the parent will try to lure you away by issuing loud alarm calls and feigning a broken wing. Most predators take the bait and are led far enough away for the parent to suddenly recover from its injury and fly off, sounding its piercing calls. Similar distraction displays are widespread phenomena in the bird world, but, in our region, the Killdeer's broken wing act is by far the gold medal winner. • The scientific name *vociferus* aptly describes this vocal bird, but double-check all calls in spring, when the Killdeer is often imitated by frisky European Starlings.

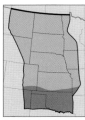

ID: brown back and head; white underparts with 2 black breast bands; black forehead band; white "eyebrow"; white patch above bill; long, pale legs; tail projects beyond wing tips at rest. *Immature:* downy; less distinction between breast bands. *In flight:* whitish underwing has broad, brownish gray trailing edge; rusty rump.
Size: *L* 9–11 in; *W* 24 in.
Habitat: open ground, fields, lakeshores, sandy beaches, mudflats, gravel streambeds, wet meadows and grasslands.

Nesting: on open ground; in a shallow, usually unlined, depression; pair incubates 4 darkly spotted and blotched, pale buff eggs for 24–28 days; occasionally raises 2 broods.
Feeding: run-and-stop foraging technique; eats mostly insects; also takes spiders, snails, earthworms and crayfish.
Voice: loud, distinctive *kill-dee kill-dee kill-deer* and variations, including *deer-deer*.
Similar Species: *Semipalmated Plover* (p. 122): smaller; 1 breast band; orangy yellow legs. *Piping Plover* (p. 123): smaller; lighter, grayer upperparts; 1 breast band; orangy yellow legs.

MOUNTAIN PLOVER

Charadrius montanus

Don't let the name fool you—the Mountain Plover favors dry grasslands and vast, open areas far from the Rockies. And even in this habitat, the Mountain Plover is far from common. Many birdwatchers have made pilgrimages just to find it. • Like the Upland Sandpiper, the Mountain Plover does little to announce its shorebird heritage, only rarely approaching shorelines. It is indeed more of a "grass-piper" than a sandpiper. • After their nesting duties are complete, many Mountain Plovers migrate to northern Mexico or southern California, crossing both the Rockies and the Coast Ranges before settling on their wintering grounds, and then repeating the journey in reverse the following spring. A few Mountain Plovers migrate south through Texas and New Mexico, however. Members of this species cling to their traditional migratory routes as tightly as any shorebird, and "lost" individuals are rarely encountered.

ID: sandy upperparts; light underparts; white forehead; thin, dark bill; light-colored legs. *Breeding:* black fore-crown; thin, black eye line. *In flight:* whitish underwing has broad, brownish gray trailing edge.

Size: *L* 9 in; *W* 23 in.

Habitat: sparse, dry prairies, heavily grazed pastures and mudflats.

Nesting: near a dry hummock, cactus or cow chips (probably as a landmark); in a shallow scrape lined with small amounts of grass, cow chips and roots; pair incubates 3 olive buff eggs with black markings for about 30 days.

Feeding: gleans the ground for insects, especially grasshoppers.

Voice: shrill call note; whistles during spring and summer.

Similar Species: *Upland Sandpiper* (p. 133): dark-marked, brownish upperparts; longer, slimmer neck; longer, yellow bill; yellow legs. *Killdeer* (p. 124): 2 breast bands; rusty rump; longer tail.

125

BLACK-NECKED STILT

Himantopus mexicanus

The Black-necked Stilt is a bird of contrasts. Black above and white below, it wades with dignity along the margins of a smelly sewage lagoon or a stark, white, alkaline lakeshore. All semblance of dignity disappears if an intruder appears, when agitated nesters will scream at the would-be predator and generally stir things up. Soon afterward, the parents return to taking their turns at sheltering their eggs from the warmth of the hot sun; sometimes they even wet their belly feathers to cool off their young during their next incubation duty. Later in the day, a border dispute may erupt between two neighboring pairs because, unlike colonial-nesting American Avocets, Black-necked Stilts are fiercely territorial. • With the longest legs relative to height of any bird—they account for 60 percent of its total height—the Black-necked Stilt can catch prey in water more than 6 inches deep.

ID: dark upperparts; white underparts; black hood; small, white "eyebrow"; long, straight, dark, needlelike bill; reddish orange legs and feet. *Male:* glossy, black back. *Female:* dark brown back. *In flight:* feet trail far behind tail.

Size: *L* 14–15 in; *W* 29 in.

Habitat: along the margins of freshwater, brackish and saltwater marshes and on the marshy shorelines of lakes, ponds and mudflats; also forages in flooded agricultural fields and saline ponds and lakes.

Nesting: in a shallow depression on slightly raised ground near water; nest is lined with shells, pebbles or vegetative debris; pair incubates 4 darkly blotched, buff eggs for about 25 days; both adults tend the precocial young.

Feeding: picks prey from the water's surface or from the bottom substrate; primarily eats insects, crustaceans and other aquatic invertebrates; rarely eats seeds of aquatic plants.

Voice: not vocal in migration; loud, sharp *yip-yip-yip-yip* in summer; *kek-kek-kek-kek* in flight.

Similar Species: *American Avocet* (p. 127): chunkier; broad, black and white stripes on upperparts; head and neck are either all peachy red (breeding) or light gray (nonbreeding); upturned bill; pale, bluish pink legs.

AMERICAN AVOCET

Recurvirostra americana

With its long, peachy red neck accentuating the length of its slender bill and stiltlike legs, an American Avocet in full breeding plumage is a strikingly elegant bird. The peach-colored "hood" is replaced, often by August, with a more subdued winter gray that the bird will wear for most of the year. This avocet is the only one in the world to undergo a yearly color change. • American Avocets walk rapidly or run about in fairly deep water, swinging their bills from side to side. Although they look bent out of shape, the upcurved bills are ideal for efficiently skimming aquatic vegetation and invertebrates off the surface of shallow water. At other times, these birds use their webbed feet to swim and feed by tipping up like dabbling ducks. • If an American Avocet is disturbed while standing in its one-legged resting position, it will take off, switch legs in midair and land on the rested leg.

♂

breeding

breeding

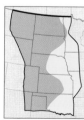

ID: upperparts show broad, alternating, black and white bands, with white at center; white underparts; long, upturned, black bill (more upturned and shortest on female); long, pale bluish pink legs. *Breeding:* peachy red head, neck and breast. *Nonbreeding:* light gray head, neck and breast. *In flight:* long neck; feet trail well behind tail.

Size: *L* 17–18 in; *W* 31 in.

Habitat: lakeshores, alkaline wetlands and exposed mudflats.

Nesting: semi-colonial; in a shallow depression along a dried mudflat, exposed shoreline or open area, always near water; pair digs a shallow scrape or builds a vegetation mound and lines it with pebbles or other debris; pair incubates 4 darkly splotched, buffy olive eggs for 23–25 days.

Feeding: sweeps bill from side to side along the water's surface, picking up minute crustaceans, aquatic insects and occasionally seeds; male sweeps lower in the water than female; occasionally swims and tips up like a duck.

Voice: harsh, shrill *plee-eek plee-eek*.

Similar Species: *Black-necked Stilt* (p. 126): dark nape and head markings; straight bill; reddish orange legs. *Willet* (p. 131): grayish upperparts, becoming dark-mottled in breeding plumage; straight bill; feet trail just behind tail in flight.

GREATER YELLOWLEGS

Tringa melanoleuca

The Greater Yellowlegs is the more solitary of the two yellowlegs species, but it can be seen in small flocks during migration, when it takes on the role of lookout among mixed flocks of shorebirds. At the first sign of danger, this large sandpiper bobs its head and calls incessantly. In escaping a perceived threat, the Greater Yellowlegs will usually retreat into deeper water, becoming airborne only as a last resort. • During migration, many shorebirds, including the Greater Yellowlegs, often stand or hop around beachflats on one leg. These stubborn "one-leggers" may be mistaken for crippled individuals, but this stance may be an adaptation that conserves body heat.

nonbreeding

nonbreeding

ID: brownish upperparts with light and dark flecking; white underparts; slightly upturned, dark bill, noticeably longer than head width; long, bright yellow legs and feet. *Breeding:* darker, heavier flecking on upperparts; fine, dense, dark streaking on head and neck; dark barring on breast often extends onto belly and flanks; subtle, dark eye line; light lores. *Nonbreeding:* light brownish streaking on neck, breast and head. *In flight:* brown upperwings; white and grayish brown underwings.
Size: *L* 13–15 in; *W* 28 in.

Habitat: almost all wetlands, including lakeshores, marshes, flooded fields and river shorelines.
Nesting: does not nest in the Great Plains.
Feeding: usually wades in water over its knees; sometimes sweeps its bill from side to side; primarily eats aquatic invertebrates but will also eat small fish; occasionally snatches prey from the water's surface.
Voice: quick, whistled, usually 3-note series: *tew-tew-tew*.
Similar Species: *Lesser Yellowlegs* (p. 129): smaller; bill length similar to width of head; call is generally 2 higher notes: *tew-tew*. *Willet* (p. 131): more muted speckling; heavier, shorter bill; greenish gray legs; black-and-white wings.

LESSER YELLOWLEGS

Tringa flavipes

With a series of continuous, rapid-fire *tew-tew* calls, Lesser Yellowlegs streak across the surface of wetlands and lakeshores. Their spring visits are relatively brief, but these birds can also be seen during their lengthy fall migration period from mid-July to mid-October. • Many birders find it a challenge to distinguish Lesser Yellowlegs and Greater Yellowlegs in the field. With practice, you will notice that the Lesser's bill is finer, straighter and only about as long as the width of its head. The Lesser appears to have longer legs and wings, making it seem slimmer and taller than the Greater, and it is also more commonly seen in flocks. If your sight proves inadequate, open your ears: the Lesser Yellowlegs gives a pair of peeps, whereas the Greater gives three. If you are still puzzled by the bird's identity, simply write "yellowlegs spp." in your field notes and try again next time. • The scientific name *flavipes* is derived from Latin words meaning "yellow foot."

nonbreeding

nonbreeding

ID: brownish upperparts with light and dark flecking; white underparts; dark bill, similar in length to head width; long, bright yellow legs and feet. *Breeding:* darker, heavier flecking on upperparts; fine, dense, dark streaking on head and neck; dark barring on breast and upper flanks; subtle, dark eye line; light lores. *Nonbreeding:* light brownish streaking on neck, breast and head. *In flight:* brown upperwings; white and grayish brown underwings.
Size: *L* 10–11 in; *W* 24 in.

Habitat: shorelines of lakes, rivers, marshes and ponds.
Nesting: does not nest in the Great Plains.
Feeding: snatches prey from the water's surface; frequently wades in shallow water; primarily eats aquatic invertebrates but also takes small fish and tadpoles.
Voice: typically a high-pitched pair of *tew* notes.
Similar Species: *Greater Yellowlegs* (p. 128): larger; noticeably longer, slightly upturned bill; *tew* call is usually given in 3-note series. *Solitary Sandpiper* (p. 130): white eye ring; duller, greenish legs; dark underwings. *Willet* (p. 131): much bulkier; more muted speckling; heavier bill, greenish gray legs; black-and-white wings.

SOLITARY SANDPIPER

Tringa solitaria

True to their name, Solitary Sandpipers are usually seen alone, bobbing their bodies like spirited dancers as they forage for insects around our wetlands. However, every so often a lucky observer may happen upon a small group of these birds during spring or fall. • Sometimes the Solitary Sandpiper forages by wading in shallow water, advancing slowly while vibrating the leading foot, thus stirring the bottom sufficiently to disturb prey. In this way it captures aquatic insects and their larvae, including water boatmen and small crustaceans. • Shorebirds lay very large eggs and incubate them for comparatively long periods of time. Once sandpiper chicks break out of their eggs, they are ready to run, hide and feed on their own. These highly developed hatchlings, known as precocial young, are immediately able to fend for themselves in a dangerous world.

ID: white-speckled, grayish brown back; fine, white streaks on grayish brown head, neck and breast; white eye ring; white lores; dark, yellowish gray bill with black tip; short, dull green legs. *In flight:* dark underwings; dark upper tail feathers with white bars on sides.
Size: *L* 7½–9 in; *W* 22 in.
Habitat: wet meadows, sewage lagoons, muddy ponds, sedge wetlands, beaver ponds and wooded streams.

Nesting: does not nest in the Great Plains.
Feeding: stalks shorelines, picking up aquatic invertebrates such as water boatmen and damselfly nymphs; also gleans for terrestrial invertebrates; occasionally stirs the water with its foot to spook out prey.
Voice: high, thin *peet-wheet* or *wheat wheat wheat*.
Similar Species: *Lesser Yellowlegs* (p. 129): less prominent eye ring; longer, bright yellow legs; whitish underwings. *Spotted Sandpiper* (p. 132): dark eye line breaks eye ring; black-tipped, orangy bill; black-spotted breast in breeding plumage. *Other sandpipers* (pp. 130–46): inconspicuous or no white eye ring; black bills and legs.

WILLET

Catoptrophorus semipalmatus

A Willet on the ground cuts a rather dull figure. The moment it takes flight or displays, however, its black-and-white wings add sudden pizzazz while it calls out a loud, rhythmic *will-will willet, will-will-willet!* If you look closely, you may notice that the white markings across the Willet's wingspan form a rough "V" as it flies away. Other shorebirds may use these bright, bold flashes of the Willet's wings as alerts to imminent danger. • Willets are loud, social, easily identified birds—a nice change when dealing with sandpipers. Most Willet sightings occur when the birds are foraging among large, mixed flocks of shorebirds. Of the two distinct sub-species of the Willet, the larger, longer-legged, longer-billed western race is the one we see breeding in the northern Great Plains. It migrates east and west to overwinter on both the Atlantic and Pacific coasts, and a few move southward. The eastern race rarely ventures far from the Atlantic coast.

breeding

breeding

ID: light brownish gray upperparts and sides; whitish belly, undertail coverts and throat; heavy, straight, blackish bill; greenish gray legs. *Breeding:* dark streaking and barring overall. *In flight:* black-and-brown wings with wide, white "V" pattern above and below.

Size: *L* 14–16 in; *W* 26 in.

Habitat: wet fields and shorelines of marshes, lakes and ponds.

Nesting: frequently colonial; usually on the ground in a field or pasture several hundred yards from water; shallow depression is lined with grass; pair incubates 4–5 brown-splotched, grayish eggs for 22–30 days.

Feeding: feeds by probing muddy areas; also gleans the ground for insects; occasionally eats shoots and seeds.

Voice: loud, rolling *will-will willet, will-will-willet!*

Similar Species: *Marbled Godwit* (p. 137) and *Hudsonian Godwit* (p. 136): larger body; much longer, yellowish orange bill with dark, slightly upturned tip; darker legs; plainer wing coloration. *Greater Yellowlegs* (p. 128): migrant only; white-speckled upperparts; longer, yellow legs; all-brown upperwings; pale underwings.

131

SPOTTED SANDPIPER

Actitis macularia

It wasn't until 1972 that the unexpected details of the Spotted Sandpiper's breeding activities were realized. In this species, the female defends a territory and mates with more than one male in a single breeding season, leaving the males to tend the nests and eggs. This unusual nesting behavior, known as polyandry, is found in about one percent of all bird species. • Even though its breast spots are not noticeable from a distance, the Spotted Sandpiper's stiff-winged, quivering flight pattern and tendency to burst from the shore are easily recognizable. This bird is also known for its continuous "teetering" behavior as it forages. • The scientific name *macularia* is Latin for "spot," referring to the spots on this bird's underparts in breeding plumage.

breeding

breeding

ID: brown upperparts and head; white underparts; brown at sides of breast; white "eyebrow." *Breeding:* dark spotting all over, heaviest on breast; black-tipped, orangy yellow bill; orangy legs. *Nonbreeding:* duskier bill; dull yellow legs. *In flight:* flies close to the water's surface with very rapid, shallow wingbeats; thin, white upperwing stripe; dark trailing edge adjoins long, white triangle on underwing.
Size: *L* 7–8 in; *W* 15 in.
Habitat: shorelines, gravel beaches, ponds, marshes, alluvial wetlands, rivers, streams, swamps and sewage lagoons; occasionally seen in cultivated fields.

Nesting: polyandrous; usually near water; often under overhanging vegetation among logs or under bushes; in a shallow depression lined with grass; almost exclusively the male incubates 4 creamy buff, heavily brown-blotched and spotted eggs and raises the young.
Feeding: picks and gleans along shorelines for terrestrial and aquatic invertebrates; also snatches flying insects from the air.
Voice: sharp, crisp *eat-wheat, eat-wheat, wheat-wheat-wheat-wheat.*
Similar Species: *Solitary Sandpiper* (p. 130): fine, white streaks on grayish brown head, neck and breast; complete white eye ring; yellowish gray bill with black tip. *Other sandpipers* (pp. 133–46): black bills and legs; no black spotting on breast.

UPLAND SANDPIPER

Bartramia longicauda

Upland Sandpipers are sometimes seen in spring, perched atop fence posts and then flying high, emitting shrill "wolf-whistle" calls. Excited males will even launch into the air to perform courtship flight displays, combining song with shallow, fluttering wingbeats. At the height of the breeding season, however, these large-eyed inland shorebirds are rarely seen, because they prefer to remain hidden in the tall grass of abandoned fields and ungrazed pastures.
• An American birder accustomed to seeing the Upland Sandpiper in our grassy fields and meadows might be shocked to meet it during a visit to the grasslands of Argentina. Twice each year, this wide-ranging shorebird makes the incredible journey to and from its breeding grounds to overwinter in South America. • During the late 1800s, high market demand for this bird's meat led to severe overhunting and a catastrophic reduction in its abundance across much of North America. Its numbers have since rebounded, but recent declines in grassland habitats again threaten its welfare.

ID: mottled, dark-marked, brownish upperparts; whitish underparts; horizontal, dark streaks on breast, sides and flanks; long, slim, streaked neck; small head; large, dark eyes; dark-tipped, yellow bill is about same length as head; yellow legs and feet. *In flight:* finely black-barred, white underwings.

Size: *L* 11–12½ in; *W* 26 in.

Habitat: hay fields, ungrazed pastures, grassy meadows, abandoned fields, natural grasslands and airports.

Nesting: in dense grass or along a wetland; in a depression, usually with grass arching over the top; pair incubates 4 pale to pinkish buff eggs, lightly spotted with reddish brown, for 22–27 days; pair tends the young.

Feeding: gleans the ground for insects, especially grasshoppers and beetles.

Voice: *quip-ip-ip* alarm call. *Male:* airy, whistled *whip-whee-ee you* courtship song.

Similar Species: *Willet* (p. 131): longer, heavier, darker bill; greenish gray legs; boldly black-and-white wings in flight. *Buff-breasted Sandpiper* (p. 146): smaller; buffier overall; shorter neck; larger head; no streaking on "cheek" and foreneck; daintier, dark bill. *Pectoral Sandpiper* (p. 143): smaller; vertical streaking on breast has crisp lower edge; shorter neck; smaller eyes; usually seen in larger numbers.

WHIMBREL

Numenius phaeopus

Whimbrels enjoy a widespread distribution, nesting across northern North America and Eurasia and spending their winters on the shores of six continents. In migration, Whimbrels are primarily coastal and oceanic, but some birds fly overland and find their way to our region. During late spring and late fall, wide scatterings of Whimbrels can sometimes be seen on expansive mudflats or in plowed fields. The birds forage individually, yet remain in contact with others of their kind, ever prepared to take flight as a flock. • It is impossible to talk about the Whimbrel without mentioning the Eskimo Curlew *(N. borealis)*. Both of these birds suffered devastating losses to their populations during the commercial hunts of the late 1800s. Whereas the Whimbrel population slowly recovered, the Eskimo Curlew seemed to vanish into thin air—the last confirmed sighting of this bird was in 1963. Encouraging reports from South American wintering grounds in 1993 offer a glimmer of hope that a few still remain.

ID: brown upperparts with dark brown mottling; buffy brown underparts with brown barring on breast and flanks; striped crown; dark eye line; long, downcurved, dull, amber bill with black tip becomes all-dark from spring through fall; long, gray legs. *In flight:* dark barring on pale brown underwings.
Size: *L* 18 in; *W* 32 in.
Habitat: mudflats, sandy beaches, farmlands, grassy lakeshores, airports and flooded agricultural fields.

Nesting: does not nest in the Great Plains.
Feeding: probes and pecks for invertebrates in mud or vegetation; also eats berries in fall.
Voice: flocks utter a distinctive, rippling *bibibibibibibi* on approach.
Similar Species: *Eskimo Curlew:* likely extinct; darker upperparts; shorter, slightly straighter bill; unbarred primaries; pale cinnamon wing linings. *Long-billed* Curlew (p. 135): larger; buffier underparts; plainer face; much longer bill. *Willet* (p. 131): smaller; grayer overall; shorter, straight bill; plain, unmarked crown; prominent, black-and-white wing markings in flight. *Marbled Godwit* (p. 137): buffier underparts; slightly upturned bill; darker legs.

LONG-BILLED CURLEW

Numenius americanus

L ong-billed Curlews are fun to watch during the breeding season. Male curlews put on spectacular displays over their prairie nesting territories, issuing loud, ringing calls as they flutter higher and higher before gliding down again in an undulating flight. • The Long-billed Curlew occasionally visits shorelines, but it is more commonly seen in pastures and stubble fields. Its long, downcurved bill is a wonderfully dexterous tool for picking up grasshoppers while it keeps a watchful eye above the prairie grass. This remarkably long bill also serves as an excellent field mark for birders. • Habitat loss has led to the decline of the Long-billed Curlew. Its future concerns conservationists, who point out that our current abundance of rangeland habitats should not be taken for granted.

ID: dark-mottled, brown upperparts; buffy brown underparts; unstriped head; very long, downcurved, yellowish-and-gray bill (distinctly longer on female); long, gray legs. *In flight:* rusty buff underwing with brown trailing edge.

Size: *L* 23 in; *W* 35 in.

Habitat: shortgrass prairie and tame pastures; less commonly grain fields, fallow or stubble. *In migration:* often near water.

Nesting: usually on dry prairie; in a slight depression sparsely lined with grass and debris; pair incubates 4 pale, uniformly dark-spotted eggs for 27–30 days.

Feeding: *Breeding:* picks grasshoppers and other invertebrates from grass and sloughs; also known to feed on the nestlings of grassland songbirds. *In migration:* probes shorelines and mudflats for soft-bodied invertebrates.

Voice: most common summer call is a loud whistle: *cur-lee cur-lee cur-lee*; also, a melodious, rolling *cuurrleeeuuu*.

Similar Species: *Whimbrel* (p. 134): smaller; striped crown; shorter bill; dark-barred underwing. *Marbled Godwit* (p. 137): shorter, slightly upturned bill with more orange at base; darker legs.

135

HUDSONIAN GODWIT

Limosa haemastica

Each fall, a great number of Hudsonian Godwits gather on the shores of Canada's Hudson Bay and then embark on a nonstop journey to southern South America, fueled solely by fat reserves built up on their staging grounds. As a result of this migration marathon, these godwits are not often seen at typical stopover sites. Fortunately, not all Hudsonian Godwits fly directly south in early fall, so birders scouting local wetlands—even as late as November—may be able to enjoy their presence. During their spring migration northward, most Hudsonian Godwits tend to fly an inland route and are even easier to find in the Great Plains. • Hudsonian Godwits probing sandy depths for prey sometimes have their bills buried up to their eyes! Longer bills allow female godwits and curlews to consistently outcompete the males in probing deeply for food. • In flight, the Hudsonian Godwit is easily distinguished from the Marbled Godwit by its distinctive, largely black underwings.

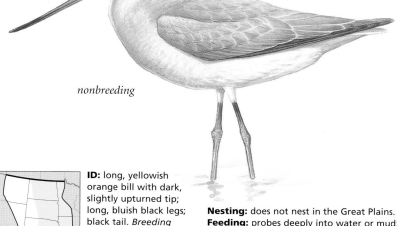

nonbreeding

ID: long, yellowish orange bill with dark, slightly upturned tip; long, bluish black legs; black tail. *Breeding male:* dark grayish brown upperparts with large white speckles; chestnut red underparts with dark and gray barring. *Breeding female:* less chestnut on underparts. *Nonbreeding:* lightly mottled, grayish upperparts and neck; pale underparts often show some barring. *Immature:* dark grayish brown upperparts; pale underparts; brownish neck and breast. *In flight:* white rump; black "wing pits," wing linings and tail.
Size: *L* 14–15½ in; *W* 29 in.
Habitat: flooded fields, marshes, mudflats and lakeshores.

Nesting: does not nest in the Great Plains.
Feeding: probes deeply into water or mud; walks into deeper water than most shorebirds but rarely swims; eats mollusks, crustaceans, insects and other invertebrates; also picks earthworms from plowed fields.
Voice: usually quiet in migration; sometimes gives a sharp, rising *god-WIT!*
Similar Species: *Marbled Godwit* (p. 137): buffy overall, with darker barring on upperparts, including rump and tail; cinnamon buff underwings. *Greater Yellowlegs* (p. 128): smaller; shorter, all-dark bill; bright yellow legs; no black on underwing. *Long-billed Dowitcher* (p. 148) and *Short-billed Dowitcher* (p. 147): smaller; straight, all-dark bills; yellowish green legs; reddish buff underparts in breeding plumage.

MARBLED GODWIT

Limosa fedoa

Even though the Marbled Godwit has a bill that, to us, looks long enough to reach buried prey, this bird doesn't seem content with its reach. It is frequently seen with its head submerged beneath the water or with its face pressed into a mudflat. These deep probings seem to pay off for this large, resourceful shorebird, however, and a Marbled Godwit looks genuinely pleased with a freshly extracted meal and a face covered in mud. • Unlike Hudsonian Godwits, which undertake long migrations from the Arctic to South America, Marbled Godwits migrate relatively short distances to coastal wintering areas in the southern U.S. and Central America. • The genus name *Limosa*, meaning "muddy," refers to this bird's preferred foraging habitats.

breeding

breeding

ID: buffy plumage, heavily barred in dark brown on upperparts; long, yellowish orange bill with dark, slightly upturned tip; long neck; long, mottled, bluish black legs. *Breeding:* fine, dark barring on underparts. *In flight:* cinnamon buff wing linings.
Size: *L* 16–20 in; *W* 30 in.
Habitat: flooded fields, wet meadows, marshes, mudflats and lakeshores.
Nesting: on dry ground in grass or sedges, usually near water; in a slight depression lined with grass; nest may have a partial canopy; pair is believed to share incubation of 4 brown-spotted, olive buff to greenish eggs for 21–23 days.

Feeding: probes deeply in soft substrates for worms, insect larvae, crustaceans and mollusks; picks insects from grass; may also eat the tubers and seeds of aquatic vegetation.
Voice: loud, ducklike, 2-syllable squawks: *co-rect co-rect* or *god-wit god-wit*.
Similar Species: *Hudsonian Godwit* (p. 136): stronger facial markings; white rump; chestnut red neck and underparts in breeding plumage; gray overall in non-breeding plumage. *Greater Yellowlegs* (p. 128): little or no buff in plumage; shorter, all-dark bill; bright yellow legs. *Long-billed Dowitcher* (p. 148) and *Short-billed Dowitcher* (p. 147): smaller; straight, all-dark bills; yellowish green legs; white rump wedge.

SEMIPALMATED SANDPIPER

Calidris pusilla

Highly efficient as breeders, Semipalmated Sandpipers raise up to four young per pair in just a few weeks of arctic summer, then fly 2000 miles nonstop over water back to their wintering grounds. They travel almost the entire length of the Americas during migration, so their staging sites must provide ample food sources. Each spring, large numbers of Semipalmated Sandpipers touch down on suitable wetlands, pecking and probing in mechanized fury to replenish their body fat for the remainder of their long journey. • Small and plain in appearance, Semipalmated Sandpipers can be difficult to identify among the swarms of similar-looking *Calidris* sandpipers that appear on beaches and mudflats each spring. Known collectively as "peeps" because of the similarity in their high-pitched calls, these strikingly similar "miniatures," which include the Semipalmated, Least, Western, White-rumped and Baird's sandpipers, can make shorebird identification either a complete nightmare or an uplifting challenge.

nonbreeding

nonbreeding

ID: white underparts; white "eyebrow"; short, straight, black bill; black legs; folded wings extend to tip of tail. *Breeding:* mottled, gray-and-brown upperparts; slight rufous tinge to scapulars, crown and ear patch; faint brown streaks on upper breast and flanks. *Nonbreeding:* grayish brown upperparts; light brown wash on sides of upper breast. *In flight:* narrow, white wing stripe; dark line through white rump and gray tail.
Size: *L* 5½–7 in; *W* 14 in.
Habitat: mudflats; shores of ponds and lakes.

Nesting: does not nest in the Great Plains.
Feeding: probes soft substrates and gleans for aquatic insects and crustaceans.
Voice: harsh *cherk* flight call; sometimes gives a longer *chirrup* or a chittering alarm call.
Similar Species: *Least Sandpiper* (p. 140): slightly darker upperparts; yellowish legs. *Western Sandpiper* (p. 139): longer, slightly downcurved bill; bright rufous wash on scapulars, crown and ear patch in breeding plumage. *Sanderling* (p. 361): nonbreeding is larger with pale gray upperparts and more contrast on upperwing. *White-rumped Sandpiper* (p. 141): larger; folded wings extend beyond tail; all-white rump. *Baird's Sandpiper* (p. 142): larger; longer bill; folded wings extend beyond tail.

WESTERN SANDPIPER

Calidris mauri

Most Western Sandpipers stick to the Pacific Coast, but some adventurous individuals traverse the continent, often flying through the prairies on their way to the Atlantic and Gulf coasts for winter. • Many identification guides will tell you to look for this bird's downcurved bill, and on paper this seems like a sensible plan. In the field, however, as angles and lighting change, the bills of "peeps" can look downcurved one moment, straight the next, and anything in between when double-checked. It is a good idea to spend some time getting to know the peeps before trying to identity them. The Western Sandpiper can be easily confused with other peeps, in particular the Semipalmated Sandpiper. • To track down the rare Western Sandpiper, try calling local birding hotlines to find out the locations of the most recent local sightings. Unless you are particularly keen to find them on your own, why not let more experienced birders do most of the work for you?

nonbreeding

nonbreeding

ID: white underparts; white "eyebrow"; black, slightly down-curved bill; black legs; folded wings extend to tip of tail. *Breeding:* black-mottled, grayish brown upperparts with rufous scapulars, crown and ear patch; V-shaped dark markings on upper breast and flanks. *Nonbreeding:* grayish brown upperparts; streaky, light brown wash on upper breast. *In flight:* narrow, white wing stripe; dark line through white rump and gray tail.
Size: *L* 6–7 in; *W* 14 in.
Habitat: pond edges, lakeshores and mudflats.
Nesting: does not nest in the Great Plains.

Feeding: gleans and probes mud and shallow water; occasionally submerges head; primarily eats aquatic insects, worms and crustaceans.
Voice: high-pitched *cheep* flight call.
Similar Species: *Semipalmated Sandpiper* (p. 138): shorter, straight bill; less rufous on scapulars, crown and ear patch of breeding bird. *Least Sandpiper* (p. 140): smaller; yellowish legs; darker breast wash; no rufous patches. *White-rumped Sandpiper* (p. 141): larger; all-white rump; folded wings extend beyond tail; much less rufous. *Baird's Sandpiper* (p. 142): larger; folded wings extend beyond tail; no rufous patches. *Sanderling* (p. 361): non-breeding has paler upperparts and bolder, white upperwing stripe.

139

LEAST SANDPIPER

Calidris minutilla

The Least Sandpiper is the smallest North American shorebird, but its size does not deter it from performing migratory feats, with some of these arctic-breeding birds flying to South America for winter (although others are content to move to the southern shores of North America). • To maximize their breeding efforts during the incredibly short arctic summers, Least Sandpipers lay large eggs relative to those of other sandpipers—the entire clutch might weigh over half the weight of the female! The young hatch in an advanced state of development, getting an early start on preparations for the fall migration. These tiny shorebirds begin moving southward as early as the first week of July, so they are some of the first fall migrants. • Although the yellowish legs are a good field mark for this species, bad lighting or mud can make a bird's legs look darker or lighter than they really are. • The apt scientific name *minutilla* is Latin for "very small."

breeding

ID: black bill; yellowish legs. *Breeding:* dark-mottled, brownish back with faint white "V"; lightly brown-streaked, buffy brown breast; buffy brown head and nape. *Non-breeding:* brownish areas are more grayish overall. *Immature:* similar to adult, but with faintly streaked breast. *In flight:* broad, dark gray edge on whitish under-wing.
Size: *L* 5–6½ in; *W* 13 in.

Habitat: sandy beaches, lakeshores, ditches, sewage lagoons, mudflats and wet-land edges.
Nesting: does not nest in the Great Plains.
Feeding: probes or pecks for insects, crustaceans, small mollusks and occasionally seeds.
Voice: high-pitched *kreee.*
Similar Species: *Semipalmated Sandpiper* (p. 138): slightly lighter upperparts; black legs. *Western Sandpiper* (p. 139): slightly larger; lighter breast wash; black legs; rufous patches on crown, ear and scapulars in breeding plumage. *Other peeps* (pp. 138–42): larger; dark legs.

WHITE-RUMPED SANDPIPER

Calidris fuscicollis

Just as a die-hard shorebird watcher is about to go into a peep-induced stupor, small brownish heads emerge from hiding, back feathers are ruffled, wings are stretched and, almost without warning, the birds take flight and flash pure white rumps. There is no doubt that the beautiful White-rumped Sandpiper has been identified. • This sandpiper's white rump may serve the same purpose as the tail of a white-tailed deer—to alert others of its kind that danger threatens. When flocks of White-rumps and other sandpipers take to the air, they often defecate in unison. This spontaneous evacuation might benefit the birds by reducing their weight for takeoff. Flocks of White-rumped Sandpipers have also been known to collectively rush at a predator and then suddenly scatter in its face. • Like many sandpipers, White-rumps are accomplished long-distance migrants, often flying for stretches of 60 hours nonstop. • The scientific name *fus-cicollis* means "brown neck," a characteristic that this bird shares with many of its close relatives.

breeding

breeding

ID: black bill, about as long as head width; black legs. *Breeding:* dark-mottled, brown upperparts; dark streaking on breast, sides and flanks. *Nonbreeding:* grayer overall. *In flight:* all-white rump; grayish brown tail.

Size: *L* 7–8 in; *W* 17 in.

Habitat: shores of lakes, marshes, sewage lagoons and reservoirs; flooded and cultivated fields.

Nesting: does not nest in the Great Plains.
Feeding: gleans the ground and shorelines for insects, crustaceans and mollusks.
Voice: flight call is a characteristic, squeal-like *tzeet,* higher than for any other peep.
Similar Species: *Other peeps* (pp. 138–42): all have dark line through rump. *Baird's Sandpiper* (p. 142): breast streaking does not extend onto flanks. *Stilt Sandpiper* (p. 145) and *Curlew Sandpiper:* nonbreeding birds have legs that trail beyond tail in flight.

141

BAIRD'S SANDPIPER
Calidris bairdii

The Baird's Sandpiper is one of the most difficult sandpipers to identify correctly. One clue is that although it often migrates with other sandpipers, upon landing it leaves them and feeds alone. • Like their *Calidris* relatives, these modest-looking shorebirds have extraordinary migratory habits—they fly from South America to the Arctic and back each year. Baird's Sandpipers remain on their northern breeding grounds for only a short time. Soon after the chicks hatch and are able to fend for themselves, the adults flock together to begin their southward migration. After a few weeks of accumulating fat reserves, the young gather in a second wave of southbound migrants. • In the 19th century, Elliott Coues named this bird in recognition of Spencer Fullerton Baird, an early director of the Smithsonian Institute who organized several natural history expeditions across North America.

breeding

breeding

ID: dark-and-white-mottled, grayish brown upperparts; buffy breast with faint brown speckling; black bill and legs; folded wings extend beyond tail. *Breeding:* dark mottling becomes more prominent, making back distinctively "scaly." *In flight:* mostly grayish brown rump.
Size: *L* 7–7½ in; *W* 17 in.
Habitat: sandy beaches, mudflats and wetland edges.
Nesting: does not nest in the Great Plains.

Feeding: gleans aquatic invertebrates, especially larval flies; also eats beetles and grasshoppers; rarely probes.
Voice: soft, rolling *kriit kriit.*
Similar Species: *White-rumped Sandpiper* (p. 141): all-white rump; breast streaking extends onto flanks. *Pectoral Sandpiper* (p. 143): larger; dark breast ends sharply at edge of white belly. *Least Sandpiper* (p. 140): smaller; yellowish legs. *Western Sandpiper* (p. 139) and *Sanderling* (p. 361): nonbreeding bird is whiter with mostly unstreaked breast. *Semipalmated Sandpiper* (p. 138): smaller; shorter bill; back is less "scaly" in breeding plumage; paler, less streaked breast in nonbreeding plumage.

PECTORAL SANDPIPER

Calidris melanotos

This widespread traveler has been observed in every state and province in North America during its epic annual migrations. In spring and fall, the Pectoral Sandpiper is conspicuous along wetlands and in wet, grassy fields, often in large flocks of over 1000 birds, with numbers peaking from late August to late October. If threatened, these flocks will suddenly launch into the air and converge into a single, swirling mass. • Unlike most sandpipers, the Pectoral exhibits sexual dimorphism—the female is only two-thirds the size of the male. • Pectoral Sandpipers are sometimes referred to as "Grass Snipes" because of their preference for wet meadows and grassy marshes. The name "pectoral" refers to the location of the male's prominent air sacs. When displaying on the species' arctic breeding grounds, the male will inflate these air sacs, causing his feathers to rise. Meanwhile, he emits a hollow hooting call that has been likened to the sound of a foghorn.

ID: dark-mottled, brown upperparts; dark crown and back may have faintly rusty tones; brown "bib" formed by breast streaks that end abruptly at edge of white belly; white undertail coverts; black bill has slightly down-curved tip; long, yellow legs. *Immature:* less spotting on breast; broader white edges on back feathers form 2 thin, white "V"s.
Size: *L* 9 in; *W* 18 in (female is noticeably smaller).

Habitat: lakeshores, marshes, mudflats and flooded fields or pastures.
Nesting: does not nest in the Great Plains.
Feeding: probes and pecks for small insects; eats mainly flies but also takes beetles and some grasshoppers; may eat small mollusks, amphipods, berries, seeds, moss, algae and some plant material.
Voice: sharp, short, low *krrick krrick*.
Similar Species: *Least Sandpiper* (p. 140): smaller; more compact shape; weaker streaking on breast. *Other peeps* (pp. 138–42): no well-defined, dark "bib" combined with yellow legs.

143

DUNLIN

Calidris alpina

With their black legs and the black bellies of their fairly distinctive breeding attire, Dunlins look as though they have been wading belly-deep in puddles of ink. • Outside the breeding season, Dunlins form dynamic, synchronous flocks. Sometimes hundreds of these birds are seen flying wing tip to wing tip, and numbers in the tens of thousands have been documented. These tight flocks are generally more exclusive than other shorebird troupes and rarely include other species. Unlike many of their shorebird relatives, Dunlins overwinter in North America, mostly in coastal areas, and few ever cross the equator. • This bird was originally called "Dunling," meaning "little dark one," but with the passage of time the "g" was dropped. Because of its rufous back in breeding plumage, this shorebird was also known as "Red-backed Sandpiper."

breeding

ID: slightly down-curved, black bill; black legs. *Breeding:* black-mottled, rufous-and-gray wings, back and crown; black belly; gray-streaked, white sides and neck. *Nonbreeding:* grayish brown upperparts; whitish underparts; light brown streaking on breast and nape, increasingly dense on head.

Size: *L* 7½–9 in; *W* 17 in.

Habitat: mudflats and the shores of ponds, marshes and lakes.

Nesting: does not nest in the Great Plains.

Feeding: gleans and probes mudflats for aquatic crustaceans, worms, mollusks and insects.

Voice: flight call is a grating *cheezp* or *treezp*.

Similar Species: *Other sandpipers* (pp. 130–46): belly is not black. *Western Sandpiper* (p. 139) and *Semipalmated Sandpiper* (p. 138): nonbreeding birds are smaller, slightly paler overall with shorter, less downcurved bills. *Least Sandpiper* (p. 140): nonbreeding bird is smaller with dark-mottled upperparts, more white on face, yellowish legs. *Sanderling* (p. 361): nonbreeding bird has gray upperparts, more white on face, straight bill.

STILT SANDPIPER

Calidris himantopus

Nearly 90 percent of eastern North America's Stilt Sandpiper population stops off at Great Plains sites, yet, with the silhouette of a small Lesser Yellowlegs and the foraging behavior of a dowitcher, this shorebird is easily overlooked. • The Stilt Sandpiper prefers to dig for food in shallow water, often dunking its head completely underwater. Because its bill is shorter than a dowitcher's, it has to lean farther forward when digging—a characteristic that can aid in identification. Moving on tall, stiltlike legs, this sandpiper will also wade in water up to its breast in search of a meal. To snag freshwater shrimp, insect larvae or tiny minnows from just below the water's surface, the Stilt occasionally sweeps its bill from side to side like an American Avocet. • Unlike many of their *Calidris* relatives, Stilt Sandpipers never gather in large flocks. At most, you may see a gathering of 50 or so Stilts between mid-August and the end of September.

breeding

nonbreeding

ID: white "eyebrow"; long, mildly down-curved, black bill; long, greenish yellow legs. *Breeding:* dark brown upperparts with white streaks; horizontal, dark barring on white underparts; streaked, brown-and-white neck; chestnut red ear patch; duskier legs. *Nonbreeding:* dark, brownish gray upperparts; white belly; grayish white neck and breast. *In flight:* all-dark upperwing; white-centered, gray underwing; white rump; legs trail well behind tail.
Size: *L* 8–9 in; *W* 18 in.
Habitat: shores of lakes, reservoirs and marshes.

Nesting: does not nest in the Great Plains.
Feeding: probes deeply in shallow water; omnivorous, but eats mostly invertebrates; occasionally picks insects from the water's surface or the ground; also eats seeds, roots and leaves.
Voice: simple, sharp *querp* or *kirr* in flight; also gives a clearer *whu*.
Similar Species: *Greater Yellowlegs* (p. 128) and *Lesser Yellowlegs* (p. 129): larger; straight or mildly upturned bill; no red ear patch; yellower legs; feet trail closer to tail in flight. *Curlew Sandpiper:* nonbreeding bird has more white on face, more downcurved bill, black legs, white upperwing stripe, mostly white underwing. *Dunlin* (p. 144): nonbreeding has darker upperparts, shorter, black legs, white upperwing stripe, mostly white underwing.

BUFF-BREASTED SANDPIPER

Tryngites subruficollis

Shy in behavior and humble in appearance, the Buff-breasted Sandpiper never-theless exudes class if you care to take a closer look. The head is perfectly round, the body is perfectly shaped, the eye is large and limpid, and the underwings are mostly a shimmering white—what a beauty! • The Buff-breast prefers drier habitats than most other sandpipers. When feeding, this subtly colored bird stands motionless, blending beautifully into a backdrop of cultivated fields, mudflats or managed sod farms. Only when it catches sight of moving prey does it become visible, making a short, forward sprint to snatch a fresh meal. • Buff-breasts migrate through the center of the continent, and many birds seen here are juveniles heading south for the first time. These sandpipers regularly mingle with flocks of foraging Black-bellied Plovers and American Golden-Plovers.

breeding

ID: buff-edged, brown feathers give "scaly" look to back and upperwings; buffy underparts; small, brown dots on crown, nape, breast, sides and flanks; buffy, unpat-terned face and fore-neck; large, dark eyes; very thin, straight, black bill; yellow to orangy legs. *In flight:* pure white under-wing with gray trailing edge.
Size: *L* 7½–8 in; *W* 18 in.
Habitat: shores of lakes, reservoirs and marshes; also sod farms and cultivated and flooded fields.

Nesting: does not nest in the Great Plains.
Feeding: gleans the ground and shorelines for insects, spiders and small crustaceans; sometimes eats seeds.
Voice: usually silent; calls include *chup* or *tick* notes; *preet* flight call.
Similar Species: *Upland Sandpiper* (p. 133): larger; more whitish underparts; bolder streaking on breast; longer neck; smaller head; streaking on foreneck and "cheek"; larger, dark-tipped, yellow bill. *Pectoral Sandpiper* (p. 143): breast streak-ing forms brown "bib" that ends abruptly at edge of white belly; streaked face; dark-centered rump. *Ruff:* immature is rare and larger and heavier with dark eye line.

SHORT-BILLED DOWITCHER
Limnodromus griseus

Short-billed Dowitchers are seen on mudflats, marshes and beaches during spring migration, but the largest concentrations usually occur during the protracted fall migration, which begins as early as mid-July. • Dowitchers tend to be stockier than most shorebirds, and they generally avoid venturing into deep water. While foraging along shorelines, these shorebirds use their bills to "stitch" up and down into the mud with a rhythm like a sewing machine. This drilling motion liquefies the mud or sand, allowing the dowitchers to reach their hidden prey. This behavior is fascinating to watch and is also helpful for long-range field identification. • The best way to distinguish between Short-billed Dowitchers and the very similar Long-billed Dowitchers is by their flight calls or by listening to them feeding—Long-bills chatter softly while feeding, but Short-bills feed silently.

breeding

nonbreeding

ID: chunky body; white "eyebrow"; long, straight, dark bill; dull, yellowish green legs. *Breeding:* dark brown upperparts with reddish buff and white feather markings; white to reddish buff underparts with dark barring or spotting on sides, flanks, neck and upper breast. *Nonbreeding:* dirty gray upperparts; dirty white underparts with some gray barring or spotting. *In flight:* white wedge on rump and lower back.
Size: *L* 11–12 in; *W* 19 in.
Habitat: shores of lakes, reservoirs and marshes.
Nesting: does not nest in the Great Plains.

Feeding: wades in shallow water or mud, probing deeply into the substrate with a rapid up–down bill motion; eats aquatic invertebrates, including insects, mollusks, crustaceans and worms; sometimes feeds on seeds, aquatic plants and grasses.
Voice: generally silent; mellow, repeated *tututu, toodulu* or *toodu* flight call.
Similar Species: *Long-billed Dowitcher* (p. 148): slightly longer bill; in breeding plumage, darker upperparts, black-and-white barring on reddish flanks and little or no white on belly; flight call is a high-pitched *keek*. *Red Knot:* rare; much shorter bill; shorter, darker legs; no barring on underparts in breeding plumage; finely dark-barred, white rump; longer wings. *Wilson's Snipe* (p. 149): white stripes along back and on head; shorter, pale grayish green legs.

LONG-BILLED DOWITCHER
Limnodromus scolopaceus

Each spring and fall, mudflats and marshes host enthusiastic Long-billed Dowitchers. These chunky, sword-billed shorebirds diligently forage up and down through shallow water and mud in a quest for invertebrate sustenance. A diet of insects, freshwater shrimp, mussels, clams and snails provides migrating Long-bills with plenty of fuel for flight and essential calcium for bone and egg development. • Dowitchers have shorter wings than most shorebirds that migrate long distances. These shorter wings make it more practical for dowitchers to take flight from shallow water, where a series of hops helps them to become airborne. • Mixed flocks of shorebirds demonstrate a variety of foraging styles, with some species probing deeply and others picking at the water's surface or gleaning the shorelines. It is thought that these different foraging styles and specialized diets help large numbers of shorebirds of various species to coexist.

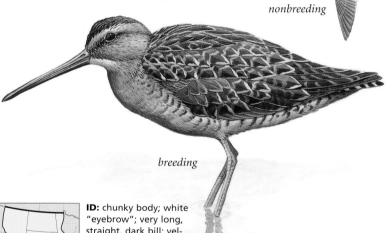

nonbreeding

breeding

ID: chunky body; white "eyebrow"; very long, straight, dark bill; yellowish green legs. *Breeding:* dark brown upperparts with reddish buff and white feather markings; reddish buff underparts with black-and-white barring on sides, flanks, neck and upper breast; little or no white on belly. *Nonbreeding:* dirty gray overall; dirty white underparts. *In flight:* white wedge on rump and lower back.
Size: *L* 11–12½ in; *W* 19 in.
Habitat: lakeshores, shallow marshes and mudflats.
Nesting: does not nest in the Great Plains.
Feeding: probes in shallow water and mudflats with a repeated up-down bill motion; frequently plunges its head under-

water; eats shrimps, snails, worms, larval flies and other soft-bodied invertebrates.
Voice: flight call is a loud, high-pitched *keek*, occasionally given in series.
Similar Species: *Short-billed Dowitcher* (p. 147): slightly shorter bill; in breeding plumage, upperparts are usually brighter, underparts are often partly white instead of entirely reddish buff and sides are more spotted than barred; lower-pitched *toodu* or *tututu* call. *Red Knot:* rare; much shorter bill; shorter, darker legs; no barring on underparts in breeding plumage; finely dark-barred, white rump; longer wings. *Wilson's Snipe* (p. 149): white stripes along back and on head; shorter, pale grayish green legs.

WILSON'S SNIPE

Gallinago delicata

Visit almost any open wetland in the northern Great Plains in spring or early summer, day or night, and you will hear the eerie, hollow, winnowing sound of courting male Wilson's Snipes. Their specialized outer tail feathers vibrate rapidly in the air as they perform daring headfirst dives high above their marshland habitat. • Outside the courtship season, this well-camouflaged bird is shy and secretive and remains concealed in vegetation. When flushed from cover by an intruder's close approach, it will perform a series of aerial zigzags as an evasive maneuver designed to confuse predators. Hunters sufficiently skilled to shoot a snipe came to be known as "snipers," a term later adopted by the military. • The placement of the snipe's eyes far back on its head allows the bird to see both forward and backward. • Until recently, this bird was considered to be the same species as Eurasia's "Common Snipe" (*G. gallinago*).

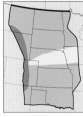

ID: dark brown upperparts with heavy, whitish stripes; white underparts with dark barring on sides, flanks and breast; bold, white stripes on brown head; long, sturdy, dusky yellow bill with dark tip; relatively short, pale grayish green legs. *In flight:* quick zigzags on takeoff.

Size: *L* 10½–11½ in; *W* 18 in.

Habitat: cattail and bulrush marshes, sedge meadows, poorly drained floodplains, bogs and fens; willow and red osier dogwood tangles.

Nesting: usually in dry grass, often under vegetation; nest is made of grass, moss and leaves; female incubates 4 dark-marked, olive buff to brown eggs for 18–20 days; pair raises the young, often splitting the brood.

Feeding: probes soft ground for larvae, earthworms and other soft-bodied invertebrates; also eats mollusks, crustaceans, spiders, small amphibians and some seeds.

Voice: often sings *wheat wheat wheat* from an elevated perch; nasal *scaip* alarm call. *Male:* eerie, accelerating *woo-woo-woo-woo-woo-woo* courtship song is produced in flight.

Similar Species: *Short-billed Dowitcher* (p. 147) and *Long-billed Dowitcher* (p. 148): breeding birds are slimmer with no bold, white stripes, longer legs and usually in flocks. *American Woodcock* (p. 150): plumper; plain, brown upperparts; plain, buff underparts. *Marbled Godwit* (p. 137): breeding is much larger and slimmer, has no bold white stripes, much longer, dark legs.

AMERICAN WOODCOCK

Scolopax minor

The American Woodcock's behavior usually mirrors its cryptic and incon-spicuous attire. This occupant of moist woodlands and damp thickets nor-mally goes about its business in a quiet and reclusive manner, but during courtship the male reveals his true character. Just before dawn or just after sunset, he struts provocatively in an open woodland clearing or a brushy, abandoned field while calling out a series of loud *peeent* notes. He then launches into the air, twitter-ing upward in a circular flight display until, with wings partly folded, he plummets to the ground in the zigzag pattern of a falling leaf, chirping at every turn. At the end of this stunning "sky dance," he lands precisely where he started. • The secretive American Woodcock has suffered greatly from the clearing of forests and the drain-ing of woodland swamps that form its breeding habitat, resulting in a decline in its populations.

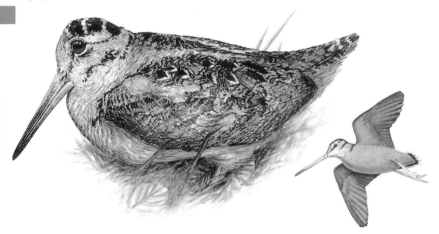

ID: chunky body; brown upperparts with dark mottling; unmarked, warm buffy underparts; short neck; large head; light-colored bars on black crown and nape; large, dark eyes; very long, sturdy, yellowish orange bill with dark tip; very short, warm buffy legs. *In flight:* rounded wings.

Size: *L* 11 in; *W* 18 in.

Habitat: moist woodlands and brushy thickets adjacent to grassy clearings or abandoned fields.

Nesting: on the ground in the woods or an overgrown field; female digs a scrape and lines it with dead leaves and other debris; female incubates 4 pinkish buff eggs, blotched with brown and gray, for 20–22 days; female tends the young.

Feeding: probes in soft, moist or wet soil for earthworms and insect larvae; also takes spiders, snails, millipedes and some plant material, including seeds, sedges and grasses.

Voice: twittering sound when flushed from cover. *Male:* nasal *peent* and high-pitched, twittering, whistling sounds during courtship.

Similar Species: *Wilson's Snipe* (p. 149): bold, white stripes on head, back, neck and breast; dark-barred sides. *Long-billed Dowitcher* (p. 148) and *Short-billed Dowitcher* (p. 147): breeding bird has reddish buff and white feather markings on upper-parts, no light bars on crown and nape, all-dark bill, longer legs, is usually in flocks.

WILSON'S PHALAROPE

Phalaropus tricolor

Phalaropes are among the most colorful and unusual shorebirds. In their uncommon mating strategy (polyandry), each female mates with several males and often produces a clutch of eggs with each male. She then usually abandons her mate, leaving him to incubate the eggs and tend the precocial young. This reversal of typical gender roles, which extends to the female being more brightly colored than her male counterpart, fooled even naturalist John James Audubon, who mislabeled the male and female birds in his phalarope illustrations. • Of the three North American phalarope species, the Wilson's Phalarope is the only one that breeds in our area, and it is the most numerous one during migration. • Most phalaropes have lobed (individually webbed) toes that help with swimming in the shallows of wetlands, but the more terrestrial Wilson's Phalarope lacks this characteristic.

nonbreeding

breeding

ID: white underparts, "cheeks" and "eyebrow"; dark, needle-like bill. *Breeding female:* chestnut brown on neck and upper breast and along edges of grayish brown back; thick, black line from bill down side of neck onto back; light gray "cap"; black legs. *Breeding male:* much duller overall; dark "cap." *Nonbreeding:* light gray upperparts; gray eye line; yellowish or greenish legs. *In flight:* unpatterned upperwing.
Size: *L* 9–9½ in; *W* 17 in.
Habitat: *Breeding:* cattail marshes and grass or sedge margins of sewage lagoons. *In migration:* lakeshores, marshes and sewage lagoons.
Nesting: often near water; well concealed in a depression lined with grass and other

vegetation; male incubates 4 brown-blotched, buffy eggs for 18–27 days; male rears the young.
Feeding: whirls in tight circles in water to stir up aquatic insects, worms and small crustaceans and picks them from the water's surface or just below; makes short jabs for land invertebrates.
Voice: deep, grunting *work work* or *wu wu wu*, usually given on the breeding grounds.
Similar Species: *Red-necked Phalarope* (p. 152): gray sides and rufous neck without black stripe in breeding plumage; black eye line and white forehead in nonbreeding plumage. *Red Phalarope:* nonbreeding bird is rare and has black eye line and white forehead. *Lesser Yellowlegs* (p. 129): larger; light- and dark-flecked, brownish upperparts; gray- or brown-streaked neck; bright yellow legs.

151

RED-NECKED PHALAROPE

Phalaropus lobatus

A local sewage lagoon may not be your idea of a venue for an aesthetically pleasing birdwatching experience, but it could be one of the best places to meet many species of birds, including the Red-necked Phalarope. • Most Red-necked Phalaropes migrate to and from their arctic wintering grounds via the Atlantic Coast, but a few pass through the Great Plains. • When foraging on the water with other shorebirds, phalaropes can usually be singled out by their unusual behavior—they spin and whirl about in tight circles, stirring up tiny crustaceans, mollusks and other aquatic invertebrates. As prey funnel toward the water's surface, these birds daintily pluck at them with their needlelike bills. • "Phalarope" is the Greek word for "coot's foot." Like coots and grebes, Red-necked Phalaropes have individually webbed, or "lobed," toes, a feature that makes them proficient swimmers.

nonbreeding

ID: white belly; thin, black bill; long, dark gray legs. *Breeding female:* 2 rusty buff stripes at edge of back; chestnut brown stripe on neck and throat; black head; white "chin"; partial white eye ring. *Breeding male:* less intense colors than female; white "eyebrow." *Nonbreeding:* brown-mottled, gray upperparts with pale streaks; white underparts; dark "cap"; broad, dark band from eye to ear. *In flight:* long, white stripe on upperwing.
Size: *L* 7 in; *W* 15 in.

Habitat: open water bodies, including ponds, lakes, marshes and sewage lagoons.
Nesting: does not nest in the Great Plains.
Feeding: whirls in tight circles in shallow or deep water to stir up prey, then picks insects, mollusks and small crustaceans from the water's surface; makes short jabs for land invertebrates.
Voice: often noisy in migration; soft *krit krit krit.*
Similar Species: *Wilson's Phalarope* (p. 151): gray "cap" and black line from bill down side of neck and onto back in breeding plumage (most visible on female); light gray eye line and yellow legs in nonbreeding plumage. *Red Phalarope:* nonbreeding bird is rare and has lighter, plainer gray back.

FRANKLIN'S GULL

Larus pipixcan

The Franklin's Gull is not a typical "seagull." A large part of its life is spent inland, where it often follows tractors across agricultural fields, snatching up insects from the tractor's path in much the same way its maritime cousins follow fishing boats. On its traditional nesting territory on the prairies, it is affectionately known as "Prairie Dove" because of its dovelike profile. • Large Franklin's Gull colonies are found in the northern Great Plains, and there are smaller, less stable colonies as far south as Nebraska, but in most of the region the species is mainly a fall migrant. • Franklin's Gull overwinters mainly along the Pacific coast of Peru and Chile. It is one of just two gull species that migrate long distances between breeding and wintering grounds.

nonbreeding

breeding

ID: dark gray mantle; white underparts; broken, white eye ring. *Breeding:* black head; orangy red bill and legs; breast can have pinkish tinge. *Nonbreeding:* front of face and forehead turn white; dark bill. *In flight:* black crescent on white wing tip; mostly white underwing.
Size: *L* 13–15 in; *W* 3 ft.
Habitat: agricultural fields, marshlands, river and lake shorelines, river mouths and landfills.
Nesting: colonial, in a marsh; pair builds a large, floating platform using cattails and bulrushes; pair incubates 2–4 blotched and spotted, greenish to buff-colored eggs for 23–26 days.
Feeding: opportunistic; gleans agricultural fields and meadows for grasshoppers and other insects; often catches dragonflies, mayflies and other flying invertebrates in midair; also eats small fish and some crustaceans.
Voice: mewing, shrill *weeeh-ah weeeh-ah* while feeding and in migration.
Similar Species: *Bonaparte's Gull* (p. 154): breeding bird has thinner eye ring, black bill, white forewing wedge. *Little Gull:* rare; smaller; paler mantle; mostly dark underwing. *Black-headed Gull:* breeding bird is rare, has paler mantle, more white on back of head, white wedge on forewing. *Sabine's Gull:* uncommon; dark, yellow-tipped bill; no eye ring in breeding plumage; more white on head in non-breeding plumage; large, black, white and gray upperwing triangles.

153

BONAPARTE'S GULL

Larus philadelphia

Many people have great disdain for gulls, but they might change their minds when they meet the Bonaparte's Gull. This graceful, reserved gull is nothing like its contentious, aggressive relatives. Delicate in plumage and behavior, this small gull avoids landfills, preferring to dine on insects caught in midair or plucked from the water's surface. Only when a school of fish or an intruder is spied does this bird raise its soft, scratchy voice in excitement. • Seen in small numbers in much of the Great Plains during spring and fall migrations, Bonaparte's Gulls will take advantage of local food supplies, with large flocks gathering to feast on any abundant food items to fuel the rest of their long journey north or south. In years with mild winter weather, many of these gulls will remain until early December, but most Bonaparte's Gulls move out of the Great Plains region well before year's end. Some remain in Oklahoma with other gulls and any lingering terns.

nonbreeding

breeding

ID: gray mantle; white underparts; black bill. *Breeding:* black head; thin, white eye ring; orange legs. *Nonbreeding:* white head; small, dark ear patch and marking above eye; paler legs. *In flight:* white forewing wedge; black-tipped outer flight feathers.

Size: *L* 11½–14 in; *W* 33 in.

Habitat: large lakes, rivers and marshes.

Nesting: does not nest in the Great Plains.

Feeding: dabbles and tips up for aquatic invertebrates, small fish and tadpoles; gleans the ground for terrestrial invertebrates; also captures insects in the air.

Voice: scratchy, soft *ear ear* while feeding.

Similar Species: *Franklin's Gull* (p. 153): larger; black crescent on white wing tip; orange bill in breeding plumage; nonbreeding bird has more black on head. *Little Gull:* rare; smaller; daintier bill; white wing tips; breeding bird has more black at back of head and no white eye ring; nonbreeding bird has small, dark "cap"; mostly dark underwings. *Sabine's Gull:* uncommon; yellow-tipped bill; no eye ring in breeding plumage; more gray on head in nonbreeding plumage; large, black, white and gray upperwing triangles.

RING-BILLED GULL

Larus delawarensis

The Ring-billed Gull's numbers have greatly increased in recent years, and its tolerance for humans has made it a part of our everyday lives. Some people consider this gull to have become a pest, however. Indeed, many parks, beaches, golf courses and even fast-food outlet parking lots are inundated with marauding gulls looking for handouts. Like many of its larger relatives, the Ring-billed Gull has taken to scavenging our litter, and it is often responsible for fouling the windshields of our vehicles. Few species, however, have fared as well as the Ring-billed Gull in the face of human development, which, in itself, is something to appreciate. • The Ring-billed Gull nests on wetlands in the northern Great Plains, and it is found as a migrant or winter resident throughout the rest of our region.

nonbreeding

breeding

ID: pale gray mantle; white underparts; red-ringed, yellow eyes; yellow bill with black ring near tip; yellow legs. *Breeding:* all-white head. *Nonbreeding:* some light gray streaking on head. *Immature:* brown mottling on upperparts, head, breast and wings; blackish band at tail tip. *In flight:* black wing tip with a white spot; all-white tail.
Size: *L* 18–20 in; *W* 4 ft.
Habitat: *Breeding:* sparsely vegetated islands, open beaches, breakwaters and dredge-spoil areas. *In migration* and *winter:* lakes, rivers, landfills, golf courses, fields and parks.

Nesting: colonial; in a shallow scrape on the ground lined with plants, debris, grass and sticks; pair incubates 2–4 brown-blotched, gray to olive eggs for 23–28 days.
Feeding: gleans the ground for human food waste, spiders, insects, rodents, earthworms, grubs and some waste grain; scavenges for carrion; surface-tips for aquatic invertebrates and fish.
Voice: high-pitched *kakakaka-akakaka;* also a low, laughing *yook-yook-yook.*
Similar Species: *California Gull* (p. 156): larger; dark eyes; black and red spots near tip of bill but no ring. *Herring Gull* (p. 157); larger; pinkish legs; red spot near tip of bill and no black ring. *Lesser Black-backed Gull:* larger; uncommon; much darker mantle; red spot near bill tip and no black ring.

CALIFORNIA GULL

Larus californicus

For a novice gull watcher, spotting a California Gull might be the first assurance that it is possible to see something other than Ring-bills in your average gang of white-headed gulls. It takes a keen eye to recognize this bird, but once you learn how, you'll see it all the time. Distinguishing the California Gull from the larger Herring Gull and the slightly smaller Ring-bill when all three are present is a good test of a birder's skill. • The California Gull breeds in the northern and western Great Plains and migrates to the Pacific Coast for winter. It is a casual visitor to the southern Great Plains. • In 1848 and 1855, Utah's harvests were threatened by swarms of grasshoppers until large numbers of California Gulls appeared and ate the pests. A monument in Salt Lake City honors this prairie gull, which is now the state bird of Utah. • California Gulls tend to nest communally on low-lying islands, but generally no closer than the distance two gulls can bridge with aggressive bill jabs from atop their eggs.

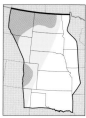

ID: gray mantle; white underparts; red-ringed, dark eyes; yellow bill with red spot and black spot near tip; yellowish green legs. *Breeding:* white head. *Nonbreeding:* dusky streaking on back of head and nape.
Immature: mottled brown overall; pale bill with black tip; light pinkish legs. *In flight:* white spots on edge of large black area at wing tip.
Size: *L* 18–20 in; *W* 4–4½ ft.

Habitat: large lakes, wetlands, farmlands, landfills and parks.
Nesting: colonial; often on open beaches or shorelines; usually on the ground in a shallow scrape lined with plants, grass, feathers and small sticks; pair incubates 2–3 buff to olive or brown eggs with darker blotches for 23–27 days.
Feeding: gleans the ground for terrestrial invertebrates, especially grasshoppers, earthworms and cutworms; scavenges; surface-tips for aquatic invertebrates.
Voice: most often heard at breeding colonies; high-pitched, nasal *kiarr-kiarr*.
Similar Species: *Ring-billed Gull* (p. 155): smaller; yellow eyes; yellow bill with black ring near tip. *Herring Gull* (p. 157): larger; yellow eyes; pink legs.

HERRING GULL

Larus argentatus

One of the world's most widespread and adaptable birds, the large Herring Gull lives up to its genus name *Larus*, which is from the Greek word for "ravenous seabird." It is as adept as the smaller Ring-billed Gull at scrounging handouts on beaches, but it prefers wilderness areas to urban settings. • The Herring Gull followed its human benefactors westward from the East Coast to colonize inland lakes. It now breeds primarily north and east of the Great Plains, but its range extends into Minnesota, and this gull is widely distributed in our region in migration and winter. • The small red spot on the lower mandible of many gulls serves as a target for nestlings. A peck here cues the parent to regurgitate its meal. • By rotating their bodies to face the sun on hot, calm days, exposing less of the body and only their highly reflective white parts, gulls reduce radiative heat gain. Standing in water also prevents overheating.

nonbreeding

breeding

ID: light gray mantle; white underparts; orange-ringed, yellow eyes; yellow bill with red spot near tip; pink legs. *Breeding:* white head. *Nonbreeding:* brown streaking on nape, sides of neck and head. *Immature:* mottled brown overall. *In flight:* white spots on edge of black wing tip.
Size: *L* 23–26 in; *W* 4 ft.
Habitat: large lakes, wetlands, rivers, landfills and urban areas.
Nesting: singly or colonially with other gulls and cormorants; on an open beach or island; on the ground in a shallow scrape lined with plants and sticks; pair incubates

3 darkly blotched, olive to buff eggs for 31–32 days; young are fed by regurgitation.
Feeding: surface-tips for aquatic invertebrates and fish; gleans the ground for insects and worms; scavenges dead fish and human food waste; eats other birds' eggs and young.
Voice: loud, buglelike *kleew-kleew;* also gives an alarmed *kak-kak-kak*.
Similar Species: *California Gull* (p. 156): smaller; dark eyes; black spot and red spot near bill tip; yellowish green legs. *Ring-billed Gull* (p. 155): smaller; black bill ring; yellow legs. *Thayer's, Glaucous* and *Iceland gulls:* uncommon; paler mantles; little or no black on wings. *Lesser Black-backed Gull:* uncommon; much darker mantle.

157

COMMON TERN

Sterna hirundo

During fall and spring, Common Terns can be seen patrolling the shorelines of wetlands, lakes and rivers. In summer, they settle in large nesting colonies, usually on islands. Both males and females perform aerial courtship dances, and for most pairs the nesting season commences when the female accepts her suitor's gracious fish offerings. • Tern colonies are noisy and chaotic, and they are often associated with even noisier gull colonies. The most successful colonies seem to be the larger ones, which can number well into the thousands. Should an intruder approach a tern nest, the parent will dive repeatedly, often defecating on the offender. It is wise, therefore, to keep a respectful distance from nesting terns—and from all nesting birds, for that matter. • Terns are effortless fliers, as well as being some of the most impressive long-distance migrants. One Common Tern banded in Great Britain was recovered in Australia.

breeding

breeding

ID: light gray mantle; white rump. *Breeding:* pale gray underparts; black nape and "cap"; thin, red bill with black tip; red legs; white tail with gray outer edges. *Nonbreeding:* white underparts; black nape; white forehead; black bill; dark legs. *In flight:* long, pointed wings, gray above and white below, with dark trailing edge near tip; shallowly forked tail.

Size: *L* 13–16 in; *W* 30 in.

Habitat: *Breeding:* natural and human-made islands, breakwaters and beaches. *In migration:* large lakes, open wetlands and slow-moving rivers.

Nesting: primarily colonial; typically on an island with nonvegetated areas; in a small scrape lined sparsely with pebbles, vegetation or shells; pair incubates 1–3 variably marked eggs for up to 27 days.

Feeding: hovers over water and plunges headfirst after small fish and aquatic invertebrates.

Voice: heard mostly at colonies but also while foraging; high-pitched, drawn-out *keee-are.*

Similar Species: *Forster's Tern* (p. 159): white underparts year-round; dark-tipped, orange bill in breeding plumage; white nape and black eye patch in nonbreeding plumage; upper primaries have silvery look; deeper fork in tail. *Caspian Tern* (p. 361): much larger; much heavier bill; dark legs year-round; larger dark area at wing tip.

FORSTER'S TERN

Sterna forsteri

The Forster's Tern so closely resembles the Common Tern that the two often seem indistinguishable to many observers. It is usually not until these terns acquire their distinctive fall plumages that most birders begin to note the Forster's presence. • Most terns are known for their extraordinary ability to catch fish in dramatic headlong dives, but the Forster's Tern excels at gracefully snatching flying insects in midair. • The Forster's tern has an exclusively North American breeding distribution, but it bears the name of a man who never visited the continent. German naturalist Johann Reinhold Forster, who examined specimens sent from Hudson Bay, was first to recognize the bird as a distinct species. Agreeing, Thomas Nuttall named this species "Forster's Tern" in his *A Manual of the Ornithology of the United States and of Canada* in 1834.

breeding

ID: light gray mantle; white underparts; white rump. *Breeding:* black nape and "cap"; thin, orange bill with black tip; orange legs. *Nonbreeding:* white nape and head; black eye patch; duskier legs. *In flight:* long, pointed wings; upperwing is silvery white near tip; deeply forked, gray tail with white outer edges.

Size: *L* 14–16 in; *W* 31 in.

Habitat: *Breeding:* cattail marshes. *In migration:* lakes and marshes.

Nesting: colonial; in a cattail marsh, atop floating vegetation; occasionally on a muskrat lodge or an old grebe nest; pair incubates 3 brown-marked, buff to olive eggs for 23–25 days.

Feeding: hovers above water and plunges headfirst after small fish and aquatic invertebrates; catches flying insects and snatches prey from the water's surface.

Voice: short, nasal *keer keer* flight call; also gives a grating *tzaap.*

Similar Species: *Common Tern* (p. 158): gray underparts and darker red bill and legs in breeding plumage; black nape and dark legs in nonbreeding plumage; dark trailing edge near wing tip; more shallowly forked, mostly white tail. *Caspian Tern* (p. 361): much larger; much heavier, redder bill; black legs year-round.

LEAST TERN

Sterna antillarum

The plight of the endangered Least Tern, which today persists at only a few places on the Great Plains, dramatizes the impact that human activities can have on birds of estuarine and river beaches. Huge numbers were slaughtered by plume hunters in the late 1800s until high prices caused the decline of the millinery trade. Development and disturbance since then have caused breeding habitat for this species to diminish. However, in places where this tern and its habitat are protected, its numbers have remained remarkably stable. • As is true for many colonial waterbirds, breeding success varies from year to year in response to food supply, weather, predation and disturbance. Least Terns show little site loyalty because their beach, sandbar and bank colony sites are frequently subject to flooding. These birds occasionally appear elsewhere on the Great Plains beyond their usual breeding sites.

breeding

ID: gray mantle; white underparts; black nape, small "cap" and eye line; white forehead. *Breeding:* dark outermost wing feathers; black "cap" and eye line lengthen; thin, yellow bill with small, black tip; orangy yellow legs. *Nonbreeding:* black bill; duskier legs. *Immature:* brownish gray "cap"; brownish outer upperwing. *In flight:* dashing, rapid wingbeats; mostly pale gray wings.
Size: *L* 9 in; *W* 20 in.
Habitat: largely restricted to major river systems.
Nesting: colonial; on undisturbed flat ground near water; shallow scrape is often

lined with pebbles, grass or debris; pair incubates 1–3 dark-blotched, buffy or greenish white eggs for 20–22 days and raises the young; chicks leave the nest shortly after hatching.
Feeding: typically hovers above water and plunges to or below the surface; eats mostly fish, crustaceans and insects; sometimes eats mollusks and other invertebrates; will take insects on the wing or snatch prey from the ground or water's surface.
Voice: loud, high-pitched *chirreek!* or *kip kip kip.*
Similar Species: *Black Tern* (p. 161): nonbreeding is larger with darker mantle, black "sideburns," darker legs. *Common Tern* (p. 158) and *Forster's Tern* (p. 159): much heavier; breeding birds have black foreheads and orange or red bills.

BLACK TERN
Chlidonias niger

Black Terns have dominion over the winds, and these acrobats slice through the sky with grace, even in a stiff wind. Wheeling about in foraging flights, they pick small minnows from the water's surface or catch flying insects in midair. • Black Terns are finicky nesters and refuse to return to nesting areas that show even slight changes in water level or in the density of emergent vegetation. This selectiveness, coupled with the degradation of marshes across North America, has contributed to a significant decline in populations of this bird over recent decades. Commitment to restoring and protecting valuable wetland habitats will eventually help the Black Tern to reclaim its once prominent place in our wetlands. • Terns of the genus *Chlidonias* are named for their swallowlike, darting flight as they pursues insects. In order to spell this genus name correctly, one must misspell *chelidonias,* the Greek word for "swallow." • When they leave our region in August and September, these terns head for the warmer climates of Central and South America.

breeding

breeding

ID: dark gray back, wings and tail. *Breeding:* black head and underparts; white undertail coverts; black bill; reddish black legs. *Nonbreeding:* white underparts and forehead; white head with partially black crown and "sideburns"; molting fall birds may be mottled with brown. *In flight:* long, pointed wings, gray above and below; slightly forked tail.
Size: *L* 9–10 in; *W* 24 in.

Habitat: shallow, freshwater cattail marshes, wetlands, lake edges and sewage ponds with emergent vegetation.
Nesting: loosely colonial; flimsy nest of dead plant material is built on floating vegetation, a muddy mound or a muskrat house; pair incubates 3 darkly blotched, olive to pale buff eggs for 21–22 days.
Feeding: snatches insects from the air, tall grass or the water's surface; also eats small fish.
Voice: greeting call is a shrill, metallic *kik-kik-kik-kik-kik;* typical alarm call is *kreea.*
Similar Species: *Other terns* (pp. 158–60): lighter in color with dark "cap" or eye patch only; bills and legs are mostly yellow, orange or red in breeding plumage.

ROCK PIGEON
Columba livia

Introduced to North America in the early 17th century, Rock Pigeons, which were until recently known as "Rock Doves," have settled wherever cities, towns and farms are found. Most birds seem content to nest on buildings or farmhouses, but "wilder" individuals can occasionally be seen nesting on tall cliffs, usually along lakeshores. • It is believed that Rock Pigeons were domesticated from Eurasian birds as a source of meat around 4500 BC. They have been used as message couriers (both Caesar and Napoleon used them), scientific subjects and even pets. Much of our understanding of bird migration, endocrinology and sensory perception derives from experiments involving Rock Pigeons. • Pigeons and doves feed their young with "pigeon milk," a nutritious liquid produced by glands in the bird's crop, which the chicks consume by inserting their bills down a parent's throat. • No other "wild" bird varies as much in coloration—a result of semi-domestication and extensive inbreeding over time.

ID: highly variable color (commonly bluish gray with an iridescent, green-and-purple neck and two dark wing bars, but sometimes reddish brown, black, piebald or tan overall); red to yellow eyes; white cere; orange or dark bill; usually has white rump and orange feet; dark-tipped tail. *In flight:* fan-shaped tail; wings clap on takeoff; holds wings in a deep "V" while gliding.
Size: *L* 12–13 in; *W* 28 in.
Habitat: urban areas, railroad yards and agricultural areas; high cliffs provide a more natural habitat for some.

Nesting: on a ledge in a barn or on a cliff, bridge, building or tower; flimsy nest is built of sticks, grass and assorted vegetation; pair incubates 1–2 white eggs for 16–19 days; pair feeds the young "pigeon milk"; may raise broods year-round.
Feeding: gleans the ground for waste grain, seeds and fruits; occasionally eats insects.
Voice: soft, cooing *coorrr-coorrr-coorrr.*
Similar Species: *Mourning Dove* (p. 163): smaller; slimmer; pale brown plumage; short wings; long, pointed tail. *Merlin* (p. 108): not as heavy bodied; wings quiet on takeoff and held flatter in flight; longer, narrower tail. *Band-tailed Pigeon:* accidental here; white nape patch; yellow bill and feet; gray rump; dark band at base of gray tail.

MOURNING DOVE

Zenaida macroura

A soft cooing heard filtering through our broken woodlands, farmlands and suburban parks and gardens is often mistaken for the muted sounds of a hooting owl. However, the source is usually discovered to be one or two Mourning Doves perched upon a fence, tree branch or utility wire. • One of North America's most abundant and widespread native birds and one of our most popular game birds, the Mourning Dove has increased both its numbers and its distribution as a result of human-induced changes to the landscape. Encountered in both rural and urban habitats, it avoids heavily forested areas. • Despite its fragile look, the Mourning Dove is a swift, direct flier with wings that often whistle as it cuts through the air at high speed. Upon bursting into flight, its wings clap above and below its body. • This bird's common name reflects its sad, cooing song. The scientific name *Zenaida* honors Zénaïde, Princess of Naples in the early 1800s and the wife of Charles-Lucien Bonaparte, who was a naturalist and the nephew of the noted French emperor.

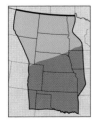

Habitat: open and riparian woodlands, woodlots, forest edges, agricultural and suburban areas and open parks.

Nesting: in the fork of a shrub or tree, occasionally on the ground; male supplies twigs for female to build a fragile, shallow platform nest; pair incubates 2 white eggs for 14 days; young are fed "pigeon milk."

Feeding: gleans the ground and vegetation for seeds; visits feeders.

Voice: mournful, soft, slow *oh-woe-woe-woe.*

Similar Species: *Inca Dove:* smaller; rufous on wings. *White-winged Dove:* larger; short, square tail; white patch on wings.

ID: sleek body; buffy, grayish brown upperparts with several black spots on wings; pale rosy brown underparts; small head; dark, shiny patch below ear; dark eyes; dark bill; dull red legs. *In flight:* long, tapering, white-trimmed, diamond-shaped tail.

Size: *L* 11–13 in; *W* 18 in.

163

BLACK-BILLED CUCKOO
Coccyzus erythropthalmus

Shrubby field edges, hedgerows, tangled riparian thickets and abandoned, over-grown fields provide the elusive Black-billed Cuckoo with its preferred nesting haunts. Although not particularly rare, it remains an enigma to many would-be observers as it quietly hops, flits and skulks through low, dense, deciduous vegetation in its ultra-secret search for sustenance. • The species arrives here in spring, and, when vegetation is in full bloom, the males issue loud, long, irregular calls to advertise to the females that it is time to nest. After a brief courtship, newly joined Black-billed Cuckoo pairs construct a makeshift nest, incubate their eggs and raise their young, then promptly return to their covert lives. • The Black-billed Cuckoo is one of the few birds to thrive on hairy caterpillars, particularly tent caterpillars, and evidence suggests that its populations increase when a caterpillar infestation occurs. • Although reluctant to fly more than a short distance during nesting, this cuckoo will migrate as far as northwestern South America to avoid the North American winter.

ID: olive brown upperparts; whitish underparts and lower face; red-ringed, dark eyes; downcurved, dark bill; long tail with paired white spots on underside. *Immature:* possible buff tinge to throat yellow eye ring. *In flight:* whitish underwing with brown trailing edge and tip.
Size: *L* 11–13 in; *W* 18 in.
Habitat: dense second-growth woodlands, shrubby areas and thickets; often in tangled riparian areas and abandoned farmlands with low deciduous vegetation and adjacent open areas.

Nesting: in a shrub or small deciduous tree; flimsy twig nest is lined with grass and other vegetation; pair incubates 2–5 bluish green, possibly mottled eggs for 10–14 days; occasionally lays eggs in other birds' nests.
Feeding: gleans hairy caterpillars from leaves, branches and trunks; also eats other insects and berries.
Voice: fast, repeated *cu-cu-cu* or *cu-cu-cu-cu-cu;* also gives a *ca, cow* and *coo* note series.
Similar Species: *Yellow-billed Cuckoo* (p. 165): dull yellow eye ring; thicker, largely yellow bill; larger undertail spots; largely rufous flight feathers. *Mourning Dove* (p. 163): black spots on upperwing; pale rosy brown underparts; smaller, straight bill; broader, diamond-shaped tail.

YELLOW-BILLED CUCKOO

Coccyzus americanus

Most of the time, the Yellow-billed Cuckoo skilfully negotiates its tangled home within impenetrable, deciduous undergrowth in silence, relying on obscurity for survival. Then, for a short period during the breeding season, the male cuckoo tempts fate by issuing a barrage of loud, rhythmic courtship calls. Some people have suggested that this cuckoo has a propensity for calling on dark, cloudy days in late spring and early summer, and it is even called "Rain Crow" in some parts of its North American range. • The Yellow-billed Cuckoo is now a fairly common nesting species throughout the Great Plains north to the southern borders of Montana and North Dakota. Although some Yellow-billed Cuckoos may lay eggs in the unattended nests of neighboring Black-billed Cuckoos, neither of these cuckoos is considered to be a "brood parasite." • Yellow-billed Cuckoos migrate as far south as Argentina for winter.

ID: olive brown upperparts; white underparts and lower face; yellow eye ring; downcurved, largely yellow bill with black on top; long tail with large white spots separated by black on underside. *In flight:* largely rufous flight feathers; mostly white underwing.

Size: *L* 11–13 in; *W* 18 in.

Habitat: semi-open deciduous habitats; dense tangles and thickets at the edges of orchards, urban parks, agricultural fields and roadways; sometimes woodlots.

Nesting: on a horizontal branch in a deciduous shrub or small tree, within 7 ft of the ground; builds a flimsy platform of twigs lined with roots and grass; pair incubates 3–4 pale bluish green eggs for 9–11 days.

Feeding: gleans insect larvae, especially hairy caterpillars, from deciduous vegetation; also eats various other insects, berries, small fruits, small amphibians and occasionally small bird eggs.

Voice: long, deep, hollow *kuk* series, slowing near the end: *kuk-kuk-kuk-kuk kuk kop kow kowlp kowlp.*

Similar Species: *Black-billed Cuckoo* (p. 164): thinner, all-dark bill; smaller undertail spots; red eye ring; immature has yellow eye ring and possible buff wash on throat and undertail coverts; underwing has brown trailing edge and tip. *Mourning Dove* (p. 163): black spots on upperwing; pale rosy brown underparts; short, straight, dark bill; broader, diamond-shaped tail.

GREATER ROADRUNNER

Geococcyx californianus

Commonly seen dashing along and across roadways traversing its brushy habitat, the celebrated Greater Roadrunner lives up to its reputation for spirit and speed. This large member of the cuckoo family spends much of its time pursuing prey on foot at speeds of up to 15 miles per hour. It seldom flies; when the need arises, it passes quickly and directly over short distances. • Roadrunner courtship is an energetic affair involving high-speed foot chases followed by long, breath-catching pauses. The male typically leads the performance by running away from his mate with both tail and wings held over his body, and after a few graceful bows and some affectionate tail wagging, both adults seal their bond by exchanging offerings of sticks or vegetation. A breeding pair may mate for life and defend its breeding territory year-round. • Wildfire suppression and suburban sprawl have diminished and fragmented Greater Roadrunner habitat, resulting in population decreases throughout much of its distribution.

ID: streaked, brown and white or buff overall, with unstreaked white to buff belly and undertail coverts; head crest (raised in alarm or interest); bare, blue-and-red skin patch behind eye; long, thick, hook-tipped bill; thick, scaly legs. *In flight:* short flights; short, rounded wings; very long tail.

Size: *L* 23 in; *W* 22 in.

Habitat: open chaparral; brushy areas in open country; arid woodlands of pine and juniper; also uses dry limestone hills, forest edges, agricultural lands and suburbs; ranges up to elevations of 7500 ft.

Nesting: usually low in a cactus, dense shrub or tree; bulky platform nest of sticks, vegetation and feathers may include snakeskin and cattle dung; largely the male incubates 3–6 whitish eggs for 20 days.

Feeding: dashes toward and runs down insects, small mammals, lizards, snakes and small birds or leaps into the air to catch flying prey; also eats scorpions, snails, spiders, fruit and seeds.

Voice: descending, dovelike cooing; loud bill clattering is often the first sign of this bird's presence.

Similar Species: *Ring-necked Pheasant* (p. 65): female has mottled brown upperparts, no head crest or colorful facial skin, shorter bill, dark-barred tail, prefers croplands.

BARN OWL

Tyto alba

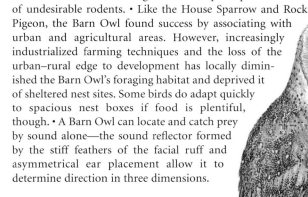

The Barn Owl's haunting look has inspired many superstitions, and naked faces and black, piercing eyes give even downy nestling owls an eerie look. In truth, this skilled night hunter helps keep farmlands and even city yards free of undesirable rodents. • Like the House Sparrow and Rock Pigeon, the Barn Owl found success by associating with urban and agricultural areas. However, increasingly industrialized farming techniques and the loss of the urban–rural edge to development has locally diminished the Barn Owl's foraging habitat and deprived it of sheltered nest sites. Some birds do adapt quickly to spacious nest boxes if food is plentiful, though. • A Barn Owl can locate and catch prey by sound alone—the sound reflector formed by the stiff feathers of the facial ruff and asymmetrical ear placement allow it to determine direction in three dimensions.

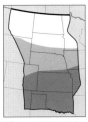

ID: golden brown upperparts mottled with gray; dark-spotted, creamy white underparts; heart-shaped, rufous-edged, white facial disc; dark eyes; pale bill; long legs. *In flight:* white underwings and undertail.

Size: *L* 12½–18 in; *W* 45 in.

Habitat: cliffs, hollow trees, barns and other unoccupied buildings, mine shafts, caves, bridges, tree groves and riverbanks for roosting and nesting; requires open areas such as fields, lawns, meadows or beach edges for hunting.

Nesting: in a natural or artificial cavity, such as a sheltered, secluded hollow of a building, a hole in a dirt bank or a nest box; no nest material is used; female incubates 3–8 whitish eggs for 29–34 days; male feeds incubating female.

Feeding: eats mostly small mammals, especially rodents; also takes small numbers of snakes, lizards, birds and large insects; rarely takes frogs and fish.

Voice: calls include harsh, raspy screeches and hisses; also makes metallic clicking sounds; often heard flying high over cities and residential areas late at night.

Similar Species: *Short-eared Owl* (p. 174): yellow eyes set in black sockets; vertical, dark streaks on breast and belly; dark "wrist" crescents; erratic flight pattern. *Barred Owl* (p. 172): horizontally barred chest; vertically streaked belly; darker facial disc.

EASTERN SCREECH-OWL
Megascops asio

The diminutive Eastern Screech-Owl is a year-round resident of deciduous woodlands, but its presence is rarely detected. Its daylight hours are usually spent snuggled safely inside a tree cavity or a nest box, but a daytime sighting opportunity might be signaled by a mobbing horde of chickadees or squawking gangs of Blue Jays, often following their loss of a family member during the night. More commonly, you will find this owl at night by listening for the male's eerie "horse-whinny" courtship calls and loud, spooky trills. • This small but adaptable hunter has a varied diet that ranges from insects, small rodents, earthworms and fish to birds larger than itself. • Unique among the owls found in our region, the Eastern Screech-Owl is polychromatic (has multiple color morphs). Gray morphs account for most Great Plains birds (about 90 percent). Red morphs, which dominate along the Atlantic Coast, are less common in our region because they are less able to withstand cold winters. Mixed-color pairs may produce young that are an intermediate buffy brown.

gray morph

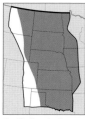

ID: white stripes on upperparts; sparse, vertical, dark streaking on paler breast and belly; short "ear" tufts; dark outline around face; yellow eyes; pale grayish bill. *Gray morph:* grayish overall. *Red morph:* rufous overall. *In flight:* dark gray "wrist" patch; short tail.
Size: *L* 8–9 in; *W* 20–22 in.
Habitat: mature deciduous forests, open deciduous and riparian woodlands, orchards and shade trees with natural cavities.
Nesting: in a natural cavity or nest box; no lining is added; female incubates 4–5 white

eggs for about 26 days; male brings food to the incubating female.
Feeding: feeds at dusk and at night; takes small mammals, earthworms, fish, birds and insects, including moths in flight.
Voice: descending, horselike "whinny"; also a long, trilled tremolo.
Similar Species: *Western Screech-Owl* (p. 362): limited range; never rufous; best distinguished by its accelerating "bouncing ball" song. *Northern Saw-whet Owl* (p. 175): long, rusty streaks on white underparts; no "ear" tufts; dark bill. *Long-eared Owl* (p. 173): much longer, slimmer body; "net" pattern on underparts; longer, closer-set "ear" tufts; 2 wide-set, rusty half-discs on face.

GREAT HORNED OWL

Bubo virginianus

The familiar *hoo-hoo-hoooo hoo-hoo* that resounds through campgrounds, suburban parks and farmyards is the call of the adaptable and superbly camouflaged Great Horned Owl. This formidable, primarily nocturnal hunter uses its acute hearing and powerful vision to hunt a wide variety of prey. It is the only consistent predator of skunks—apparently it has a poorly developed sense of smell—but almost any moving small creature is fair game. • Their hooting courtship calls make Great Horned Owls quite conspicuous, often as early as January. By February and March, females are already incubating their eggs, and by the time most migratory birds have moved into our region, Great Horned owlets have already fledged. • The large eyes of an owl are fixed in place. To look up, down or to the side, the bird must move its entire head—the flexible neck gives a range of 180 degrees to either side and 90 degrees up and down!

ID: varies from light gray to dark brown overall; heavily mottled, gray, brown and black upperparts; fine, horizontal barring on pale underparts; white "chin"; tall, wide-set "ear" tufts; facial disc is rusty orange to grayish brown and outlined with black. *In flight:* pale underwing with brown "wrist" patch.
Size: *L* 18–25 in; *W* 3–5 ft.
Habitat: fragmented forests, agricultural areas, woodlots, meadows, riparian woodlands, wooded suburban parks and the wooded edges of landfills.
Nesting: in the abandoned stick nest of another bird or sometimes on a cliff; adds little or no nest material; mostly the female incubates 2–3 dull whitish eggs for 28–35 days.
Feeding: mostly nocturnal but also hunts at dusk or by day in winter; usually swoops from a perch; eats small mammals, birds, snakes, amphibians and even fish.
Voice: breeding season call is 4–6 deep hoots: *hoo-hoo-hoooo hoo-hoo* or *Who's awake? Me too. Male:* also gives higher-pitched hoots.
Similar Species: *Long-eared Owl* (p. 173): smaller; much thinner; "net" pattern on underparts; close-set "ear" tufts. *Eastern Screech-Owl* (p. 168): much smaller; vertical breast streaks. *Great Gray, Short-eared* (p. 174) and *Barred* (p. 172) *owls:* tiny "ear" tufts or none.

169

SNOWY OWL
Bubo scandiacus

When the mercury drops and the landscape hardens in winter's icy grip, ghostly white Snowy Owls appear on fence posts, utility poles, fields and lakeshores throughout the northern Great Plains. They are yearly visitors, but their numbers can fluctuate quite dramatically. When lemming and vole populations crash in the Arctic, large numbers of Snowy Owls venture southward in search of food. • People with an eye for Snowies can often find them, even though these birds blend in perfectly against almost any flat, snow-covered landscape. Snow cover is not a prerequisite for a Snowy Owl visit—many of these birds perch conspicuously on earth-toned fields in snow-free portions of our region each winter. • Feathered to the toes, a Snowy Owl can remain active at low temperatures that often send other owls to the woods for shelter. • As Snowy Owls age, their plumage becomes lighter in color, and old males are often pure white. • Snowy Owls are recognizable in the oldest prehistoric cave art and may have inspired the first bird painting.

ID: predominantly white; no "ear" tufts; yellow eyes; black bill and talons. *Male:* almost entirely white with very little dark flecking. *Female:* prominent dark barring or flecking on breast and upperparts. *Immature:* heavy dark barring, particularly on upperparts.
Size: *L* 20–27 in; *W* 4½–6 ft.
Habitat: open country, including croplands, meadows, airports and lakeshores; often perches on fence posts, buildings and utility poles.
Nesting: does not nest in the Great Plains.
Feeding: swoops from a perch, often punching through the snow to take mice, voles, grouse, hares, and weasels; rarely takes songbirds and waterbirds.
Voice: quiet in winter.
Similar Species: no other owl in the region is all or largely white and has no "ear" tufts. *Barn Owl* (p. 167): smaller; in flight, upperparts are golden brown mottled with gray, bill does not protrude in front, and feet trail behind tail.

BURROWING OWL

Athene cunicularia

Burrowing Owls were once common in the Great Plains, but their numbers have declined significantly in recent years. The reduction of prairie dog and ground squirrel populations as a result of the conversion of native grasslands to croplands and residential areas has greatly diminished the number of suitable burrows to use as nest sites. Other factors relating to a decline in Burrowing Owls include poisonings, collisions with vehicles and the use of agricultural chemicals. Fortunately, some landowners have agreed to protect Burrowing Owl habitat, and some even support the introduction of artificial burrows to attract these birds to areas where ground squirrels are rare or absent. • During the day, this ground-dwelling bird can often be seen atop a fence post or rock in open grassland habitat. When perched at the entrance to its burrow, it looks very similar to the ground squirrels with which it closely associates.

ID: brown upperparts flecked with white; white underparts with horizontal, brown barring; bold, white "chin" stripe; rounded head; no "ear" tufts; white around eyes; pale, yellowish bill; long legs; short tail. *Immature:* brownish breast band; pale, unbarred underparts. *In flight:* weak "wrist" markings.

Size: *L* 8–9 in; *W* 21–24 in.

Habitat: open shortgrass hayfields, pastures and prairies; occasionally on lawns and golf courses.

Nesting: singly or in loose colonies; in an abandoned natural or artificial burrow; nest is lined with bits of dry manure, food debris, feathers and fine grass; female incubates 5–11 white eggs for 29 days.

Feeding: eats mostly ground insects such as grasshoppers, beetles and crickets; also eats small rodents, some birds, amphibians and reptiles.

Voice: calls include a harsh *chuk* and a chattering *quick-quick-quick;* rattlesnake-like warning call inside burrow. *Male: coo-hooo!* courtship call resembles higher-pitched Mourning Dove's *coo.*

Similar Species: *Short-eared Owl* (p. 174): larger; heavy, vertical streaks on underparts; tiny "ear" tufts; black eye sockets; long wings with bolder "wrist" marks; nests aboveground. *Northern Saw-whet Owl* (p. 175): smaller; bold, vertical, rusty streaks on underparts; short legs.

171

BARRED OWL

Strix varia

Each spring, the distinctive courting calls of the Barred Owl (frequently called "Old Eight-Hooter") echo through the forests and suburban woodlots of the easternmost Great Plains. The escalating laughs, hoots and gargling howls reinforce the pair bond. At the height of courtship and when raising young, a pair may continue their calls well into daylight hours, and they may hunt actively day and night. A full moon and calm air also tend to make this owl more vocal during early evening or early morning. Normally, the Barred Owl is most active between midnight and 4 AM, when the forest floor rustles with rodent movements. • With its relatively weak talons, this owl preys mostly on small mammals such as voles, but it sometimes takes small birds, including smaller owls. • Barred Owls were once common inhabitants of the moist deciduous woodlands and swamps that covered our region, but their numbers have declined with the destruction of these habitats. Lacking suitable tree hollows—their preferred nest sites—Barred Owls may resort to abandoned stick nests or even nest on the ground.

ID: mottled, dark grayish brown upperparts; horizontal barring around neck and upper breast; vertical streaking on belly; no "ear" tufts; dark eyes; pale, yellowish bill. *In flight:* weak "wrist" markings. **Size:** *L* 17–24 in; *W* 3½–4 ft.

Habitat: mature deciduous and mixed-wood forests, especially in dense stands near swamps, streams and lakes.

Nesting: in a natural tree cavity, broken treetop or abandoned stick nest with very little added material; male brings food as female incubates 2–3 white eggs for 28–33 days.

Feeding: nocturnal; swoops down on prey from a perch; eats mostly mice, voles and squirrels; also takes amphibians and small birds.

Voice: most characteristic of all our owls; *Who cooks for you? Who cooks for you all?* loud, hooting, rhythmic, laughing call is heard mostly in spring.

Similar Species: *Great Horned Owl* (p. 169): chunkier; finer, horizontal barring throughout underparts; prominent "ear" tufts; yellow eyes. *Short-eared Owl* (p. 174): dense, vertical streaking on breast; sparser streaking on belly; yellow eyes. *Spotted Owl:* limited range in Southwest; white-spotted, brown underparts.

LONG-EARED OWL

Asio otus

A Long-eared Owl will often scare off an intruder by spreading its wings and expanding its air sacs to puff out its feathers to look as large as possible. If it chooses to hide instead, it can flatten its feathers and compress itself into a long, thin, vertical form. • Widespread but scarce, Long-eared Owls are easily overlooked because of their cryptic plumage and reclusive habits. Only at dusk do they emerge from their secret hideouts to prey upon the small creatures of the night. Long-eared Owls are most noticeable during winter, when they roost together in groups of 10 to 20 birds in woodlots, hedgerows or isolated tree groves. • All owls (along with many other birds, such as herons, gulls, crows and hawks) regurgitate "pellets" that consist of the indigestible parts of the bird's prey compressed into an elongated ball. The feathers, fur and bones that make up the pellets are fascinating to analyze, because they reveal the bird's diet.

ID: slim body; mottled, brown upperparts; "net" of vertical streaks and horizontal barring on underparts; long, relatively close-set "ear" tufts; widely split, rusty brown facial disc; yellow eyes; white around bill. *In flight:* dark "wrist" patches.

Size: *L* 13–16 in; *W* 3–4 ft.

Habitat: *Breeding:* dense coniferous, mixed and riparian forests and areas with tall shrubs. *Winter:* woodlots, dense riparian woodlands, hedgerows and isolated tree groves in meadows, fields, cemeteries, farmyards and parks.

Nesting: in a tree in an abandoned hawk or crow nest; male brings food as female incubates 2–6 white eggs for 26–28 days.

Feeding: nocturnal; flies low, pouncing on prey from the air; eats mostly voles and mice; occasionally takes shrews, moles, small rabbits, small birds and amphibians.

Voice: low, soft, ghostly *quoo-quoo* breeding call; *weck-weck-weck* alarm call; also issues various shrieks, hisses, whistles, barks, hoots and dovelike coos.

Similar Species: *Great Horned Owl* (p. 169): much heftier; no vertical streaking on underparts; rounder face; wide-set "ear" tufts. *Short-eared Owl* (p. 174): no horizontal barring on breast and upper belly; tiny "ear" tufts; nests on the ground. *Eastern Screech-Owl* (p. 168): much stouter; shorter, wider-set "ear" tufts.

SHORT-EARED OWL

Asio flammeus

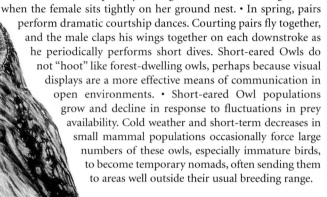

Habitats such as wet meadows, marshes, fields and bogs attract the Short-eared Owl, which, like the Snowy Owl of the Arctic, fills a niche in open country that has been left unoccupied by forest-dwelling owls. However, this bird can be difficult to locate, especially during the summer breeding season, when the female sits tightly on her ground nest. • In spring, pairs perform dramatic courtship dances. Courting pairs fly together, and the male claps his wings together on each downstroke as he periodically performs short dives. Short-eared Owls do not "hoot" like forest-dwelling owls, perhaps because visual displays are a more effective means of communication in open environments. • Short-eared Owl populations grow and decline in response to fluctuations in prey availability. Cold weather and short-term decreases in small mammal populations occasionally force large numbers of these owls, especially immature birds, to become temporary nomads, often sending them to areas well outside their usual breeding range.

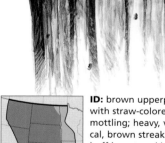

ID: brown upperparts with straw-colored mottling; heavy, vertical, brown streaking on buff breast and belly; inconspicuous "ear" tufts; yellow eyes in black sockets; black bill. *In flight:* deep wingbeats; erratic flight pattern; dark "wrist" patches.
Size: *L* 13–17 in; *W* 3–4 ft.
Habitat: open areas, including grasslands, wet meadows, marshes, fields, airports and forest clearings.
Nesting: on dry ground in an open, often wet area, such as a hummocky marsh; a slight depression is sparsely lined with

grass; male brings food as female incubates 4–7 white eggs for 24–37 days.
Feeding: mostly at dawn and dusk; flies low over marshes, wet meadows and tall vegetation and pounces on prey, mostly voles and other small rodents, from the air; also takes insects, small birds and amphibians.
Voice: generally quiet; produces a soft *toot-toot-toot* during the breeding season; also squeals and barks like a small dog.
Similar Species: *Long-eared Owl* (p. 173) and *Great Horned Owl* (p. 169): long "ear" tufts; rarely hunt by day. *Barred Owl* (p. 172): taller; much heavier; horizontal barring on upper breast; dark eyes; pale bill; nocturnal hunter. *Burrowing Owl* (p. 171): much longer legs; pale bill; shorter tail; much shorter wings.

NORTHERN SAW-WHET OWL

Aegolius acadicus

The tiny Northern Saw-whet Owl is an opportunistic hunter that takes whatever it can, whenever it can. If temperatures are below freezing, it may choose to catch more than it can eat in a single sitting, storing the excess in trees to freeze. When hunting efforts fail, the hungry Saw-whet returns to "incubate" its frozen cache as if it were a clutch of eggs! • In our area, Saw-whets normally breed only in coniferous forests along the western margin of the plains and in northern Minnesota, but they are regular winter visitors to the Great Plains, hunting at night and hiding by day, usually in dense conifers. They are most conspicuous in October, when they can be found in considerable numbers at some sites, and "owl prowls" during Christmas bird counts frequently concentrate much energy on Saw-whets. Saw-whets are usually heard more than they are seen, and from midwinter to early spring their slow, whistled notes— sometimes compared to the "bleeps" emitted by a large truck backing up—are often surprisingly common, but these birds can sometimes be frustratingly silent. • The scientific name *acadicus,* Latin for "from Acadia," refers to the Canadian region where this bird was first collected.

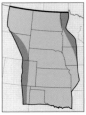

ID: small body; white-spotted, brown upperparts; vertical, rusty streaks on white underparts; large, rounded head; white-streaked forehead; unbordered, light facial disc; white "eyebrows" form "Y"; yellow eyes; dark bill; short legs; short tail.
Size: *L* 7–9 in; *W* 17–22 in.
Habitat: forests, often mixed or coniferous; wooded city parks and ravines.
Nesting: in an abandoned woodpecker cavity, natural tree hollow or nest box; male provides food as female incubates 5–6 white eggs for 27–29 days.

Feeding: nocturnal; swoops down on prey from a perch; may cache food; eats mostly mice and voles; also large insects, songbirds, shrews, moles and occasionally amphibians.
Voice: easily imitated, continuous, evenly spaced, whistled notes are repeated about 100 times per minute: *whew-whew-whew-whew.*
Similar Species: *Boreal Owl:* less common; white-spotted, dark forehead; dark-bordered facial disc; vertical, dark "eyebrows"; pale bill. *Gray-morph Eastern Screech-Owl* (p. 168) and *Western Screech-Owl* (p. 362): vertical, dark streaking on pale breast and belly; prominent "ear" tufts; paler, grayish bill.

COMMON NIGHTHAWK

Chordeiles minor

Each May and June, the male Common Nighthawk can be seen flying high above forest clearings and lakeshores, gaining elevation in preparation for the climax of his noisy aerial dance. From a great height, he dives swiftly, thrusting his wings forward in a final braking action as he strains to pull out of the steep dive. This quick thrust of the wings produces a deep, hollow *vroom* that attracts female nighthawks. • Like other goatsuckers, the Common Nighthawk has feather shafts placed to funnel insects into its gaping mouth in midair. • Nighthawks are generally less nocturnal than other goatsuckers, but they still spend most of the daylight hours resting on tree limbs or on the ground. These birds have very short legs and small feet and sit along the length of a tree branch, rather than across the branch as do most perched birds.

ID: cryptic, mottled, brownish gray upperparts; paler, horizontally barred underparts. *Male:* white throat. *Female:* buff throat. *In flight:* bold, white "wrist" patches on long, pointed wings; shallowly forked, barred tail; erratic flight.
Size: *L* 8½–10 in; *W* 24 in.
Habitat: *Breeding:* in forest openings as well as burns, bogs, rocky outcroppings, gravel rooftops and sometimes fields with sparse cover or bare patches. *In migration:* anywhere large numbers of flying insects can be found; usually roosts in trees, often near water.

Nesting: on bare ground; no nest is built; female incubates 2 well-camouflaged, heavily dark-spotted, pale eggs for about 19 days; pair feeds the young.
Feeding: primarily at dawn and dusk; catches insects such as mosquitoes, blackflies, midges, beetles, flying ants and moths in flight, often high in the air; may fly around streetlights at night to catch prey attracted to the light.
Voice: frequently repeated, nasal *peent peent. Male:* deep, hollow *vroom* from wings during courtship flight.
Similar Species: *Common Poorwill* (p. 177), *Chuck-will's-widow* (p. 178) and *Whip-poor-will* (p. 179): more rounded, barred wings; no white "wrist" patches; round-tipped tail.

COMMON POORWILL

Phalaenoptilus nuttallii

The discovery of a Common Poorwill that appeared to be hibernating through winter in a rock crevice surprised the scientific community in 1946. The bird was cold to the touch and had no detectable breath or heartbeat. Although Poorwills do not enter true hibernation like some mammals, birds that choose not to migrate to warmer climates will enter a short-term torpor in which their body temperature drops as low as 41° F and their oxygen intake is reduced by over 90 percent. This overwintering strategy of the Common Poorwill was known to the Hopi Indians, who named the species *Holchoko*, "the sleeping one," and to Meriwether Lewis, who, in 1804, found a mysterious goatsucker "to be passing into the dormant state." The seemingly dead birds may actually sleep for up to three months, exposing them to potential predation. Upon awakening, a good meal is a high priority. • Another trait this species shares with few other birds is a tendency to carry its eggs and young to a safer location after a disturbance. • The scientific name celebrates 19th-century ornithologist and botanist Thomas Nuttall.

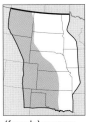

ID: cryptic, mottled, light to dark brown upperparts; finely barred, white-and-dark underparts; pale throat. *In flight:* rounded wings; barred flight feathers; rounded tail with white (male) or buff (female) corners.
Size: *L* 7–8 in; *W* 17 in.
Habitat: dry, open, grassy environments and rocky canyons.
Nesting: typically on bare ground with no additional material; pair incubates 2 white eggs for 20–21 days.

Feeding: on the wing; eats mainly moths, beetles and other flying insects.
Voice: calls are rarely heard. *Male:* frequently sings at dusk and through the night: *poor-will poor-will;* at close range, a hiccuplike sound can be heard at the end of the phrase.
Similar Species: *Chuck-will's-widow* (p. 178): mostly in southeast; larger; browner overall; male has striped tail corners. *Whip-poor-will* (p. 179): mostly in east; dark-edged, pale stripe along edge of back; darker wings; male has more white on tail corners. *Common Nighthawk* (p. 176): long, pointed wings; white "wrist" patches; shallowly forked tail.

CHUCK-WILL'S-WIDOW

Caprimulgus carolinensis

During daylight, you are lucky if you see the perfectly camouflaged Chuck-will's-widow roosting on the furrowed bark of a horizontal tree limb or sitting among scattered leaves on the forest floor. Even while nesting, this bird is virtually undetectable as it incubates its eggs and raises its young on the forest floor. At dusk, however, the Chuck-will's-widow is easily noticed as it calls its own name while patrolling the evening skies for flying insects. • Chuck-will's-widows roost more in trees than their closest relatives and suffer less from road collisions and owl predation than Whip-poor-wills and Common Poorwills. • Chuck-will's-widows (and other members of the family) can be found at night by shining a flashlight and looking for the reflected orangy red light from their eyes, but keep in mind that other animals' eyes also can be spotted in this way. This trick should, however, be attempted outside the breeding season only, so as not to disrupt the incubating and feeding of young or to encourage predation by nearby owls and squirrels.

ID: cryptic, mottled, brown-and-buff body with overall reddish tinge, barred on underparts; pale brown to buff throat, whitish "necklace" and dark breast. *In flight:* long, rounded tail; white stripes on corners of male's tail.

Size: *L* 12 in; *W* 26 in.

Habitat: riparian woodlands, swamp edges and hardwood and pine woodlands.

Nesting: on bare ground; no nest is built; female incubates 2 heavily blotched,

creamy white eggs for about 21 days and raises the young alone.

Feeding: catches beetles, moths and other large flying insects on the wing or by hawking.

Voice: calls are rarely heard. *Male:* song of 3 loud, whistling notes is often paraphrased as *chuck-will's-widow.*

Similar Species: *Whip-poor-will* (p. 179): smaller; grayer coloration overall; pale "necklace" contrasts with black throat; male shows much more white on tail feathers; female's dark tail feathers are bordered with buff on outer tips. *Common Nighthawk* (p. 176): smaller; throat is white (male) or buffy (female); white "wrist" patches; shallowly forked tail.

WHIP-POOR-WILL
Caprimulgus vociferus

This nocturnal hunter fills the late evening with calls of its own name: *whip-poor-will*. Although the Whip-poor-will is heard throughout many open woodlands, this cryptic bird is rarely seen. Because of the Whip-poor-will's camouflaged plumage, sleepy daytime habits and secretive nesting behavior, a hopeful observer must usually literally stumble upon it to see it. Only occasionally is this bird seen roosting on an exposed tree branch or alongside a quiet road. • Birds in this family were named "goatsuckers" during the days of Aristotle. According to a widely believed superstition, they would suck milk from the udders of female goats, causing the goats to go blind! • Within days of hatching, young Whip-poor-wills scurry away from their nest site in search of protective cover. For the first 20 days after hatching, the parents feed them regurgitated insects.

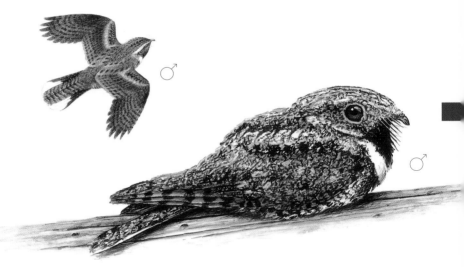

ID: cryptic, mottled, brownish gray upperparts with black flecking; dark-barred, gray to buffy underparts; black throat. *Male:* white "necklace." *Female:* buff "necklace." *In flight:* reddish tinge on rounded wings; long, rounded tail; conspicuous white patches near corners of male's tail.

Size: *L* 9–10 in; *W* 16–20 in.

Habitat: open hardwood and pine woodlands; often along forest edges.

Nesting: frequently along a clearing edge under herbaceous plant growth; on the ground in leaf or pine needle litter; no nest is built; female incubates 2 whitish eggs, blotched with brown and gray, for 19–20 days; pair feeds the young by regurgitation.

Feeding: catches large, night-flying insects in flight; eats mostly moths, beetles and mosquitoes; some grasshoppers are taken and swallowed whole.

Voice: loud, whistled *whip-poor-WILL.*

Similar Species: *Chuck-will's-widow* (p. 178): larger; more reddish overall; darker breast; pale brown to buff throat; whitish "necklace"; much less white on male's tail; different call. *Common Nighthawk* (p. 176): throat is white (male) or buffy (female); white "wrist" patches; shallowly forked, barred tail; much more conspicuous behavior.

179

CHIMNEY SWIFT

Chaetura pelagica

Chimney Swifts are the "frequent fliers" of the bird world—they feed, drink, bathe, collect nest material and even mate while in flight! They spend much of their time scooping up flying insects high above urban neighborhoods, and only the business of nesting or resting keeps these birds off their wings. • Chimney Swifts are most conspicuous while foraging in huge flocks on warm summer evenings and during fall migration, frequently alongside large numbers of Common Nighthawks. • Declining Chimney Swift populations may be the result of a decrease in available tree cavities for nesting. Their second choice for nest sites—brick chimneys—is the source of their name. • The legs of Chimney Swifts are so weak and small that if one of these birds lands on the ground, it may not be able to gain flight again. Swifts do have strong claws, though, which allow them to cling to vertical surfaces.

ID: slim body; brown overall; usually paler at throat. *In flight:* boomerang-shaped profile; long, thin, pointed, crescent-shaped wings; squared tail with "needle points"; rapid wing-beats; erratic flight pattern.

Size: *L* 4½–5½ in; *W* 12–13 in.

Habitat: forages over cities and towns; roosts and nests in chimneys; may nest in tree cavities in remote areas.

Nesting: often colonial; nests deep in the interior of a chimney or tree cavity or in an abandoned attic; pair uses saliva to attach a half-saucer nest of short, dead twigs to a vertical wall; pair incubates 4–5 white eggs for 19–21 days; pair feeds the young.

Feeding: swallows flying insects whole during continuous flight.

Voice: rapid, chattering *chitter-chitter-chitter* in flight; also gives a rapid series of *chip* notes.

Similar Species: *White-throated Swift* (p. 181): mostly in west; dark gray overall with white throat, belly and sides of rump. *Swallows* (pp. 225–31): pale underparts; broader, shorter wings; smoother flight patterns; most have forked or notched tail.

WHITE-THROATED SWIFT

Aeronautes saxatalis

True to its genus name *aeronautes*, which means "sky sailor" in Greek, this avian marvel certainly earns its wings. The White-throated Swift feeds, drinks, bathes and even mates while flying. Only brief, cliff-clinging rest periods and annual nesting duties keep it grounded. During its lifetime, the average White-throated Swift is likely to travel more than a million miles—enough to take this aerial insectivore around the world more than 40 times, yet it remains remarkably site loyal! Furthermore, it has been clocked at up to 200 miles per hour, which is fast enough to avoid any Prairie Falcons wanting to make a meal of it. • White-throats are easily recognized by their loud, sharp, scraping notes, black-and-white coloring and rapid, rather erratic flight. They can be a familiar sight in mountainous areas and even some cities along the western edge of the Great Plains.

ID: small, slender body; generally blackish overall, with white on throat tapering to a point on belly. *In flight:* long, tapering wings angled backward; white-tipped flight feathers; white patches at sides of rump; long, slightly forked tail, often held in a point.

Size: *L* 6–7 in; *W* 15 in.

Habitat: *Breeding:* high cliffs and crags in open country, especially dry escarpments surrounded by conifer forest, high desert fault blocks and river canyons; ranges widely in search of food. *In migration:* mostly at low elevations.

Nesting: high in a crevice on a cliff or building; cup made of materials gathered on the wing, including feathers, grass, moss, cotton, straw and plant down, is stuck together with gluelike saliva; pair incubates 4–5 pale creamy to white eggs for 24 days; young fledge in about 45 days and are expert fliers upon leaving the nest.

Feeding: snatches insects and other arthropods in midair; eats almost anything edible carried aloft by wind currents.

Voice: loud, shrill, descending *skee-jee-ee-ee-ee-ee-ee*.

Similar Species: *Chimney Swift* (p. 180): slightly smaller; brown overall with paler throat; "needle points" on square-ended tail. *Swallows* (pp. 225–31): all-white or pale underparts; stubbier-looking wings.

RUBY-THROATED HUMMINGBIRD

Archilochus colubris

Each year, many Ruby-throated Hummingbirds migrate across the Gulf of Mexico—an incredible, nonstop journey of more than 500 miles. To accomplish this feat, these little birds double their body mass by fattening up on nectar and insects before departing. • Like bees, hummingbirds visit flowers to feed on the sweet, energy-rich nectar and pollinate them in the process. Many avid gardeners and birders have long understood this interdependence and cultivate nectar-producing native plants in their yards to attract these delightful birds. Nongardeners can attract hummingbirds by maintaining a clean sugarwater feeder in a safe location. • Weighing about as much as a nickel, hummingbirds are capable of briefly achieving speeds of up to 62 miles per hour. They are also among the few birds that are able to fly vertically and in reverse. In straight-ahead flight, hummingbirds beat their wings up to 80 times per second, and their hearts can beat up to 1200 times per minute!

ID: iridescent, green upperparts; light underparts; long bill; dark tail. *Male:* ruby red throat (can appear dark purplish); black "chin." *Female and immature:* fine, dark streaking on whitish throat.

Size: *L* 3½–4 in; *W* 4½ in.

Habitat: open, mixed woodlands, wetlands, orchards, tree-lined meadows, flower gardens and backyards with trees and feeders.

Nesting: on a horizontal tree limb; tiny, deep cup nest of plant down and fibers is bound with spiderwebs; lichens and leaves are pasted on the nest's exterior wall; female incubates 2 white eggs for 13–16 days; female feeds the young.

Feeding: uses long bill and tongue to probe blooming flowers and sugar water from feeders; also eats small insects and spiders.

Voice: loud *chick* and other high squeaks; soft buzzing of the wings is most noticeable.

Similar Species: *Black-chinned Hummingbird* (p. 362): much less common; limited range; shorter bill; male has purple throat (never red) and more black on "chin"; female typically has grayer crown. *Rufous Hummingbird* (p. 362): less common; male has bright reddish orange on flanks and back; female has gray- and red-spotted throat and rust-washed flanks.

BELTED KINGFISHER
Ceryle alcyon

Many Great Plains lakes, rivers, streams, marshes and beaver ponds are monitored closely by the boisterous Belted Kingfisher. Never far from water, this bird is often found uttering its distinctive, rattling call while perched on a bare branch that extends out over a productive pool. With a precise headfirst dive, the Kingfisher can catch fish at depths of up to 23 inches or snag a frog immersed in only a few inches of water. The Kingfisher has even been observed diving into water to elude avian predators. • During the breeding season, a pair of kingfishers typically takes turns excavating the nest burrow. The birds use their bills to chip away at an exposed sandbank and then kick loose material out of the tunnel with their feet. The female kingfisher has the traditional female reproductive role for birds but is more colorful than her mate—she has an extra, rust-colored band across her belly. • In Greek mythology, Alcyon (Halcyon), the daughter of Aeolus, the wind god, grieved so deeply for her drowned husband that the gods transformed them both into kingfishers.

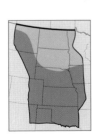

ID: bluish upperparts; bluish gray breast band; white "collar"; unkempt crest; white spot ahead of eye; long, sturdy, straight bill; short legs. *Female:* rust-colored "belt" (may be incomplete) on belly. *In flight:* white underwings; dark tail with pale barring.
Size: *L* 11–14 in; *W* 20 in.
Habitat: rivers, large streams, lakes, marshes and beaver ponds, especially near exposed soil banks, gravel pits or bluffs.

Nesting: pair uses bills and claws to dig a horizontal burrow, often up to 6 ft long, and nest cavity in a steep, sandy bank; pair incubates 6–7 white eggs for 22–24 days; pair feeds the young.
Feeding: dives headfirst into water, either from a perch or from a hovering flight; eats mostly small fish, aquatic invertebrates and tadpoles.
Voice: fast, repetitive, cackling rattle, a little like a teacup shaking on a saucer.
Similar Species: *Blue Jay* (p. 218): more intense blue color; smaller head and bill; black "necklace"; completely different behavior.

183

LEWIS'S WOODPECKER

Melanerpes lewis

This green-and-pink woodpecker does much of its foraging in the manner of a tyrant flycatcher, catching insects on the wing more often than probing into tree bark for them like most woodpeckers. Lewis's Woodpecker is also the only woodpecker that perches on wires, although it is most likely to be seen in semi-open country at the top of oaks or pines or atop poles or snags. • Lewis's Woodpecker often flies in a crowlike fashion, crossing the sky with slow, floppy wingbeats like a miniature Pileated Woodpecker. • Competition with European Starlings for nest holes and the loss of favored snag habitats for feeding has greatly diminished this woodpecker's numbers. • The Lewis's Woodpecker is named for Meriwether Lewis of the western "Expedition of Discovery" in the early 1800s. Although he was not a formal naturalist, Lewis detailed in his diary a great many concise and original natural history observations.

ID: glossy, dark green upperparts; pinkish belly; dark undertail coverts; light gray breast and "collar"; dusky red face; sharp, stout bill. *Immature:* brown breast, head and face; no light gray "collar." *In flight:* underwing shows pale gray flight feathers and dark lining; all-dark tail.
Size: *L* 11 in; *W* 21 in.
Habitat: broken or burned-over pine forests, pinyon-juniper and gray pine–oak woodlands, open riparian woodlands, ranch windbreaks and isolated groves.
Nesting: excavates a cavity in a dead or dying tree; pair incubates 6–7 white eggs for about 15 days.
Feeding: mostly flycatches for flying invertebrates; probes into cracks and crevices for invertebrates; eats acorns and mistletoe berries locally in winter.
Voice: nearly silent away from the nest; utters a harsh series of *chur* notes.
Similar Species: *Other woodpeckers* (pp. 185–92): upperparts not dark green; pronounced undulations in flight.

RED-HEADED WOODPECKER

Melanerpes erythrocephalus

Easily distinguished by its red head, black-and-white upperparts and white underparts, the Red-headed Woodpecker is a favorite visitor to feeders because of its beauty. • Like other members of the *Melanerpes* genus, Red-headed Woodpeckers will, during the breeding season, hawk for flying insects and store them, as well as acorns and other nuts, in cracks and bark crevices. • Red-headed Woodpeckers were once common throughout their range, but their numbers have declined dramatically over the past century. Since the introduction of the European Starling, Red-headed Woodpeckers have been largely outcompeted for nest cavities. As well, these birds are frequent traffic fatalities, often struck by vehicles when they dart from their perches and over roadways to catch flying insects. • This bird's scientific species name, *erythrocephalus*, means "red head" in Greek.

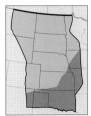

ID: black upper back and tail; white lower back and underparts; bright red "bib" (with black boundary), neck and head. *Immature:* dark areas are brownish; brown head; slight brown streaking on white underparts. *In flight:* rump, over half of flight feathers and inner half of underwing are white.
Size: *L* 9–9½ in; *W* 17 in.
Habitat: open hardwood woodlands (especially oak woodlands), urban parks, river edges and roadsides with groves of scattered trees.

Nesting: male excavates a nest cavity in a dead tree or limb; pair incubates 4–5 white eggs for 12–13 days; pair feeds the young.
Feeding: flycatches for insects; hammers dead and decaying wood for grubs; eats mostly insects, earthworms, spiders, nuts, berries, seeds and fruit but possibly also some young birds and eggs.
Voice: loud series of *kweer* or *kwrring* notes; occasionally a chattering *kerr-r-ruck*; drums softly in short bursts.
Similar Species: *Other woodpeckers* (pp. 184–92): no large white area across lower back or completely red head.

RED-BELLIED WOODPECKER

Melanerpes carolinus

In the eastern half of the Great Plains, the nattily attired Red-bellied Woodpecker is an uncommon but year-round breeding resident with a rapidly expanding range. In North Dakota, this bird is close to the extreme limit of its range in North American, where numbers fluctuate depending on the availability of habitat and the mildness of winter conditions. In recent years, mild winter weather has enabled the Red-bellied Woodpecker to increase its numbers in most of eastern North America. • These birds are often noisy as they poke around wooded landscapes in search of food. Unlike most woodpeckers, Red-bellies consume large amounts of plant material, seldom excavating wood for insects. When they occupy an area along with Red-headed Woodpeckers, Red-bellies will nest in the trunk, below the foliage, and the Red-heads will nest in dead branches among the foliage. • Studies of banded Red-bellied Woodpeckers have shown that they have a lifespan in the wild of more than 20 years.

Habitat: mature hardwood woodlands; occasionally in wooded residential areas.
Nesting: female selects one of several cavities excavated by the male, a natural cavity or the abandoned cavity of another woodpecker; pair incubates 4–5 white eggs for 12–14 days; pair raises the young.
Feeding: forages in trees, on the ground or occasionally on the wing; eats mostly insects, seeds, nuts and fruit; sometimes eats tree sap, small amphibians, bird eggs and small fish.
Voice: soft, rolling *churr;* drums in second-long bursts.
Similar Species: *Northern Flicker* (p. 191): pale brown, black-barred back and wings; spotted, buff to whitish underparts; gray (sometimes brown) crown; black "bib"; yellow (sometimes reddish) underwings. *Red-headed Woodpecker* (p. 185): all-red head; unbarred, black back and wings; large white patch on wing's trailing edge.

ID: black-and-white-barred back; whitish to pale brown underparts and face; red nape; often inconspicuous reddish tinge on belly. *Male:* red crown. *Female:* pale brown crown. *Immature:* dark gray crown; streaked breast. *In flight:* dark flight feathers at wing tips; white "wrist" patches; black-speckled, white rump.
Size: *L* 9–10½ in; *W* 16 in.

YELLOW-BELLIED SAPSUCKER

Sphyrapicus varius

Yellow-bellied Sapsuckers are migrants and winter residents in most of the Great Plains, breeding only in the northeastern portion of the region. • The drumming of sapsuckers—with its irregular rhythm reminiscent of Morse code—differs from the steadier patterns of other local woodpeckers. • Lines of parallel, freshly drilled sap wells in tree bark are a sure sign that sapsuckers are nearby.

A pair of sapsuckers might drill a number of sites within their forest territory. The wells fill with sweet, sticky sap that attracts insects; the sapsuckers then make their rounds, eating both the trapped bugs and the pooled sap. Sapsuckers do not actually "suck" sap—they lap it up with a tongue that resembles a paintbrush. • Other species, such as hummingbirds, kinglets, warblers and waxwings also eat from the wells made by Yellow-bellied Sapsuckers, especially early in the season when flying insects, fruits and nectar are rare.

♂

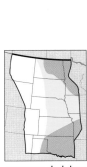

ID: white-barred, black upperparts; brown-barred, whitish flanks; yellow wash on lower breast and belly; black "bib"; white head with black stripes; red fore-crown. *Male:* red "chin." *Female:* white "chin." *Immature:* dark areas are dark brown; pale areas (except for white wing stripe) are light brown. *In flight:* broad, diagonal, white upperwing stripe.
Size: *L* 7–9 in; *W* 16 in.
Habitat: hardwood and mixed forests, especially dry second-growth woodlands.
Nesting: usually in a live poplar or birch with heart rot; in a cavity, often lined with wood chips; pair incubates 5–6 white eggs for 12–13 days.

Feeding: hammers trees for insects; drills "wells" in live trees to collect sap and trap insects; also flycatches for insects.
Voice: nasal, catlike *meow*; territorial and courtship hammering has a quality and rhythm similar to Morse code.
Similar Species: *Red-naped Sapsucker* (p. 363): limited range; usually reddish nape and throat. *Red-headed Woodpecker* (p. 185): immature has paler underparts, streaked face and different pattern of white on wings. *Downy Woodpecker* (p. 189) and *Hairy Woodpecker* (p. 190): white back and underparts; red restricted to spot on nape; less white on upperwing.

LADDER-BACKED WOODPECKER

Picoides scalaris

The Ladder-backed Woodpecker is a common visitor to ranches and rural towns throughout much of the Southwest, taking over in areas where the Downy Woodpecker will not go. Formerly called "Cactus Woodpecker," the Ladder-back frequents cacti, both to feed from them and to live in them. This small, speckled woodpecker will also flit between small scrub, dried riverbeds and pine-oak woodlands. • The male and the female have very different foraging techniques, perhaps as an adaptation to low food availability. The female prefers to glean insects off the bark's surface near the tops of scrub or trees. The male is more likely be found on the ground or near the bottoms of trees, picking off ants from underneath the bark. • When a male finds something thick enough to drum, a sporadic staccato will ring through the desert, sometimes followed by a characteristic *Picoides* whinny.

ID: black back with thick, white, horizontal stripes turning to spots on wings; white to buffy underparts with black spotting; whitish throat; white face with black eye line that loops back to join black bill line; black tail with white and black striped outer coverts. *Male:* extensive red crown patch with white dots on forehead; larger bill. *Female:* black crown. *Immature male:* smaller crown patch. *In flight:* white-barred, black wings.
Size: *L* 7–7½ in; *W* 13 in.
Habitat: mesquite, desert savanna and scrubland.

Nesting: in a large tree, agave, cactus, pole or similar site; excavates cavity and lines it with wood chips; probably the pair incubates 2–7 eggs for 13 days.
Feeding: mainly invertebrates, such as ants and beetles; cactus flowers. *Female:* gleans surfaces on the upper parts of trees. *Male:* prefers the ground and lower tree parts; digs under the bark.
Voice: quick, descending laugh with a raspy ending; fast *chip* contact call; drumming burst lasts about 1 second.
Similar Species: *Downy Woodpecker* (p. 189) and *Hairy Woodpecker* (p. 190): white patch on upper back; unbarred, white underparts, different facial striping; red on male is restricted to back of crown. *Red-bellied Woodpecker* (p. 186): less dark marking on underparts; red nape; no black on head.

DOWNY WOODPECKER

Picoides pubescens

Often the first woodpecker a novice birder will identify with confidence, the widely common Downy Woodpecker is a regular patron of backyard suet feeders. Generally more approachable and tolerant of human activities than are most birds, it is easily recognized by its dainty appearance, soft taps and brisk, staccato calls. However, the closely related but larger Hairy Woodpecker looks remarkably similar. • The Downy Woodpecker's small bill is extremely effective for poking into tiny crevices and extracting invertebrates such as wood-boring grubs. • Like other woodpeckers, the Downy has evolved a number of features that help to cushion the repeated shocks of a lifetime of hammering. These characteristics include a strong bill, strong neck muscles, a flexible, reinforced skull and a brain that is tightly packed in its protective cranium. Another feature that Downies share with other woodpeckers is feathered nostrils that filter out the sawdust produced by hammering.

♂

♀

ID: mostly unmarked, white back; white belly; white face with black crown, eye line and "mustache"; short, stubby bill; black tail with black-spotted, white outer feathers. *Male:* small red patch on back of head. *In flight:* white-barred, black wings with mostly white linings.

Size: *L* 6–7 in; *W* 12 in.

Habitat: wooded environments, especially hardwood and mixed forests and areas with tall hardwood shrubs.

Nesting: in a dying or decaying trunk or limb; pair takes over 2 weeks to excavate a cavity and lines it with wood chips; pair incubates 4–5 white eggs for 11–13 days; pair feeds the young.

Feeding: forages on trunks and branches, often in saplings and shrubs; chips and probes for insect eggs, cocoons, larvae and adults; also eats nuts and seeds; visits suet feeders.

Voice: long, unbroken trill is most common; other calls include a sharp *pik* or *ki-ki-ki* and whiny *queek queek;* drums more than the Hairy Woodpecker and at a higher pitch, usually on smaller trees and dead branches.

Similar Species: *Hairy Woodpecker* (p. 190): larger; bill as long as head is wide; completely white outer tail feathers. *Yellow-bellied Sapsucker* (p. 187): white-barred, black back; red forecrown; white nape; large, white upperwing stripe.

HAIRY WOODPECKER

Picoides villosus

A second or third look is often required to confirm the identity of the Hairy Woodpecker because it is so similar in appearance to its smaller cousin, the Downy Woodpecker. A convenient way to learn to distinguish the two birds is by watching them at a backyard feeder. It is not uncommon to see both species vying for food, with the larger Hairy Woodpecker being more aggressive. • The secret to woodpeckers' feeding success is hidden in their skulls. Most woodpeckers have very long tongues—sometimes more than four times the bill length—made possible by twin structures that wrap around the perimeter of the skull. These structures store the tongue in much the same way that a measuring tape is stored in its case. Besides being long and maneuverable, the tongue has a finely barbed tip coated with sticky saliva to help seize reluctant wood-boring insects. • Rather than singing during courtship, woodpeckers drum rhythmically on trees.

ID: mostly unmarked, white back; white belly; white face with black crown, eye line and "mustache"; bill is about as long as head is wide; black tail with completely white outer feathers. *Male:* small red patch on back of head. *In flight:* white-barred, black wings with gray-marked, white linings.
Size: *L* 8–9½ in; *W* 15 in.
Habitat: hardwood and mixed forests.
Nesting: in a live or decaying tree trunk or limb; pair takes over 2 weeks to excavate a cavity and lines it with wood chips; pair

incubates 4–5 white eggs for 12–14 days; pair feeds the young.
Feeding: forages on tree trunks and branches; chips, hammers and probes bark for insect eggs, cocoons, larvae and adults; also eats nuts, fruit and seeds; attracted to suet feeders, especially in winter.
Voice: loud, sharp *peek peek* call; long, unbroken *keek-ik-ik-ik-ik-ik* trill; drums less regularly and at a lower pitch than the Downy Woodpecker, always on tree trunks and large branches.
Similar Species: *Downy Woodpecker* (p. 189): smaller; shorter bill; dark spots on white outer tail feathers. *Yellow-bellied Sapsucker* (p. 187): white-barred, black back; red forecrown; white nape; large, white upperwing stripe.

NORTHERN FLICKER

Colaptes auratus

Unlike most woodpeckers, this species spends much of its time on the ground, feeding mostly on ants. It appears almost robinlike as it hops about on ant hills and in grassy meadows, fields and forest clearings. • Flickers are often seen bathing in dusty depressions. The dust particles absorb oils and bacteria that are harmful to the birds' feathers. To clean even more thoroughly, flickers will squish captured ants and then preen themselves with the remains: ants contain formic acid, which can kill small parasites on the flickers' skin and feathers. • Like many woodpeckers, the Northern Flicker has zygodactyl feet—each foot has two toes facing forward and two toes pointing backward—which allow the bird to move vertically up and down tree trunks. Woodpeckers are also aided by their stiff tail feathers, which they use to help to prop up their bodies as they scale trees and excavate cavities. • "Yellow-shafted Flickers" are most prevalent in the Great Plains, but winter brings some "Red-shafted Flickers" to the region.

♂

"Yellow-shafted Flicker"

♀

ID: black-barred, pale brown back and wings; spotted, buff to whitish underparts; black "bib"; long bill; black tail. *Yellow-shafted:* red nape patch; gray crown; brownish throat and face; male has black "mustache." *Red-shafted:* mostly gray throat and face with brownish crown area; male has red "mustache." *In flight:* white rump; yellow (Yellow-shafted) or reddish (Red-shafted) underwings.
Size: *L* 12½–13 in; *W* 20 in.
Habitat: open woodlands and forest edges; fields and meadows; beaver ponds and other wetlands.

Nesting: in a dead or dying hardwood tree; pair takes about 2 weeks to excavate a cavity and lines it with wood chips or uses a nest box; pair incubates 5–8 white eggs for 11–16 days; pair feeds the young.
Feeding: forages on the ground for ants and other terrestrial insects and probes bark; also eats berries and nuts; occasionally flycatches.
Voice: loud, laughing, rapid *kick-kick-kick-kick-kick-kick; woika-woika-woika* issued during courtship.
Similar Species: *Red-bellied Woodpecker* (p. 186): smaller; white-barred, black back; more red on head; black-and-white wings with dark flight feathers at tips.

191

PILEATED WOODPECKER
Dryocopus pileatus

With its flaming red crest, swooping flight and maniacal call, this impressive, deep-forest dweller can stop hikers in their tracks. • Using its powerful, dagger-shaped bill and stubborn determination, the Pileated Woodpecker chisels out uniquely shaped rectangular cavities in its unending search for grubs and ants. These cavities are often the first indication that a breeding pair is resident in an area. Because a breeding pair generally needs more than 100 acres of mature forest for its home territory, this magnificent bird is not encountered with much frequency. • As a primary cavity nester, the Pileated Woodpecker plays an important role in forest ecosystems. Certain ducks, small falcons and owls—and even flying squirrels—are some of the frequent users of abandoned Pileated Woodpecker cavities for their nests. • Not surprisingly, a woodpecker's bill becomes shorter as the bird ages. In his historic painting of the Pileated Woodpecker, John James Audubon correctly depicted the bills of juveniles as slightly longer than those of the adults. • Whether this bird's name is pronounced "pie-lee-ated" or "pill-ee-ated" remains a matter of good-natured debate.

ID: predominantly black; flaming red crest; white "chin"; yellow eyes; white stripe runs from bill to shoulder; stout, dark bill. *Male:* red patch extends from bill to nape; red "mustache." *Female:* grayish brown forehead. *In flight:* white "wrist" patch on upperwing; white wing linings.
Size: *L* 16–19 in; *W* 29 in.

Habitat: extensive tracts of mature forest; sometimes in riparian woodlands or woodlots in suburban and agricultural areas.
Nesting: in a dead or dying tree trunk; pair takes 3–6 weeks to excavate a cavity and lines it with wood chips; pair incubates 4 white eggs for 15–18 days; pair feeds the young.
Feeding: often hammers the base of rotting trees, creating rectangular holes, fist-sized or larger; eats carpenter ants, wood-boring beetle larvae, berries and nuts.
Voice: loud, fast, laughing, rolling *woika-woika-woika-woika;* long series of *kuk* notes; loud, resonant drumming.
Similar Species: *Other woodpeckers* (pp. 184–91): much smaller. *American Crow* (p. 222): all black; no crest; dark eyes.

PASSERINES

Flycatchers

Shrikes & Vireos

Jays & Crows

Larks & Swallows

Chickadees,
Nuthatches & Wrens

Kinglets, Gnatcatchers
& Thrushes

Mimics, Starlings
& Waxwings

Wood-warblers
& Tanagers

Sparrows, Grosbeaks
& Buntings

Blackbirds
& Orioles

Finchlike Birds

Passerines are also commonly known as songbirds or perching birds. Although these terms are easier to comprehend, they are not as strictly accurate, because some passerines neither sing nor perch, and many nonpasserines do sing and perch. In a general sense, however, these terms represent passerines adequately: they are among the best singers, and they are typically seen perched on a branch or wire.

It is believed that passerines, which all belong to the order Passeriformes, make up the most recent evolutionary group of birds. Theirs is the most numerous of all orders, representing about 47 percent of the bird species in the Great Plains region, and nearly three-fifths of all living birds worldwide.

Passerines are grouped together based on the sum total of many morphological and molecular similarities, including such things as the number of tail and flight feathers and reproductive characteristics. All passerines share the same foot shape: three toes face forward and one faces backward, and no passerines have webbed toes. Also, all passerines have a tendon that runs along the back side of the bird's knee and tightens when the bird perches, giving it a firm grip.

Some of our most common and easily identified birds are passerines, such as the Black-capped Chickadee, American Robin and House Sparrow, but the passerines also include some of the most challenging and frustrating birds to identify, until their distinct songs and call are learned.

OLIVE-SIDED FLYCATCHER

Contopus cooperi

An early morning hike through a conifer forest often reveals a most curious and incessant wild call: *quick-three-beers! quick-three-beers!* This interpretation of the male Olive-sided Flycatcher's courtship song may seem silly, but it is surprisingly accurate. Once nesting begins, this flycatcher quickly changes its tune to an equally enthusiastic, but less memorable, territorial *pip-pip-pip*. Like other "tyrant flycatchers," Olive-sided Flycatchers fiercely defend their nests, harassing and chasing off squirrels and other predators. • Olive-sided Flycatchers nest high in the forest canopy, far above the daily hubbub of the forest floor. There, they have easy access to an abundance of flying insects, especially the honeybees and adult wood-boring and bark beetles that inhabit the sunny forest heights. • This feisty bird is difficult to spot, so look for a big-headed silhouette perched at the tip of a mature conifer or dead branch. Like all flycatchers, it perches with a distinctive, upright, attentive stance that allows it to quickly launch out and snatch flying insects in midair.

ID: olive gray to olive brown upperparts; white patches on side of rump sometimes show; dark, olive gray "vest"; light throat and belly; inconspicuous eye ring; dark bill with dull yellowish orange base to lower mandible. *In flight:* grayish brown underwings.
Size: *L* 7–8 in; *W* 13 in.
Habitat: semi-open mixed and conifer forests near water; prefers burned areas and wetlands.
Nesting: high in a conifer, usually on a horizontal branch far from the trunk; nest

of twigs and plant fibers is bound with spider silk; female incubates 3 white to pinkish buff eggs, with dark spots concentrated at the larger end, for 14–17 days.
Feeding: flycatches insects from a perch.
Voice: descending *pip-pip-pip* when excited. *Male:* chipper and lively *quick-three-beers!* song has the 2nd note highest in pitch.
Similar Species: *Eastern Wood-Pewee* (p. 196): smaller; 2 faint, whitish wing bars; no white rump patches; gray breast. *Eastern Phoebe* (p. 202): paler overall; no white rump patches; less peaked crown; all-dark bill; often wags tail. *Eastern Kingbird* (p. 207): darker upper face; white sides; no white rump patches; all-dark bill; white-tipped tail.

WESTERN WOOD-PEWEE

Contopus sordidulus

Following this bird's characteristic down-slurred call leads to the middle level of the forest, where the male Western Wood-Pewee sings persistently throughout the day. When he's not singing, he launches himself in long, looping foraging ventures. Not as faithful to its perches as many other flycatchers, the Western Wood-Pewee sometimes alights upon a different perch from the one it left when it set out to chase down a tasty insect. • The nest of the Western Wood-Pewee is well camouflaged by both its shape and color—the completed structure resembles little more than a bump on a horizontal limb. As if this concealing masterpiece didn't provide enough protection, this small flycatcher vigorously defends its nest by chasing and vocalizing against hawks, jays and chipmunks. • The scientific name *sordidulus* refers to this bird's "dirty," dusky color.

ID: dark olive brown upperparts with 2 faint, whitish wing bars; lighter underparts; faintly darker "vest"; light-colored throat and undertail coverts; no eye ring; partly yellowish orange lower mandible. *In flight:* plain, grayish brown underwings.

Size: *L* 6–6½ in; *W* 10½ in.

Habitat: open woodlands and hardwood, ponderosa pine and riparian forests.

Nesting: on a horizontal tree limb; small cup nest of plant fibers is bound with spider silk; female incubates 3 brown-blotched, off-white eggs for 12–13 days.

Feeding: flycatches insects.

Voice: dry *chip* call.

Similar Species: *Eastern Wood-Pewee* (p. 196): very similar; typically has greener tinge on back and bolder wing bars (buffy on immature); higher, clearer, whistled song and drier calls. *Olive-sided Flycatcher* (p. 194): larger; more contrasting plumage; white rump patches; explosive song and calls. Empidonax *flycatchers* (pp. 197–201): generally more compact, with more contrast in plumage, more distinct wing bars and conspicuous eye rings. *Eastern Phoebe* (p. 202): inconspicuous wing bars; all-dark bill; very pale wing linings; often pumps its tail. *Eastern Kingbird* (p. 207): larger; more contrast in plumage; all-dark bill; white-tipped tail.

EASTERN WOOD-PEWEE

Contopus virens

Perched on an exposed tree branch in a suburban park, woodlot edge or neighborhood yard, the male Eastern Wood-Pewee whistles his plaintive *pee-ah-wee pee-oh* all day long throughout summer. Some of the keenest suitors will even sing their charms late into the evening, long after most birds have silenced their weary courtship songs. • The Eastern Wood-Pewee is hard to distinguish from the Western Wood-Pewee; song and range are often the best clues. • Like other flycatchers, the Eastern Wood-Pewee loops out from exposed perches to snatch flying insects in midair, a technique known as "flycatching" or "hawking." • Many insects have evolved defense mechanisms—such as camouflage, bad taste or toxins—to avert the Eastern Wood-Pewee and other potential predators. Some insects flaunt their foul nature with vivid colors; however, some mimics also exhibit warning colors even though they are perfectly tasty.

ID: olive gray to olive brown upperparts; 2 narrow, white wing bars; faint, grayish "vest"; whitish to yellowish belly and undertail coverts; whitish throat; partly yellowish orange lower mandible; no eye ring. *In flight:* plain, grayish brown underwings.
Size: *L* 6–6½ in; *W* 10 in.
Habitat: open mixed and hardwood woodlands with a sparse understory, especially woodland openings and edges.
Nesting: on the fork of a horizontal hardwood branch, far from the trunk; open cup of grass, plant fibers and lichen is bound with spider silk; female incubates 3 dark-blotched, whitish eggs for 12–13 days.
Feeding: flycatches from a perch; sometimes gleans insects from foliage, especially while hovering.

Voice: *chip* call. *Male:* song, sometimes with pauses, is a clear, slow, plaintive *pee-ah-wee*, with the 2nd note lower, plus a downslurred *pee-oh*.
Similar Species: *Western Wood-Pewee* (p. 195): typically browner back and weaker wing bars; lower, less clear song and less dry calls. *Olive-sided Flycatcher* (p. 194): larger; inconspicuous wing bars; white rump patches; darker "vest." *Empidonax flycatchers* (pp. 197–201): generally more compact, with more contrasting plumage and bolder wing bars and eye rings. *Eastern Phoebe* (p. 202): inconspicuous wing bars; pale wing linings; often pumps tail. *Eastern Kingbird* (p. 207): larger; more contrasting plumage; white-tipped tail.

YELLOW-BELLIED FLYCATCHER

Empidonax flaviventris

Sometimes the Yellow-bellied Flycatcher shows more yellow below than its cousins, but this field mark is not dependable. With few visual clues to depend on, distinguishing among the *Empidonax* flycatchers is a real test for birders. Learning the calls and songs of this group is the best way to identify them. A plain, soft, liquidy *che-lek* song indicates a male Yellow-bellied Flycatcher. Using a good pair of binoculars and paying close attention to fine details in plumage and voice should help you identify this flycatcher. • The Yellow-bellied Flycatcher migrates through the eastern Great Plains as it moves between its wintering grounds in southern Mexico and its nesting areas in Canada's boreal forests. This reclusive species migrates later in spring than most other flycatchers and is usually found in deep shade in moist woods. It perches low, darting out to catch flying insects, or it gleans spiders and caterpillars from foliage.

ID: olive green upperparts; 2 whitish wing bars; yellow underparts; pale olive breast; yellowish throat; yellowish eye ring. *In flight:* relatively pale underwings.
Size: *L* 5–6 in; *W* 8 in.
Habitat: coniferous bogs and fens and shady spruce and pine forests with a dense shrub understory.
Nesting: does not nest in the Great Plains.
Feeding: flycatches for insects at low to middle levels of the forest; also gleans vegetation for larval and adult invertebrates while hovering.

Voice: calls include a chipper *pe-wheep, preee, pur-wee* or *killik. Male:* song is a soft *che-luck* or *che-lek* with a lower-pitched 2nd syllable.

Similar Species: *Acadian* (p. 198), *Willow* (p. 200), *Alder* (p. 199) and *Least* (p. 201) *flycatchers:* generally browner upperparts; little or no yellow wash from throat to belly; generally whiter eye rings; different songs. *Dusky Flycatcher* (p. 363): white eye ring; longer tail; usually clearer whistles and 3-phrased song. *Cordilleran Flycatcher* (p. 363): browner upperparts with yellowish wash; fainter wing bars; slight crest; longer tail.

197

ACADIAN FLYCATCHER

Empidonax virescens

As most experienced birders will agree, one of the keys to identifying a flycatcher is to listen for the male's distinctive song; for the Acadian Flycatcher, it's a quick, forceful *peet-sa*. • Learning to identify this bird is only half the fun. The speedy, aerial courtship chases and the male's hovering flight displays are sights to behold—that is, if you can survive the swarming hordes of bloodsucking mosquitoes deep within the swampy woodlands where this flycatcher is primarily found. • Maples and beeches provide preferred nest sites for the Acadian Flycatcher. The nest is built on a horizontal branch up to 20 feet above the ground, and it can be quite conspicuous because of the loose material that often dangles from it, giving a sloppy appearance. • *Empidonax* flycatchers are members of the family Tyrannidae or "Tyrant Flycatchers"—so named because of their feisty, aggressive behavior.

ID: olive green upperparts; 2 buff to yellowish wing bars; faint, olive yellow breast; yellow belly and undertail coverts; white throat; narrow, yellowish eye ring; dark upper mandible; pinkish yellow lower mandible.

Size: *L* 5½–6 in; *W* 9 in.

Habitat: fairly mature hardwood woodlands, riparian woodlands and wooded swamps.

Nesting: in a beech or maple, usually 6–20 ft above the ground; female builds a loose cup of bark strips, catkins, fine twigs and grass bound with spider silk; female incubates 3 creamy white, lightly brown-spotted eggs for 13–15 days; pair raises the young.

Feeding: primarily hawks or gleans from foliage while hovering; takes insect adults and larvae, including wasps, bees, ants and spiders; sometimes eats berries and other small fruits.

Voice: soft *peet* call; may issue a loud, flickerlike *ti-ti-ti-ti-ti* during breeding season. *Male:* forceful *peet-sa* song.

Similar Species: *Alder Flycatcher* (p. 199) and *Willow Flycatcher* (p. 200): browner overall; smaller heads relative to bodies; less conspicuous, white eye rings; male sings *fee-bee-o* (Alder) or an explosive *fitz-bew* (Willow). *Least Flycatcher* (p. 201): smaller overall; rounder head; white eye ring; smaller bill; clear *che-bek* song. *Yellow-bellied Flycatcher* (p. 197): yellow wash from throat to belly; liquid *che-lek* song.

ALDER FLYCATCHER

Empidonax alnorum

Until the nondescript male Alder Flycatcher utters his hearty *fee-bee-o* or *free beer*, his identity usually remains concealed. The well-named Alder Flycatcher is often found in alders, which is an aid to identification. However, where ranges overlap, it frequently competes against the closely related Willow Flycatcher for control over dense alder and willow riparian habitat. These two species were once grouped together as "Traill's Flycatcher" (*E. traillii*). • The Alder Flycatcher is a migrant through much of the eastern Great Plains. Once spotted, this feisty and aggressive bird can often be observed without distraction as it drives away rivals and pursues flying insects. • Many birds have to learn their songs and calls, but Alder Flycatchers (and Willows) instinctively know the simple phrase of their species. Even a young bird isolated from the sounds of other Alder Flycatchers will, on maturing, produce a perfectly acceptable song.

W 8½ in.

ID: olive brown upperparts; 2 dull white to buff wing bars; pale yellowish belly; pale olive breast; white throat; faint, whitish eye ring; orangy yellow lower mandible; long tail.
Size: *L* 5½–6 in;

Habitat: riparian alder or willow thickets.
Nesting: does not nest in the Great Plains.
Feeding: flycatches from a perch for beetles, bees, wasps and other flying insects; also eats berries and occasionally seeds.

Voice: *wheep* or *peep* call. *Male:* song is a snappy *free beer* or *fee-bee-o*.
Similar Species: *Willow Flycatcher* (p. 200): very similar; range mostly differs; explosive *fitz-bew* song; will use drier areas. *Least Flycatcher* (p. 201): bolder, white eye ring; smaller bill; clear *che-bek* song. *Acadian Flycatcher* (p. 198): greener upperparts; bolder, yellowish eye ring; forceful *peet-sa* song. *Yellow-bellied Flycatcher* (p. 197): greener upperparts; yellower underparts; yellowish eye ring; liquid *che-lek* song. *Eastern Wood-Pewee* (p. 196): grayer overall; slightly peaked crown; inconspicuous eye ring.

WILLOW FLYCATCHER

Empidonax traillii

When warm spring winds flood the Great Plains with migrant songbirds, the characteristic, sneezy *fitz-bew* call of male Willow Flycatchers occasionally rises above the sounds of the crowd. Upon arriving in a suitable shrubby area of thick willows and tangled dogwood, the males swing energetically on their perches to do vocal battle over preferred territory. Once the boundaries are drawn and the business of nesting begins, these flycatchers become shy, inconspicuous birds that prefer to remain out of sight. Only when an avian intruder violates an established boundary does a resident aggressively reveal itself. • After raising their young and fattening themselves up in late summer and early fall, Willow Flycatchers begin their journey to Central and South America. • John James Audubon originally named this species after Thomas Stewart Traill, an Englishman who helped him to find a British publisher for his book *Ornithological Biography*.

ID: olive brown upperparts; 2 whitish wing bars; yellowish belly; pale olive breast; white throat; faint or no eye ring; orangy yellow lower mandible; long tail.
Size: *L* 5½–6 in; *W* 8½ in.

Habitat: shrubby areas of hawthorn, apple, red-osier dogwood or willow on abandoned farmlands and in riparian corridors.
Nesting: in a fork or on a branch of a dense shrub, usually 3–7 ft above the ground; female builds an open, down-lined cup nest of grass, bark strips and plant fibers; female incubates 3–4 whitish to pale buff eggs, with brown spots concentrated toward the larger end, for 12–15 days.
Feeding: flycatches insects and gleans them from vegetation, usually while hovering.
Voice: quick *whit* call. *Male:* quick, sneezy *fitz-bew* song drops off at the end and is repeated up to 30 times a minute.
Similar Species: *Alder Flycatcher* (p. 199): very similar; range mostly differs; often in wetter areas; *fee-bee-o* song. *Least Flycatcher* (p. 201): bolder, white eye ring; smaller bill; clear *che-bek* song. *Acadian Flycatcher* (p. 198): greener upperparts; bolder, yellowish eye ring; forceful *peet-sa* song. *Yellow-bellied Flycatcher* (p. 197): greener upperparts; yellower underparts; yellowish eye ring; liquid *che-lek* song. *Eastern Wood-Pewee* (p. 196): grayer overall; slightly peaked crown.

LEAST FLYCATCHER

Empidonax minimus

This small bird might not look like a bully, but the Least Flycatcher is one of the boldest and most pugnacious songbirds of our hardwood woodlands, even though it is our smallest *Empidonax*. During the nesting season, the male is noisy and conspicuous, forcefully repeating his simple, two-part *che-bek* call throughout much of the day. Intense song battles normally eliminate the need for physical aggression, but feathers fly in fights that are occasionally required to settle disputes over territory and courtship privileges. • These birds often fall victim to nest parasitism by the Brown-headed Cowbird—its hatchlings often smother the much smaller young of Least Flycatchers'. • This genus of flycatchers is aptly named: the literal translation of *Empidonax*, which reflects the birds' insect-hunting prowess, is "mosquito king."

ID: olive brown upperparts; 2 white wing bars; grayish white to yellowish belly and undertail coverts; gray breast; white throat; bold, white eye ring; dark bill with yellowish orange on lower mandible; fairly long, narrow tail.

Size: *L* 4½–6 in; *W* 7½–8 in.

Habitat: open hardwood or mixed woodlands; forest openings and edges; often in second-growth woodlands and occasionally near human habitation.

Nesting: in a fork of a small tree or shrub, often against the trunk; female builds a small cup nest of plant fibers and bark lined with fine grass, plant down and

feathers; female incubates 4 creamy white eggs for 13–15 days; pair feeds the young.

Feeding: flycatches insects; gleans trees and shrubs for insects while hovering; sometimes eats fruits and seeds.

Voice: call is a seldom-heard *wit*. *Male:* song is a constantly repeated, dry *che-bek che-bek*.

Similar Species: *Alder Flycatcher* (p. 199) and *Willow Flycatcher* (p. 200): faint or no eye ring; longer bill; *fee-bee-o* (Alder) or explosive *fitz-bew* (Willow) song. *Acadian Flycatcher* (p. 198): slightly greener upperparts; larger bill; forceful *peet-sa* song. *Yellow-bellied Flycatcher* (p. 197): greener upperparts; yellower underparts; yellowish eye ring; liquid *che-lek* song. *Eastern Wood-Pewee* (p. 196): grayer overall; slightly peaked crown; inconspicuous eye ring. *Ruby-crowned Kinglet* (p. 247): smaller; smaller upper wing bar; elongated eye ring; daintier bill; shorter tail.

EASTERN PHOEBE

Sayornis phoebe

Whether you are poking around your summer cottage, a campground picnic shelter or your backyard shed, you are quite likely to stumble upon an Eastern Phoebe family and its marvelous mud nest. Once limited to nesting on natural cliffs and fallen riparian trees, this adaptive flycatcher has gradually found success in nesting on buildings and bridges, with a preference for sites near water. The Eastern Phoebe's nest building and territorial defense is normally well underway by the time most other songbirds arrive in our region. • Some people have caught on to the benefits of having phoebe tenants, because these birds can be effective at controlling pesky insects. Too often, though, people unnecessarily destroy the phoebes' mud nests, which the birds will sometimes happily reuse for many years. • Some other birds pump their tails while perched, but few of them match the Eastern Phoebe's zest and frequency of pumping.

ID: grayish brown upperparts; no obvious wing bars; whitish underparts; gray wash on breast and sides; belly and undertail coverts may be washed with yellow in fall; no eye ring; all-black bill; dark legs; frequently pumps tail. *In flight:* brown flight feathers; pale wing linings.
Size: *L* 6½–7 in; *W* 10½ in.
Habitat: open hardwood woodlands, forest edges and clearings, usually near water.
Nesting: under a ledge on a structure, culvert, cliff or well; cup-shaped mud nest is lined with moss, grass, fur and feathers; female incubates 4–5 white eggs, often with a few reddish brown spots, for about 16 days; pair feeds the young.

Feeding: flycatches beetles, flies, wasps, grasshoppers, mayflies and other insects; occasionally plucks aquatic invertebrates and small fish from the water's surface.
Voice: sharp *chip* call. *Male:* delivers hearty, snappy *fee-bee* song frequently.
Similar Species: *Eastern Wood-Pewee* (p. 196): smaller; pale wing bars; yellowish orange on lower mandible; plainer underwings; does not pump tail. *Olive-sided Flycatcher* (p. 194): dark "vest"; white, fluffy patches border rump; pointier wings, plainer below. Empidonax *flycatchers* (pp. 197–201): most have eye rings and conspicuous wing bars. *Eastern Kingbird* (p. 207): white-tipped tail; black upperparts; white lower face.

SAY'S PHOEBE

Sayornis saya

Unlike its close relative the Eastern Phoebe, the Say's Phoebe is partial to dry environments. It thrives in sun-parched grassy valleys and hot, dry canyons. This flycatcher is particularly common where an abandoned or little-used farm building provides a safe, sheltered nest site that can be reused every year and where livestock conveniently stir up insects. The Say's Phoebe "hawks" these insects from a fence post or other low perch, resorting to hovering in the absence of perches. • The Say's Phoebe is the only bird whose genus and species names are both derived from the same person's name. Thomas Say was a versatile, initially self-taught, 19th-century U.S. naturalist whose primary contributions were in the field of entomology. The name "phoebe" comes from the call of the Eastern Phoebe.

ID: brownish gray upperparts and breast; very faint wing bars; apricot buff belly, flanks and undertail coverts; brownish gray head; no eye ring; dark tail constantly bobs. *In flight:* pale flight feathers; apricot buff wing linings.

Size: *L* 7½ in; *W* 13 in.

Habitat: hot, dry canyons, ravines, rim-rocks, valleys and gullies dominated by grasses and shrubs; sometimes uses agricultural areas and scrublands.

Nesting: in a niche on a cliff face, beneath a building eave or under a bridge; shallow, open, cup-shaped nest consists of grass, moss and fur; female incubates 4–5 white, sometimes brown-spotted eggs for up to 17 days.

Feeding: flycatches for aerial insects; also gleans buildings, vegetation, streamsides and the ground for insects; sometimes runs short distances in pursuit of prey.

Voice: softly whistled *pee-ur* call. *Male: pitseedar* song.

Similar Species: *Other flycatchers* (pp. 194–208): bellies are not apricot buff; often have eye rings; lower mandibles are generally partly yellowish orange.

ASH-THROATED FLYCATCHER

Myiarchus cinerascens

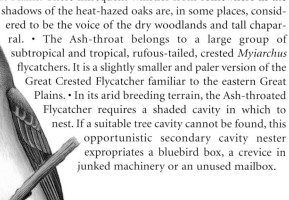

The shrill, whistled calls of the Ash-throated Flycatcher are some of the most familiar summer sounds in canyons and river valleys along the southwestern edge of the Great Plains. These infrequent whistles from somewhere in the shadows of the heat-hazed oaks are, in some places, considered to be the voice of the dry woodlands and tall chaparral. • The Ash-throat belongs to a large group of subtropical and tropical, rufous-tailed, crested *Myiarchus* flycatchers. It is a slightly smaller and paler version of the Great Crested Flycatcher familiar to the eastern Great Plains. • In its arid breeding terrain, the Ash-throated Flycatcher requires a shaded cavity in which to nest. If a suitable tree cavity cannot be found, this opportunistic secondary cavity nester expropriates a bluebird box, a crevice in junked machinery or an unused mailbox.

ID: grayish brown upperparts; 2 pale wing bars; pale gray throat and breast; light yellow belly and under-tail coverts; fluffy crown; no eye ring; stout, dark bill; long, dark brown tail (some rufous in webbing). *In flight:* rufous-tinged, brown flight feathers; yellowish wing linings.

Size: *L* 7–8 in; *W* 12 in.

Habitat: *Breeding:* tall mixed chaparral, oak groves and woodlands, riparian corridors with large, old trees. *In migration:* varied tree and shrub associations.

Nesting: in a natural or artificial cavity; pair builds a nest made of soft vegetation, hair and feathers; female incubates 4–5 brown-blotched, cream eggs for about 15 days; pair feeds the young.

Feeding: flies out from perch to snatch prey from foliage or other surface; tends to forage low among trees and shrubs; eats mostly insects but also fruit and, rarely, small lizards and even mice.

Voice: voice quality vaguely suggests a referee's whistle; distinctive, year-round *prrrt* call; also issues a *ka-BREER!* or a harsh, abrupt *ka-brick*.

Similar Species: *Great Crested Flycatcher* (p. 205): brighter yellow underparts and wing linings; darker breast, throat and face; different calls and range. Empidonax *flycatchers* (pp. 197–201): smaller; bolder wing bars; eye rings. *Western Kingbird* (p. 206) and *Cassin's Kingbird* (p. 363): yellower below; no wing bars or crest; white "cheek"; pointier wings.

GREAT CRESTED FLYCATCHER

Myiarchus crinitus

L ike other *Myiarchus* flycatchers, the Great Crested Flycatcher uses tree cavity nests instead of cup nests. Once in a while, the Great Crested will decorate the entrance of its nest cavity with a shed snakeskin. The purpose of this practice is not fully understood, but it might make any would-be predators think twice! In some instances, this versatile bird has even been known to substitute translucent plastic wrap for genuine reptilian skin. • A common summer resident throughout much of the Great Plains, the Great Crested Flycatcher prefers open or semi-open hardwood forests. • We usually think of songbirds such as the Great Crested Flycatcher as birds that fly south for winter. However, it would be more correct to say that these migrants are subtropical or tropical birds of Central and South America that fly north to visit our area only briefly to raise their young before returning home.

ID: dark olive brown upperparts; 2 pale wing bars; medium gray upper breast and throat; bright yellow belly and undertail coverts; peaked, "crested" head; no eye ring; heavy, black-tinged bill; long, dark brown tail (rufous in webbing). *In flight:* rufous-tinged, brown flight feathers; bright yellow wing linings.

Size: *L* 8–9 in; *W* 13 in.

Habitat: hardwood and mixed woodlands and forests, usually near openings or edges.

Nesting: in a natural tree cavity, abandoned woodpecker hole, nest box or other artificial cavity lined with grass, bark strips and feathers; female incubates 5 creamy to pale buff eggs, marked with brownish tints, for 13–15 days.

Feeding: often in the upper branches of hardwood trees, where it flycatches for insects; may also glean caterpillars and occasionally fruit.

Voice: loud, whistled *wheep!* and a rolling *prrrrreet!*

Similar Species: *Ash-throated Flycatcher* (p. 204): paler underparts, wing linings, breast, throat and face; different calls and range. *Yellow-bellied Flycatcher* (p. 197): smaller; yellowish throat; finer bill, mostly yellowish orange below; no rufous in wings and tail. *Western Kingbird* (p. 206) and *Cassin's Kingbird* (p. 363): yellower below; no wing bars or crest; white "cheek"; pointier wings.

205

WESTERN KINGBIRD

Tyrannus verticalis

Often observed surveying for prey from a fence post, power line or utility pole, the Western Kingbird is a common sight in the Great Plains. When a kingbird spots an insect, it may chase it for up to 50 feet before a capture is made. • Once you have witnessed a kingbird's brave attacks against much larger birds, such as crows and hawks, it is easy to understand why these brawlers were awarded the name "kingbird." The scientific name *verticalis* refers to the Western Kingbird's normally hidden red crown patch, which the male flares during courtship displays and while in combat with rivals. • In his courtship aerobatics, the male Western Kingbird twists and turns as he rises to heights of 65 feet above the ground; then he stalls and tumbles, flips and twists his way back to earth. • Western Kingbirds have been known to hybridize with Eastern Kingbirds on several occasions.

ID: ashy gray-and-brown upperparts; yellow belly and undertail coverts; pale gray breast and head; thin, orangy red crown patch (rarely seen); white "chin" and "cheek"; black bill; faintly darker eye line; white-edged, black tail. *In flight:* yellow underwing with grayish brown-and-white flight feathers.

Size: *L* 8–9 in; *W* 15½ in.

Habitat: open scrubland areas with scattered patches of brush or hedgerows; along the edges of open fields.

Nesting: near the trunk in a hardwood tree; bulky cup nest of grass, weeds and twigs is lined with fur, plant down and feathers; female incubates 3–5 whitish, heavily blotched eggs for 18–19 days.

Feeding: flycatches aerial insects, including bees, wasps, butterflies, moths, grasshoppers and flies; occasionally eats berries.

Voice: chatty, twittering *whit-ker-whit;* also a short *kit* or extended *kit-kit-keetle-dot.*

Similar Species: *Cassin's Kingbird* (p. 363): limited range; darker head and breast; smaller white area on face; light tip on tail instead of white edges. *Eastern Kingbird* (p. 207): black upperparts; white underparts. *Great Crested Flycatcher* (p. 205) and *Ash-throated Flycatcher* (p. 204): brownish upperparts; yellowish wing bars; slightly crested head; longer bill; brown-and-rufous tail.

EASTERN KINGBIRD

Tyrannus tyrannus

When you think of a "tyrant," an image of a ruthless despot might spring to mind. Most people wouldn't think of a small bird, except maybe those who are familiar with the exploits of the tyrant flycatchers, of which the Eastern Kingbird is North America's most widespread representative. This brawler will fearlessly attack crows, hawks and even humans that pass through its territory. Intruders are often vigorously pursued, pecked and plucked for some distance until the kingbird is satisfied that there is no further threat. In contrast, the male's butterfly-like courtship flight, which is characterized by short, quivering wingbeats, reveals a gentler side of this bird. • Almost any trip through the countryside is likely to reveal at least one Eastern Kingbird sitting on a fence line or utility wire along a roadside. • Eastern Kingbirds rarely walk or hop on the ground—they prefer to fly, even for very short distances.

Nesting: on a horizontal tree or shrub limb, standing stump or an upturned tree root; pair builds a cup nest of weeds, twigs and grass lined with root fibers, fine grass and fur; female incubates 3–4 darkly blotched, white to pinkish eggs for 14–18 days.

Feeding: flycatches aerial insects; infrequently eats berries.

Voice: call is a quick, loud, chattering *kit-kit-kitter-kitter;* also a buzzy *dzee-dzee-dzee.*

Similar Species: *Western Kingbird* (p. 206) and *Cassin's Kingbird* (p. 363): paler above; yellow below. *Tree Swallow* (p. 226): female has smaller bill, shorter, forked tail and more streamlined body. *Olive-sided Flycatcher* (p. 194): brown back, head, sides and undertail coverts; longer bill; 2 white patches border rump; all-brown tail. *Eastern Wood-Pewee* (p. 196): smaller; drabber coloration.

ID: dark gray to black upperparts; white underparts and lower face; small head crest; thin, orangy red crown patch (rarely seen); black bill; black legs; white-tipped, dark tail. *In flight:* gray underwing with whitish stripe.

Size: *L* 8½ in; *W* 15 in.

Habitat: rural fields with scattered trees or hedgerows, clearings in fragmented forests, open roadsides, burned areas and near human settlements.

SCISSOR-TAILED FLYCATCHER

Tyrannus forficatus

Endowed with the refined, long tail feathers of a tropical bird of paradise, the Scissor-tailed Flycatcher certainly remains one of the top birds on most "must-see" lists. This lovely bird is often seen perched on roadside fences and utility wires, allowing keen observers to marvel at its periodic hawking flights to gracefully snatch flying insects out of the air. • The Scissor-tail derives its name from the male's habit of opening and closing the gap between his long tail feathers during his cackling, roller-coaster courtship flight. This display often includes dazzling backward somersaults that showcase the beauty of the streaming tail. • Although the Scissor-tail breeds primarily in Texas and northward through Oklahoma into Kansas, birders in most of the lower 48 states have a chance to be left glowing by the sight of far-wandering post-breeding strays. • Like the closely related kingbirds, this bird aggressively defends its nest, giving piercing, shrill calls and attacking much larger birds, including jays, magpies, crows and hawks.

ID: whitish to grayish back, breast and head; dark brown to black wings; salmon pink flanks and lower underparts; very long tail, especially on male. *Immature:* paler; shorter tail. *In flight:* bright to salmon pink "wing pits" and wing linings; tail's extremely long, black-and-white outer feathers give forked appearance.

Size: *Male: L* 15 in (tail is up to 9 in long); *W* 15 in. *Female: L* 10 in; *W* 15 in.

Habitat: grasslands, pastures, roadsides and semi-open country with scattered groves of trees and shrubs or utility poles for nesting.

Nesting: in a tree or shrub, utility pole or other suitable structure; female builds a messy nest cup of twigs, vegetation and animal hair; female incubates 3–6 brown-blotched, off-white eggs for 14–17 days; pair raises the young.

Feeding: hawks for insects; sometimes seizes insects on the ground, while flying or by gleaning them from foliage while hovering.

Voice: calls include a repeated *ka-leap* and a sharp, harsh *kek*.

Similar Species: none; long tail and mostly white upperparts and head are distinctive.

LOGGERHEAD SHRIKE
Lanius ludovicianus

The Loggerhead Shrike resembles a Northern Mockingbird in body shape and color, but its hunting method is very different. This predatory songbird has very acute vision, and it often perches atop trees and on wires to scan for small prey, which is caught in fast, direct flight or a swooping dive. • Male Loggerheads display their hunting prowess by impaling prey on thorns or barbed wire. This behavior may also serve as a means of storing excess food during times of plenty. In spring, you may see a variety of skewered creatures baking in the sun. • Loggerhead Shrike populations have severely declined in many parts of the bird's North American range. Habitat destruction is thought to be the main reason for the population decline. Another cause is collisions with motor vehicles on their southern U.S wintering grounds as they fly low across roads to prey on insects attracted to the warm pavement.

ID: gray back and crown; black wings; white underparts; black "mask" extends above short, dark, hooked bill onto forehead; black eyes. *Immature:* brownish gray back; barred, brown-and-gray under-parts. *In flight:* white "wrist" patches above and below; white-edged, black tail.
Size: *L* 9 in; *W* 12 in.
Habitat: grazed pastures and marginal and abandoned farmlands with scattered thorny shrubs, fence posts, barbed wire and nearby wetlands.
Nesting: low in the crotch of a shrub or small tree; thorny hawthorn shrubs are often preferred; bulky cup nest of twigs and grass is lined with animal hair, feathers, plant down and rootlets; female incubates 5–6 pale buff to grayish white eggs, with dark spots concentrated at the larger end, for 15–17 days.
Feeding: swoops down on prey from a perch or attacks in pursuit; takes mostly large insects; regularly eats small birds, rodents and shrews; also eats carrion, small snakes and amphibians.
Voice: infrequent, harsh *shack-shack. Male:* high-pitched, hiccupy *bird-ee bird-ee* in summer.
Similar Species: *Northern Shrike* (p. 210): winter visitor; larger; fine barring on sides and breast; smaller black "mask"; browner immature has "scalier" underparts. *Northern Mockingbird* (p. 260): eye line instead of "mask"; brown eyes; slim bill; longer legs.

NORTHERN SHRIKE

Lanius excubitor

Northern Shrikes retreat from their taiga breeding grounds to appear throughout the northern half of the Great Plains each winter in unpredictable and highly variable numbers. They are typically seen perched like hawks on exposed snags or bushes, from which they survey open and semi-open hunting grounds. Many are also drawn to prey on the patrons of feeding stations. • Although it looks somewhat like a gray robin, the Northern Shrike has a sharp, hawklike bill and specializes in catching and killing small birds and rodents. • Shrikes are the world's only true carnivorous songbirds, and the greatest diversity of shrikes occurs in Africa and Eurasia. • The Northern Shrike's habit of impaling its kills on thorns and barbs has earned it the names "Butcher Bird" and, in Europe, "Nine-Killer." *Lanius* is Latin for "butcher," and *excubitor* is Latin for "watchman" or "sentinel"; "watchful butcher" is indeed an appropriate description of the Northern Shrike's foraging behavior.

ID: pale gray upperparts; black wings and tail; finely barred, pale gray underparts; black "mask" does not extend above hooked bill. *Immature:* light brown upperparts; brown-barred, "scaly" underparts; faint "mask"; plainer wings. *In flight:* white "wrist" patches above and below; white-edged, black tail.
Size: *L* 10 in; *W* 14½ in.
Habitat: open country, including fields, shrubby areas, forest clearings and roadsides.

Nesting: does not nest in the Great Plains.
Feeding: swoops down on prey from a perch or chases prey through the air; regularly eats small birds, shrews, rodents and large insects; may also take snakes and frogs; sometimes impales prey on a thorn or barb for later consumption.
Voice: usually silent; infrequently gives a long, grating laugh: *raa-raa-raa-raa.*
Similar Species: *Loggerhead Shrike* (p. 209): generally absent in winter; unbarred underparts; broader "mask"; immature more resembles adult but with gray barring on underparts. *Northern Mockingbird* (p. 260): slimmer overall; paler wings and tail; eye line instead of "mask"; slim bill; longer legs.

WHITE-EYED VIREO

Vireo griseus

Proclaiming its spring arrival, the male White-eyed Vireo sings *chick-ticha-wheeyou, chick-ticha-wheeyou-chick* among vibrant early spring blossoms in local forests. This species is renowned for its complex vocalizations, and a single bird may have a repertoire of a dozen or more songs. The White-eyed Vireo is also an excellent vocal mimic and may incorporate the calls of other bird species in its own songs! • Like most vireos, the White-eyed Vireo can be a challenge to spot as it sneaks through dense tangles of branches and foliage in search of insects. Even more secretive than the bird itself is the location of its precious nest. Hung between the forking branches of a tree or shrub, the nest of the White-eyed Vireo is intricately woven from grass, twigs, bark, lichen, moss, plant down, leaves and the fibrous paper from wasps' nests.

ID: olive gray upperparts; dark wings and tail; 2 whitish wing bars; white underparts with yellow sides and flanks; yellow "spectacles"; pale eyes. *In flight:* yellowish white wing linings.
Size: *L* 5 in; *W* 7½ in.
Habitat: dense, shrubby undergrowth and thickets in open, swampy, hardwood woodlands; also overgrown fields, young second-growth woodlands, woodland clearings and along woodlot edges.
Nesting: in a hardwood shrub or small tree; cup nest hangs from a horizontal fork; pair incubates 4 lightly speckled, white eggs for 13–15 days; pair feeds the young.
Feeding: gleans insects from branches and foliage during very active foraging; often hovers while gleaning.
Voice: no general call of note. *Male:* loud, snappy, 3–9-note song, usually beginning and ending with *chick*: *chick-ticha-wheeyou, chick-ticha-wheeyou-chick!*
Similar Species: *Yellow-throated Vireo* (p. 213) and *Pine Warbler* (p. 280): yellow breast and throat; grayish wing linings. *Bell's Vireo* (p. 212) and *Blue-headed Vireo* (p. 214): white "spectacles"; dark eyes; duller wing linings.

211

BELL'S VIREO
Vireo bellii

The subtle colors and markings of the Bell's Vireo can easily cause observers to mistakenly identify it as one of a number of similar birds, especially because some of the finer whitish markings around the eyes may be present in some individuals but not in others. Confusion is particularly likely during migration, when the olive-and-yellow midwestern birds can easily cross paths with the gray southwestern ones. • Destruction of streamside habitat and nest parasitism by the Brown-headed Cowbird (facilitated by habitat fragmentation) have caused noticeable declines in Bell's Vireo populations throughout much of its range. • This vireo is named after John Graham Bell (1812–89), a famous New York taxidermist and bird collector who accompanied John James Audubon and John Cassin on various expeditions to the western frontier.

ID: gray or olive upperparts and head; pale underparts, with yellow-washed sides and undertail coverts on midwestern birds; 2 whitish wing bars (upper bar is often faint); "eyebrow," eye ring and lores often appear whitish; bluish black legs and feet. *In flight:* pale gray or grayish yellow wing linings.
Size: *L* 4½–5 in; *W* 7 in.
Habitat: dense riparian shrubs and thorny thickets in the Southwest; brushy fields and second-growth scrub in the Midwest; may also use chaparral, hedgerows, scrub oaks or woodland edges.
Nesting: small hanging cup of woven vegetation is suspended in a horizontal fork of a shrub branch, usually within 5 ft of the ground; mostly the female incubates 3–5 dark-dotted, white eggs for about 14 days.
Feeding: catches insects by hawking, hovering or gleaning from foliage; sometimes eats spiders and a few berries.
Voice: sharp, high-pitched calls. *Male:* song is a rapid, nonmusical series of harsh notes, *chu-che-chu-che-chu-che*, increasing in volume, often with an upward or downward inflection on the last note.
Similar Species: *Warbling Vireo* (p. 215): lankier; no wing bars; finer bill; sings an extended, slurred whistle series. *Philadelphia Vireo* (p. 216): migrant only; longer proportions; no wing bars; more yellow on underparts. *Blue-headed Vireo* (p. 214): more contrasting plumage. *Ruby-crowned Kinglet* (p. 247): bolder wing bars; bold, elongated eye ring; sings 3-part descending phrases.

YELLOW-THROATED VIREO

Vireo flavifrons

Singing tirelessly as he searches his large territory for nest sites, a male Yellow-throat often places a few pieces of nest material in several locations. When a female appears, he dazzles her with his displays and leads her on a tour of potential sites. A devoted parent, the male participates in all aspects of brood-rearing. • The Yellow-throat is North America's most colorful vireo and the only one with a bright yellow throat and breast (*flavifrons* means "yellow front") and a white belly. • The Yellow-throated Vireo forages high above the forest floor, making it difficult to observe. Usually found in mature hardwood woodlands with little or no understory, it particularly likes tall oaks and maples. Once widespread in the eastern U.S., the Yellow-throated Vireo disappeared from towns, suburbs and large cities following heavy spraying of insecticides on shade trees to prevent the spread of Dutch elm disease. It may now be recovering as woodlands mature, but it remains unevenly distributed in the eastern Great Plains.

ID: olive upperparts; dark wings and tail; 2 white wing bars; white belly and under-tail coverts; bright yellow breast, throat, "chin" and "spectacles"; bluish gray legs. *In flight:* gray-and-white wing linings; gray rump.

Size: *L* 5½ in; *W* 9½ in.

Habitat: mature hardwood woodlands with minimal understory.

Nesting: pair builds an intricately woven, hanging cup nest in the fork of a horizontal hardwood tree branch; pair incubates 4 creamy to pinkish eggs, with dark spots toward the larger end, for 14–15 days;

each parent cares for half the fledged young.

Feeding: inspects branches and foliage in the upper canopy, mostly for insects, but also for berries.

Voice: calls include a throaty *heh heh heh*. *Male:* song is a slowly repeated series of hoarse phrases with long pauses in between: *ahweeo, eeoway, away.*

Similar Species: *Pine Warbler* (p. 280): faint, darkish streaking along sides; yellow belly; faint "spectacles"; thinner bill; olive yellow rump. *White-eyed Vireo* (p. 211): white breast, throat and "chin"; more gray on head; white eyes. *Blue-headed Vireo* (p. 214): white breast, throat and "chin"; bluish gray head; white "spectacles."

213

BLUE-HEADED VIREO

Vireo solitarius

From the canopies of shady woodlands, the purposeful, liquid notes of the male Blue-headed Vireo penetrate the dense foliage. Preferring different habitat than many of its relatives, this vireo is the only one to commonly occupy conifer forests. • During courtship, male Blue-headed Vireos fluff out their yellowish flanks and bob ceremoniously to their prospective mates. When mating is complete and the eggs are in the nest, the parents become extremely quiet. Once the young hatch, however, Blue-headed parents will readily scold an intruder long before it gets close to the nest. Even so, Brown-headed Cowbirds manage to find temporarily vacated vireo nests in which to lay their eggs. As human development continues to fragment our forests, cowbirds pose an increasing threat to their Blue-headed hosts. • This vireo's distinctive "spectacles" provide a good field mark. They are among the boldest of the eye rings seen on our songbirds. • Until 1997, the now newly named Blue-headed, Cassin's *(V. cassinii)* and Plumbeous *(V. plumbeus)* vireos were lumped together as "Solitary Vireo"—all three species have been noted on the Great Plains.

ID: olive green upperparts; yellow highlights on dark wings and tail; 2 white wing bars; white underparts; yellow sides and flanks; bluish gray head; white "spectacles"; stout bill; dark legs.

Size: *L* 5–6 in; *W* 9½ in.

Habitat: remote, mixed conifer–hardwood forests; also pure coniferous forests and pine plantations.

Nesting: in a horizontal fork in a coniferous tree or tall shrub; hanging, basketlike cup nest is made of grass, roots, plant down, spider silk and cocoons; pair incubates 3–5 whitish eggs, lightly spotted with black and brown, for 12–14 days.

Feeding: gleans branches for insects; frequently hovers to pluck insects from vegetation.

Voice: *churr* call. *Male:* slow, purposeful, slurred, robinlike notes with moderate pauses in between: *chu-wee, taweeto, toowip, cheerio, teeyay.*

Similar Species: *Plumbeous Vireo* (p. 364) and *Cassin's Vireo:* mostly restricted to southwestern edge of region; gray completely (Plumbeous) or partly (Cassin's) replaces yellows and greens. *White-eyed Vireo* (p. 211): yellow "spectacles"; light-colored eyes. *Yellow-throated Vireo* (p. 213): yellow "spectacles" and throat.

WARBLING VIREO
Vireo gilvus

The charming Warbling Vireo is a common summer resident across most of the Great Plains. By early May, the male's wondrous voice fills many local parks and backyards. Because this vireo often settles close to urban areas, its bubbly, warbling songs will be familiar to most people. • The Warbling Vireo has no splashy field marks and is readily observed only when it moves from one leaf-hidden perch to another. Searching treetops for this generally inconspicuous vireo may literally be a "pain in the neck," but the satisfaction of visually confirming this bird's identity is exceptionally rewarding. • During the breeding season, the hanging nests of vireos are usually much harder to find than the birds themselves. In winter, though, the nests are revealed as they swing precariously from bare hardwood branches.

ID: olive gray upperparts; white to pale gray underparts; greenish flanks; gray crown; white "eyebrow"; faint eye line; bluish gray legs. *In flight:* slightly yellowish white wing linings.
Size: *L* 5–5½ in; *W* 8½ in.

Habitat: open hardwood woodlands; parks and gardens with hardwood trees.
Nesting: in a horizontal fork in a hardwood tree or shrub; hanging, basketlike cup nest is made of grass, roots, plant down, spider silk and a few feathers; pair incubates 4 darkly speckled, white eggs for 12–14 days.

Feeding: gleans foliage for insects; occasionally hovers to glean insects from vegetation.
Voice: call is seldom heard. *Male:* long, musical warble of slurred whistles.
Similar Species: *Philadelphia Vireo* (p. 216): typically yellower breast, sides and flanks; bolder eye line; smaller bill; pauses in song. *Bell's Vireo* (p. 212): wing bars; stouter, pinker bill; stubbier wings. *Red-eyed Vireo* (p. 217): bluish gray crown; more conspicuous "eyebrow"; black eye line; red eyes; pauses in song. *Tennessee Warbler* (p.): migrant only; breeding male has olive green back, bluish gray "cap" and nape, slimmer bill, pinkish black legs and plainer underwings.

215

PHILADELPHIA VIREO

Vireo philadelphicus

Many similar-looking birds sound quite different, but the Philadelphia Vireo and the Red-eyed Vireo sound very similar. Because most forest songbirds are initially identified by voice, the less common Philadelphia Vireo is often overlooked. The two species are easy to tell apart once you locate them with your binoculars, but managing to track down greenish vireos among the rich green foliage where they prefer to forage is never easy. • The Philadelphia Vireo nests in mixed boreal forests, mostly in Canada, where it fills a niche left unoccupied by the strictly hardwood-dwelling Warbling Vireo. • This bird bears the name of the city in which the first scientific specimen of this species was collected. In the early 1800s, Philadelphia was the center of America's budding scientific community, and much of the nation's study of birds and other natural sciences originated in Pennsylvania.

ID: dark olive green upperparts; pale yellow breast, sides and flanks; white belly (underparts may be completely yellow in fall); gray "cap"; full, dark eye line borders bold, white "eyebrow"; pale eyes; robust bill. *In flight:* yellowish white wing linings.
Size: *L* 4½–5 in; *W* 8 in.
Habitat: woodlands with aspen and alder.
Nesting: does not breed in the Great Plains.
Feeding: gleans vegetation for insects; frequently hovers to glean food from foliage.

Voice: no general calls of note. *Male:* song resembles that of the Red-eyed Vireo but is usually slower, slightly higher pitched and not as variable: *Look-up way-up tree-top see-me.*
Similar Species: *Red-eyed Vireo* (p. 217): larger; whitish breast and throat; black-bordered, bluish gray "cap"; red eyes; longer bill. *Warbling Vireo* (p. 215): whitish breast and throat; less prominent eye line; longer bill; longer song. *Bell's Vireo* (p. 212): wing bars; stouter, pinker bill; stubbier wings. *Tennessee Warbler* (p. 269): migrant only; breeding male has whitish breast, bluish gray "cap" and nape, slimmer bill, pinkish black legs and plainer underwings.

RED-EYED VIREO

Vireo olivaceus

The male Red-eyed Vireo is the undisputed champion of vocal endurance in our region. In spring and early summer, he will sing continuously through the day, carrying on long after most songbirds have curtailed their courtship melodies. One particularly vigorous Red-eye male was documented delivering a record 22,000-plus songs in one day! Beginning birders are often delighted to discover this nifty bird hiding behind a familiar-sounding song that resembles an American Robin's. • A distinctive hunched-over stance marks the Red-eyed Vireo when it perches or hops along branches, and it moves with its body diagonal to the direction of travel. • Why this vireo has red eyes remains the subject of scientific debate. Very unusual among songbirds, red eyes tend to be more prevalent in nonpasserines, such as accipiters, grebes and some herons. • The Red-eyed Vireo is among the most common and widespread vireos, and its ability to adapt has enabled it to become part of many of our communities.

ID: olive green upperparts; white to pale gray underparts (possible yellow wash on sides, flanks and undertail coverts, especially in fall); black-bordered, bluish gray "cap"; white "eyebrow"; dark eye line; olive "cheek"; red eyes (seen at close range); bluish gray legs and feet. *In flight:* dull yellowish white wing linings.

Size: *L* 6 in; *W* 10 in.

Habitat: hardwood woodlands with a shrubby understory.

Nesting: in a horizontal fork in a hardwood tree or shrub; hanging, basketlike cup nest is made of grass, roots, spider silk and cocoons; female incubates 4 white eggs, darkly spotted at the larger end, for 11–14 days.

Feeding: gleans foliage for insects, especially caterpillars; often hovers; also eats berries.

Voice: short, scolding *neeah* call. *Male:* song is a continuous, variable, robinlike run of quick, short phrases separated by distinct pauses: *Look-up, way-up, tree-top, see-me, here-I-am!*

Similar Species: *Philadelphia Vireo* (p. 216): smaller; yellow breast; unbordered "cap"; shorter bill; slightly higher pitched song. *Warbling Vireo* (p. 215): unbordered "cap"; less prominent eye line; shorter bill. *Tennessee Warbler* (p. 269): migrant only; breeding male has bluish gray "cap" and nape, slimmer bill, pinkish black legs and plainer underwings.

BLUE JAY

Cyanocitta cristata

Beautiful, resourceful and vocally diverse, the Blue Jay embodies all the admirable traits and aggressive qualities of the corvid family, which also includes magpies, crows and ravens. Whether as a solo bird or gathered in a mob, the Blue Jay will rarely hesitate to drive away smaller birds, squirrels or even cats when threatened. In addition, it seems that no predator, not even the Great Horned Owl, is too formidable for this bird to harass. The Blue Jay also occasionally raids nests and bullies other feeder occupants. • The large trees and bushy ornamental shrubs of our suburban neighborhoods and rural communities provide perfect habitat for the adaptable Blue Jay. Common wherever there are fruit-bearing plants or backyard feeding stations maintained with a generous supply of sunflower seeds and peanuts, this jay is one of the most recognizable songbirds. Because it often takes food to store in caches strategically placed around the neighborhood, it can appear a bit "piggish" at the feeder.

ID: blue upperparts; white underparts; white bar and flecking on wings; blue crest; black "necklace" and eye line; black bill; blue tail with dark bars. *In flight:* dark gray underwing with white arc; white trailing edge on wing near body; white corners on tail.

Size: *L* 11–12½ in; *W* 16 in.

Habitat: mixed hardwood forests, agricultural areas, scrubby fields and townsites.

Nesting: in the crotch of a tree or tall shrub; pair builds a bulky stick nest; pair incubates 4–5 greenish, buff or pale blue eggs, spotted with gray and brown, for 16–18 days.

Feeding: forages on the ground and among vegetation for nuts, berries, eggs, nestlings and birdseed; also eats insects and carrion.

Voice: noisy, screaming *jay-jay-jay;* nasal *queedle queedle queedle-queedle* sounds a little like a muted trumpet; often imitates sounds.

Similar Species: difficult to misidentify. *Most other jays:* no crest. *Steller's Jay:* rare transient; blue overall with crested, black head.

WESTERN SCRUB-JAY

Aphelocoma californica

In the southwestern part of our region, the slender Western Scrub-Jay is often seen foraging among leaf litter or surveying its tree-dotted habitat from a perch atop a tall shrub. Although this jay eats mostly insects in summer, acorns are a staple of its winter diet. Each fall, it harvests fallen acorns and stores them individually in holes dug in the ground with its strong bill. This intelligent bird often uses a rock or concrete slab as an "anvil" to assist in cracking open the shielding coat. At the end of winter, many uneaten acorns germinate, thereby regenerating the oak stand.
• The Western Scrub-Jay was previously considered to be the same species as the Florida Scrub-Jay (*A. coerulescens*) and the Island Scrub-Jay (*A. insularis*), which inhabits California's Santa Cruz Island.

ID: slim body; sky blue upperparts with gray back; light gray underparts; gray-streaked, white throat bordered by bluish "necklace"; faint white "eyebrow"; dark gray "cheek"; heavy, dark bill; long, all-blue tail. *In flight:* blue-tinged, gray underwing; round-ended tail is gray below and grayish blue above.
Size: *L* 11½ in; *W* 15–16 in.
Habitat: chaparral and dry, brushy open areas of oak and pinyon pine–juniper woodlands, mixed oak–conifer forests,

broken mixed hardwood–conifer woodlands and riparian woodlands; also uses suburban parks and gardens, urban shrubbery and roadside tree plantations to 8000 ft (may wander to 11,000 ft).
Nesting: in a small conifer or small shrub; pair builds a bulky stick nest, usually with an inner cup lined with moss, grass and fur; female incubates 3–6 dark-spotted, pale green eggs for 15–17 days.
Feeding: forages on the ground for insects and small vertebrates; also eats other birds' eggs and nestlings, as well as acorns, pinyon nuts and many fruits.
Voice: harsh, repetitive *ike-ike-ike* perch call; rough, frequently repeated *quesh, quesh, quesh* in flight.
Similar Species: *Pinyon Jay* (p. 220): grayish blue overall; shorter tail. *Blue Jay* (p. 218): white wing markings; black "necklace"; crested head; whitish "cheeks"; black-barred tail. *Steller's Jay:* rare transient; blue overall with crested, black head.

PINYON JAY
Gymnorhinus cyanocephalus

Loud and highly gregarious, Pinyon Jays behave much like American Crows. During the nonbreeding season, they forage in enormous flocks that consist of many smaller family groups. While foraging, Pinyon Jays adhere to an orderly social structure, with some birds taking turns acting as the lookout as the others concentrate on feeding. • Nesting takes place in late winter, with loose colonies of up to 150 birds. Pinyon pines and junipers provide preferred nest sites, and a single tree may support up to three nests. Cached seeds and nuts help to supplement freshly harvested foods when it comes time to feed the growing young. Pinyon Jays might nest again in late summer if pinyon pine seed crops are sufficient. When the pinyon crop fails, these jays become nomadic and disperse widely in search of other food.

W 19 in.

ID: generally grayish blue overall; blue streaks on whitish throat; bright blue head; long, dark, pointed bill; all-blue tail. *In flight:* wing feathers have more grayish tips.
Size: *L* 9–11½ in;

Habitat: *Breeding:* pinyon pine–juniper forest and woodlands at elevations of 4000–7500 ft; ranges among stands of ponderosa pine. *Foraging:* sagebrush flats, montane chaparral, pine forests and tall sagebrush.
Nesting: loosely colonial; in pinyon pines, junipers, shrubs and occasionally oaks; large, bulky nest consists of sticks, twigs and fibers; female incubates 4–5 dark-

speckled, grayish to greenish eggs for up to 17 days.
Feeding: searches the ground and vegetation for pinyon nuts, seeds and insects; also eats berries and other birds' eggs and nestlings.
Voice: low *krawk-krawk-krawk* warning call; flight call is a high, piercing *mew* or laughing *hah-hah*.
Similar Species: *Western Scrub-Jay* (p. 219): sky blue upperparts with gray back; light gray underparts; dark gray "cheek"; longer tail. *Blue Jay* (p. 218): white wing markings; black "necklace"; crested head; whitish "cheeks"; black-barred tail. *Steller's Jay:* rare transient; blue overall with crested, black head. *Mountain Bluebird* (p. 251): smaller; male has smaller bill, pointier wings, forked tail and different behavior.

BLACK-BILLED MAGPIE
Pica hudsonica

The saying "familiarity breeds contempt" is well illustrated by the Black-billed Magpie, which is resident throughout the northwestern two-thirds of the Great Plains but is not commonly found elsewhere in the region. Truly among North America's most beautiful birds, this magpie is too often disliked because of its raucous and aggressive demeanor, a trait for which many other members of the crow family are also known. Luckily for today's birders, this hardy species managed to survive persecution by farmers and ranchers during the early 1900s. • The Black-billed Magpie is one of the most exceptional architects among our birds. Its elaborate domed nest might be found in a spruce or hardwood or even on an iron bridge. Constructed of sticks and held together with mud, the domed compartment conceals and protects the eggs and young from harsh weather and predators. The nest is so well constructed that an abandoned site can remain intact for years, often serving as a nest site for nonbuilders such as owls.

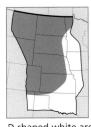

ID: white-edged, black back; blue-and-black wings; white belly; black undertail coverts, breast, neck and head; black eyes and bill; black legs and feet; long, blue-and-black tail. *In flight:* rounded wings with large, D-shaped white areas above and below.
Size: *L* 18–22 in; *W* 24–26 in.
Habitat: open forests, agricultural areas, riparian thickets, townsites and campgrounds.

Nesting: in a tree or tall shrub; domed stick-and-twig nest is often held together with mud; female incubates 5–8 brown-spotted, dull greenish eggs for up to 24 days; pair feeds the young.
Feeding: forages on the ground for insects, carrion and garbage; picks insects and ticks off large ungulates; fruits, nuts and seeds often feature in the winter diet.
Voice: loud, nasal, frequently repeated *ueh-ueh-ueh;* also gives many other vocalizations.
Similar Species: none.

AMERICAN CROW

Corvus brachyrhynchos

Despite considerable human effort, over many generations, to reduce its numbers, the wary and intelligent American Crow has flourished. This bird is an ecological generalist, and much of its strength lies in its ability to adapt to a variety of habitats. • American Crows are common throughout much of the Great Plains. In fall, they group together in flocks numbering in the hundreds or thousands. Such aggregations of crows were once commonly known as "murders." In some places, many thousands of these birds may roost together on any given winter night. • Crows are impressive mimics, able to whine like a dog, squawk like a hen, cry like a child and laugh like an adult. Some crows in captivity are able to repeat simple spoken words. • The American Crow's cumbersome-sounding scientific name, *Corvus brachyrhynchos,* is Latin for "raven with the small nose."

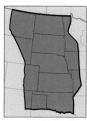

ID: black overall; slim, sleek head and throat; robust, black bill; black legs and feet. *In flight:* round-ended tail; never soars.
Size: *L* 17–21 in; *W* 3 ft.
Habitat: urban areas, agricultural fields and other open areas with scattered woodlands; also among clearings, marshes, lakes and rivers in densely forested areas.
Nesting: in a tree or on a utility pole; large stick-and-branch nest is lined with fur and soft plant materials; female incubates

4–6 grayish green to bluish green eggs, blotched with brown and gray, for about 18 days.
Feeding: very opportunistic; feeds on carrion, small vertebrates, other birds' eggs and nestlings, berries, seeds, invertebrates and human food waste; also visits bird feeders.
Voice: distinctive, far-carrying, repetitive *caw-caw-caw.*
Similar Species: *Fish Crow* (p. 364): limited range; slightly smaller and browner; simpler calls. *Chihuahuan Raven* (p. 223) and *Common Raven* (p. 364): limited ranges; larger; shaggy throats; heavier bills; wedge-shaped tails; often soar.

CHIHUAHUAN RAVEN

Corvus cryptoleucus

Unless it is a blustery day, you may not see the Chihuahuan Raven's hidden white neck feathers, the main characteristic distinguishing it and the slightly larger Common Raven. The easiest way to tell the two apart is to examine your surroundings and open your ears. The Chihuahuan Raven resides in habitat the Common Raven usually snubs—the flat, scrubby grasslands of the Texas and Oklahoma panhandles, northeastern New Mexico, southeastern Colorado, western Kansas and southwestern Nebraska. Though the two species have similar vocalizations, the calls of the Chihuahuan Raven tend to be higher pitched.

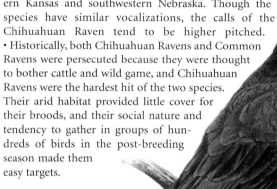

• Historically, both Chihuahuan Ravens and Common Ravens were persecuted because they were thought to bother cattle and wild game, and Chihuahuan Ravens were the hardest hit of the two species. Their arid habitat provided little cover for their broods, and their social nature and tendency to gather in groups of hundreds of birds in the post-breeding season made them easy targets.

ID: black overall; hidden, white neck feathers; heavy, black bill; black legs and feet. *In flight:* somewhat wedge-shaped tail. **Size:** *L* 19–20 in; *W* 3½ ft. **Habitat:** brushy areas, arid grasslands, yuccas and garbage dumps.
Nesting: in a tree or on a utility pole or a yucca; platform of thorns and sticks is lined with grass, bark and hair; pair incubates

5–6 dull greenish, brown-splotched eggs for 18–21 days.
Feeding: eats carrion, other birds' eggs, insects, grains, berries, cactus fruit and garbage.
Voice: flat, croaking *craaaaag, craaaag* call is typical.
Similar Species: *Common Raven* (p. 364): larger; much heavier; shaggier throat area; longer bill; very wide vocal repertoire. *American Crow* (p. 222): widespread; smaller; sleek head and throat; smaller bill; shorter, rounder wings; rounded tail; higher-pitched calls.

HORNED LARK

Eremophila alpestris

Flying and gliding in circles as high up as 800 feet, male Horned Larks issue their sweet, tinkling songs before closing their wings and plummeting in dramatic, high-speed dives that they abort at the last second to avoid hitting the ground. The songs of these birds as they fly over pastures and fields in their elaborate song-flight courtship displays are a sure sign that another spring has arrived. • Horned Larks are commonly found along the shoulders of gravel roads, where they search for seeds. These open-country inhabitants are most common in spring and fall migration and in early winter as they congregate in flocks on farm fields, beaches and airfields, sometimes in the company of longspurs and Snow Buntings. The birds are easy to see but often tough to identify because they fly off into the adjacent fields at the approach of vehicles.

ID: dull brown upperparts; white underparts; brownish white sides. *Male:* black breast band; whitish to yellowish throat; small, black "horns" (rarely raised); light yellow to white face; broad, black stroke under eye extends from bill to "cheek." *Female:* duller plumage overall, with dull brown instead of black; no "horns." *In flight:* underwing shows yellowish white lining and brownish flight feathers; dark tail with white outer feathers.
Size: *L* 7 in; *W* 12 in.
Habitat: *Breeding:* open areas, including pastures, croplands, sparsely vegetated fields, weedy meadows and airfields. *In migration* and *winter:* croplands, fields and roadside ditches.
Nesting: female chooses a site on the ground; in a shallow scrape lined with grass, plant fibers and roots; female incubates 3–4 pale gray to greenish white eggs, blotched and spotted with brown, for 10–12 days; young are fed insects.
Feeding: gleans the ground for seeds; also takes insects.
Voice: call is a tinkling *tsee-titi* or *zoot*. *Male:* flight song is a long series of tinkling, twittered whistles.
Similar Species: *Sparrows* (pp. 300–25), *Lapland Longspur* (p. 327) and *American Pipit* (p. 265): most have plainer faces and stouter bills; no "horns" or solid black breast band.

PURPLE MARTIN

Progne subis

Purple Martins once nested in natural tree hollows and cliff crevices, but with today's modern martin "condo" complexes, these birds have all but abandoned natural nest sites. To successfully attract these large swallows to your backyard, make the complex with right size of cavity openings for Purple Martins and place the martin condo high on a pole in a large, open area, preferably near water. Remove any aggressive House Sparrows and European Starlings that drive away the rightful owners and move in. The condo must be cleaned out and closed up each winter. If all goes well, a Purple Martin colony will return to your martin complex each spring. The result will be an endlessly entertaining summer spectacle as the martin adults spiral around the house in pursuit of flying insects, and the young birds perch clumsily at the opening of their apartment cavity. • The scientific name *Progne* refers to Procne, the daughter of the king of Athens, who, according to Greek mythology, was transformed into a swallow.

ID: glossy, very dark blue and blackish brown upperparts; small bill. *Male:* dark blue underparts. *Female:* sooty gray underparts with indistinct streaking and barring. *In flight:* pointed wings; slightly forked tail.

Size: *L* 7–8 in; *W* 18 in.

Habitat: semi-open areas, often near water.

Nesting: communal; usually in a human-made, apartment-style birdhouse; also in a hollowed-out gourd; rarely in a tree cavity or cliff crevice; nest materials include feathers, grass, mud and vegetation; female incubates 4–5 white eggs for 15–18 days.

Feeding: mostly while in flight; usually eats flies, ants, bugs, dragonflies and mosquitoes; may also walk on the ground, taking insects and rarely berries.

Voice: rich, fluty, robinlike *pew-pew,* often heard in flight.

Similar Species: *European Starling* (p. 264): breeding bird has green-and-purple gloss, longer, yellow bill and slightly rounded tail tip. *Barn Swallow* (p. 231): rufous brown throat and forehead; rusty to buffy underparts; deeply forked tail. *Tree Swallow* (p. 226): greenish blue and brown upperparts; whitish underparts.

TREE SWALLOW

Tachycineta bicolor

Tree Swallows favor natural tree hollows and woodpecker cavities in standing dead trees for their nests. Increasingly, landowners, park managers and forestry company employees are realizing the value of dead trees as homes for wildlife and are choosing to leave them standing. Where cavities are scarce, Tree Swallows will use nest boxes. When conditions are favorable, these busy birds are known to return to their young 10 to 20 times per hour, providing observers with numerous opportunities to watch and photograph the birds in action at their fence-post nest boxes. • In bright spring sunshine, the iridescent back of the Tree Swallow appears dark blue, but prior to fall migration it appears green. Unlike other North American swallows, a female Tree Swallow does not acquire her full adult plumage until her second or third year. • The scientific name *bicolor*, Latin for "two colors," refers to the bird's contrasting dark upperparts and white underparts.

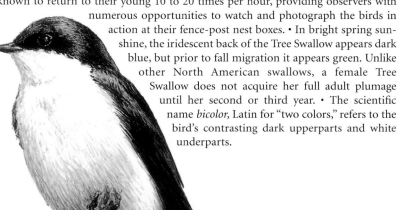

ID: iridescent, dark blue or green upperparts and head; white underparts and lower face; small, dark bill. *Female:* duller upperparts and head can appear brown. *Immature:* brown upperparts; white underpats. *In flight:* long, pointed wings; dark rump; shallowly forked tail.
Size: *L* 5½ in; *W* 14½ in.
Habitat: open areas, such as beaver ponds, marshes, lakeshores, field fence lines, townsites and open woodlands.

Nesting: in a tree cavity or nest box lined with weeds, grass and feathers; female incubates 4–6 white eggs for up to 19 days.
Feeding: catches airborne flies, midges, mosquitoes, beetles and ants on the wing; also takes stoneflies, mayflies and caddisflies over water; sometimes eats berries and seeds.
Voice: metallic, buzzy *klweet* alarm call. *Male:* song is a liquid, chattering twitter.
Similar Species: *Violet-green Swallow* (p. 227): bluish green upperparts with dark violet to brown areas; white area extends above eye; female often has smudgy brown face; white-sided rump. *Purple Martin* (p. 225): larger; female has sooty gray underparts. *Barn Swallow* (p. 231): rufous brown throat and forehead; deeply forked tail. *Eastern Kingbird* (p. 207): larger; dark gray to blackish upperparts; longer bill; longer, rounded tail.

VIOLET-GREEN SWALLOW

Tachycineta thalassina

The Violet-green Swallow can routinely be seen darting above cliffs and rivers in the leisurely pursuit of flying insect prey. Considered the western equivalent of the Tree Swallow, the Violet-green demonstrates a greater aptitude for taking advantage of western montane habitats, and it is found around cliffs and treeless open areas far more than its cousin. • At first sight, Violet-greens look an awful lot like Tree Swallows, which is to be expected, given their close relationship. The extent of the white areas is often the best clue to a bird's identity. • Swallows occasionally eat mineral-rich soil, eggshells and exposed shellfish fragments, possibly to recoup the minerals lost during egg laying. • Swallows are swift and graceful flyers, routinely traveling at speeds of 30 miles per hour. • The scientific name *thalassina* is Latin for "sea green," a tribute to this bird's distinguishing body color.

ID: iridescent, bluish green upperparts with dark violet to brown areas; white underparts; small, dark bill. *Male:* white area extends behind and above eye. *Female:* duller and more bronze and brown than male; face is often smudgy brown with short, white "eyebrow." *In flight:* long, pointed wings; white patches alongside rump; shallowly forked tail.

Size: *L* 5–5½ in; *W* 13½ in.

Habitat: open environments, including beaver ponds, marshes, townsites and mixed woodlands.

Nesting: in a tree cavity, rock crevice or nest box; nest consists of weeds, grass and feathers; female incubates 4–6 white eggs for up to 15 days.

Feeding: catches flying insects such as leafhoppers, leafbugs, flies, ants and wasps; drinks on the wing.

Voice: buzzy, trilling *tweet tweet;* harsh *chip-chip.*

Similar Species: *Tree Swallow* (p. 226): heavier; white ends lower on face; dark rump. *Bank Swallow* (p. 229): brown upperparts and breast band. *Northern Rough-winged Swallow* (p. 228): brown upperparts; light brown breast and head. *Purple Martin* (p. 225): larger; female has sooty gray underparts. *Barn Swallow* (p. 231): rufous brown throat and forehead; deeply forked tail. *Eastern Kingbird* (p. 207): larger; dark gray to blackish upperparts; longer bill; longer, rounded tail.

NORTHERN ROUGH-WINGED SWALLOW

Stelgidopteryx serripennis

Enjoying its own private piece of waterfront, the inconspicuous Northern Rough-winged Swallow typically nests in sandy banks along rivers and streams. This swallow is usually seen in single pairs, but it doesn't mind joining a crowd, often gulping down insects in the company of other swallow species—it is most likely to be seen feeding over water, picking off insects on or near the water's surface. In the wheeling flocks of feeding birds, the Northern Rough-winged Swallow is often completely overlooked among its similar-looking cousins. Once in a while, a pair may nest among a large colony of Bank Swallows. • Unlike other swallows, male Northern Rough-wings have curved barbs along the outer edge of their primary wing feathers. The resulting sawtooth edge may serve to produce sound during courtship displays. The ornithologist who initially named this bird must have been very impressed with its wings: *Stelgidopteryx* means "scraper wing" and *serripennis* means "saw feather."

ID: brown upperparts; light brownish gray underparts; light brown breast and head; pale throat; small, dark bill. *In flight:* long, pointed wings; dark rump; squarish tail tip.
Size: *L* 5½ in; *W* 14 in.

Habitat: open and semi-open areas, including fields and open woodlands, usually near water; also gravel pits.

Nesting: usually solitary, occasionally in small colonies; pair excavates a long burrow in a steep earth bank and lines the end with leaves and dry grass; sometimes reuses a kingfisher or rodent burrow or occupies a crevice; mostly the female incubates 4–8 white eggs for 12–16 days.

Feeding: catches flying insects on the wing; occasionally eats insects from the ground; drinks while flying.

Voice: generally quiet; occasionally gives a quick, short, squeaky *brrrtt.*

Similar Species: *Bank Swallow* (p. 229): whiter underparts and lower face; dark brown breast band. *Tree Swallow* (p. 226): heavier; dark, iridescent bluish to greenish and brown upperparts; distinctly white underparts. *Violet-green Swallow* (p. 227): bluish green upperparts with dark violet to brown areas; distinctly white underparts; white-sided rump. *Cliff Swallow* (p. 230): chunkier; brown-and-blue upperparts; rusty buff forehead and nape; rusty chestnut lower face.

BANK SWALLOW

Riparia riparia

A colony of Bank Swallows can be a constant flurry of activity as eager parents pop in and out of their earthen burrows with mouthfuls of insects for their insatiable young. Somehow, the parents can quickly distinguish their own nestlings' demanding squeaks among the thousands of cries for food in the colony's bankside chambers. All this activity tends to attract attention, but few predators are able to catch these swift and agile birds. • Bank Swallows usually excavate their own nest burrows, first using their small bills and later digging with their feet. Most nestlings are safe from predators within their nest chamber, which is typically at the end of a burrow 2 to 3 feet in length. • In medieval Europe, when swallows vanished each fall, they were believed to have gone into the mud at the bottom of swamps. In those days, it was beyond imagination that these birds might fly south. • *Riparia* is from the Latin for "riverbank," which is a common nest site for this bird.

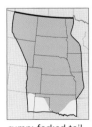

ID: brown upperparts; whitish underparts; brown breast band and vertical stripe; white throat; grayish brown crown; dark ear patch; small, dark bill; short legs; small feet. *In flight:* long, pointed wings; light brown rump; forked tail.

Size: *L* 5½ in; *W* 13 in.

Habitat: steep banks, lakeshore bluffs and gravel pits.

Nesting: colonial; pair excavates or reuses a long burrow in a steep earthen bank and lines the end with grass, rootlets, weeds, straw and feathers; pair incubates 4–5 white eggs for 14–16 days.

Feeding: catches flying insects; drinks on the wing.

Voice: twittering chatter: *speed-zeet speed-zeet.*

Similar Species: *Northern Rough-winged Swallow* (p. 228): light brown breast and head; square-ended tail. *Tree Swallow* (p. 226) and *Violet-green Swallow* (p. 227): bluish or greenish and brown upperparts; all-white breast. *Cliff Swallow* (p. 230): chunkier; brown-and-blue upperparts; rusty buff forehead and nape; rusty chestnut lower face.

CLIFF SWALLOW
Petrochelidon pyrrhonota

If the Cliff Swallow were to be renamed today, it would probably be called "Bridge Swallow" because so many of eastern North America's river bridges have a colony living under them. If you stop to inspect the underside of a bridge, you may see hundreds of gourd-shaped mud nests stuck to the pillars and structural beams. Clouds of Cliff Swallows will often swirl up along either side of the roadway, dazzling passersby with their acrobatics and impressive numbers. • Master mud masons, Cliff Swallows roll mud into balls with their bills and press the pellets together to form their characteristic nests. Brooding parents peer out of the circular

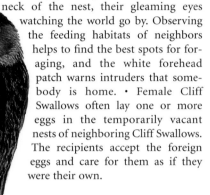

neck of the nest, their gleaming eyes watching the world go by. Observing the feeding habitats of neighbors helps to find the best spots for foraging, and the white forehead patch warns intruders that somebody is home. • Female Cliff Swallows often lay one or more eggs in the temporarily vacant nests of neighboring Cliff Swallows. The recipients accept the foreign eggs and care for them as if they were their own.

ID: dark bluish gray back with 2 faint, whitish stripes; dark brown wings and tail; brown-spotted, white undertail coverts; white belly; buffy breast and "collar"; dark bluish gray crown; buffy forehead; rusty chestnut "cheek" and throat; dark bill. *In flight:* pale brown underwings; orangy buff rump; squarish tail tip.
Size: *L* 5½ in; *W* 13½ in.

Habitat: steep banks, cliffs, bridges and buildings, often near watercourses.
Nesting: colonial; under a bridge or on a cliff or building, often under the eaves of a barn; pair builds a gourd-shaped mud nest with a small opening near the bottom; pair incubates 4–5 brown-spotted, white to pinkish eggs for 14–16 days.
Feeding: forages over water, fields and marshes; catches flying insects and drinks on the wing; occasionally eats berries.
Voice: twittering, chattering *churrr-churrr; nyew* alarm call.
Similar Species: *Barn Swallow* (p. 231): bluish black extends to wings; rust- to buff-colored underparts; rufous brown throat and forehead; dark rump; deeply forked tail. *Other swallows* (pp. 225–29): different forehead and rump colors.

BARN SWALLOW

Hirundo rustica

Barn Swallows do not form impressive colonies, but their choice of human-made structures as nest sites makes them very familiar birds. Although these swallows once nested on cliffs and in cave entrances, their cup-shaped mud nests are now found under house eaves, in barns and boathouses, under bridges or on any other structure that provides shelter.
• Unfortunately, not everyone appreciates nesting Barn Swallows—the young can be very messy—and people often scrape barn swallow nests off buildings just as the nesting season begins. However, these graceful birds are natural pest controllers, and their close association with urban areas and tolerance for human activity affords us the wondrous opportunity to observe and study the normally secretive reproductive cycle of birds. • *Hirundo* is Latin for "swallow," and *rustica* refers to this bird's preference for rural habitats.

ID: bluish black upperparts; rust- to buff-colored underparts; rufous brown throat and forehead; small, dark bill. *In flight:* long, pointed wings; buffy to rusty underwing with broad, bluish black trailing edge; long, deeply forked tail.
Size: *L* 7 in; *W* 15 in.
Habitat: open rural and urban areas with structures suitable for nesting located near water.
Nesting: singly or in small, loose colonies; on a vertical or horizontal building structure under a suitable overhang, on a bridge or in a culvert; half or full cup nest consists of mud and grass or straw; pair incubates 4–7 white eggs, spotted with brown, for 13–17 days.
Feeding: catches flying insects on the wing.
Voice: continuous, twittering chatter: *zip-zip-zip*; also *kvick-kvick*.
Similar Species: *Cliff Swallow* (p. 230): chunkier; brown wings; pale underparts; buffy breast, "collar" and forehead; orangy buff rump; squarish tail tip. *Purple Martin* (p. 225): communal nester; larger; underparts are dark blue (male) or sooty gray (female); shallowly forked tail. *Tree Swallow* (p. 226) and *Violet-green Swallow* (p. 227): iridescent, bluish or greenish and brown upperparts; all-white underparts; shorter, shallowly forked tail.

CAROLINA CHICKADEE
Poecile carolinensis

Visitors to the southeastern part of our region may be forgiven for mistaking this garden and woodland chickadee for its more widespread cousin, the Black-capped Chickadee. The Carolina Chickadee replaces the Black-cap in this area, overlapping only in some southern Kansas counties. Unlike the Black-capped Chickadee, which roves all over the Great Plains in search of food, the Carolina Chickadee rarely leaves its breeding territory, but a few birds will join marauding bands of chickadees, nuthatches and kinglets in fall and winter. In areas of overlap, both species interchange songs, which may lead to hybridization, although most birds choose their own kind. • Carolina Chickadees are particularly partial to nest boxes, whereas Black-capped Chickadees prefer to nest in natural cavities, if they are available.

ID: gray upperparts; white underparts; buffy sides and flanks; black "cap" and "bib"; white "cheek," often grayish toward rear; small, dark bill; dark legs. *In flight:* rounded wings; pale buff underwings with grayish flight feathers; round-tipped tail.
Size: *L* 4½–5 in; *W* 7½ in.
Habitat: hardwood and mixed woods, riparian woodlands, groves and isolated shade trees.
Nesting: pair excavates a cavity in rotting wood, enlarges the interior of a natural tree cavity or uses a nest box or a woodpecker cavity; cavity is lined with soft plant material and animal hair; probably just the

female incubates the 5–8 chestnut-speckled, white eggs; pair raises the young.
Feeding: gleans a variety of insects, seeds and berries from vegetation; sometimes hawks for insects, hangs upside down on branches to glean items and gleans while hovering; visits feeders for seeds and suet.
Voice: call is a faster, higher version of the Black-capped Chickadee's *chick-a-dee-dee-dee. Male:* clear, 4-note whistled song: *fee-bee fee-bay.*
Similar Species: *Black-capped Chickadee* (p. 233): almost identical; color is often more vibrant on fresh plumage; lower edge of black "bib" is not as defined; folded wing shows whiter feather edges.
Mountain Chickadee: limited to far west of region; grayer sides; prominent, white "eyebrow." *Blackpoll Warbler* (p. 284): breeding male has 2 white wing bars, dark-streaked underparts; no buff on sides; longer, paler bill; pale orange legs.

BLACK-CAPPED CHICKADEE

Poecile atricapillus

Flocks of energetic Black-capped Chickadees can be seen year-round as they flit from tree to tree, scouring branches and shriveled leaves for insects, and sometimes hanging upside down to catch the fleeing bugs. These spunky birds remind us that winter can never keep a good bird down, even as most species appear to retreat into a slower mode of living or escape to warmer climes. As if inspired, other residents seem to fall into step with the lively, active chickadees, and in spring and fall, migrants appear to rely on the local knowledge of Black-caps for finding the best foraging areas. • Most songbirds, including the Black-capped Chickadee, have both songs and calls. This chickadee's *swee-tee* song is heard primarily during spring courtship, and its *chick-a-dee-dee-dee* call keeps flocks together and maintains contact among flock members year-round. • The scientific name *atricapillus* is Latin for "black crown."

ID: gray upperparts with whitish edging on wing feathers; white underparts; light buff sides and flanks; black "cap" and "bib"; white "cheek"; small, dark bill; dark legs. *In flight:* rounded wings; dingy buff underwings with grayish flight feathers; round-tipped tail.
Size: *L* 5–6 in; *W* 8 in.
Habitat: hardwood and mixed forests and woodlands, riparian woodlands, wooded urban parks and backyards with bird feeders.
Nesting: pair excavates a cavity in rotting wood, enlarges the interior of a natural tree cavity or uses a nest box or a woodpecker cavity; cavity is lined with fur,

feathers, moss, grass and cocoons; female incubates 6–8 white eggs with fine, reddish brown dots for 12–13 days.
Feeding: gleans vegetation, branches and the ground for small insects and spiders; visits backyard feeders; also eats conifer seeds and invertebrate eggs.
Voice: chipper, whistled *chick-a-dee-dee-dee* call; song is a slow, whistled *swee-tee* or *fee-bee*.
Similar Species: *Carolina Chickadee* (p. 232): limited range; almost identical and sometimes hybridizes; less conspicuous wing-feather edges; neater edge to black "bib"; higher-pitched call. *Mountain Chickadee:* limited to far west of region; grayer sides; prominent, white "eyebrow." *Blackpoll Warbler* (p. 284): 2 white wing bars; dark-streaked underparts; no buff on sides; longer, paler bill; pale orange legs.

233

TUFTED TITMOUSE

Baeolophus bicolor

The amusing feeding antics of the Tufted Titmouse and its insatiable appetite keep curious observers entertained at bird feeders. Grasping an acorn or sunflower seed with its tiny feet, this dexterous bird strikes its dainty bill repeatedly against the hard outer coating, exposing the inner core. • A breeding pair of Tufted Titmice will maintain their bond throughout the year, even when joining small, multispecies flocks for the coldest months of winter. The titmouse family bond is so strong that the young from one breeding season will often stay with their parents long enough to help them with nesting and feeding duties the following year. • If you are fortunate enough to have titmice living in your area, you might be able to attract nesting pairs by setting out the hair that has accumulated in your hairbrush. There is a good chance that these curious birds will gladly incorporate your offering into the construction of their nest, allowing you the pleasure of knowing you are helping to keep titmice eggs and young as snug as can be.

ID: gray upperparts; white underparts; pinkish buff flanks; gray crest; black forehead; white oval around dark eye; small, dark bill. *In flight:* short, rounded wings with white linings and brownish gray flight feathers.

Size: *L* 6–6½ in; *W* 10 in.

Habitat: hardwood woodlands, groves and suburban parks with large, mature trees.

Nesting: in a natural cavity or woodpecker cavity lined with soft vegetation and animal hair; female incubates 5–6 brown- or purple-speckled, white eggs for 12–14 days; pair and occasionally a "helper" raise the young; male may feed the female from courtship until hatching time.

Feeding: forages on the ground and in trees, often hanging upside down like a chickadee; eats insects, supplemented with seeds, nuts and fruits; takes seeds and suet from feeders.

Voice: noisy, scolding, chickadee-like call. *Male:* song is a whistled *peter peter* or *peter peter peter.*

Similar Species: *Black-crested Titmouse* (p. 365): restricted to far south; black forecrest. *Juniper Titmouse* (p. 364): restricted to the Southwest; smaller; brownish gray all over.

RED-BREASTED NUTHATCH

Sitta canadensis

Like a rusty rocket, the Red-breasted Nuthatch streaks toward a neighborhood bird feeder from the cover of a conifer. Ejecting empty shells left behind by other birds, it selects its own meal and speeds off, never lingering longer than it takes to pick up a seed. • Red-breasted Nuthatches frequently join in on bird waves—groups of warblers, chickadees, kinglets, titmice and small woodpeckers that often forage together through woodlands in migration and winter. Nuthatches stand out because of their unusual body form and their headfirst foraging down tree trunks. Their loud, nasal *eenk eenk eenk* calls, which are frequently heard in spring, are also distinctive. • This bird smears the entrance of its nest cavity with pitch from pine or spruce trees, possibly to inhibit ants and other animals from entering. Because they can transmit fungal infections or parasitize nestlings, invertebrates can be the most serious threat to nesting success. • *Sitta* means "nuthatch" in Greek, and *canadensis* refers to this bird's partially Canadian distribution.

ID: grayish blue upperparts; rusty underparts; white "cheek"; white "eyebrow"; black eye line; straight bill; short legs. *Male:* deeper rust on breast; black crown. *Female:* lighter wash on breast; dark gray crown. *In flight:* short, rounded wings with light rusty linings and gray flight feathers; pale diagonal stripes on short, rounded tail.
Size: *L* 4½ in; *W* 8½ in.
Habitat: *Breeding:* spruce–fir and pine forests; pine plantations. *In migration* and *winter:* mixed woodlands, especially near feeders.
Nesting: excavates a cavity or uses an abandoned woodpecker nest; nest consists of bark shreds, grass and fur; female

incubates 5–6 white eggs, spotted with reddish brown, for about 12 days.
Feeding: moves down a tree, probing under loose bark for larval and adult invertebrates; eats pine and spruce seeds in winter; often visits feeders.
Voice: slow, continually repeated, nasal *eenk eenk eenk* call is higher than the White-breasted Nuthatch's; also a short *tsip*.
Similar Species: *White-breasted Nuthatch* (p. 236): more widespread breeder; larger; all-white face and breast. *Pygmy Nuthatch* (p. 365): limited range in west; buffy to whitish underparts; brown "cap" extends to eye line and nape.

WHITE-BREASTED NUTHATCH
Sitta carolinensis

To a novice birder, seeing a White-breasted Nuthatch calling repeatedly while clinging to the underside of a branch is an odd sight. Moving headfirst down a tree trunk, this bird forages for invertebrates, sometimes pausing to survey its surroundings and occasionally issuing a noisy call. Unlike woodpeckers and creepers, nuthatches do not use their tails to brace themselves against tree trunks, relying solely on their feet. • The White-breasted Nuthatch is a regular visitor to most backyard feeders, but, like its Red-breasted cousin, it sticks around just long enough to grab a seed. Only an offering of suet can persuade this tiny bird to remain in the same spot for any length of time. • Nuthatches are presumably named for their habit of wedging seeds and nuts into crevices and hacking them open with their bills. The scientific name *carolinensis* means "of Carolina"—the first White-breasted Nuthatch specimen was collected in South Carolina.

Nesting: in a natural cavity or an abandoned woodpecker nest in a large hardwood; female lines the cavity with bark, grass, fur and feathers; female incubates 5–8 white eggs, spotted with reddish brown, for 12–14 days.

Feeding: forages down trees headfirst in search of larval and adult invertebrates; also eats nuts and seeds; regularly visits feeders.

Voice: calls include *ha-ha-ha ha-ha-ha, ank ank* and *ip*. *Male:* song is a fast, nasal *yank-hank yank-hank* song, lower than the Red-breasted Nuthatch's.

Similar Species: *Red-breasted Nuthatch* (p. 235): largely a winter resident; smaller; light rusty underparts; black eye line; shorter bill. *Pygmy Nuthatch* (p. 365): limited range in west; smaller; buffy to whitish underparts; brown "cap" extends to eye line and nape. *Carolina Chickadee* (p. 232) and *Black-capped Chickadee* (p. 233): black "bibs."

ID: grayish blue back; white underparts; grayish flanks; rusty brown undertail covert markings; white face; straight bill; short legs. *Male:* black "cap." *Female:* dark gray "cap." *In flight:* rounded, gray wings with white crescents on undersides; pale, diagonal stripes on short, rounded tail.

Size: *L* 5½–6 in; *W* 11 in.

Habitat: mixedwood forests, woodlots and backyards.

BROWN CREEPER

Certhia americana

The cryptic Brown Creeper is never easy to find. Inhabiting old-growth forests for much of the year, it often goes unnoticed until what appeared to be a flake of bark suddenly takes the shape of a bird. If a creeper is frightened, it will freeze and flatten itself against a tree trunk, becoming even more difficult to see. • The Brown Creeper feeds by slowly spiraling up a tree trunk, searching for hidden invertebrates. When it reaches the upper branches, the creeper floats down to the base of a neighboring tree to begin another foraging ascent. Its long, stiff tail feathers prop it up against vertical tree trunks as it hitches its way skyward. • Like the call of the Golden-crowned Kinglet, the thin whistle of the Brown Creeper is so high pitched that many birders fail to hear it. To increase the confusion, the creeper's song often takes on the boisterous, warbling quality of a wood-warbler song. • Many species of creepers inhabit Europe and Asia, but the Brown Creeper is the only North American member of its family.

ID: brown-and-black back with buffy white streaks; white under-parts; white "eye-brow"; downcurved bill; rusty rump; long, pointed tail feathers. *In flight:* rounded, dark wings with buffy stroke across flight feathers above and below; white wing linings.

Size: *L* 5–5½ in; *W* 7½ in.

Habitat: mature forests and woodlands, especially in wet areas with large dead trees; also found near bogs.

Nesting: under loose bark; nest of grass and conifer needles is woven together with spider silk; female incubates 5–6 whitish eggs, dotted with reddish brown, for 14–17 days.

Feeding: hops up tree trunks and large limbs, probing loose bark for adult and larval invertebrates.

Voice: high *tseee* call. *Male:* song is a faint, high-pitched *trees-trees-trees see the trees.*

Similar Species: *Red-breasted Nuthatch* (p. 235) and *White-breasted Nuthatch* (p. 236): grayish blue upperparts; straight bills; forage downward on trunk. *Woodpeckers* (pp. 184–92): larger; different plumage patterns, many with some red; straight bills.

ROCK WREN

Salpinctes obsoletus

Well-camouflaged plumage, secretive habits and echoing songs and calls can make it difficult to spot this endearing, mysterious bird among its rocky habitat. When singing, the male Rock Wren is an expert in the art of bouncing his buzzy, trilling songs off surrounding rocks to maximize their range and aural effect while remaining comfortably concealed from onlookers. • Rock Wrens generally nest in a sheltered, rocky crevice or an animal burrow—or even in a crack in the concrete or wood of an abandoned building. The nest entrance is typically "paved" with a few (or up to 1500!) small pebbles, bones and other pieces of debris. This "welcome mat" might protect the nest from moisture or make it easier to find in confusing rocky terrain. • Rock Wrens are typically identified at long range by their habit of bobbing atop prominent boulders. • *Salpinctes*, from the Greek word for "trumpeter," refers to this bird's exclamatory call, and *obsoletus* is Latin for "indistinct," reflecting the dull, cryptic plumage.

ID: bluish gray to grayish brown upperparts with intricate light and dark flecking; white to buffy underparts; finely brown-streaked, white throat and breast; faint, buffy "eyebrow"; long, slender, slightly downcurved, gray bill. *In flight:* rounded wings; 2-tone gray underwings; cinnamon rump; broad, grayish tail has broken, buffy terminal band.
Size: *L* 6 in; *W* 9 in.
Habitat: talus slopes, scree, outcrops, stony barrens and similar substrates with abundant crevices.

Nesting: in a crevice, hole or burrow; often places small stones at the opening; nest of grass and rootlets is lined with a variety of items; probably the female incubates 5–6 eggs for up to 14 days.
Feeding: forages among rocks, boulders, logs and on the ground for insects and spiders.
Voice: *tick-EAR* alarm call. *Male:* song consists of repeated, accented 1–2-note phrases: *tra-lee tra-lee tra-lee.*
Similar Species: *Canyon Wren* (p. 239): generally rufous brown with speckles; white throat and breast; longer bill. *House Wren* (p. 242): more compact; darker upperparts; drabber underparts; shorter, paler bill. *Bewick's Wren* (p. 241): plain, browner upperparts and rump; white throat and breast; bolder "eyebrow."

CANYON WREN

Catherpes mexicanus

The lively song of the Canyon Wren is heard far more often than the bird itself is seen. Echoing hauntingly across broad canyons, rippling and cascading downward in pitch, it is as if the song were recounting the action of tumbling boulders. • Canyon Wrens forage tirelessly, even during the hottest parts of the day, searching nooks and crevices with great vigilance for hidden insects and spiders. Their quick, gliding movements suggest small rodents, and their somewhat flattened body shape allows them to pass easily through narrow crevices. A quick raising and lowering of the hindquarters every few seconds provides a clue to the identity of these small birds.

ID: black-and-white flecking on brown to orangy upperparts and flanks and grayer crown; orangy brown belly, often with indistinct, black barring; white throat and upper breast; grayish face; long, downcurved bill; thin, black barring on bright orange tail. *In flight:* rounded wings, gray below; rounded tail tip.
Size: *L* 5½–6 in; *W* 7½ in.
Habitat: precipitous cliffs, steep-walled streamside canyons, boulder piles and rocky slopes and outcroppings; post-breeding birds may be found at up to 12,000 ft; much more partial to cliffs than the Rock Wren.

Nesting: in a crevice under rocks, on a ledge or on a shelf in a cave; cup nest of moss, twigs and spider silk is lined with fur and feathers; female incubates 5–6 brown-speckled, white eggs for up to 18 days; pair feeds the young.
Feeding: gleans rocks, exposed ground and vegetation for insects and spiders.
Voice: flat *jeet* call. *Male:* song is a startling, descending, whistled *dee-ah dee-ah dee-ah dah-dah-dah.*
Similar Species: *Rock Wren* (p. 238): bluish gray to grayish brown upperparts; white to buffy underparts; finely brown-streaked throat and breast; faint, buffy "eyebrow." *Other wrens* (pp. 240–45): much shorter bills; most have prominent "eyebrows."

CAROLINA WREN

Thryothorus ludovicianus

The energetic and cheerful Carolina Wren can be shy and retiring, often hiding deep inside dense shrubbery. The best opportunity for viewing this large wren is when it sits on a conspicuous perch while unleashing its impressive song. Pairs perform lively "duets" at any time of day and in any season. The performance often begins with introductory chatter by the female, followed by innumerable ringing variations of *tea-kettle tea-kettle tea-kettle tea* from her mate. • When winters are mild, Carolina Wren populations remain stable, but a winter of frigid temperatures with ice and snow can decimate an otherwise healthy population. Fortunately, the effects of such disasters are temporary, and populations normally recover within a few years. • Carolina Wrens readily nest in the brushy thickets of an overgrown backyard or in an obscure nook or crevice in a house or barn. Under favorable conditions, two broods may be raised in a single season.

ID: rusty brown upperparts; richly buffy underparts; whitish throat; prominent, long, white "eyebrow"; slightly downcurved bill; orangy pink legs and feet. *In flight:* buffy wing lining; gray flight feathers; whitespotted rump; rounded, weakly brown-barred tail.

Size: *L* 5½ in; *W* 7½ in.

Habitat: dense forest undergrowth, especially shrubby tangles and thickets.

Nesting: in a natural or artificial cavity or a nest box; pair builds a nest cup, possibly domed, with twigs and vegetation (and sometimes snakeskin) lined with finer materials; female incubates 4–5 brown-blotched, white eggs for 12–16 days; pair feeds the young.

Feeding: usually forages in pairs on the ground and among vegetation; eats mostly insects and other invertebrates; also takes berries, fruits and seeds; visits feeders for peanuts and suet.

Voice: varied calls include a scolding chatter and a soft *dedup. Male:* offers loud, repetitious *tea-kettle tea-kettle tea-kettle* song year-round at any time of day. *Female:* often chatters while male sings.

Similar Species: *House Wren* (p. 242) and *Winter Wren* (p. 243): smaller; duller coloration; less conspicuous "eyebrow"; unspotted rump. *Marsh Wren* (p. 245): smaller; white-streaked, black upper back; prefers marsh habitat. *Sedge Wren* (p. 244): smaller; white-streaked, dark back and crown; indistinct "eyebrow"; shorter bill.

BEWICK'S WREN

Thryomanes bewickii

This charming brown mite seems to investigate all the nooks and crevices of its territory with endless curiosity and exuberant animation. As the Bewick's Wren briefly perches to scan its surroundings for sources of food, its long, narrow tail flits and waves from side to side, occasionally flashing with added verve as the bird scolds an approaching intruder. • Bewick's Wren populations in the West are better off than those of the East, where numbers are declining because of a loss of habitat. • John James Audubon chose to honor Thomas Bewick in the name of this spirited bird. A respected friend of Audubon, Bewick was an exceptionally talented wood engraver who wrote and illustrated *A History of British Birds* in the early 19th century.

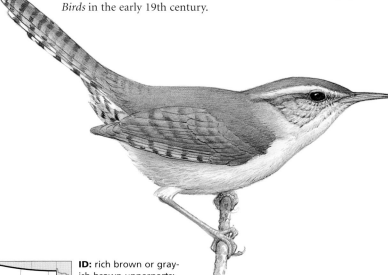

ID: rich brown or grayish brown upperparts; unmarked, whitish underparts; long, bold, white or cream "eyebrow"; slender, downcurved bill. *In flight:* pale gray wing linings; long, dark-barred, pale grayish brown tail with white-tipped outer feathers.

Size: *L* 5–5½ in; *W* 7 in.

Habitat: chaparral, riparian thickets and brush piles; dense vines and shrubby tangles bordering woodlands, parks and gardens; shrublands within pinyon–juniper woodlands and oak woodlands.

Nesting: in a natural cavity, abandoned woodpecker nest or nest box; nest of sticks and grass is lined with feathers; female incubates 5–7 brown-splotched, white eggs for up to 14 days.

Feeding: gleans vegetation for insects (especially caterpillars, grasshoppers and beetles) and spiders.

Voice: peevish *dzeeeb* or *knee-deep* alarm call. *Male:* sings clear, bold *chick-click, for me-eh, for you.*

Similar Species: *Marsh Wren* (p. 245): black area streaked with white on upper back; shorter tail; brownish to pale rufous wash on flanks. *Carolina Wren* (p. 240): buffy underparts. *Sedge Wren* (p. 244): dark back and crown streaked with white; brownish to pale rufous wash on flanks; indistinct "eyebrow"; shorter bill. *House Wren* (p. 242) and *Winter Wren* (p. 243): browner underparts; faint, buffy "eyebrows"; shorter tails. *Rock Wren* (p. 238): flecked upperparts; lightly streaked throat and breast; fainter "eyebrow."

241

HOUSE WREN

Troglodytes aedon

The House Wren's bubbly song and energetic demeanor make it a welcome addition to any neighborhood. A small cavity in a standing dead tree or a custom-made nest box is usually all it takes to attract this joyful bird to most backyards. Sometimes even an empty flowerpot or unused drainpipe is deemed a suitable nest site, provided insects are sufficiently abundant. Occasionally, you may find that your nest site offering is packed full of twigs and left abandoned without any nesting birds in sight. Male wrens often build numerous nests to serve as decoys or "dummy" nests. In such a case, if the male and his mate have moved in elsewhere, you can just clean out the cavity and hope that another pair of wrens will find your real estate more appealing. • In Greek mythology, Zeus transformed Aedon, the queen of Thebes, into a nightingale, and the species name *aedon* reflects the nightingale-like qualities of the male House Wren's wonderfully warbled song.

ID: brown upperparts; fine, dark barring on upper wings and lower back; faintly barred, pale brown flanks; whitish to buff underparts; faint, pale "eyebrow" and eye ring; whitish throat; short, upraised tail and undertail coverts finely barred with black. *In flight:* all-gray underwing, lightest at lining.
Size: *L* 4½–5 in; *W* 6 in.
Habitat: thickets and shrubby openings in or at the edge of hardwood or mixed woodlands; often in shrubs and thickets near buildings.

Nesting: in a natural cavity or abandoned woodpecker nest or in a nest box or other artificial cavity; nest of sticks and grass is lined with soft materials; female incubates 6–8 white eggs, heavily dotted with reddish brown, for 12–15 days.
Feeding: gleans the ground and vegetation for spiders and insects, especially beetles, caterpillars and grasshoppers.
Voice: *Male:* song is a smooth, running, bubbly warble: *tsi-tsi-tsi-tsi oodle-oodle-oodle-oodle,* lasting about 2–3 seconds.
Similar Species: *Winter Wren* (p. 243): slightly smaller; darker overall; prominent, dark barring on flanks; much shorter, stubby tail. *Sedge Wren* (p. 244): faint, white streaking on dark back and crown; brighter, buffier flanks.

WINTER WREN
Troglodytes troglodytes

The Winter Wren is a much-anticipated fall-to-spring visitor to the southeastern portion of the Great Plains. The best way to find one in its wintering grounds is to check every brush pile in the forest. Eventually you'll flush one out. • The song of the male Winter Wren is distinguished by its explosive delivery, melodious, bubbly tone and extended duration—up to 10 music-packed seconds. Few other singers can sustain their songs for as long. When the Winter Wren is not singing, it skulks through the forest understory, quietly probing the myriad nooks and crannies for invertebrates. • *Troglodytes* is Greek for "creeping in holes" or "cave dweller." • The Winter Wren is the only North American wren that is also found across Europe and Asia, where it is a common garden bird known simply as "Wren."

ID: dark brown upperparts; lighter brown underparts; prominent, dark barring on flanks; very short, stubby, upraised tail; fine, pale buff "eyebrow." *In flight:* uniformly gray underwing.

Size: *L* 4 in; *W* 5½ in.

Habitat: woodland thickets.

Nesting: does not nest in the Great Plains.

Feeding: forages on the ground and on trees for beetles, wood-boring insects and other invertebrates.

Voice: call is a sharp *chip-chip*. *Male*: song is a warbled, tinkling series of quick trills and twitters, often up to 10 seconds long.

Similar Species: *House Wren* (p. 242): paler overall; less conspicuous barring on flanks; longer tail. *Carolina Wren* (p. 240): larger; brighter, buffy underparts; long, bold, white "eyebrow"; longer tail. *Marsh Wren* (p. 245): black upper back with white streaking; unbarred flanks; bold, white "eyebrow." *Sedge Wren* (p. 244): white streaking on dark back and crown; paler underparts; longer tail.

SEDGE WREN

Cistothorus platensis

Like most wrens, the Sedge Wren is secretive and difficult to observe. Because it keeps itself well concealed in dense stands of sedges and tall, wet grass, it is the least familiar of all our wrens. The Sedge Wren is also less loyal to specific sites than other wrens, and it may totally disappear from an area after a few years for no apparent reason. • Sedge Wrens are feverish nest builders, and construction begins immediately after a pair settles on a nesting territory. Each energetic male may build several incomplete nests throughout his territory before the females arrive. The decoys or "dummy" nests often serve as dormitories for young and adult birds later in the season. • The scientific name *platensis* refers to the Rio de la Plata in Argentina, where another isolated population of this wren is found. • This bird used to be known as "Short-billed Marsh Wren."

Nesting: usually less than 3 ft from the ground; well-built, woven globe nest of sedges and grass has a side entrance; female incubates 4–8 all-white eggs for about 14 days.

Feeding: picks and probes low in dense vegetation for adult and larval insects and spiders; occasionally catches flying insects.

Voice: sharp *chat* or *chep* call. *Male:* sings a few short, staccato notes followed by a rattling trill: *chap-chap-chap-chap, chap, churr-r-r-r-r-r.*

ID: faintly white-streaked, dark brown-and-black back and crown; barred, dark-and-pale wing coverts; whitish underparts with buffy orange sides, flanks and undertail coverts; faint, pale "eyebrow"; short, narrow tail (often upraised). *In flight:* pale, buffy orange wing linings.

Size: *L* 4–4½ in; *W* 5½ in.

Habitat: wet sedge meadows, wet grassy fields (often with low, shrubby willows and alders), alfalfa hay fields, marshes, bogs and beaver ponds.

Similar Species: *Marsh Wren* (p. 245): boldly white-streaked, black upper back; unstreaked crown; conspicuous, white "eyebrow"; prefers cattail marshes. *Winter Wren* (p. 243): darker overall; unstreaked crown; finer bill; shorter, stubby tail. *House Wren* (p. 242): unstreaked, dark brown back and crown; barred undertail coverts; fainter "eyebrow."

MARSH WREN

Cistothorus palustris

Fueled by newly emerged aquatic insects, the Marsh Wren zips about in short bursts through tall stands of cattails and bulrushes. This expert hunter catches flying insects with lightning speed, but don't expect to see it in action—it is a reclusive bird that prefers to remain hidden deep within its dense marshland habitat. A patient observer might be rewarded with a brief glimpse of a Marsh Wren, but it is more likely that the male's distinctive song, reminiscent of an old-fashioned treadle sewing machine, will reveal the bird's presence. • The Marsh Wren occasionally destroys the nests and eggs of other Marsh Wrens and other marsh-nesting songbirds such as the Red-winged Blackbird. Other birds are usually prevented from doing the same because the Marsh Wren's globe nest keeps the eggs well hidden, and several decoy nests help to divert predators from the real nest. • The scientific name *palustris* is Latin for "marsh." This bird was formerly known as "Long-billed Marsh Wren."

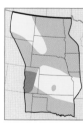

ID: white to light brown upperparts; black triangle on upper back is streaked with white; white belly and "chin"; unstreaked brown crown; bold, white "eyebrow"; long, thin, downcurved bill; tail usually sharply upraised when perching. *In flight:* buffy gray wing lining.

Size: *L* 5 in; *W* 6 in.

Habitat: large cattail and bulrush marshes interspersed with open water; occasionally in tallgrass-sedge marshes.

Nesting: in a marsh among cattails or tall emergent vegetation; globelike nest is woven from cattails, bulrushes, weeds and grass and lined with cattail down; female incubates 4–6 white to pale brown eggs, heavily dotted with dark brown, for 12–16 days.

Feeding: gleans vegetation and flycatches for adult aquatic invertebrates, especially dragonflies and damselflies.

Voice: harsh *chek* call. *Male:* rapid, rattling, staccato warble sounds like an old-fashioned treadle sewing machine.

Similar Species: *Sedge Wren* (p. 244): slightly smaller; more uniformly patterned upperparts; streaked crown; weaker "eyebrow"; shorter bill. *House Wren* (p. 242): brown back without white streaking; dark-barred wings; faint "eyebrow"; less upraised tail. *Carolina Wren* (p. 240): larger; buffy underparts; rusty brown upperparts without white streaking; less upraised tail.

GOLDEN-CROWNED KINGLET

Regulus satrapa

As they feed on insects and berries, Golden-crowned Kinglets use tree branches as swings and trapezes, flashing their regal crowns and constantly flicking their tiny wings. During summer, these dainty forest sprites are often too busy to make an appearance for admiring observers. Not much larger than hummingbirds, Golden-crowned Kinglets can be difficult to spot as they flit and hover among conifer treetops. • In winter, Golden-crowned Kinglets are commonly seen and heard among multispecies flocks that often include chickadees, Red-breasted Nuthatches and Brown Creepers. Golden-crowned Kinglets manage to survive low winter temperatures by roosting together in groups or in empty squirrel nests. Like chickadees, these birds can lower their body temperature at night to conserve energy. • The Golden-crowned Kinglet's extremely high-pitched call is very faint and is often lost in the slightest woodland breeze.

ID: olive back; darker wings and tail; 1 prominent, white wing bar and 1 weak one; light underparts; black crown border, eye line and thin "mustache"; white "eyebrow"; gray "cheek"; small, black bill; black legs; yellow feet. *Male:* orange crown. *Female:* yellow crown. *In flight:* rounded wings, dingy gray below; forked, dark tail.

Size: *L* 4 in; *W* 7 in.

Habitat: *Breeding:* mixed and pure mature coniferous forests (especially spruce-dominated) and conifer plantations. *In migration* and *winter:* forests and woodlands.

Nesting: usually in a spruce or other conifer; hanging nest consists of moss, lichen, twigs and leaves; female incubates 8–9 whitish to pale buff eggs, spotted with gray and brown, for 14–15 days.

Feeding: gleans and hovers among the forest canopy for insects, berries and occasionally sap.

Voice: very high-pitched *tsee tsee tsee* call. *Male:* faint, high-pitched, accelerating song: *tsee-tsee-tsee-tsee, why do you shilly-shally?*

Similar Species: *Ruby-crowned Kinglet* (p. 247): olive green head; elongated, white eye ring; just the male has a colorful crown (usually hidden). *Mountain Chickadee:* limited to far west of region; black "bib"; no colorful crown; heavier eye line.

RUBY-CROWNED KINGLET

Regulus calendula

The loud, rolling song of the male Ruby-crowned Kinglet is a familiar tune that echoes through conifer forests in the western Great Plains and the Black Hills of South Dakota and Wyoming. As he sings to impress prospective mates during courtship, he also erects his brilliant red crown. Throughout most of the year, though, his red crown remains hidden among dull gray feathers and is impossible to see, even through binoculars. • While in migration, the Ruby-crowned Kinglet is regularly seen flitting among treetops, intermingling with a colorful assortment of warblers and vireos. It might be mistaken for an *Empidonax* flycatcher, but the kinglet's frequent hovering and energetic wing-flicking behavior set it apart from look-alikes. The wing flicking is thought to startle insects into movement, allowing the kinglet to spot them and pounce.

ID: olive green upperparts; dark wings (frequently flicked) and tail; 2 bold, white wing bars; grayish white to dull buff underparts; bold, elongated, broken eye ring; small, dark bill; black legs; yellow feet. *Male:* small, red crown (usually hidden). *In flight:* rounded wings, gray below; forked, dark tail.
Size: *L* 4 in; *W* 7½ in.
Habitat: mixed woodlands and pure conifer forests, especially those dominated by spruce; often found near wet forest openings and edges.
Nesting: usually in a conifer, typically spruce or hemlock; female builds a hanging

nest made of moss, lichen, twigs and leaves and lines it with feathers, fur and plant down; female incubates 7–8 brown-spotted, whitish to pale buff eggs for 13–14 days.
Feeding: gleans and hovers for insects and spiders; also eats seeds and berries.
Voice: dry *che-dit* call. *Male:* song is an accelerating and rising *tea-tea-tea-tew-tew-tew look-at-ME, look-at-ME, look-at-ME.*
Similar Species: *Golden-crowned Kinglet* (p. 246): black-bordered, yellow or orange crown remains exposed; black eye line and thin "eyebrow"; white "eyebrow"; gray "cheek." *Orange-crowned Warbler* (p. 270): generally yellow overall; no wing bars or eye ring. Empidonax *flycatchers* (pp. 197–201): no red crown; complete eye ring or no eye ring; larger bill; black feet; longer tail; more upright perching posture.

BLUE-GRAY GNATCATCHER

Polioptila caerulea

Fidgety and constantly on the move, the Blue-gray Gnatcatcher issues a quiet, banjolike *twang* as it flits restlessly from shrub to shrub, gleaning insects from branches and leaves. When perched, this woodland inhabitant holds its tail upward, like a wren. • Gnatcatcher pairs remain close once a bond is established, and both parents share the responsibilities of nest building, incubation and raising the young. As soon as the young gnatcatchers are ready to fly, they leave the nest for the cover of dense shrubby tangles along woodland edges. Like most songbirds, Blue-gray Gnatcatchers mature quickly and will fly as far as South America within months of hatching. • Although this bird undoubtedly eats gnats, they are only a small part of the Blue-gray Gnatcatcher's insectivorous diet. • The scientific name *Polioptila* means "gray feather," and *caerulea* means "blue."

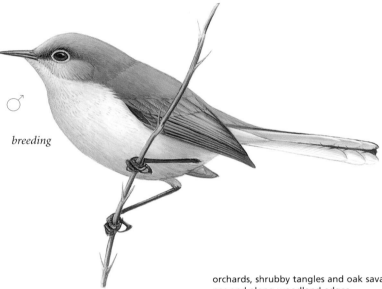

♂

breeding

ID: bluish gray upperparts; no wing bars; pale gray underparts; bluish gray head; white eye ring; long, black tail with white outer feathers. *Breeding male:* darker upperparts; black border along edge of forecrown. *In flight:* pale gray underwing with darker edges on flight feathers; roughly triangular tail, widest near tip.
Size: *L* 4½ in; *W* 6 in.
Habitat: hardwood woodlands along streams, ponds, lakes and swamps; also in orchards, shrubby tangles and oak savannas and along woodland edges.

Nesting: on a branch, usually halfway between tip and trunk; cup nest is made of plant fibers and bark chips, decorated with lichen and lined with fine vegetation, hair and feathers; female incubates 3–5 pale bluish white eggs, dotted with reddish brown, for 11–15 days; male feeds the female and young.
Feeding: gleans vegetation and flycatches for insects, spiders and other invertebrates.
Voice: call is a banjolike, high-pitched *twang*. *Male:* song is a faint, airy *puree*.
Similar Species: *Golden-crowned Kinglet* (p. 246) and *Ruby-crowned Kinglet* (p. 247): olive green upperparts; white wing bars; shorter, forked, dark olive tails.

EASTERN BLUEBIRD

Sialia sialis

Perhaps no other bird is as cherished and admired in rural areas as the lovely Eastern Bluebird. With the colors of the cool sky on its back and the warm setting sun on its breast, the male Eastern Bluebird looks like a piece of pure sky come to life. • When Eastern Bluebirds were forced to compete with introduced House Sparrows and European Starlings for nest sites, bluebird numbers began to decline. The creation of bluebird nest boxes with entrances too small for starlings has helped. Also, the development of "bluebird trails" (consisting of nest boxes mounted on fence posts along highways and rural roads) has allowed bluebird populations to recover gradually throughout much of their original range. • Eastern Bluebirds are fond of fields, uncultivated farmlands and mature wood edges, but an elevated perch is necessary as a base from which to hunt insects.

ID: rusty breast, sides, throat and "chin"; white belly and under-tail coverts; dark bill and legs. *Male*: deep blue upperparts. *Female*: grayish brown back and head tinged with blue; gray-and-blue wings and tail; paler rusty areas; thin, white eye ring. *In flight*: gray underwing with whitish stripe; shallowly forked tail.

Size: *L* 7 in; *W* 13 in.

Habitat: cropland fence lines, meadows, fallow and abandoned fields, pastures, forest clearings and edges; also golf courses, large lawns and cemeteries.

Nesting: in an abandoned woodpecker cavity, natural cavity or nest box; female builds a cup nest of grass, weed stems and small twigs and lines it with finer materials; mostly the female incubates 4–5 pale blue eggs for 13–16 days.

Feeding: swoops from a perch to pursue flying insects; also forages on the ground for invertebrates.

Voice: chittering *pew* call. *Male:* song is a rich, warbling *turr, turr-lee, turr-lee.*

Similar Species: *Western Bluebird* (p. 250): male has blue throat, belly and undertail coverts and some rusty coloration on sides of back; female has grayer underparts and gray sides to neck. *Mountain Bluebird* (p. 251): female has paler upperparts, faint or no rust on grayish breast and sides and grayer belly.

WESTERN BLUEBIRD

Sialia mexicana

Western Bluebird feathers, like those of other blue birds, are not actually pigmented blue. The blue color is a result of the feather's microscopic structure: shiny blues that change hue and intensity with the angle of view are produced by iridescence (as with soap bubbles); dull blues come from "Tyndall scatter," the same process that produces the blue of the sky. • In some areas, Western Bluebirds manage to raise two broods of young each year. A second clutch of eggs is often laid just as the first brood has left the nest, even though the first set of young still rely on their parents for food. • In fall and over the winter months, Western Bluebirds often flock together with Yellow-rumped Warblers around good crops of berries on mistletoe and other berry-producing shrubs.

ID: rusty breast; light gray belly and under-tail coverts; dark bill and legs. *Male:* deep blue back, wings, throat and head; rusty sides of back, sides and flanks. *Female:* grayish brown back and head; bluish wings and tail; paler rusty areas; light eye ring. *In flight:* gray underwing with whitish stripe; shallowly forked tail.

Size: *L* 7 in; *W* 13½ in.

Habitat: *Breeding:* broken oak and oak–conifer woodlands, oak savannas, riparian woodlands and open pine forests. *In migration* and *winter:* lowland valleys, agricultural lands interspersed with treed areas.

Nesting: in an abandoned woodpecker cavity, natural cavity or nest box; nest is built of stems, conifer needles and twigs;

female incubates 4–6 light blue eggs for up to 17 days.

Feeding: swoops from a perch to pursue flying insects; also forages on the ground for invertebrates; highly reliant on ground foraging and berries in winter.

Voice: soft *few* or harsh *chuck* call. *Male:* song is a harsh *cheer cheerful charmer.*

Similar Species: *Eastern Bluebird* (p. 249): white belly and undertail coverts; rusty at side of neck; male has all-blue back and rusty throat area; female has white to rusty throat. *Mountain Bluebird* (p. 251): female has paler upperparts, paler blue areas and faint or no rust on grayish breast. *Townsend's Solitaire* (p. 252): mostly gray; peach-colored wing patches.

MOUNTAIN BLUEBIRD

Sialia currucoides

The color of a piece of spring sky, the male Mountain Bluebird has few rivals for good looks, cheerful disposition and boldness—it is not surprising that bluebirds are viewed as the "birds of happiness." • Human activities have brought both good and bad for bluebirds. The birds have profited from the clearing of forests, raising of livestock and erection of nest boxes, but they have clearly suffered from fire suppression and the manicuring of overgrown pastures. • The spring and fall migrations of the Mountain Bluebird routinely consist of small groups of birds, but on occasion Mountain Bluebirds migrate in flocks numbering more than a hundred. • The Mountain Bluebird appears to enjoy open areas to a greater degree than other bluebirds. Despite its name, it is by no means restricted to the mountains.

ID: black eyes, bill and legs. *Male:* sky blue overall, becoming paler on underparts, especially toward undertail coverts. *Female:* sky blue wings, tail and rump; bluish gray back and head; gray underparts; possible rufous tint to breast area; whitish undertail coverts. *In flight:* bluish gray underwing with whitish stripe; shallowly forked tail.
Size: *L* 7–7½ in; *W* 14 in.
Habitat: open forests, forest edges, burned forests, agricultural areas and grasslands.
Nesting: in an abandoned woodpecker cavity, natural cavity or nest box; nest is built of plant stems, grass, conifer needles and twigs and frequently lined with a few feathers; female incubates 5–6 pale blue eggs for 13 days.
Feeding: swoops from a perch for flying and terrestrial insects; also forages on the ground for a variety of invertebrates, such as beetles, ants and bugs.
Voice: low *turr turr* call. *Male:* short, warbling song of *chur* notes.
Similar Species: *Eastern Bluebird* (p. 249) and *Western Bluebird* (p. 250): female has stronger hues overall and breast is always pale rusty in color. *Pinyon Jay* (p. 220): larger; larger bill; rounder wings; rounded tail; more raucous behavior. *Townsend's Solitaire* (p. 252): mostly gray; peach-colored patches on wings and tail; longer tail with white outer feathers.

TOWNSEND'S SOLITAIRE

Myadestes townsendi

Few birds characterize the mountain forests of the West better than the slim and graceful Townsend's Solitaire. The Townsend's Solitaire is an inconspicuous bird, perching for minutes at a time at the top of a tall tree or snag or on the upturned roots of a fallen tree. From its perch, it flutters out to catch insects in midair or follows them to the ground and grasps them with a soft pounce reminiscent of a bluebird. The male makes up for the relatively plain plumage with remarkable bursts of sustained song. In flight, the warm, peachy wing linings of this beautiful bird shine like sunlight through a bedroom window. • The Townsend's Solitaire has the unusual habit of picking fruit off trees while in flight. In winter it will defend its feeding grounds of berry-loaded junipers and other fruit-bearing trees. • True to its name, the Townsend's Solitaire is only rarely seen in groups.

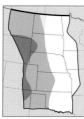

ID: gray overall; darker wings with peach-colored markings; white eye ring; small, dark bill; long, dark tail with white outer feathers. *Immature:* brown body is heavily spotted with buff; buffy eye ring. *In flight:* peach-colored stripe is boldest on underwing; triangular shape to tail.

Size: *L* 8½ in; *W* 14½ in.

Habitat: woodland edges, especially in areas with fruit-bearing shrubs and trees.

Nesting: on the ground, in a bank or among upturned tree roots; cup nest of twigs and grass is well lined with conifer needles; female incubates 4 pale blue eggs, patterned with brown, for up to 13 days.

Feeding: flycatches and gleans vegetation and the ground for invertebrates and berries; plucks berries from branches while in flight.

Voice: harsh *piink* call. *Male:* long, bubbly, warbling song.

Similar Species: *Gray Catbird* (p. 259): black "cap"; no eye ring; chestnut undertail coverts; rounder, all-gray wings and black tail. *Bluebirds* (pp. 249–51): females have bluish areas on wings without peach-colored markings, pale bellies, forked, bluish tails without white edges and most have pale rust on breast.

VEERY

Catharus fuscescens

Navigating its way across the forest floor, the Veery travels in short, springy hops, flipping leaves and scattering leaf litter in search of worms and grubs. This shy, well-camouflaged bird is always attuned to the sounds of wiggling prey or approaching danger. The Veery is the most terrestrial of the North American thrushes and is often difficult to find. Listen for it in spring and early summer, when the male's fluty, cascading song is easily detected. • When startled by an intruder, the Veery either flushes or faces the threat with its faintly streaked, buffy breast exposed, hoping for concealment. • This bird's name is an imitation of its airy song. The scientific name *fuscescens*, from the Latin word for "dusky," refers to the Veery's color. • These birds migrate to South America each winter, so there's a very good chance that the Veery pairs nesting in your local ravine might soon be traveling to the rainforests of the Amazon!

ID: reddish brown or tawny upperparts; whitish gray underparts; faintly brown-streaked upper breast and buff throat; gray flanks and face patch; very thin, grayish eye ring; pale, pinkish legs. *In flight:* buff stripe on dark gray underwing with paler lining; round-tipped tail.
Size: *L* 6½–7½ in; *W* 12 in.
Habitat: cool, moist hardwood and mixed forests and woodlands with a dense understory of shrubs and ferns; often in disturbed woodlands. *In migration:* variety of forested areas, parks and backyards.
Nesting: on the ground or in a shrub; female builds a bulky nest of leaves, weeds, bark strips and rootlets; female incubates 3–4 pale greenish blue eggs for 10–15 days.
Feeding: gleans the ground and lower vegetation for invertebrates and berries.
Voice: high, whistled *feeyou* call. *Male:* fluty, descending *da-vee-ur, vee-ur, vee-ur, veer, veer, veer* song.
Similar Species: *Swainson's Thrush* (p. 255): olive brown upperparts; dark brown spotting on throat and upper breast; bolder, buffy eye ring. *Hermit Thrush* (p. 256): brownish back; buffy brown flanks; large, dark brown spots on throat and breast; bolder, white eye ring. *Gray-cheeked Thrush* (p. 254): grayish brown upperparts; dark breast spots; brownish gray flanks.

GRAY-CHEEKED THRUSH

Catharus minimus

Few people have ever heard of the Gray-cheeked Thrush, but keen birders find this inconspicuous bird a source of great interest. A champion migrant, this thrush winters as far south as Peru and regularly summers farther north in the Arctic than any other North American thrush. Unfortunately for us, the inaccessibility of this remote northern region has prevented most birders and ornithologists from documenting more than a few nesting records for this elusive bird. • In migration, the Gray-cheeked Thrush travels primarily at night, so it is most often seen or heard rustling through shrub-covered leaf litter early in the morning. Its migration route takes it through the Great Plains, but it does not stay for long, rarely uttering more than a simple warning note during its brief refueling stops, although the male's song may sometimes be heard. Spring birds seen in our region are usually en route to nesting among willows and stunted black spruce in Canada's Hudson Bay Lowlands.

ID: grayish brown upperparts; pale underparts; heavily dark-spotted breast; brownish gray flanks; gray "cheek"; whitish eye ring (often inconspicuous); pink legs. *In flight:* buff stripe on pale-lined, brownish gray underwing; round-tipped tail.
Size: *L* 7–8 in; *W* 13 in.
Habitat: a variety of forested areas, parks and backyards.
Nesting: does not nest in the Great Plains.

Feeding: hops along the ground, picking up insects and other invertebrates; may also feed on berries during migration.
Voice: call is a downslurred *wee-o. Male:* song is typically thrushlike in tone, ending with a clear, descending whistle: *wee-a, wee-o, wee-a, titi wheeee.*
Similar Species: *Swainson's Thrush* (p. 255): warmer browns on flank and face; more obvious eye ring; buffier upper breast. *Hermit Thrush* (p. 256): olive brown upperparts; warmer browns on face; reddish tail. *Veery* (p. 253): reddish brown or tawny upperparts; very light breast streaking. *Wood Thrush* (p. 257): darker, more extensive spotting on underparts.

SWAINSON'S THRUSH

Catharus ustulatus

With the upward spiral of his song, the male Swainson's Thrush lifts the soul of any listener at each note. He is an integral part of the morning chorus, even in migration. His inspiring song is also heard at dusk, and he is routinely the last forest singer silenced by nightfall. • Most thrushes are ground-feeders, but the Swainson's is also adept at gleaning food from the airy heights of trees, sometimes briefly hover-gleaning like a warbler or vireo. • On its breeding grounds, the Swainson's Thrush is typically seen perched high in a treetop, cast in silhouette against the sky. In migration, this bird skulks low on the ground under shrubs and tangles, occasionally appearing in backyards and local parks. A wary bird, this thrush does not allow many viewing opportunities, and it often gives a sharp warning call from some distance. • William Swainson was an English zoologist and illustrator in the early 19th century. His name also graces the Swainson's Hawk.

ID: olive brown upperparts; whitish belly and undertail coverts; brownish gray flanks; dark brown spots form streaks on throat and breast; buff-washed upper breast and "cheek"; noticeable, buffy eye ring; pink legs. *In flight:* buffy stripe on pale-lined, brownish gray underwing; round-tipped tail.
Size: *L* 7 in; *W* 12 in.
Habitat: edges and openings of conifer and mixed forests; prefers moist areas with spruce and fir. *In migration:* a variety of forested areas, parks and backyards.
Nesting: usually in a shrub or small tree; small cup nest of grass, moss, leaves, roots

and lichen is lined with fur and soft fibers; female incubates 3–4 brown-spotted, pale blue eggs for 12–14 days.
Feeding: gleans vegetation and forages on the ground for invertebrates; also eats berries.
Voice: sharp *wick* call. *Male:* song is a slow, rolling, rising spiral: *Oh, Aurelia will-ya, will-ya will-yeee.*
Similar Species: *Gray-cheeked Thrush* (p. 254): less or no buff wash on breast; gray "cheek"; usually inconspicuous eye ring. *Hermit Thrush* (p. 256): grayish brown upperparts; darker spotting on whiter breast; reddish rump and tail. *Veery* (p. 253): more reddish upperparts; faint breast streaking; inconspicuous eye ring.

HERMIT THRUSH

Catharus guttatus

If beauty were gauged by sound, the male Hermit Thrush would doubtless be deemed one of the world's most beautiful forest birds. On his nesting grounds, his familiar theme is as much a part of the forest ecosystem as are the trees and wildflowers. His song, like that of the Swainson's Thrush, is normally preceded with a single questioning note, as if asking if the coast is clear. • When a female arrives in his territory, for the first two days the male will attack and chase her. If she remains, the male gradually accepts her, and the union is formed. She then builds a cryptic cup nest on the ground, often hiding it in a natural hollow between raised, mossy hummocks under the low branches of a spruce or fir. She incubates the eggs alone while the male defends the territory. The minimized activity around the nest probably benefits the vulnerable eggs. • The scientific name *guttatus*, Latin for "spotted" or "speckled," refers to this bird's breast.

ID: grayish brown upperparts; dark brown spotting on throat and breast; pale underparts; gray flanks; thin, whitish eye ring; thin bill; pink legs; reddish brown rump and tail. *In flight:* buff stripe on pale-lined, brownish gray underwing; round-tipped tail.

Size: *L* 7 in; *W* 11½ in.

Habitat: woodlands; conifer-bordered bogs.

Nesting: usually on the ground; occasionally in a small tree or shrub; female builds a bulky cup nest of grass, twigs, moss, ferns and bark strips; female incubates 4 pale blue to greenish blue, possibly dark-flecked eggs for 11–13 days.

Feeding: forages on the ground and gleans vegetation for insects and other invertebrates; also eats berries.

Voice: faint *chuck* and fluty *treee* calls. *Male:* song is a series of beautiful, flutelike notes, both rising and falling in pitch.

Similar Species: *Swainson's Thrush* (p. 255): grayish brown back and tail; buff-washed upper breast and "cheek." *Veery* (p. 253): reddish brown upperparts and tail; lightly streaked upper breast. *Gray-cheeked Thrush* (p. 254): gray "cheek"; inconspicuous eye ring. *Fox Sparrow* (p. 318): stockier; more spotting and streaking on breast and sides; conical bill.

WOOD THRUSH
Hylocichla mustelina

The Wood Thrush is North America's largest spotted thrush. It is instantly recognizable on the few occasions it ventures out into the open, but the male's loud, warbled songs are not always recognized by Great Plains inhabitants. Forest fragmentation and urban sprawl have eliminated much of this bird's nesting habitat, allowing the less melodic song of the American Robin to prevail. Broken forests and diminutive woodlots have permitted the invasion of open-area predators and parasites, such as raccoons, skunks, crows, jays and cowbirds, which traditionally had little access to nests insulated deep within vast hardwood stands. • The Wood Thrush's wintering grounds extend from southeastern Mexico down to Panama, and the species breeds primarily in the East, from the Gulf Coast to southern Canada. • Nineteenth-century naturalist and author Henry David Thoreau considered the song of the male Wood Thrush—which can even sing two notes at once!—to be the most beautiful of avian sounds.

ID: rusty head and back; brown wings, rump and tail; large blackish spots on white breast, sides and flanks; dark-streaked, white "cheeks"; bold, white eye ring. *In flight:* buff stripe on pale-lined, dark gray underwing; round-tipped tail.

Size: *L* 8 in; *W* 13 in.

Habitat: moist, mature and preferably undisturbed hardwood woodlands and mixed forests.

Nesting: low in a fork of a hardwood; female builds a bulky cup nest of grass, twigs, moss, weeds, bark strips and mud lined with softer materials; female incubates 3–4 pale, greenish blue eggs for 13–14 days.

Feeding: forages on the ground and gleans vegetation for insects and other invertebrates; also eats berries.

Voice: calls include *pit pit* and *bweebee-beep. Male:* bell-like phrases of 3–5 notes, with each note at a different pitch, followed by a trill: *Will you live with me? Way up high in a tree, I'll come right down and…seeee!*

Similar Species: *Swainson's Thrush* (p. 255): olive brown upperparts; less extensive, browner spotting; buff-washed upper breast and "cheek"; buffy eye ring; rising, flutelike song. *Hermit Thrush* (p. 256): reddish brown restricted mostly to rump and tail; flutelike song has ascending and descending phrases.

AMERICAN ROBIN

Turdus migratorius

American Robins are widely heralded as harbingers of spring, but they are found year-round throughout the American Great Plains, albeit with a significant southward movement in winter. Widespread and abundant in many of our natural habitats, they are familiar to most of us from residential lawns, gardens and parks. • A hunting robin may appear to be listening for prey, but it is actually looking for movements in the soil—with its eyes placed on the sides of its head, it must tilt its head to look downward. Robins seen hunting with their bills already stuffed full of earthworms and grubs are a sign that hungry young are close at hand. Young robins are easily distinguished by their disheveled appearance and heavily spotted underparts. • English colonists named the American Robin after the distantly related Robin *(Erithacus rubecula)* of their native land, which looks and behaves similarly.

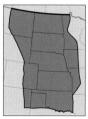

ID: grayish brown back; black-streaked, white throat; white undertail coverts; incomplete, white eye ring; black-tipped, yellow bill; dark legs. *Male:* deep orangy red breast; black head. *Female:* mottled, light reddish orange breast; dark gray head. *Immature:* heavily gray-spotted, whitish breast and orangy flanks. *In flight:* gray wings with orangy linings; round-tipped, blackish tail with white corners.
Size: *L* 10 in; *W* 17 in.
Habitat: residential lawns and gardens, pastures, urban parks, broken forests, bogs and river shorelines.
Nesting: in a tree or shrub; sturdy cup nest of grass, moss and loose bark is cemented with mud; female incubates 4 light blue eggs for 11–16 days; up to 3 broods each year.
Feeding: forages on the ground and among vegetation for larval and adult insects, earthworms, other invertebrates and berries.
Voice: rapid *tut-tut-tut* call. *Male:* evenly spaced, warbling song: *cheerily cheer-up cheerio.*
Similar Species: *Varied Thrush:* rare transient; peach-colored wing markings; black or gray "necklace" and "mask." *Swainson's Thrush* (p. 255) and *Hermit Thrush* (p. 256): paler upperparts; little or no red or orange on underparts; pink legs. *Orchard Oriole* (p. 349): smaller; male has white and red wing bars and chestnut underparts. *Spotted Towhee* (p. 300) and *Eastern Towhee* (p. 301): smaller; white lower breast and belly; conical bill.

GRAY CATBIRD

Dumetella carolinensis

True to its name, the Gray Catbird has a call that sounds like a mewing cat. It shares the vocal dexterity of other members of the mimic thrush family and has the ability to use each side of its syrinx separately. The Gray Catbird's characteristic call and boisterous, hectic, mimicked phrases are often the only evidence of this bird's presence, because it prefers to remain in the underbrush and dense riparian shrubs. The male does come out in the open, however, to perform a most unusual "mooning" courtship display: he raises his long, slender tail to show off his only bright color, his rusty undertail coverts. • Near homes, Gray Catbirds can sometimes be seen at dawn, feeding on insects attracted to electric lights. • *Dumetella* is Latin for "small thicket," apparently in reference to this bird's preferred habitat. • Catbird parents will usually recognize and destroy Brown-headed Cowbird eggs deposited in their nests.

ID: dark gray overall; black "cap"; chestnut undertail coverts; black eyes, bill and legs; long tail may be dark gray to black. *In flight:* rounded wings and tail.
Size: *L* 8½–9 in; *W* 11 in.
Habitat: dense thickets, brambles, shrubby or brushy areas and hedgerows, often near water.
Nesting: in a dense shrub or thicket; loosely built, bulky cup nest of twigs, leaves and grass is lined with fine material; female incubates 4 greenish blue eggs for 12–15 days.

Feeding: forages on the ground and in vegetation for a wide variety of insects (such as ants, beetles, grasshoppers, caterpillars and moths) and spiders; also eats berries and visits feeders.
Voice: calls include a catlike *meoow* and a harsh *check-check*. *Male:* song is a variety of warbles, squeaks and mimicked phrases repeated only once and often interspersed with a *mew* call.
Similar Species: *Gray Jay* (p. 364), *Northern Mockingbird* (p. 260) and *Townsend's Solitaire* (p. 252): different wing and facial markings; smaller or no black "cap"; whitish or gray undertail coverts.

NORTHERN MOCKINGBIRD
Mimus polyglottos

In winter, Northern Mockingbirds rely heavily on wild and ornamental fruits, especially the bounty of nutritious rose hips. Generous offerings of suet, raisins and fruit at feeders can go a long way toward luring these and other birds into your yard. • The male Northern Mockingbird's vocal repertoire is amazing—over 400 different song types have been attributed to this bird! It can imitate almost anything, from the vocalizations of other birds and animals to musical instruments, hence the scientific name *polyglottos*, which is Greek for "many tongues." This mimic's sound replications are so accurate that even computerized auditory analysis may be unable to distinguish them from the original sources. • The Northern Mockingbird's energetic territorial dance is delightful to watch, as males square off in what appears to be a swordless fencing duel.

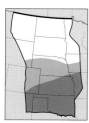

ID: gray upperparts; dark wings with 2 thin, white bars; light gray underparts; yellowish eyes; dark legs; long, dark tail with white outer tail feathers. *Immature:* gray- or brown-spotted breast. *In flight:* large, white patch near wing tip; round-tipped tail.
Size: *L* 10 in; *W* 14 in.
Habitat: hedges, suburban gardens and orchard margins with an abundance of available fruit; hedgerows of multiflora roses are especially important in winter.
Nesting: often in a small shrub or small tree; cup nest is built with twigs, grass, fur

and leaves; female incubates 3–4 brown-blotched, bluish gray to greenish eggs for 12–13 days.
Feeding: gleans vegetation and forages on the ground for beetles, ants, wasps and grasshoppers; also eats berries and wild fruit; visits feeders.
Voice: calls include a harsh *chair* and *chewk. Male:* song is a medley of mimicked phrases, with the phrases often repeated 3 times or more.
Similar Species: *Loggerhead Shrike* (p. 209) and *Northern Shrike* (p. 210): black "masks"; thicker, hooked bills; shorter legs. *Townsend's Solitaire* (p. 252): peach-colored wing markings; gray underparts; prominent eye ring. *Gray Catbird* (p. 259): gray overall; black "cap"; chestnut undertail coverts; all-dark tail.

SAGE THRASHER

Oreoscoptes montanus

The Sage Thrasher is intricately linked to open flats of sagebrush. It is less particular in migration, but in summer it is only rarely found in other habitats. In breeding season, the male can regularly be seen perched on the top of a sage plant or other shrub, belting out long, warbling phrases to defend his territory. • While perched, the Sage Thrasher slowly raises and lowers its tail, and while running along the ground, it holds its tail high. Because of these mockingbird-like mannerisms, this bird was formerly known as "Mountain Mockingbird" or "Sage Mockingbird." • Thrashers belong to the family Mimidae, the mimic thrushes, and "thrasher" is derived from "thrush." *Oreoscoptes* is Greek for "mimic of the mountains"—really a misconception, because most of these birds don't live in mountainous regions.

ID: grayish brown upperparts; 2 white wing bars (often faded); white to buffy underparts with heavy, dark streaking (often faded); yellow to orangy eyes; short, slim, straight, dark bill; dark legs and feet; long tail. *In flight:* pale buff wing linings; white tail corners.
Size: *L* 8½ in; *W* 12 in.
Habitat: *Breeding:* sagebrush and grease-wood flats, and shrublands dominated by tall sagebrush. *In migration:* sagebrush flats, open brushland and coastal sage scrub.
Nesting: usually in a large sagebrush; bulky cup nest of grass, twigs and leaves is lined with fine vegetation; pair incubates 3–5 brown-spotted, greenish blue eggs for up to 17 days.
Feeding: runs across the ground among vegetation looking for invertebrates and larvae; also eats berries.

Voice: calls include a high *churr* and a *chuck. Male:* complex, warbled song is sustained, lasting up to 2 minutes, with the phrases usually repeated without a pause; notable night singer.
Similar Species: *Brown Thrasher* (p. 262): larger; reddish brown upperparts; bolder streaking; larger bill. *Curve-billed Thrasher* (p. 263): larger; drabber; larger bill. *Northern Mockingbird* (p. 260): immature has less heavily streaked underparts, large, white wing patches and all-white outer tail feathers. *Swainson's Thrush* (p. 255) and *Hermit Thrush* (p. 256): smaller; unstreaked belly; dark eyes; pinkish legs; inhabit treed areas. *Greater Roadrunner* (p. 166): much larger; darker overall; longer tail.

BROWN THRASHER

Toxostoma rufum

Amid the various chirps and warbles that rise from woodland and lakefront edges in spring and early summer, the song of the male Brown Thrasher stands alone with its unique, lengthy, complex chorus of twice-repeated phrases. This thrasher has the most extensive vocal repertoire of any North American bird, with up to an estimated 3000 distinctive combinations of various phrases! • Although relatively large, the Brown Thrasher generally goes unnoticed in its shrubby domain. A typical sighting consists of nothing more than a flash of reddish brown as it zips from one tangle to another. • Because the Brown Thrasher nests on or close to the ground, its eggs and nestlings are particularly vulnerable to predation by snakes, weasels, skunks and other animals. Brown Thrasher parents are aggressive, vigilant nest defenders, sometimes to the point of drawing blood, but their spirited efforts are not always enough to protect their progeny.

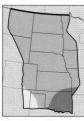

ID: reddish brown upperparts; 2 white wing bars; pale underparts with heavy brown spotting and streaking; yellow or orangy eyes; long, slender, downcurved bill; pinkish legs; long, reddish brown tail. *In flight:* buffy wing linings; buffy tail corners.
Size: *L* 11½ in; *W* 13 in.
Habitat: dense shrubs and thickets, overgrown pastures (especially with hawthorns), woodland edges and brushy areas.
Nesting: usually in a low shrub or on the ground; cup nest of grass, twigs and leaves is lined with fine vegetation; pair incubates

4 bluish white to pale blue eggs, dotted with reddish brown, for 11–14 days.
Feeding: gleans the ground and vegetation for larval and adult invertebrates; occasionally tosses leaves aside with its bill; also eats seeds and berries.
Voice: calls include a loud crackling note, a harsh *shuck,* a soft *churr* and a whistled, 3-note *pit-cher-ee. Male:* sings a large variety of typically duplicated phrases: *dig-it dig-it, hoe-it hoe-it, pull-it-up pull-it-up.*
Similar Species: *Curve-billed Thrasher* (p. 263): drabber; larger, more downcurved bill; inhabits arid open and brushy areas. *Sage Thrasher* (p. 261): grayer overall; smaller bill; inhabits sagebrush areas. *Wood Thrush* (p. 257) and *Hermit Thrush* (p. 256): smaller; no wing bars; dark eyes; shorter bills and tails.

CURVE-BILLED THRASHER

Toxostoma curvirostre

Deserts filled with cholla (pronounced *CHOY-ah*), prickly-pear and saguaro cacti provide favored feeding, nesting and roosting habitat for this sassy, familiar bird. Like its neighbor, the ubiquitous, chattery Cactus Wren, the Curve-billed Thrasher prefers to build its nest among the nearly impenetrable fortress of spines provided by the cholla cactus. Brutally sharp spines help to protect both cactus and bird from predators but require that the birds quickly learn to become expert flyers and landers—fledglings leaving the nest for the first time must succeed in their first flight or risk being fatally pricked in a faulty attempt. • Like a prospector searching for oil, gold or precious water, a foraging Curve-billed Thrasher may penetrate the dusty soil with heavy, purposeful blows. Without the advantage of hands for wielding tools, the thrasher props its tail against the ground to give added force to the strikes of its sharp bill. • *Toxostoma* (from Greek words meaning "archer's bow" and "mouth") and *curvirostre* (Latin for "curved bill") both refer to the bird's bill.

Nesting: loose, bulky cup of grass, thorny twigs, feathers and animal hair is built in cholla cactus, yucca or thorny shrub; pair incubates 3 bluish green eggs with brown spots for 12–15 days.

Feeding: forages on the ground for insects, berries and seeds; often digs in the soil with its long bill; cactus fruit and seeds are readily taken.

Voice: sharp, liquidy *whit-wheat* call. *Male:* song is a long series of variable whistled phrases.

Similar Species: *Sage Thrasher* (p. 261): smaller; grayer overall; dark streaks on underparts; yellow eyes; short, straight bill; different breeding range. *Brown Thrasher* (p. 262): reddish brown upperparts; pale underparts with bolder streaking and spotting; shorter bill; prefers shrubby areas and thickets.

ID: pale brownish gray upperparts; possibly 2 white wing bars; brownish to buffy gray underparts; large, blurry, brown breast spots; bright yellow to orange eyes; long, dark, downcurved bill. *In flight:* plain, buffy gray underwing; long tail may have mostly whitish tip.

Size: *L* 9½–11½ in; *W* 13–14 in.

Habitat: arid, brushy lowlands, desert and grasslands, preferably with cholla cactus.

EUROPEAN STARLING

Sturnus vulgaris

The European Starling was brought to North America in 1890 and 1891, when about 100 birds were released into New York's Central Park as part of the local Shakespeare society's plan to introduce all the birds mentioned in their favorite author's writings. The European Starling quickly established itself in the New York landscape and then spread rapidly across the continent, often at the expense of many native cavity-nesting birds, such as the Tree Swallow, Eastern Bluebird and Red-headed Woodpecker. Despite many concerted efforts to control or even eradicate this species, the European Starling will no doubt continue to assert its claim in the New World. The more than 200 million starlings in North America today are believed to have sprung from these first 100 birds. • Courting European Starlings are infamous for their ability to reproduce the sounds of birds such as Killdeers, Red-tailed Hawks, Soras and meadowlarks.

breeding

ID: shiny black overall; orangy wing-feather edges; dark eyes; straight, pointed bill; orangy pink legs. *Breeding:* greenish back; pinkish buff spots on upperparts and undertail coverts; glossy, purple breast, neck and head; yellow bill. *Nonbreeding:* white-spotted back and underparts; finely white-streaked head; black bill. *Immature:* grayish brown overall; brown bill. *In flight:* pointed wings; blunt tail.

Size: *L* 8½ in; *W* 16 in.

Habitat: agricultural areas, townsites, woodland and forest edges, landfills and roadsides.

Nesting: in an abandoned woodpecker cavity, natural cavity or artificial cavity; nest consists of grass, twigs and straw; largely the female incubates 4–6 bluish to greenish white eggs for 12–14 days.

Feeding: mostly a ground forager; diverse diet includes many invertebrates, berries, seeds and human food waste.

Voice: very variable call. *Male:* various whistles, squeaks and gurgles comprise the song; imitates other birds.

Similar Species: *Rusty Blackbird* (p. 344): male has yellow eyes, longer tail and no spotting; nonbreeding bird shows rusty tinges. *Brewer's Blackbird* (p. 345): no spotting; dark legs; longer tail; male has iridescent, bluish green body, purplish head and yellow eyes; female is brown overall. *Brown-headed Cowbird* (p. 348): smaller; stouter bill; dark legs; male has brown head; female has paler head than immature European Starling; immature has streaked underparts.

AMERICAN PIPIT

Anthus rubescens

Each fall, agricultural fields and open wetlands serve as refueling stations for large concentrations of migratory American Pipits. Flocks of pipits may go unnoticed to untrained eyes because the dull brown-and-buff plumage of these birds blend into the landscape. But to keen observers, their plain attire, white outer tail feathers and habit of continuously wagging their tails makes them readily identifiable. The best indicator that pipits are near is their telltale, two-syllable call of *pip-it pip-it*, which is usually given in flight. • Although American Pipits may pair up prior to arriving on their nesting grounds—a strategy that is thought to save valuable nesting time—a conspicuous courtship display helps each pair establish and defend the boundaries of its exclusive nesting territory in the Arctic or above timberline in alpine habitats. • This bird was formerly known as "Water Pipit" (*A. spinoletta*).

ID: faintly streaked, grayish brown upperparts; buff edges on wing feathers; whitish buff to pale peach-colored underparts; heavy to little or no streaking on flanks, sides and upper breast; slim, dusky bill; dark legs. *In flight:* brownish gray flight feathers; grayish white wing lining; dark tail with white outer feathers.
Size: *L* 6–7 in; *W* 10½ in.
Habitat: agricultural fields, pastures and shores of wetlands, lakes and rivers.

Nesting: does not nest in the Great Plains.
Feeding: gleans the ground and vegetation for terrestrial and aquatic invertebrates and for seeds, which can constitute up to nearly half the food intake in migration and winter.
Voice: familiar flight call is *pip-it pip-it*. *Male:* gives a harsh, sharp *tsip-tsip* or *chi-wee* call.
Similar Species: *Sprague's Pipit* (p. 266): lighter back with strong buffy streaking; paler buff on breast. *Horned Lark* (p. 224): female has whitish belly, well-defined, dark breast band and dark tail with pale center.

265

SPRAGUE'S PIPIT

Anthus spragueii

The uplifting melody carries across the open landscape as the male Sprague's Pipit delivers his courtship song from high above the ground. This prairie songster flies in a continuous circle, sometimes for more than an hour at a time, as he does so. Although the Sprague's Pipit is becoming less common, it seems that every patch of healthy prairie rangeland still has at least one bird singing overhead. • The Sprague's Pipit has few musical rivals, but it seems to have been cheated out of a matching plumage. Instead, it wears a pattern common to many prairie passerines: camouflaged browns with white outer tail feathers that only show in flight. • Unlike most of the world's pipits, this species does not habitually wag its tail. • Isaac Sprague was a talented illustrator who accompanied John J. Audubon across the Great Plains in the mid-1800s. He later became one of America's foremost botanical artists.

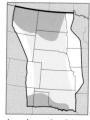

ID: grayish brown upperparts, heavily streaked with buff; lighter underparts with brown breast streaks; thin, pinkish yellow bill; pinkish yellow legs. *In flight:* brownish gray flight feathers; grayish white wing lining; broad, white edges on tail.
Size: *L* 6 in; *W* 10 in.
Habitat: native shortgrass prairie.
Nesting: in a depression in the ground, often with overarching grass; well-built cup nest is made of woven grass; female incubates 4–5 heavily purple-spotted, white eggs for about 11 days.

Feeding: walks along the ground picking grasshoppers, beetles, moths and other invertebrates from vegetation and the ground; may also eat seeds.
Voice: seldom-heard flight call is a nasal *squeep*. *Male:* song is a swirling and descending, bell-like *choodly choodly choodly choodly chooodly*.
Similar Species: *American Pipit* (p. 265): darker upperparts and face; variable breast streaking; darker legs; wags its tail. *Vesper Sparrow* (p. 309): chestnut shoulder patch; crisper eye ring; shorter, stouter bill; longer tail with broader tip. *Baird's Sparrow* (p. 314): smaller; darker browns; buff to pale orange tints on face and crown; tail edges are just faintly pale.

BOHEMIAN WAXWING

Bombycilla garrulus

Faint, quavering whistles attract attentive naturalists who take pleasure in watching Bohemian Waxwings descend on berry-filled mountain-ashes and other ornamental plantings. After nesting in northern forests in Alaska and western Canada, these birds visit more southern areas in search of winter food. They thrill us with their unpredictable appearances, usually arriving just in time to be tallied in reasonable numbers in Christmas bird counts and departing for their boreal homes before most songbirds arrive back on the Great Plains. Although they sometimes appear in great flocks, in most years Bohemians are seen only in small groups, usually intermingled with overwintering flocks of similar-looking Cedar Waxwings. Chestnut undertail coverts readily distinguish the Bohemians from their counterparts, however. • Waxwings get their name from the spots on their secondary feathers. These "waxy" spots are actually colorful enlargements of the feather shafts, whose pigments are derived from the birds' berry-filled diet. The smaller pigment spots on young birds grow in size until maturity.

ID: soft brownish gray overall, grayer on belly; small white, red and yellow markings on folded wings; chestnut red undertail coverts; cinnamon crest; reddish forehead, "eyebrow" area and cheek tinges; black "mask" and throat; yellow terminal tail band. *Immature:* grayer upperparts; heavily gray-streaked, whitish underparts and throat; no "mask"; reddish markings restricted to undertail coverts. *In flight:* pointed, grayish brown wings with narrow trailing edge near body; dark outer half of upperwing has white "wrist" crescent.

Size: *L* 8 in; *W* 14 in.

Habitat: natural and residential areas with wild berries and other fruit.

Nesting: does not nest in the Great Plains.

Feeding: gleans vegetation for insects and wild fruit or catches flying insects on the wing; depends on berries and other fruit in winter; also eats some tree seeds.

Voice: call is a faint, high-pitched, quavering whistle.

Similar Species: *Cedar Waxwing* (p. 268): smaller; browner overall; white undertail coverts; no yellow and less white on wings.

267

CEDAR WAXWING

Bombycilla cedrorum

Cedar Waxwing pairs perform a wonderful courtship dance: the male first lands slightly away from the female, then tentatively hops toward her and offers her a berry. The female accepts the berry and hops away from the male; then she stops, hops back and offers him the berry. This gentle ritual can last for several minutes. • Planting native berry-producing trees and shrubs in your backyard can attract Cedar Waxwings and will often encourage them to nest in your area. These birds are late nesters, which ensures that the berry crops will be ripe when the nestlings are ready to be fed. In fall and winter, Cedar Waxwings gorge themselves on fruit left hanging on tree and shrub branches and occasionally eat themselves to flightless intoxication on fermented fruit. • Unlike the Bohemian Waxwing, which appears in our region strictly in winter, the smaller Cedar Waxwing is found year-round in the northern Great Plains and in winter through the southern plains. • Practiced observers learn to recognize this bird by its high-pitched, trilling calls.

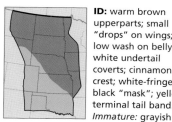

ID: warm brown upperparts; small red "drops" on wings; yellow wash on belly; white undertail coverts; cinnamon crest; white-fringed, black "mask"; yellow terminal tail band. *Immature:* grayish brown overall; unmarked wings; streaked underparts; small "mask." *In flight:* pointed, unmarked, grayish brown wings.
Size: *L* 7 in; *W* 12 in.
Habitat: wooded residential parks and gardens, overgrown fields and forest edges; second-growth, riparian and open woodlands.
Nesting: in a tree or shrub; cup nest of twigs, grass, moss and lichen is lined with fine grass; female incubates 3–5 pale gray to bluish gray eggs with fine, dark spotting for 12–16 days.
Feeding: catches flying insects on the wing or gleans vegetation; also eats large amounts of berries and other wild fruit, especially in fall and winter.
Voice: call is a faint, high-pitched, trilled whistle: *tseee-tseee-tseee.*
Similar Species: *Bohemian Waxwing* (p. 267): larger; white, red and yellow markings on wings; chestnut red undertail coverts; reddish forehead, "eyebrow" area and facial tinges; immature has chestnut undertail coverts and white wing patches.

TENNESSEE WARBLER

Vermivora peregrina

Without the kinds of bold, bright features found on many other warblers, Tennessee Warblers are harder to identify and are easily confused with Warbling Vireos and Philadelphia Vireos. • Fall migration starts very early and accounts for some late summer reports, but no evidence exists of any Tennessee Warblers attempting to nest in the northern Great Plains, although they occur along the Canadian border, in northern Michigan and northeastern Minnesota. Migrating Tennessee Warblers often sing their tunes and forage for insects high in the forest canopy. Inclement weather and the need for food after a long flight can force these birds to lower levels in the forest. • Tennessee Warblers thrive during spruce budworm outbreaks. During times of plenty, these birds may produce more than seven young in a single brood, resulting in a larger number of migrants through our region. • In the 19th century, the noted ornithologist Alexander Wilson discovered this bird along the Cumberland River in Tennessee and named it after that state, though it is only a migrant in Tennessee.

breeding

ID: dark eye line; thin bill. *Breeding male:* olive green back, wings and tail edgings; white underparts; bluish gray "cap" and "cheek"; white "eyebrow." *Breeding female:* yellow wash on breast and "eyebrow"; olive gray "cap" and "cheek." *Nonbreeding:* olive yellow upperparts; yellow "eyebrow"; yellow underparts except for white undertail coverts; male may have white belly. *In flight:* light gray wing lining; yellowish gray tail.
Size: *L* 4½–5 in; *W* 8 in.
Habitat: woodlands or areas with tall shrubs.

Nesting: does not nest in the Great Plains.
Feeding: gleans foliage and buds for small insects, caterpillars and other invertebrates; also eats berries; occasionally visits suet feeders.
Voice: sweet *chip* call. *Male:* song is a loud, sharp, accelerating *ticka-ticka-ticka swit-swit-swit-swit chew-chew-chew-chew-chew.*
Similar Species: *Orange-crowned Warbler* (p. 270): yellower underparts, particularly undertail coverts; no "eyebrow." *Warbling Vireo* (p. 215): stouter overall; thicker bill; much less green on upperparts; paler, yellowish wing lining. *Philadelphia Vireo* (p. 216): stouter overall; yellow sides, breast and throat; plainer "cheek"; thicker bill.

ORANGE-CROWNED WARBLER

Vermivora celata

D on't be disappointed if you can't see the Orange-crowned Warbler's orange crown, because it rarely shows. One might say that this bird's most distinguishing characteristic is its lack of field marks—wing bars, eye rings and color patches are all absent. • When encountered, the Orange-crowned Warbler usually appears as a blurred, olive yellow bundle flitting nervously among the leaves and branches of low shrubs. In addition, its drab, olive yellow appearance makes it frustratingly similar to females of other warbler species. • The Orange-crowned Warbler is often the most common species to capitalize on the sap wells drilled by Yellow-bellied Sapsuckers. • *Vermivora* is Latin for "worm eating," and *celata* is derived from the Latin word for "hidden," a reference to this bird's inconspicuous crown.

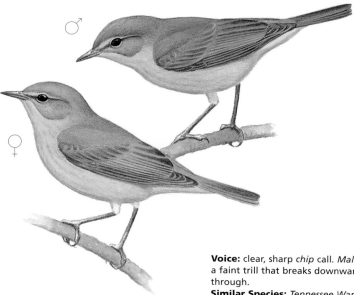

Voice: clear, sharp *chip* call. *Male:* song is a faint trill that breaks downward halfway through.

Similar Species: *Tennessee Warbler* (p. 269): bold "eyebrow"; mostly or all-white underparts, including undertail coverts; breeding male has bluish gray head. *Wilson's Warbler* (p. 294): brighter yellow underparts; unstreaked breast; dark olive or black crown; complete, bright yellow eye ring; pale pinkish legs. *Yellow Warbler* (p. 273): brighter underparts and head (especially the male); reddish streaks on breast and side (faint or absent on female); pale pinkish legs. *Common Yellowthroat* (p. 293): female has browner upperparts, flanks and face, yellow, unstreaked breast, throat and undertail coverts. *Ruby-crowned Kinglet* (p. 247): smaller; white wing bars; daintier bill; elongated, white eye ring.

ID: olive yellow to olive gray overall; faintly olive-streaked underparts; bright yellow undertail coverts; faint, orange crown patch (rarely seen); bright yellow "eyebrow" and broken eye ring; thin, faint, dark eye line; thin bill. *In flight:* dull olive gray wings and tail.
Size: *L* 5 in; *W* 7 in.
Habitat: woodlands or areas with tall shrubs.
Nesting: does not nest in the Great Plains.
Feeding: gleans foliage for invertebrates, berries, nectar and sap; often hover-gleans.

NASHVILLE WARBLER

Vermivora ruficapilla

Nashville Warblers are fairly common migrants across the eastern Great Plains and rare, local breeders in the northeast. They are best found in overgrown farmland and second-growth forest as they forage low in trees and thickets, often at the edge of a dry forest or burn area. The thin, two-part trill song of the male is infrequently issued if competing Nashvilles are absent from the area. • The unusual breeding distribution of the Nashville Warbler, with two separated populations—one in the eastern U.S. and the other in the West—is believed to have been created thousands of years ago when continental glaciation split apart a single core population. • This warbler was first described near Nashville, Tennessee, but it does not breed in that state. This misnomer is not an isolated incident: the Tennessee, Cape May and Connecticut warblers all bear names that misrepresent their breeding distributions.

breeding

ID: yellowish green upperparts; yellow underparts; white between legs; bold, white eye ring. *Male:* bluish gray head; may show a small, chestnut red crown patch. *Female* and *immature:* duller overall; bluish gray nape; olive gray head. *In flight:* gray underwing with paler lining; olive gray tail.
Size: *L* 4½–5 in; *W* 7½ in.
Habitat: prefers second-growth mixed woodlands; also wet conifer forests, riparian woodlands, cedar–spruce swamps and moist, shrubby, abandoned fields.
Nesting: on the ground under a fern, sapling or shrubby cover; female builds

a cup nest of grass, bark strips, ferns and moss lined with conifer needles, fur and fine grass; female incubates 4–5 chestnut-spotted, white eggs for 11–12 days.
Feeding: gleans foliage for insects such as caterpillars, flies and aphids.
Voice: metallic *chink* call. *Male:* song consists of a thin, high-pitched *see-it see-it see-it see-it* followed by a trilling.
Similar Species: *Common Yellowthroat* (p. 293): female flanks and head are olive green to olive brown; less conspicuous eye ring. *Wilson's Warbler* (p. 294): female has all-yellow underparts, greenish yellow head, yellow eye ring. *Mourning Warbler* (p. 292): larger; all-yellow underparts; gray throat and upper breast; less obvious eye ring.

271

NORTHERN PARULA

Parula americana

The small, colorful Northern Parula is a summer forest resident across much of eastern North America, with the eastern Great Plains at the edge of its range. This warbler prefers open woodlands, especially near water. • Singing throughout the day and into the evening, the males are often very vocal. The distinctive song is not hard to identify, but their secretive nature makes them difficult to see. Expect to spend some time trying to chase one down. • Lichens, when available, are used to build the basketlike nest suspended from a tree branch. In the southern part of the range, Spanish moss is also used. • In fall, Northern Parulas begin a rather leisurely migration to their wintering grounds, largely in the West Indies, Greater Antilles and central and eastern Mexico, with some birds overwintering in Florida. In spring, Northern Parulas are among the earliest warblers to return to the breeding grounds.

ID: bluish gray upperparts; olive patch on back; 2 white wing bars; white belly and flanks; yellow breast with 1 black and 1 orange band (both often absent on female); yellow throat and "chin"; bold, white eye ring broken by dark eye line; yellow-and-dark bill; grayish pink legs and feet. *In flight:* white center to outer tail feathers.
Size: *L* 4½ in; *W* 7 in.
Habitat: *Breeding:* moist conifer forests, humid riparian woodlands and swampy hardwood woodlands, especially with hanging lichens. *In migration:* woodlands or areas with tall shrubs.

Nesting: usually in a conifer; female weaves a small hanging nest into hanging tree lichen strands; may add lichens to a dense cluster of conifer boughs; pair incubates 4–5 brown-marked, whitish eggs for 12–14 days.
Feeding: hovers, gleans or hawks for insects and other invertebrates, mostly at branch tips, occasionally on the ground.
Voice: sharp *tzip* call. *Male:* song is a rising, buzzy trill ending with an abrupt, lower-pitched *zip*.
Similar Species: *Cerulean Warbler* (p. 366): all-blue back; dark-streaked, white breast and sides; no white eye ring. *Blue-winged Warbler* (p. 365): yellow belly and head. *Yellow-rumped Warbler* (p. 276): grayer; black streaking on breast and sides. *Yellow-throated Warbler* (p. 279): black-and-white sides and face.

YELLOW WARBLER
Dendroica petechia

Usually arriving in early May, inquisitive Yellow Warblers seem to be in perpetual motion as they flit from branch to branch among open woodland edges and riparian shrubs in search of caterpillars, aphids, beetles and other invertebrates. • Yellow Warblers are among the most frequent victims of nest parasitism by Brown-headed Cowbirds. Unlike many birds, they can recognize the foreign eggs, and many pairs will either abandon their nest or build another nest on top of the old eggs. Some persistent Yellow Warblers build over and over, creating bizarre, multilayered, high-rise nests. • During fall migration, silent, plain-looking Yellow Warblers and other similar-looking warblers can cause confusion for birders who have been lulled into a false sense of familiarity with these birds. Yellow Warblers are unique in having yellow flashes on the sides of their tails. • Because of their bright yellow plumage, Yellow Warblers are often mistakenly called "Wild Canaries."

ID: mostly bright yellow overall; black eyes and bill; yellowish legs. *Male:* red to chestnut breast streaks. *Female:* fainter breast streaks. *In flight:* bright yellow highlights on dark, yellowish olive tail and wings.

Size: *L* 5 in; *W* 8 in.

Habitat: moist, open woodlands with dense, low scrub; also shrubby meadows, willow tangles, shrubby fencerows and riparian woodlands; usually near water.

Nesting: in a fork in a hardwood tree or small shrub; female builds a compact cup nest of grass, weeds and shredded bark lined with plant down and fur; female

incubates 4–5 brown- or gray-speckled or spotted, pale green eggs for 11–12 days.

Feeding: gleans foliage and vegetation for invertebrates, especially caterpillars, beetles, aphids and cankerworms; occasionally hover-gleans.

Voice: sharp *tzip* call. *Male:* song is a fast, frequently repeated *sweet-sweet-sweet summer sweet.*

Similar Species: *Orange-crowned Warbler* (p. 270): darker olive overall; no reddish breast streaks; white eye ring. *Wilson's Warbler* (p. 294): unstreaked underparts; dark crown; shorter, darker tail. *Common Yellowthroat* (p. 293): female has darker face and upperparts, all-olive wings, grayish belly. *Prothonotary Warbler* (p. 287): bluish gray wings and tail. *American Goldfinch* (p. 357): black wings and tail; dark crown and forehead; heavier, orangy bill.

CHESTNUT-SIDED WARBLER

Dendroica pensylvanica

When colorful waves of warbler migrants flood across the landscape each spring, Chestnut-sided Warblers consistently rank among the most anticipated arrivals. The boldly patterned males never fail to dazzle onlookers as they flit about at eye level. • Chestnut-sided Warblers tend to favor early-succession forests, which have become abundant over the past century. Although clear-cut logging has had a negative impact on other warbler species, it has created suitable habitat for the Chestnut-sided Warbler in many areas. A good indicator of this species' success is that each spring you can easily see more Chestnut-sided Warblers in a single day than John James Audubon saw in his entire life—he saw only one! • Although other warblers lose some of their brighter colors in fall yet still look familiar, the Chestnut-sided Warbler undergoes a complete transformation, looking more like a flycatcher or kinglet in its green-and-gray coat.

breeding

ID: black wings with whitish to yellow feather edges and bars; white underparts; yellow "cap"; black or gray legs. *Breeding male:* black-and-yellow back; chestnut brown sides; black "mask" and "mustache."
Breeding female: less striking than male; less chestnut on sides; dark streaking on yellow "cap"; less black on face.
Nonbreeding: greener back, nape and crown; gray sides and face; white eye ring.
In flight: whitish corners on tail.
Size: *L* 5 in; *W* 8 in.

Habitat: shrubby, hardwood second-growth woodlands, abandoned fields and orchards; especially in areas that are regenerating after logging or fire.
Nesting: low in a shrub or sapling; small cup nest is made of bark strips, grass, roots and weed fibers and lined with fine grass, plant down and fur; female incubates 4 brown-marked, whitish eggs for 11–12 days.
Feeding: gleans trees and shrubs at midlevel for insects.
Voice: musical *chip* call. *Male:* loud, clear song: *so pleased, pleased, pleased to MEET-CHA!*
Similar Species: *Bay-breasted Warbler* (p. 283): breeding male has black "cheek" and more extensive rufous on sides, breast and crown; other plumages show yellow on lower face and upper breast. *American Redstart* (p. 286): female has plainer upperparts, yellow on sides, gray crown, longer tail with large, yellow patches.

MAGNOLIA WARBLER

Dendroica magnolia

The Magnolia Warbler is widely regarded as one of the most beautiful wood-warblers. Like a customized Cadillac, the breeding male Magnolia comes fully loaded with all the fancy features: bold "eyebrows," flashy wing bars and tail patches, an elegant "necklace," a bright yellow rump and breast and a dark "mask." It frequently forages along the lower branches of trees and among shrubs, allowing for reliable, close-up observations. • Male Magnolias flash their white wing and tail patches, snap bills, chase and use *chip* notes to discourage intruders, but competitive singing is used to settle the most intense disputes. • Magnolia Warblers and many other songbirds migrate at night. Unfortunately, many birds are killed each year when they collide with tall buildings, radio towers and smokestacks.

breeding

ID: dark upperparts; yellow underparts with bold, black streaks; bluish gray crown. *Breeding male:* black upper back; 2 white wing bars (often merged); black "necklace" and "mask"; white "eyebrow."
Breeding female: duller overall; paler "mask"; yellow-streaked, olive back. *Nonbreeding:* separate wing bars; no necklace; faint or no "eyebrow." *In flight:* yellow rump; broken, white tail band.
Size: *L* 4½–5 in; *W* 7½ in.
Habitat: *Breeding:* open conifer and mixed forests, mostly in natural openings and along edges, frequently near water; often prefers areas with short balsam fir and white spruce. *In migration:* woodlands or areas with tall shrubs.

Nesting: on a horizontal limb in a conifer; loose cup nest of grass, twigs and weeds is lined with rootlets; female incubates 4 white eggs, marked with several dark tones, for 11–13 days.
Feeding: gleans vegetation and buds; occasionally flycatches for beetles, flies, wasps, caterpillars and other insects; sometimes eats berries.
Voice: *clank* call. *Male:* quick, rising *pretty pretty lady* or *wheata wheata wheet-zu* song.
Similar Species: *Yellow-rumped Warbler* (p. 276): larger; underparts have less yellow (no streaking on yellow areas); usually has white throat. *Cape May Warbler* (p. 365): male has chestnut "cheek" patch and streaking extends to "chin"; female has yellow "eyebrow" but none on lower breast or belly. *Prairie Warbler* (p. 281): faint, yellowish wing bars; partial "necklace"; yellow face with dusky eye line and "jaw stripe."

YELLOW-RUMPED WARBLER

Dendroica coronata

Your greatest chance of meeting the Yellow-rumped Warbler, North America's most abundant and widespread wood-warbler, is from late April to late May. It tends to forage among streamside and lakeshore trees during the first few hours after dawn, but it is the least choosy of all warblers in migration, spreading out and using all kinds of habitats. • Many migrating Yellow-rumps continue onward, but latecomers stay to nest in open and mixed woods in Minnesota and the north-western Great Plains. Adults are generally quiet when they have eggs or nestlings to guard. Noise and aggression usually indicate that the young have recently left the nest. • The widespread, white-throated "Myrtle Warbler" is most common, but you might encounter the very rarely seen yellow-throated western race, "Audubon's Warbler." • This bird's yellow crown inspired the scientific name *coronata*, Latin for "crowned."

ID: white underparts; dark streaking and yellow patch on sides; faint, white wing bars; white ("Myrtle") or yellow ("Audubon's") throat; white "eyebrow" (faint on "Audubon's"); broken, white eye ring. *Male:* black-streaked, bluish gray upperparts; wing bars may merge; yellow crown; black streaking, breast band and "cheek." *Female:* browner upperparts; paler streaking; fainter crown. *In flight:* yellow rump; partly white outer tail feathers.
Size: *L* 5–6 in; *W* 9 in.
Habitat: *Breeding:* conifer and mixed forests; rarely in all-hardwood stands. *In migration:* prefers woodlands or shrubby areas.

Nesting: in a conifer crotch or on a horizontal limb; female builds a compact cup nest of grass, bark strips, moss, lichen and spider silk lined with feathers and fur; female incubates 4–5 brown- and gray-marked, creamy eggs for about 12 days.
Feeding: hawks and hovers for beetles, flies, wasps, caterpillars, moths and other insects; also gleans vegetation; sometimes eats berries.
Voice: sharp *chip* or *check* call. *Male:* variable song is a tinkling trill, often in 2-note rising or falling phrases.
Similar Species: *Magnolia Warbler* (p. 275): yellow underparts; bluish gray crown. *Cape May Warbler* (p. 365): heavily streaked, yellow throat, breast and sides; grayish olive or dark crown. *Yellow-throated Warbler* (p. 279): black-sided, all-yellow breast and throat; dark crown and rump.

BLACK-THROATED GREEN WARBLER

Dendroica virens

Before the first warm rays of dawn brighten the spires of our forests, male Black-throated Green Warblers offer up their distinctive *see-see-see SUZY!* tunes. On their breeding grounds, males not only use song to defend their turf, but they also seem to thrive on chasing each other, and even other songbirds, from their territories. • In some other parts of its range, the Black-throated Green Warbler nests in pure deciduous forests or conifer plantations. • Black-throated Green females will lay one egg every day for four to five days. They begin to brood the eggs only when the last one is laid. • When foraging among the forest canopy, males are highly conspicuous as they dart from branch to branch, chipping noisily as they go. Females often prefer to feed at lower levels among the foliage of tall shrubs and sapling trees.

ID: olive back, rump and crown; dark wings and tail; 2 white wing bars; yellow-tinged, white lower breast, belly and undertail coverts; black upper breast band and side streaks; yellow face; possible faint, dusky "cheek" or eye line. *Male:* black throat. *Female:* yellow throat. *In flight:* mostly white outer tail feathers.
Size: *L* 4½–5 in; *W* 7½ in.
Habitat: *Breeding:* conifer and mixed forests; also in some woodlands composed of beech, maple or birch; may inhabit cedar swamps, hemlock ravines and conifer plantations. *In migration:* woodlands; areas with tall shrubs.
Nesting: usually in a conifer crotch or on a horizontal limb; compact cup nest of grass,

weeds, twigs, bark, lichen and spider silk is lined with soft materials; female incubates 4–5 chestnut-marked, creamy to gray eggs for 12 days.
Feeding: gleans vegetation and buds for beetles, flies, wasps, caterpillars and other insects; sometimes takes berries; frequently hover-gleans.
Voice: fairly soft *tick* call. *Male:* fast *see-see-see SUZY!* or *zoo zee zoo zoo zee* song.
Similar Species: *Blackburnian Warbler* (p. 278): female has browner back and crown, 2 white back stripes, yellower breast, angular facial patch. *Cape May Warbler* (p. 365): female has grayer upperparts, heavily streaked yellow throat and whitish breast and sides. *Pine Warbler* (p. 280): fainter streaking on yellower breast and sides; drabber face.

277

BLACKBURNIAN WARBLER

Dendroica fusca

Widely regarded as one of North America's most beautiful warblers—the male's fiery orange throat is ablaze in spring—the colorful Blackburnian Warbler breeds high among towering conifer spires, where it stays hidden for much of summer. • By foraging in different niches (such as high or low, close to the trunk or far from it) and using different feeding strategies, a number of species of wood-warblers can coexist in the same area. Blackburnians have found their niche predominantly in the outermost branches of the crowns of mature trees. • This bird's name is thought to honor the Blackburne family of England, whose members collected the type specimen and managed the museum in which it was housed. Making an odd reference to this bird's dull winter plumage, *fusca* is Latin for "dusky."

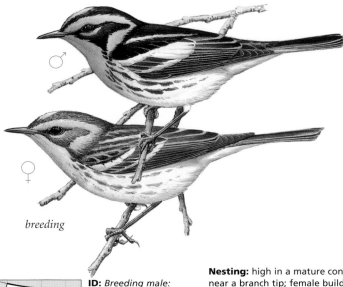

breeding

ID: *Breeding male:* blackish upperparts; large, white wing patch; dark streaking on sides and flanks; yellowish to whitish underparts; fiery, reddish orange upper breast and throat; yellowish orange head with 2 broad, black crown stripes and angular, black "mask." *Female:* like male, with brown replacing black and yellow replacing orange. *In flight:* mostly white outer tail feathers.

Size: *L* 4½–5½ in; *W* 8½ in.

Habitat: *Breeding:* mature conifer and mixed forests. *In migration:* woodlands; areas with tall shrubs.

Nesting: high in a mature conifer, often near a branch tip; female builds a cup nest of bark, twigs and plant fibers lined with conifer needles, moss and fur; female incubates 3–5 white to greenish eggs, blotched with reddish brown toward larger end, for about 13 days.

Feeding: forages on uppermost branches, gleaning budworms, flies, beetles and other invertebrates; occasionally hover-gleans.

Voice: short *tick* call. *Male:* song is a soft, faint, high-pitched *ptoo-too-too-too tititi zeee* or *see-me see-me see-me see-me.*

Similar Species: *Yellow-throated Warbler* (p. 279): bluish gray upperparts; white "eyebrow," eye crescent and ear patch; bright yellow throat. *Prairie Warbler* (p. 281): olive gray upperparts; faint, yellowish wing bars; dark facial stripes do not form solid angular patch.

YELLOW-THROATED WARBLER
Dendroica dominica

The southeastern corner of the Great Plains is just within the breeding range of the striking Yellow-throated Warbler, and fall and early winter can produce the odd wayward Yellow-throat at backyard feeders in many parts of our region. The bright lemon yellow of the throat and upper breast occasionally catches the sun and gives this bird an unexpected flamboyance at odds with its generally quiet and unassuming demeanor. Now and again the male will break into a series of sweet, clear, descending whistles ending with a two-note flourish before returning to the job at hand. • Yellow-throats are fond of wet lowland forests and prefer the upper canopy. They forage more like creepers than warblers, inserting their unusually long bills into bark cracks and crevices. Yellow-throats often forage on the undersides of horizontal branches, and sometimes on the trunk, areas also used by the Black-and-white Warbler.

ID: bluish gray upperparts; 2 white wing bars; white underparts; black-streaked sides; yellow upper breast and throat; black forehead; bold, white "eyebrow," ear patch and under-eye crescent; triangular, black "mask." *In flight:* mostly white outer tail feathers.
Size: *L* 5–5½ in; *W* 8 in.
Habitat: primarily riparian woodlands with many tall sycamore trees; occasionally at backyard feeders in winter.
Nesting: high in a sycamore tree, often near a branch tip; female builds a cup nest of fine grass, weed stems, plant down and caterpillar silk lined with sycamore down and feathers; female incubates 4 greenish

to grayish white eggs, blotched and speckled with lavender, gray and wine red, for 12–13 days.
Feeding: primarily insectivorous; gleans insects from tree trunks and foliage by creeping along tree surfaces; often flycatches insects in midair; wintering birds may eat suet from feeders.
Voice: loud *churp* call. *Male:* boisterous song is a series of downslurred whistles with a final rising note: *tee-ew tee-ew tee-ew tew-wee.*
Similar Species: *Magnolia Warbler* (p. 275): yellow upper belly and rump; black "necklace"; no white ear patch. *Blackburnian Warbler* (p. 278): male's head is all orange and black; female is browner overall. *Yellow-throated Vireo* (p. 213): larger; no dark side streaking; olive-and-yellow face.

PINE WARBLER

Dendroica pinus

Perfectly named for its habitat, the unassuming Pine Warbler is often difficult to find. It typically forages near the tops of very tall mature pines, preferring long-needled white pines and red pines and avoiding short-needled species. This preference limits its breeding to the northeastern and southeastern edges of the Great Plains. Occasionally, a foraging Pine Warbler can be seen smeared with patches of sticky pine resin. • The Pine Warbler's modest appearance, which is very similar to that of some immature and fall-plumaged warblers and vireos, forces birders to obtain a good, long look before making a positive identification. This warbler is most often confused with the Bay-breasted Warbler or Blackpoll Warbler in drab fall plumage. • The Pine Warbler is peculiar among the wood-warblers in that both its breeding and wintering ranges are located almost entirely within the U.S. and Canada.

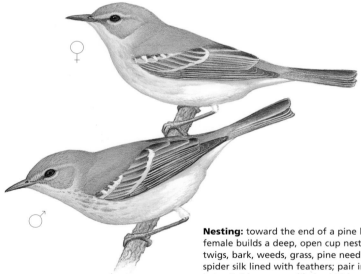

ID: *Male:* olive green back and head; dark grayish wings and tail; whitish wing bars; yellow throat and breast; dusky streaking or wash on sides; white undertail coverts and belly; faint, dark eye line; faint, broken, yellow eye ring. *Female:* similar to male but duller, especially in fall. *In flight:* mostly white outer tail feathers.
Size: *L* 5–5½ in; *W* 8½ in.
Habitat: *Breeding:* open, mature pine woodlands and mature pine plantations. *In migration:* mixed and hardwood woodlands.

Nesting: toward the end of a pine limb; female builds a deep, open cup nest of twigs, bark, weeds, grass, pine needles and spider silk lined with feathers; pair incubates 3–5 brown-speckled, whitish eggs for about 10 days.
Feeding: gleans from the ground; gleans foliage by climbing around trees and shrubs; may hang upside down on branch tips like a chickadee or a titmouse; eats mostly insects, berries and seeds.
Voice: sweet *chip* call. *Male:* song is a short, musical trill.
Similar Species: *Prairie Warbler* (p. 281): female is brighter yellow with yellowish wing bars, yellow belly, darker side streaking. *Bay-breasted Warbler* (p. 283) and *Blackpoll Warbler* (p. 284): nonbreeding birds have dark streaking on heads, backs or both and long, thin, yellow "eyebrows." *Yellow-throated Vireo* (p. 213): unstreaked sides; gray rump and tail.

PRAIRIE WARBLER

Dendroica discolor

Open scrublands host the summer activities of the inappropriately named Prairie Warbler. This bird occupies early successional areas with such poor soil conditions that the vegetation remains short and scattered. • It is thought the Prairie Warbler was rare over much of its current breeding range in the early 1800s, before North America was widely colonized. As settlers cleared land, the Prairie Warbler gradually occupied what is now its current range. Because this bird uses early successional habitats, which change over time, its breeding locations change as well. A male Prairie Warbler may return each year to a favored nest site until the vegetation in that area grows too tall and dense, at which point he moves to a new area. • On their nesting territories, song wars occasionally result in physical fights between competing males. When the dust and feathers clear, the victor resumes his slow, graceful, butterfly-like courtship flight.

ID: *Male:* olive gray upperparts; inconspicuous, chestnut streaks on back; 2 faint, yellowish wing bars; black streaking on sides; bright yellow underparts (except for white undertail coverts) and face; dark "cheek" stripe and eye line. *Female:* duller than male. *In flight:* white outer tail feathers.
Size: *L* 4½–5 in; *W* 7 in.
Habitat: shrubby sites and young pine plantations. *Breeding:* dry, open, scrubby sand dunes; young jack pine plains; burned-over sites; young pine plantations with hardwood scrub.
Nesting: sometimes loosely colonial; low in a shrub or small tree; female builds an open cup nest of soft vegetation lined with animal hair; female incubates 4 brown-spotted, whitish eggs, for 11–14 days; pair raises the young.
Feeding: gleans, hover-gleans and occasionally hawks for prey; mainly insectivorous; also eats berries and tree sap exposed by sapsuckers; caterpillars are a favored nestling food.
Voice: sweet *chip* call. *Male:* buzzy song is an ascending series of *zee* notes;
Similar Species: *Pine Warbler* (p. 280): duller overall; lighter streaking on sides. *Yellow-throated Warbler* (p. 279): white belly; white facial markings. *Bay-breasted Warbler* (p. 283) and *Blackpoll Warbler* (p. 284): nonbreeding birds have lighter, olive-streaked backs, white wing bars, white bellies.

PALM WARBLER

Dendroica palmarum

Considering this bird's subtropical wintering range, it may make sense to call it the Palm Warbler, even though it doesn't actually forage in palm trees. Based on its summer range, it could just as easily have been named "Bog Warbler" because of its preference for northern bogs and fens of sphagnum moss and black spruce. Despite its name, the Palm Warbler nests farther north than all other wood-warblers except the Blackpoll Warbler. • The Palm Warbler is unusual in its preference for foraging on the ground or in low shrubs and vegetation. It nests directly on the ground in a bog, usually below a young conifer. • Whether the Palm Warbler is hopping on the ground or perched momentarily on an elevated limb, it incessantly bobs its tail. This trait is a prominent field mark, particularly in fall, when its distinctive chestnut crown fades to olive brown.

breeding

ID: olive brown upperparts; yellow or white breast and belly; dark-streaked breast and sides; yellow undertail coverts and throat; chestnut "cap" (inconspicuous in fall); yellow "eyebrow"; frequent tail-bobbing. *In flight:* dull yellow rump; white-cornered tail.

Size: *L* 4–5½ in; *W* 8 in.

Habitat: *Breeding:* edges of mature bogs with scattered black spruce; less frequently in openings of spruce–tamarack forests with sphagnum moss and shrubs; rarely in jack pine plains. *In migration:* woodlands or areas with tall shrubs.

Nesting: on the ground or in a low shrub or spruce, often on a concealed sphagnum hummock; female builds a cup nest of grass, weeds and bark lined with feathers; female incubates 4–5 brown-marked, creamy eggs for about 12 days.

Feeding: hovers or perches to glean the ground and vegetation for a variety of insects and berries; occasionally hawks for insects; sometimes takes seeds.

Voice: sharp *sup* or *check* call. *Male:* song is a weak, buzzy trill with a quick finish.

Similar Species: *Prairie Warbler* (p. 281): olive gray upperparts; brighter yellow extends onto belly; streaking on sides only; olive crown. *Pine Warbler* (p. 280): white undertail coverts; no prominent "eyebrow." *Chipping Sparrow* (p. 305) and *American Tree Sparrow* (p. 304): unstreaked, grayish underparts; no yellow plumage; more robust bills.

BAY-BREASTED WARBLER

Dendroica castanea

Like all migratory birds, Bay-breasted Warblers face many dangers on their travels. Their annual trip north to the spruce–fir forests of Canada, however, seems well worth it for the abundance of summer food found there. Rare in some years, Bay-breasts may pass through the eastern Great Plains in large numbers in the spring following a successful preceding nesting season. • Bay-breasted Warblers are spruce budworm specialists, and their populations fluctuate from year to year along with the cyclical rise and fall of budworm numbers. These birds are invaluable when it comes to the suppression of budworm outbreaks, typically moving to where the larvae are most numerous. In outbreak situations, Bay-breasted Warblers will lay more eggs than usual to capitalize on the bountiful food supply. Although Bay-breasts are insectivorous on their breeding grounds, they switch to an almost all-fruit diet while they winter in Panama and Colombia.

breeding

ID: *Breeding male:* chestnut sides, flanks, throat and crown; dark wings with 2 white bars; creamy yellow belly, undertail coverts and patch on side of neck; black face. *Breeding female:* paler colors overall, particularly on chestnut areas and face. *Nonbreeding:* yellowish olive back and head; dark-streaked back and crown; whiter underparts; chestnut-tinged sides. *In flight:* white-cornered tail.
Size: *L* 5–6 in; *W* 9 in.
Habitat: *Breeding:* mature conifer and mixed boreal forest; almost exclusively in spruce and fir stands. *In migration:* woodlands or areas with tall shrubs.
Nesting: usually on a horizontal conifer branch; open cup nest of grass, twigs, moss, roots and lichen is lined with fine bark strips and fur; female incubates 4–5 dark-marked, whitish eggs for about 13 days.
Feeding: usually forages at the midlevel of trees; gleans vegetation and branches for caterpillars and adult invertebrates; eats numerous spruce budworms when available.
Voice: high *see* call. *Male:* song is an extremely high-pitched *seee-seese-seese-seee*.
Similar Species: *Cape May Warbler* (p. 365): female has streaked sides and no chestnut markings. *Chestnut-sided Warbler* (p. 274): smaller; yellow crown; breeding bird has white "cheek" area; nonbreeding bird has gray face and white eye ring. *Blackpoll Warbler* (p. 284): nonbreeding has white undertail coverts, olive-streaked breasts and sides.

BLACKPOLL WARBLER

Dendroica striata

The Blackpoll Warbler is the greatest warbler migrant. Weighing less than a wet teabag, this bird is known to fly south over the Atlantic, leaving land at Cape Cod and flying for 88 hours nonstop until it reaches the northern coast of Venezuela. In such a trip, a Blackpoll Warbler will cover almost 1900 miles, and in a single year it may fly up to 15,000 miles! In migration, the Blackpoll Warbler adjusts its flying altitude—sometimes traveling at heights of 20,000 feet—to best use shifting prevailing winds to reach its destination. This bird is truly an international resident, so the conservation of its habitat requires the efforts of several nations. • Blackpoll Warblers in fall plumage are easily confused with Bay-breasted Warblers, but most Blackpolls migrate later in fall than their Bay-breasted counterparts. • This bird's scientific name *striata* means "striped" in Latin.

breeding

ID: 2 white wing bars; dark-streaked, white underparts; all-white undertail coverts. *Breeding male:* black-streaked, olive gray upperparts; black "cap"; white "cheek"; black "mustache" stripe; orangy yellow legs. *Breeding female:* drabber underparts; streaked, yellowish olive back and head; pale "eyebrow"; small, dark eye line. *Nonbreeding:* resembles breeding female but is more generally olive yellow; dark legs. *In flight:* white-cornered tail.

Size: *L* 5–5½ in; *W* 9 in.
Habitat: mixed woodlands.
Nesting: does not nest in the Great Plains.
Feeding: gleans buds, leaves and branches for aphids, mosquitoes, beetles, wasps, caterpillars and many other insects; often flycatches for insects.
Voice: loud *chip* call. *Male:* song is an extremely high-pitched, uniform trill: *tsit tsit tsit.*
Similar Species: *Black-and-white Warbler* (p. 285): striped, black-and-white crown; bold, white "eyebrow"; dark legs year-round. *Chickadees* (p. 232–33): unstreaked sides; black "bib"; shorter bill. *Bay-breasted Warbler* (p. 283): nonbreeding bird has no streaking on underparts and dark legs year-round.

BLACK-AND-WHITE WARBLER

Mniotilta varia

Birders with frayed nerves and tired eyes from watching flitty warblers will be refreshed by the sight of the Black-and-white Warbler as it methodically creeps up and down tree trunks, probing bark crevices. The foraging behavior of the Black-and-white Warbler stands in sharp contrast to that of most of its kin. Rather than dancing or flitting quickly between twig perches, this bird behaves like a creeper or nuthatch, both of which are only distantly related. • Novice birders can easily identify this unique, two-tone warbler, which retains its standard plumage throughout its stay in our region. Even a trip to its wintering grounds will reveal this warbler in the same black-and-white outfit. A keen ear also helps to identify this forest-dweller: the male's gentle, oscillating song—like a wheel in need of greasing—is easily recognized and remembered.

ID: dark upperparts with white streaking; 2 white wing bars; white underparts with black streaking on sides, flanks and undertail coverts; black-and-white-striped crown; black legs. *Male:* black "cheek" and throat. *Female:* gray "cheek"; white throat. *In flight:* white-cornered tail.
Size: *L* 4½–5½ in; *W* 8 in.
Habitat: hardwood or mixed forests, often near water; also in cedar swamps and alder and willow thickets bordering muskeg and beaver ponds.
Nesting: usually on the ground next to a tree, log or large rock; in a shallow scrape, often among a pile of dead leaves; female builds a cup nest of grass, leaves, bark strips, rootlets and pine needles lined with fur and fine grass; female incubates 5 brown-flecked, creamy white eggs for 10–12 days.
Feeding: gleans insect eggs, larval insects, beetles, spiders and other invertebrates while creeping along tree trunks and branches.
Voice: sharp *pit* and soft, high *seet* calls. *Male:* song is a series of high, thin, 2-syllable notes: *weetsee weetsee weetsee weetsee weetsee weetsee.*
Similar Species: *Blackpoll Warbler* (p. 284): breeding male has solid black "cap"and all-white undertail coverts.

AMERICAN REDSTART

Setophaga ruticilla

American Redstarts are a consistent favorite among birders. These supercharged birds flit from branch to branch in dizzying pursuit of prey. Even when perched, their tails sway rhythmically back and forth. Few birds can rival a mature male for his contrasting black-and-orange plumage and amusing behavior.
• A common foraging technique used by the American Redstart is to flash its wings and tail patches to flush prey. If a concealed insect tries to flee, the redstart will give chase. The American Redstart behaves much the same way on its Central American wintering grounds, where it is known locally as *candelita,* meaning "little candle."
• Although Redstarts are common in the northern Great Plains, the male's beautiful, trilly song is so variable that identifying this species by song alone is a challenge to birders of all levels.

ID: white belly and undertail coverts. *Male:* black upperparts and breast; reddish orange foreshoulder, wing and tail patches. *Female:* olive brown upper-parts; yellow foreshoul-der, wing and tail patches; white breast; grayish green head. *In flight:* long tail with black tip and center; male has orange-tinged wing lining.
Size: *L* 5 in; *W* 8 in.
Habitat: shrubby woodland edges, open and semi-open hardwood and mixed forests with a regenerating hardwood understory of shrubs and saplings; often near water.

Nesting: in the fork of a shrub or sapling, usually 3–23 ft above the ground; female builds an open cup nest of plant down, bark shreds, grass and rootlets lined with feathers; female incubates 4 whitish eggs, marked with brown or gray, for 11–12 days.
Feeding: actively gleans foliage and hawks for insects and spiders on leaves, buds and branches; often hover-gleans.
Voice: sharp, sweet *chip* call. *Male:* song is a highly variable series of *tseet* or *zee* notes, often given at different pitches.
Similar Species: *Virginia's Warbler* (p. 365): limited range; generally gray with yellow breast and undertail coverts. *Blackbirds* (pp. 339–48): males are much larger with all-black underparts and tails. *Orioles* (pp. 349–51): much larger; white wing bars; broad expanses of yellow, orange or red on breast and often below.

PROTHONOTARY WARBLER

Protonotaria citrea

Standing dead trees and stumps riddled with natural cavities and woodpecker excavations provide perfect nesting habitat for this bird, especially if the site is near stagnant, swampy water. Much of the Prothonotary's swampy habitat is inaccessible to most birders, but if you are in the right place at the right time, you might be lucky enough to come across a Prothonotary as it forages for insects along tree trunks and decaying logs, in low, tangled thickets and on debris floating on the water's surface. • The male can be very aggressive when defending his territory and often resorts to combative aerial chases when songs and warning displays fail to intimidate an intruder. Benign cavity-nesting neighbors such as woodpeckers, wrens and bluebirds also often fall victim to this fury. • This bird's unusual name reflects the similarity in coloration between its head and the hoods worn by prothonotaries, high-ranking clerics in the Catholic Church.

breeding

In flight: gray of rump extends onto upper center of black-tipped, mostly white tail.
Size: *L* 5½ in; *W* 8½ in.
Habitat: hardwood swamps and riparian woodlands.
Nesting: natural cavity in standing dead tree or rotten stump, birdhouse or abandoned woodpecker nest, from water level to 10 ft above the ground; often reused;

ID: olive green back; unmarked, bluish gray wings and tail; yellow undersides; white undertail coverts; unmarked, yellow head; large, dark eyes; long, dark bill. *Male:* slightly orangy on yellow areas; blacker bill.

mostly the male builds a cup nest of twigs, leaves, moss and plant down lined with soft plant material; female incubates 4–6 brown-spotted, creamy to pinkish eggs for 12–14 days.
Feeding: gleans from vegetation; may hop on floating debris or creep along tree trunks; eats a variety of insects and small mollusks.
Voice: brisk *tink* call. *Male:* loud, ringing song is a 1-pitch series of *sweet* or *zweet* notes; flight song is *chewee chewee chee chee.*
Similar Species: *Blue-winged Warbler* (p. 365): white wing bars; black eye line. *Yellow Warbler* (p. 273): olive wings and tail with yellow highlights; yellow undertail coverts. *Hooded Warbler* (p. 366): female has yellowish olive upperpart and yellow undertail coverts.

287

OVENBIRD

Seiurus aurocapilla

The Ovenbird's loud and joyous "ode to teachers" is a common sound that echoes through hardwood and mixed forests in spring, but pinpointing the exact location of this resonating call is not always easy. An Ovenbird will rarely expose itself, and even when it does, active searching and patience are necessary to get a good look at it. What may sound like one long-winded Ovenbird may actually be two neighboring males singing and responding on the heels of each other's song. • The name "Ovenbird" refers to this bird's unusual, dome-shaped ground nest. An incubating female nestled within her woven dome usually feels so secure that she will choose to sit tight rather than flee when approached. The nest is so well camouflaged that few people ever find one, even though nests are often located near hiking trails and bike paths. • Robert Frost was so moved by this warbler's spring songs that he dedicated the poem "Ovenbird" to it.

ID: olive brown upperparts; no wing bars; white underparts; heavy, dark streaking on sides, flanks, breast and throat; black-bordered, rufous crown; white eye ring; pink legs. *In flight:* dark-edged, whitish underwing; dark tail.

Size: *L* 6 in; *W* 9½ in.

Habitat: *Breeding:* undisturbed, mature forests with a closed canopy and very little understory; often in ravines and riparian areas. *In migration:* dense riparian shrubbery and thickets; variety of woodlands.

Nesting: on the ground; female builds an oven-shaped, domed nest of grass, weeds, bark, twigs and dead leaves lined with animal hair; female incubates 4–5 white eggs, spotted with gray and brown, for 11–13 days.

Feeding: gleans the ground for worms, snails, insects and occasionally seeds.

Voice: brisk *chip, cheep* or *chock* call. *Male:* sings loud, distinctive *tea-cher tea-cher tea-CHER tea-CHER*, increasing in speed and volume; night song is an elaborate series of bubbly, warbled notes, often ending in *teacher-teacher*.

Similar Species: *Northern Waterthrush* (p. 289) and *Louisiana Waterthrush* (p. 290): all-dark crown; bold, whitish "eyebrow"; dark eye line; dark wing lining. *Thrushes* (pp. 254–57): larger; most have blurrier sides; plainer crowns.

NORTHERN WATERTHRUSH

Seiurus noveboracensis

Birders unsatisfied with simply hearing a Northern Waterthrush must literally get their feet wet if they hope to see one as it skulks along the shores of the hardwood swamps and conifer bogs of its nesting territory, where the fallen logs, shrubby tangles and soggy ground discourage many human visitors. During the relatively bug-free months of spring and fall, however, migrating Northern Waterthrushes typically appear within drier, upland forests or along lofty park trails and boardwalks. A backyard featuring a small garden pond may also attract migrating waterthrushes. • The voice of the Northern Waterthrush is loud and raucous for such a small bird, so it seems fitting that this bird was once known as the New York Warbler, in reference to the city so well known for its decibels. The scientific name *noveboracensis* means "of New York." • Although this bird's long body looks "thrush-like," the Northern Waterthrush is actually a wood-warbler.

ID: olive brown upperparts; pale yellowish to buff underparts with dark streaking; finely spotted throat; pale yellowish to buffy "eyebrow"; pinkish legs; frequently tail-bobbing. *In flight:* all-dark wings and tail.

Size: *L* 5–6 in; *W* 9½ in.

Habitat: wooded edges of swamps, lakes, beaver ponds, bogs and rivers; also in moist, wooded ravines and riparian thickets.

Nesting: on the ground, usually near water; female builds a cup nest of moss, leaves, bark shreds, twigs and pine needles lined with moss, hair and rootlets; female incubates 4–5 whitish eggs, spotted and blotched with brown and purple gray, for about 13 days.

Feeding: gleans foliage and the ground for invertebrates, frequently tossing aside ground litter with its bill; may also take aquatic invertebrates and small fish from shallow water.

Voice: brisk *chip* or *chuck* call. *Male:* song is a loud, 3-part *sweet sweet sweet, swee wee wee, chew chew chew chew.*

Similar Species: *Louisiana Waterthrush* (p. 290): buffy orange wash on flanks; unmarked, white throat; broader, white "eyebrow." *Ovenbird* (p. 288): rufous crown bordered by black stripes; no whitish "eyebrow"; bold, white eye ring. *Thrushes* (pp. 254–57): no conspicuous, pale "eyebrows."

LOUISIANA WATERTHRUSH

Seiurus motacilla

The Louisiana Waterthrush is often seen sallying along the shorelines of babbling streams and gently swirling pools in search of its next meal. This bird dwells in swamps and sluggish streams throughout much of its North American range, but where its range overlaps with the Northern Waterthrush's, it inhabits shorelines near fast-flowing water. • The Louisiana Waterthrush has a larger bill, pinker legs and whiter "eyebrows" than the Northern Waterthrush, along with an unstreaked throat. As the scientific name *motacilla* (Latin for "wagtail") suggests, the Louisiana Waterthrush moves its tail up and down as it walks, but more slowly than its cousin, and it tends to sway from side to side as well. Bobbing heads also mark both waterthrushes. • The Louisiana Waterthrush has never been recorded in great numbers in the Great Plains, partly because little suitable habitat remains. Its future success depends on the stewardship of private landowners to protect its nesting habitat.

ID: brownish upperparts; white underparts with buffy orange wash on flanks; long, dark streaks on breast and sides; all-white throat; "eyebrow" is buff ahead of eye and white behind; long bill; pink legs. *In flight:* all-dark wings and tail.

Size: *L* 6 in; *W* 10 in.

Habitat: moist, forested ravines alongside fast-flowing streams; rarely along wooded swamps.

Nesting: concealed within a rocky hollow or a tangle of tree roots; pair builds a cup nest of leaves, bark strips, twigs and moss lined with animal hair, ferns and rootlets;

female incubates 3–6 creamy white eggs, spotted with brown and purplish gray, for about 14 days.

Feeding: gleans terrestrial and aquatic insects and crustaceans from rocks and debris in or near shallow water; may overturn dead leaves and other debris in probing for food; occasionally catches flying insects over water.

Voice: brisk *chick* or *chink* call. *Male:* song begins with 3–4 distinctive, shrill, slurred notes followed by a warbling twitter.

Similar Species: *Northern Waterthrush* (p. 289): yellowish to buff "eyebrow" narrows behind eye; usually all-yellowish or buff underparts (occasionally white); finely spotted throat; no buffy orange on flanks. *Ovenbird* (p. 288) and *thrushes* (pp. 254–57): no broad, white "eyebrows."

KENTUCKY WARBLER

Oporornis formosus

Yet another eastern warbler found only along the eastern edge of the Great Plains, the Kentucky Warbler is the only *Oporornis* warbler to nest south of Minnesota. Never easy to see, the Kentucky Warbler rarely leaves the confines of its dense ground cover, where it forages stealthily. • The shy and elusive males sing their loud springtime song from secluded perches. As a general rule, male warblers sing most actively and feed only intermittently in the morning, but they quiet down and feed more actively in the afternoon. Once the young hatch, singing becomes rare as both the male and the female spend much of their time feeding the young. Unmated males may continue to sing throughout summer. The Kentucky Warbler's song may be confused with that of the Carolina Wren, but the Kentucky Warbler will sing the same song pattern repeatedly, whereas the Carolina Wren varies its song constantly. • Like waterthrushes and Ovenbirds, Kentucky Warblers bob their tails up and down as they walk.

ID: olive green upperparts; bright yellow underparts, throat and "spectacles." *Male:* black crown, "sideburns" and half "mask." *Female:* dark areas are more olive than black. *In flight:* olive wings and tail.

Size: *L* 5–5½ in; *W* 8½ in.

Habitat: moist hardwood and mixed woodlands with dense, shrubby cover and herbaceous plant growth, including wooded ravines, swamp edges and creek bottomlands.

Nesting: on or close to the ground; pair builds a cup nest of plant material and hair lined with rootlets and hair; female incubates 4–5 cream-colored eggs, spotted or blotched with reddish brown, for 12–13 days.

Feeding: gleans insects while walking along the ground and flipping over leaf litter; also snatches prey from the undersides of low foliage.

Voice: sharp *chick* call. *Male:* musical song (reminiscent of the Carolina Wren) is a series of 2-syllable notes: *chur-ree chur-ree.*

Similar Species: *Canada Warbler* (p. 295): dark, streaky "necklace"; bluish gray upperparts. *Yellow-throated Warbler* (p. 279): bluish gray upperparts; yellow is limited mostly to throat area. *Prairie Warbler* (p. 281): streaked sides.

MOURNING WARBLER

Oporornis philadelphia

Mourning Warblers seldom leave the protection of their dense, shrubby, often impenetrable habitat, and the males tend to utter their *cheery* song only on their breeding territory. Riparian areas, regenerating cut-blocks and patches of forest that have been recently cleared by fire provide the low shrubs and saplings—largely hardwoods—that these birds rely on for nesting and foraging. • Mourning Warblers are best seen during migration, when backyard shrubs and raspberry thickets may attract small, silent flocks. • This bird's dark hood reminded 19th-century pioneering ornithologist Alexander Wilson of someone dressed in mourning. Some birders like to remember this bird's name by thinking that it is mourning the loss of its eye ring (thus helping distinguish it from several similarly plumaged species).

breeding

ID: olive green upperparts; yellow underparts; pinkish legs; short tail. *Breeding male:* black upper breast patch; bluish gray "hood"; possible broken eye ring. *Female:* whitish throat and "chin"; gray "hood"; possible thin eye ring. *In flight:* dusky yellow wing linings.
Size: *L* 5–5½ in; *W* 7½ in.
Habitat: dense and shrubby thickets, tangles and brambles, often in moist areas of forest clearings and riparian areas.
Nesting: on the ground at the base of a shrub or plant tussock or in a small shrub; bulky nest of leaves, weeds and grass is

lined with fur and fine grass; female incubates 3–4 creamy white eggs, spotted or blotched with brown, for about 12 days.
Feeding: forages in dense, low shrubs for caterpillars, beetles, spiders and other invertebrates.
Voice: loud, low *check* call. *Male:* husky, 2-part song is variable and lower-pitched at the end: *churry, churry, churry, churry, chorry, chorry.*
Similar Species: *Connecticut Warbler:* all-gray breast; complete, bold eye ring; brown of immature's hood extends across breast. *Nashville Warbler* (p. 271): smaller; paler "hood"; bold eye ring; dark legs. *MacGillivray's Warbler* (p. 366): broken, white eye ring; at rest, tail appears longer; male has dark eye line; female has whiter throat.

COMMON YELLOWTHROAT

Geothlypis trichas

The Common Yellowthroat is one of our most common warblers. This energetic songster of our wetlands is a favorite among birders—its small size, bright plumage and spunky disposition quickly endear it to all observers. • The Common Yellowthroat favors shrubby marshes and wet, overgrown meadows, shunning the forest habitat preferred by most of its wood-warbler relatives. In May and June, the male Yellowthroat issues his distinctive *wichity-witchity-witchity* songs while perched atop tall cattails or shrubs. Observing a male in action will reveal the location of his favorite singing perches, which he visits in rotation. These strategic outposts mark the boundary of his territory, which he fiercely guards from intrusion by other males. • Unfortunately for the Common Yellowthroat, its nests are frequently parasitized by the Brown-headed Cowbird.

ID: olive green to olive brown upperparts; yellow undertail coverts, throat and breast; dingy white belly; orangy legs. *Male:* broad, black "mask" with white upper border. *Female:* all-olive face; may show faint, white eye ring. *In flight:* olive underwing with paler lining.
Size: *L* 5 in; *W* 6½ in.
Habitat: cattail marshes, riparian willow and alder clumps, sedge wetlands, beaver ponds and wet, overgrown meadows; sometimes dry, abandoned fields.
Nesting: on or near the ground, often in a small shrub or among emergent aquatic vegetation; female builds a bulky, open cup nest of weeds, grass, sedges and other materials, lined with hair and soft plant fibers; female incubates 3–5 creamy white eggs, spotted with brown and black, for 12 days.
Feeding: gleans vegetation and hovers for adult and larval insects, including dragonflies and beetles; also eats spiders and occasionally seeds.
Voice: sharp *tcheck* or *tchet* call. *Male:* song is a clear, oscillating *witchety witchety witchety-witch.*
Similar Species: male's black "mask" is distinctive. *Kentucky Warbler* (p. 291): yellow underparts; half "mask"; yellow "spectacles." *Yellow Warbler* (p. 273): female has yellow highlights on wings, yellow belly. *Wilson's Warbler* (p. 294): forehead, "eyebrow" and "cheek" are yellow like underparts; may show dark "cap." *Orange-crowned Warbler* (p. 270): dull, yellowish olive overall; faint breast streaks. *Nashville Warbler* (p. 271): bluish gray crown; complete, bold eye ring.

WILSON'S WARBLER

Wilsonia pusilla

Y ou are almost sure to catch sight of the energetic Wilson's Warbler at any migration hotspot. This lively bird flickers quickly through tangles of leaves and trees, darting frequently into the air to catch flying insects. Birders often become exhausted while pursuing a Wilson's Warbler, but the bird itself never seems to tire during its lightning-fast performances. • This bird may make brief stopovers in the shrubs of almost any backyard during spring or fall migration, but its nesting habitat is mostly in early successional stages of willow and alder near bogs and shrub-lined beaver ponds and in pioneering trees on drier sites well north and west of the Great Plains. • The Wilson's Warbler is richly deserving of its name. Named after Alexander Wilson, this species epitomizes the energetic devotion that the pioneering ornithologist exhibited in the study of North American birds in the 19th century.

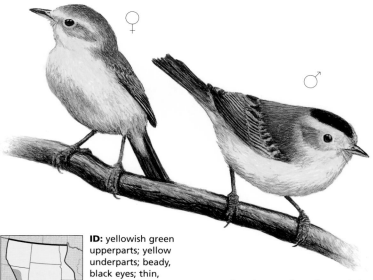

ID: yellowish green upperparts; yellow underparts; beady, black eyes; thin, pointed bill; orange legs. *Male:* black "cap." *Female:* faint "cap" or none. *In flight:* dark wing with yellowish olive lining.

Size: *L* 4½–5 in; *W* 7 in.

Habitat: *Breeding:* riparian woodlands, willow and alder thickets, bogs and wet, shrubby meadows. *In migration:* woodlands or areas with tall shrubs.

Nesting: on the ground in moss or at the base of a shrub; female builds a nest of moss, grass and leaves lined with animal hair and fine grass; female incubates 4–6 brown-marked, creamy white eggs for 10–13 days.

Feeding: hovers, flycatches and gleans vegetation for insects.

Voice: flat, low *chet* or *chuck* call. *Male:* rapid, chattering song drops in pitch at the end: *chi chi chi chi chet chet.*

Similar Species: male's black "cap" is distinctive. *Yellow Warbler* (p. 273): female has white highlights on wings, duller underparts, more uniform head coloration. *Common Yellowthroat* (p. 293): female has brownish or grayish belly and sides, all-olive face. *Kentucky Warbler* (p. 291): larger; dark, angular "half mask"; yellow "spectacles." *Orange-crowned Warbler* (p. 270): dull yellowish olive overall; faint breast streaks. *Nashville Warbler* (p. 271): bluish gray head; bold eye ring.

CANADA WARBLER

Wilsonia canadensis

Bold "spectacles" give the Canada Warbler a wide-eyed, alert appearance. Fairly inquisitive, this bird will occasionally pop up from dense shrubs in response to passersby. • Although several wood-warblers breed exclusively in Canada, the Canada Warbler isn't one of them. Most Canada Warblers nest in eastern and northern Canada, but some can be found nesting in the Appalachian and northeastern states, including northern Minnesota. • Canada Warblers live in open defiance of winter: they never stay in one place long enough to experience one! As the summer nesting season comes to a close, these warblers migrate to South America. Unlike most wood-warblers, Canadas have a strong pair bond and often migrate and overwinter together. • This active forager typically catches more insects on the wing than most of its cousins do.

ID: bluish gray upperparts, browner on wings; yellow underparts (except white undertail coverts); yellow "spectacles"; pale legs. *Male:* streaky, black "necklace"; dark, angular "half mask." *Female:* fainter "necklace" and "half mask." *In flight:* whitish wing linings.

Size: *L* 5–6 in; *W* 8 in.

Habitat: *Breeding:* wet, low-lying areas of mixed forests with a dense understory, especially riparian willow–alder thickets; also cedar woodlands and swamps. *In migration:* woodlands; areas with tall shrubs.

Nesting: on a mossy hummock or upturned root or stump; female builds a loose, bulky cup nest of leaves, grass, ferns, weeds and bark lined with animal hair and soft plant fibers; probably largely the female incubates 4 brown-spotted, creamy white eggs for 10–14 days.

Feeding: gleans the ground and vegetation for beetles, flies, hairless caterpillars, mosquitoes and other insects; frequently flycatches flushed prey; occasionally hovers.

Voice: *tick* call. *Male:* song begins with 1 sharp *chip* note and continues with a rich, variable warble.

Similar Species: *Kentucky Warbler* (p. 291): olive green upperparts; yellow undertail coverts; no black "necklace"; half eye ring. *Northern Parula* (p. 272): white wing bars; white belly and flanks; bluer head; broken, white eye ring; shorter tail.

YELLOW-BREASTED CHAT

Icteria virens

The unique Yellow-breasted Chat, measuring over 7 inches in length, is almost a warbler-and-a-half. New DNA evidence shows that it isn't really closely related to any other genus of living bird, so it may soon be removed from its position with the warblers. • On its breeding grounds throughout much of the Great Plains, the Yellow-breasted Chat keeps to dense, often thorny cover. It typically thrashes about in dense undergrowth, rarely holding back its strange vocalizations, thereby often drawing attention to itself. • The Yellow-breasted Chat is not a strong or frequent flier, but during courtship the male advertises for a mate by launching off his perch to hover in the air with head held high and legs dangling, chirping incessantly until he drops back down.

ID: olive green upperparts; yellow to orange breast and throat; white undertail coverts; white "spectacles"; white "jaw line"; heavy, black bill; grayish black legs; long tail. *Male:* black lores. *Female:* gray lores. *In flight:* usually flies only short distances.
Size: *L* 7½ in; *W* 9½ in.
Habitat: riparian thickets, brambles and shrubby tangles.
Nesting: low in a shrub or hardwood sapling; well-concealed, bulky base of leaves and weeds holds an inner woven cup nest of vine bark lined with fine grass and plant fibers; female incubates 3–4 creamy white eggs, spotted with brown toward the large end, for about 11 days.
Feeding: gleans insects from low vegetation; eats berries in fall.
Voice: calls include a *whoit, chack* and *kook. Male:* song is an assorted series of whistles, "laughs," squeaks, grunts, rattles and mews.
Similar Species: *American Robin* (p. 258): larger; darker upperparts; reddish orange breast; black-streaked, white throat; thinner, yellow bill. *Tanagers* (pp. 297–99): females have mostly yellow heads and more robust bills. *Orioles* (pp. 349–51): females have wing bars, mostly yellow to brownish heads and no eye rings.

SUMMER TANAGER

Piranga rubra

Summer Tanagers thrive on a wide variety of insects, but they are best known for their courageous attacks on wasps. These birds snatch flying wasps and bees from menacing swarms, and may even harass the occupants of a wasp nest to the point that the nest is abandoned, leaving the larvae inside free for the picking. When not foraging, Summer Tanagers tend to be hard to spot as they move slowly through leafy treetop concealment. • The northern limits of the Summer Tanager's breeding range reach southeastern Nebraska. • Breeding males are bright rosy red overall, whereas first-spring males look like females that have toppled head-first into a tub of strawberries. Eastern females have traces of red in the plumage, but occasional western females do not.

ID: robust, pale yellowish or orangy bill. *Male:* rose red overall; sometimes crest shows. *Female:* grayish yellow to greenish yellow upperparts; dusky yellow underparts; may have orange or reddish wash overall. *Immature male:* resembles female, but with patchy red, largely on head and breast. *In flight:* wing lining matches underparts.
Size: *L* 7–8 in; *W* 12 in.
Habitat: mixed woodlands, especially those with oak or hickory, or riparian woodlands with cottonwoods.
Nesting: on a horizontal tree limb; loosely constructed nest of grass, forbs and other plant material is lined with fine grass; female incubates 3–5 pale green or bluish green, brown-splotched eggs for 11–12 days.

Feeding: gleans insects from the tree canopy; may hover-glean or hawk insects in midair; also eats berries and other small fruits; known to raid wasp nests.
Voice: call is *pit* or *pit-a-tuck*. *Male:* song is a series of 3–5 sweet, clear, whistled phrases, like a faster version of the American Robin's.
Similar Species: *Scarlet Tanager* (p. 298): smaller bill; blackish wings and tail; white wing linings; female has uniformly olive upperparts and brighter underparts. *Western Tanager* (p. 299): gray to blackish back, wings and tail; wing bars; smaller bill; mostly yellow male has reddish orange on head only. *Northern Cardinal* (p. 331): male has prominent head crest, black "mask" and "bib," red bill. *Orioles* (pp. 349–51): females have wing bars and thinner, sharper bills.

SCARLET TANAGER

Piranga olivacea

Each spring, birders eagerly await the sweet, rough-edged song of the lovely male Scarlet Tanager, which is often the only thing that gives away this unobtrusive forest inhabitant. The return of the brilliant red male to wooded ravines and traditional nest sites is always a much-anticipated event. • During the cold and rainy weather that often dampens spring migration, you may find yourself in the enviable position of observing a Scarlet Tanager at eye level as it forages in the forest understory. At other times, this bird can be surprisingly difficult to spot as it darts through the forest canopy in pursuit of insect prey. • In Central and South America, over 200 tanager species represent every color of the rainbow. The Scarlet Tanager migrates farther than any other tanager—most of the others are sedentary birds in Central and South American forests.

breeding

ID: *Breeding male:* bright red overall; pure black wings and tail; pale bill. *Fall male:* red areas become patchy with greenish yellow. *Nonbreeding male:* bright yellow underparts; olive upperparts; black wings and tail. *Female:* resembles nonbreeding male, but duller. *In flight:* white wing linings.
Size: *L* 7 in; *W* 11½ in.
Habitat: fairly mature, upland hardwood and mixed forests and large woodlands.
Nesting: usually in a hardwood; on a high branch, well away from the trunk; female builds a flimsy, shallow cup of grass, weeds and twigs lined with rootlets and fine grass;

female incubates 2–5 pale bluish green, chestnut-spotted eggs for 12–14 days.
Feeding: gleans tree-canopy insects; hover-gleans or hawks insects in midair; may forage at lower levels during cold weather; takes some berries.
Voice: *chip-burrr* or *chip-churrr* call. *Male:* song is a series of 4–5 sweet, clear, whistled phrases like a slurred American Robin's.
Similar Species: *Summer Tanager* (p. 297): larger bill; breeding male has red wings and tail; duskier breeding female with paler wings is often red-tinged. *Western Tanager* (p. 299): dark back; wing bars. *Northern Cardinal* (p. 331): male has red wings, prominent crest, black "mask" and "bib." *Orioles* (pp. 349–51): females have wing bars and thinner, sharper bills. *Vermilion Flycatcher* (p. 363): male has black "mask" and fine, black bill.

WESTERN TANAGER

Piranga ludoviciana

Few birds can match the tropical splendor of the tanagers. Three species of this Central and South American family breed in the Great Plains, renewing their acquaintances with their strictly southern relatives in winter. The Western Tanager is limited mainly to the western Great Plains. • The male Western Tanager is the most colorful of the three species seen here—with a golden body accentuated by black wings and tail and an orange red face, he brings a splash of color to the foothills and lower mountain slopes. His song closely parallels the phrases of an American Robin's song. The tanager's notes are somewhat hoarser, as if the bird had a sore throat, and it ends with a distinctive, hiccuplike *pit-a-tik*. • Female tanagers are more cryptically colored than males, and the female Western Tanager is no exception.

breeding

ID: *Breeding male:* black back, wings and tail; yellow nape, underparts and rump; 1 yellow and 1 white wing bar; often has entirely red head; pale bill. *Breeding female:* olive green overall, yellower below; dark wings with faint bars. *Nonbreeding male:* drabber yellows; typically only forehead and chin areas are reddish. *In flight:* whitish olive yellow wing linings.
Size: *L* 7 in; *W* 11–12 in.
Habitat: *Breeding:* variety of foothill and mountain forests and woodlands; favors tall conifers with or without a hardwood component, from sea level to 9000 ft.

In migration: almost any stand of trees, even if small or isolated.
Nesting: in a conifer fork or on a horizontal branch, far from the trunk; loosely built cup nest of twigs and other plant materials is lined with fine vegetation; female incubates 4 eggs for 13–14 days.
Feeding: gleans vegetation and catches prey on the wing; eats wasps, beetles and other insects; also eats fruit; drinks from the ground.
Voice: unique, crisp *pritik* or *priterik* call. *Male:* song is a hoarse, rapid series of dry 2- or 3-note phrases.
Similar Species: *Summer Tanager* (p. 297): female has no wing bars and larger bill. *Scarlet Tanager* (p. 298): female has fainter or no wing bars and olive back. *Orioles* (pp. 349–51): females have paler tails and thinner, sharper bills.

SPOTTED TOWHEE

Pipilo maculatus

Even though it is shy, the Spotted Towhee is not a quiet neighbor. Scratching for food on the forest floor, it really puts both feet to full use, scratching its long claws to reveal anything hidden in the leaf litter. Expecting to find a squirrel making such a ruckus, most people are surprised to find a bird not much larger than a sparrow. • Towhees like tangled thickets and overgrown gardens, especially if there are blackberries or other small fruits for the taking. Many pairs visit urban neighborhoods, where they take turns scolding the family cat and checking out any suspicious sounds. • Spotted Towhees rarely leave their sub-arboreal world, except to perform their simple courtship song or to furtively eye a threat to their territory. These curious birds can often be enticed into view by "squeaking" or "pishing," but discerning birders would rather not disturb these busy birds, preferring instead to simply enjoy the sound of their clamorous exploits.

♂

ID: *Male:* black back, wings, tail and "hood"; bold, white wing spots; white belly; pale, rufous undertail coverts; rufous flanks; red eyes; conical dark bill; white-tipped outer tail feathers. *Female:* somewhat drabber and paler overall. *In flight:* brownish white wing linings.
Size: *L* 7–8½ in; *W* 10–11 in.
Habitat: riparian thickets, chaparral, brushy ravines; shady canyons and thick undergrowth in suburban parks and gardens.

Nesting: low in a bush, on the ground under cover or in a brushy pile; cup nest of leaves, grass and bark shreds is lined with fine materials; primarily the female incubates 3–4 brown-wreathed, white eggs for 12–13 days.
Feeding: scratches the ground vigorously for seeds and insects; periodically visits feeding stations; seldom feeds in trees; also eats berries and acorns, especially in winter.
Voice: raspy or whining *chee* or *chwaay* call. *Male:* song is a simple, querulous trilling: *here here here PLEASE.*
Similar Species: *Eastern Towhee* (p. 301): white on wing restricted mostly to "wrist" marking; chestnut or yellowish white eyes. *Black-headed Grosbeak* (p. 333): orangy nape and rump; black eyes; much heavier bill. *"Oregon" Dark-eyed Junco* (p. 325): smaller; pale rufous back; pale bill.

EASTERN TOWHEE

Pipilo erythrophthalmus

Eastern Towhees are often heard before they are seen. These noisy foragers rustle about in dense undergrowth, craftily scraping back layers of dry leaves to expose the seeds, berries or insects hidden beneath. Like Spotted Towhees, they employ an unusual two-footed technique to uncover food items—a strategy that is especially important in winter when virtually all of their food is taken from the ground. • Although you wouldn't guess it, this colorful bird is a member of the American Sparrow family, a normally drably colored group. • The Eastern Towhee and its similar western relative, the Spotted Towhee, were once grouped together as a single species called "Rufous-sided Towhee." • The scientific name *Pipilo* is derived from the Latin *pipo*, meaning "to chirp or peep," and *erythrophthalmus* is derived from Greek words that mean "red eye."

ID: *Male:* black back, wings, tail and "hood"; white belly; buff undertail coverts; rufous sides and flanks; chestnut or yellowish white eyes; conical, dark bill; white-tipped outer tail feathers. *Female:* brown upperparts and "hood." *In flight:* buffy to grayish wing linings.

Size: *L* 7–8½ in; *W* 10½ in.

Habitat: wide variety of undergrowth, including field edges, tangled thickets and berry patches, along woodland edges and in shrubby, abandoned fields.

Nesting: on the ground or low in a dense shrub; female builds a camouflaged cup nest of twigs, bark strips, grass, weeds, rootlets and animal hair; mostly the female incubates 3–4 creamy white to pale gray eggs, spotted with brown toward the larger end, for 12 to 13 days.

Feeding: scratches at leaf litter for insects, seeds and berries; sometimes forages in low shrubs and saplings.

Voice: scratchy, slurred *cheweee!* or *chewink!* call. *Male:* song is 2 high, whistled notes followed by a trill: *drink your teeeee.*

Similar Species: *Spotted Towhee* (p. 300): white-spotted wing without "wrist" marking; red eyes. *Black-headed Grosbeak* (p. 333): orangy nape and rump; black eyes; much heavier bill. *"Oregon" Dark-eyed Junco* (p. 325): smaller; pale rufous back; pale bill.

CASSIN'S SPARROW

Aimophila cassinii

Dull and plain in appearance and extremely secretive most of the year, the Cassin's Sparrow nests in pairs in dense, tall grasslands with scattered bushes. • A wet year in the prairies will most likely entice large numbers of Cassin's Sparrows to appear in the Great Plains. These birds will range large distances when the prairies are parched, following the rains to feed on the more plentiful insects and seeds that result from the moisture. • If another male enters his territory, the incumbent male Cassin's Sparrow will "skylark," launching from tall grass to float down with the notes of his sweet, trilling song. In productive years, male Cassin's Sparrows will have singing competitions from their individual grass tops as they compete for breeding territory. • S.W. Woodhouse collected the first specimen of this bird in San Antonio, Texas, in 1851. He named it for John Cassin of the Academy of Natural Sciences in Philadelphia, Pennsylvania.

ID: overall brown markings; dark-barred upperparts (sometimes with rufous spots and streaks) yield a spotted pattern, and white outlines give a "scaly" look; faintly streaked, off-white underparts; rounded head; long tail. *In flight:* obviously pale tips on outer feathers of rounded tail.

Size: *L* 5½–6 in; *W* 7½–8 in.

Habitat: sand–sage prairies, arid grasslands with scattered shrubs, yuccas, rabbitbush or low trees, especially on open slopes. *In migration:* brushy draws and canyons.

Nesting: on the ground or low in a bush; cup nest of grass, roots and bark is camouflaged by surrounding vegetation; female incubates 3–5 white eggs for 10 days; pair feeds the young.

Feeding: hops along the ground to catch insects and pick dropped seeds; will eat many invertebrates, including beetles and grasshoppers.

Voice: *chip* call. *Male:* song is 1–2 clear notes followed by a varied trill and a clear *I have-a great song!*

Similar Species: *Grasshopper Sparrow* (p. 313): bolder coloration overall; large, rufous spots on back and innermost flight feathers; unmarked, buff underparts; black-and-white-striped crown; shorter tail. *Other sparrows* (pp. 303–24): mostly have bolder head markings.

RUFOUS-CROWNED SPARROW

Aimophila ruficeps

The Rufous-crowned Sparrow is a bird of brushy and grassy areas on rocky hillsides along the southern borders of the Great Plains. It usually avoids the prairie grasslands, dense chaparral and oak-dominated woodlands that many Great Plains sparrows prefer. Instead, it remains devoted to the arid, grassy slopes and shrub-strewn, rocky outcroppings that carpet many adjacent canyons and foothills. • In winter, Rufous-crowned Sparrows are seen hopping about in search of seeds from sun-dried grasses and herbaceous plants. • When alarmed or disturbed, this sparrow will readily issue a nasal *deer-deer-deer*.

ID: chestnut-striped, gray back; unstreaked, buffy gray breast; whitish throat; rufous crown with pale central stripe; gray "eyebrow" and "cheek"; black and white "whisker" stripes; white eye ring; rufous line behind eye; gray bill. *In flight:* all-dark tail.

Size: *L* 6 in; *W* 7½–8 in.

Habitat: grassy shrublands and open woodlands on rocky hillsides and in canyons; rocky slopes of mesas.

Nesting: on the ground under a shrub or grass clump or in a low shrub; open cup of twigs, grass and plant fibers is often lined with animal hair; likely the female incubates 3–4 pale bluish white eggs for 11–13 days; pair feeds the young.

Feeding: largely searches small areas on foot; eats mostly grass and forb seeds, stems and shoots, but insects predominate in spring and summer.

Voice: sharp *deer-deer* or *deer-deer-deer* call. *Male:* song is a series of rapid, bubbling warbles and *chip* notes.

Similar Species: *Cassin's Sparrow* (p. 302): plainer crown and face. *American Tree Sparrow* (p. 304): wing bars; dark breast spot; unstriped crown; stubby bill; yellow lower mandible. *Chipping Sparrow* (p. 305) and *Clay-colored Sparrow* (p. 306): darker back stripes; wing bars; gray napes. *Swamp Sparrow* (p. 321): more rufous overall; black-and-buff back; unclear breast streaks. *Canyon Towhee* (p. 366): much heavier; more uniform upperparts.

AMERICAN TREE SPARROW

Spizella arborea

Most of us know American Tree Sparrows as winter visitors to backyard feeders, but the best time to see these rufous-capped, spot-breasted sparrows is in late March and April when they are in migration. As the small flocks migrate northward, they offer bubbly, bright songs between bouts of foraging along the ground or in low, budding shrubs. • Although its name suggests a close relationship with trees or forests, the American Tree Sparrow actually prefers treeless fields and semi-open, shrubby habitats. This bird got its name because of a superficial resemblance to the Eurasian Tree Sparrow (*Passer montanus*), which would have been familiar to many early settlers. Perhaps a more appropriate name for this bird would be "Subarctic Shrub Sparrow." With adequate food supplies, the American Tree Sparrow can survive temperatures as low as −28° F.

breeding

ID: *Breeding:* mottled, dark brown, gray and buff upperparts; 2 white wing bars; unstreaked gray underparts; central, dark breast spot; pale rufous "cap"; gray face; rufous stripe behind eye; dark upper mandible; yellow lower mandible; dark legs. *Nonbreeding:* gray central crown stripe. *In flight:* slightly notched tail.
Size: *L* 6–6½ in; *W* 9½ in.
Habitat: brushy thickets, roadside shrubs, semi-open fields and croplands.
Nesting: does not nest in the Great Plains.

Feeding: scratches exposed soil or snow for seeds in winter; takes some berries and occasionally visits bird feeders.
Voice: call is a 3-note *tsee-dle-eat. Male:* song, which may be given in late winter and during spring migration, is a high, whistled *tseet-tseet* followed by a short, sweet, musical series of slurred whistles.
Similar Species: *Chipping Sparrow* (p. 305): no dark breast spot; white "eyebrow"; black eye line. *Swamp Sparrow* (p. 321): no wing bars or dark breast spot; white throat. *Field Sparrow* (p. 308): no dark breast spot; white eye ring; orangy pink bill. *Rufous-crowned Sparrow* (p. 303): no wing bars; no dark breast spot; pale-striped crown; all-gray bill.

CHIPPING SPARROW

Spizella passerina

The Chipping Sparrow and the Dark-eyed Junco do not share the same tailor, but the males must have attended the same voice lessons, because their songs are very similar. Although the rapid trill of the Chipping Sparrow is slightly faster, drier and less musical than the junco's, even experienced birders can have difficulty identifying this singer. • Chipping Sparrows commonly nest at eye level, so you can easily watch their breeding and nest-building rituals. They are well known for their preference for conifers as nest sites and for hair as a lining material for their nests. By planting conifers in your backyard and offering some of your pet's hair—or even your own—in backyard baskets in spring, you could attract nesting Chipping Sparrows to your area and contribute to their nesting success. • Named for its call, the Chipping Sparrow is among the smallest and tamest of sparrows.

breeding

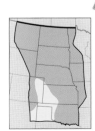

ID: buff-and-brown upperparts; 2 faint whitish wing bars; light gray, unstreaked underparts; full, black eye line. *Breeding:* prominent rufous "cap"; white "eyebrow"; all-dark bill; pale legs. *Nonbreeding:* paler crown with dark streaks; brownish "eyebrow" and "cheek"; mostly pinkish yellow bill. *In flight:* pale gray wing lining.
Size: *L* 5–6 in; *W* 8½ in.
Habitat: open conifers or mixed woodland edges; often in yards and gardens with tree and shrub borders.

Nesting: usually at midlevel in a conifer; female weaves a compact cup nest of grass and rootlets, often lined with hair; female incubates 4 pale blue eggs for 11–12 days.
Feeding: gleans seeds from the ground and from the outer branches of trees or shrubs; prefers seeds from grass, dandelions and clovers; also eats adult and larval invertebrates; occasionally visits feeders.
Voice: high-pitched *chip* call. *Male:* song is a rapid, dry trill of *chip* notes.
Similar Species: *Clay-colored Sparrow* (p. 306): stronger "jaw line" markings; eye line behind eye only. *American Tree Sparrow* (p. 304): dark central breast spot; rufous stripe behind eye; no white "eyebrow." *Swamp Sparrow* (p. 321): no wing bars; no white "eyebrow." *Field Sparrow* (p. 308): no white "eyebrow"; partial, rufous eye line; white eye ring; orangy pink bill.

CLAY-COLORED SPARROW

Spizella pallida

With their plumage, habit and voice all contributing to a cryptic lifestyle, Clay-colored Sparrows go for the most part completely unnoticed. Even when males are singing at the top of their vocal cords, they are usually mistaken for buzzing insects. • The scientific name *pallida*, Latin for "pale," refers to this bird's overall coloration. Even though it is subtle in plumage, the Clay-colored Sparrow still possesses an unassuming beauty. Birders looking closely at this sparrow to confirm its identity can easily appreciate its delicate shading, texture and form—features so often overlooked on birds with more colorful plumage. • Often found in shrubby, open bogs and willow scrub habitat, Clay-colored Sparrows will tag along with migrant and wintering Chipping Sparrows and Dark-eyed Juncos and show up in a variety of open-ground habitats.

breeding

ID: *Breeding:* dark feathers with broad buff edges on upperparts; gray nape; unstreaked, whitish underparts; buffy wash on breast and sides; brown border separates white throat and "jaw stripe"; brown crown with dark streak and pale central stripe; pale "eyebrow"; light brown "cheek" edged with darker brown; dark eye line. *Nonbreeding:* buffier overall. *In flight:* buffy wing linings.
Size: *L* 5–6 in; *W* 7½ in.
Habitat: brushy open areas along forest and woodland edges; in forest openings, regenerating burn sites, abandoned fields and riparian thickets.
Nesting: in a grassy tuft or a small shrub; female builds an open cup nest of twigs, grass, weeds and rootlets lined with rootlets, fine grass and fur; mostly the female incubates 4 brown-speckled, bluish green eggs for 10–12 days.
Feeding: takes seeds and insects from the ground and low vegetation.
Voice: soft *chip* call. *Male:* song is a series of 2–5 slow, low-pitched, insectlike buzzes.
Similar Species: *Chipping Sparrow* (p. 305): plainer "jaw line" area; dark eye line continues to bill; breeding bird has rufous crown and dark bill. *Brewer's Sparrow* (p. 307): duller colors overall; white eye ring; shorter, drabber bill. *Field Sparrow* (p. 308): less black on upperparts; gray face; no white "eyebrow"; rusty streak behind eye; white eye ring.

BREWER'S SPARROW

Spizella breweri

Strip away all the breast streaks, "caps," crown stripes and facial markings that adorn most other sparrows, and you're left with the Brewer's Sparrow. This sparrow's identity is often determined not from its visible features but from its buzzy call and its characteristic quick getaway flights, because it only infrequently obliges binocular-toting birders by perching in the open. • Brewer's Sparrow is most frequently encountered in sagebrush habitats. It is remarkably well adapted to its dry environments and can survive long periods of drought by getting sufficient water from its diet of seeds. Over time, both the sparrow and its habitat have declined in our region. • John Cassin named this bird for Dr. Thomas Mayo Brewer, a 19th-century physician and ornithologist who made significant contributions to the understanding of the breeding behavior of North American birds.

breeding

ID: finely streaked, brown upperparts; light brown, unstreaked underparts; brown cheek patch; faint eye ring; light throat; pale "eyebrow" and "jaw stripe"; short, pale, dull-colored bill; light pinkish legs.
In flight: grayish wing linings.
Size: *L* 5 in; *W* 7–8 in.
Habitat: sagebrush flats and grasslands.
Nesting: in a low, dense shrub; small, compact, woven cup nest of grass and roots is lined with fine materials and fur; pair incubates 3–5 brown-spotted, light bluish green eggs for 11–13 days.
Feeding: forages on the ground and gleans low vegetation for adult and larval invertebrates and seeds.
Voice: buzzy and *chip* calls. *Male:* extremely variable, canary-like song with buzzes and trills, up to 10 seconds long; often includes trills of different speeds and pitches in the same song.
Similar Species: *Clay-colored Sparrow* (p. 306): more pronounced facial markings and crown stripe; brighter bill color; no eye ring. *Cassin's Sparrow* (p. 302): heavier; browner overall; redder legs.

307

FIELD SPARROW

Spizella pusilla

Deserted farmland may seem unproductive to some people, but to the pink-billed Field Sparrow, which frequents overgrown fields, pastures and forest clearings, it is heaven. For nesting purposes, these places must be scattered with shrubs, herbaceous plants and plenty of tall grass. • Unlike most songbirds, a nestling Field Sparrow will leave its nest prematurely if disturbed. • The Field Sparrow can recognize when its nest has been parasitized by the Brown-headed Cowbird. Because the unwelcome eggs are usually too large for this small sparrow to eject, the nest is simply abandoned. This sparrow may be so stubborn in refusing to raise young cowbirds that an affected pair of Field Sparrows may make numerous nesting attempts in a single season.

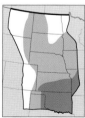

ID: gray upperparts with black and rusty stripes; 2 white wing bars; unstreaked, gray underparts; often has buffy red wash on breast, sides and flanks; gray face and throat; rusty crown with gray central stripe; white eye ring; rusty streak behind eye; orangy pink bill; pinkish legs. *In flight:* buffy wash on wing lining.

Size: *L* 5–6 in; *W* 8 in.

Habitat: abandoned or weedy and over-grown fields and pastures, woodland edges and clearings, extensive shrubby riparian areas and young conifer plantations.

Nesting: on or near the ground, often sheltered by a grass clump, shrub or sapling; female weaves an open cup nest of grass lined with animal hair and soft plant material; female incubates 3–5 brown-spotted, whitish to pale bluish white eggs for 10–12 days.

Feeding: forages on the ground, mostly for insects in summer and seeds in spring and fall.

Voice: *chip* or *tsee* call. *Male:* song is a series of woeful, musical, downslurred whistles accelerating into a trill.

Similar Species: *American Tree Sparrow* (p. 304): larger; dark, central breast spot; dark upper mandible. *Swamp Sparrow* (p. 321): white throat; dusky bill; no wing bars or eye ring. *Chipping Sparrow* (p. 305): white "eyebrow"; black eye line; dark bill; no buffy red wash on underparts.

VESPER SPARROW

Pooecetes gramineus

For birders who live near grassy fields and agricultural lands with multitudes of confusing little brown sparrows, the Vesper Sparrow offers welcome relief—white outer tail feathers and a chestnut shoulder patch announce its identity whether the bird is perched or in flight. The Vesper Sparrow is also known for the male's bold and easily distinguished song, which begins with two sets of unforgettable double notes: *here-here! there-there!* • When the business of nesting begins, the Vesper Sparrow scours the neighborhood for a potential nest site. More often than not, this bird builds its nest in a grassy hollow at the base of a clump of weeds or small shrub, thus providing camouflage, a windbreak and an umbrella to protect the young. • "Vesper" is Latin for "evening," a time when the male often sings. *Pooecetes* is Greek for "grass dweller."

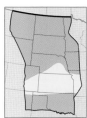

ID: streaked, black-, buff-and-brown upperparts; chestnut shoulder patch; white to creamy underparts; brown streaking on breast and (weaker) on flanks; yellowish lores; white "jaw line" and eye ring; dusky upper mandible; pale orangy lower mandible and legs. *In flight:* white-edged, rounded tail.
Size: *L* 6 in; *W* 10 in.
Habitat: open fields bordered or interspersed with shrubs, semi-open shrublands and grasslands; also in agricultural areas, open, dry conifer plantations and scrubby gravel pits.
Nesting: in a scrape on the ground, often under a grass canopy or at a shrub base;

loosely woven cup nest of grass is lined with rootlets, fine grass and hair; mostly the female incubates 3–5 brown- and gray-blotched, whitish to greenish white eggs for 11–13 days.
Feeding: walks and runs along the ground, picking up grasshoppers, beetles, cutworms, other invertebrates and seeds.
Voice: sharp *chirp* call. *Male:* song has 4 characteristic preliminary notes, with the 2nd higher in pitch, and a bubbly trill: *here-here there-there, everybody-down-the-hill.*
Similar Species: *Savannah Sparrow* (p. 312): fainter "jaw line" and eye ring; darker tail edges. *Other sparrows* (pp. 302–24): no chestnut shoulder patches; no all-white sides to tail. *American Pipit* (p. 265): plainer upperparts; plainer face; thinner bill; longer legs. *Longspurs* (pp. 326–29): white or pale "eyebrows"; slightly notched tail tips.

LARK SPARROW

Chondestes grammacus

The male Lark Sparrow's manner of singing atop small bushes or low rock outcrops in dry scrubland and open oak woodlands reminded early naturalists of the famed Sky Lark (*Alauda arvensis*) of Europe, a bird that had inspired many poets. Occasionally indulging himself in a short display flight, the male Lark Sparrow does not attain the heights reached by the Sky Lark, either in altitude or aptitude. • Although Lark Sparrows are typically seen in open, shrubby areas and "edge" habitats, they occasionally venture into meadows, grassy forest openings and wooded areas, where they might join Vesper Sparrows and Savannah Sparrows. Their unique tail pattern easily identifies them in such situations and during migration, when small flocks of Lark Sparrows are regularly seen foraging alongside juncos, other sparrows and towhees in suburban parks and gardens.

ID: mottled, soft brown back and wings; faint, pale wing bars; whitish to pale brown underparts; unstreaked, pale breast with central dark spot; distinctive "helmet" formed by chestnut red outer crown stripes and "cheek," interspersed with white throat, central crown stripe and "eyebrow" and several black lines; light-colored legs. *In flight:* black tail with mostly white tip and mostly white outer feathers.
Size: *L* 6 in; *W* 11 in.
Habitat: semi-open shrublands, sandhills, sagebrush and occasionally pastures.

Nesting: on the ground or in a low bush; occasionally reuses abandoned thrasher nests; bulky cup nest of grass and twigs is lined with finer material; female incubates 4–5 dark-spotted, whitish eggs for 11–12 days.
Feeding: walks or hops on the ground, gleaning seeds; also eats grasshoppers and other invertebrates.
Voice: sharp *tzip* call. *Male:* melodious and variable song consists of short trills, buzzes, pauses and clear notes.
Similar Species: no other sparrow has the Lark Sparrow's distinctive head pattern.

LARK BUNTING
Calamospiza melanocorys

Wherever grasslands or hay fields are found within the Lark Bunting's range, you will have a good chance of seeing the male's spectacular courtship flight. As he rises into the air, the male flutters about in circles above the prairie, beating his wings slowly and deeply. His bell-like, tinkling song spreads over the landscape until he decides to fold his wings and float to the ground like a falling leaf. Because this courtship behavior evolved on the prairie before the arrival of elevated perches such as fence posts and power poles, this bird developed the habit of delivering its song on the wing. • The numbers and breeding range of the Lark Bunting vary markedly from year to year. In drought years, it breeds farther north than usual and becomes one of the most conspicuous and abundant birds in the Great Plains. It nests in native prairie and hay fields, as well as in roadside ditches.

breeding

ID: conical, grayish blue bill; large, white wing patch (most conspicuous on male). *Breeding male:* mostly black plumage. *Female:* mottled, brown-and-buff upperparts; lightly brown-streaked, whitish underparts; pale "eyebrow." *Nonbreeding male:* like female, but streaking is darker. *In flight:* mostly white tail tip.
Size: *L* 7 in; *W* 10–11 in.

Habitat: shortgrass prairie and sagebrush, hay fields, grassy ditches.
Nesting: on the ground; sheltered by a canopy of grass or by a small bush; cup nest is loosely built with grass, roots and other plant material and lined with plant down and fur; mostly the female incubates 4–5 pale blue eggs for 11–12 days.
Feeding: walks or hops along the ground collecting insects, including grasshoppers, beetles and ants, seeds and waste grain.
Voice: soft *who-ee* call. *Male:* rich, warbling song has clear notes.
Similar Species: *Other sparrows* (pp. 302–24): no large, white wing patch. *Bobolink* (p. 339): breeding male has creamy nape, white rump and back stripes.

311

SAVANNAH SPARROW

Passerculus sandwichensis

At one time or another, most people have probably seen or heard a Savannah Sparrow, although they may not have realized it. One of the most common open-country birds, the Savannah is easily overlooked because its streaky, dull plumage resembles that of many other grassland sparrows. • From early spring to early summer, male Savannah Sparrows belt out their distinctive, buzzy tunes while perched atop prominent shrubs, tall weeds or strategic fence posts. Later in summer and throughout early fall, Savannahs are most often seen darting across roads, highways and open fields in search of food. Like most sparrows, though, they generally stay out of sight. When danger appears, Savannahs take flight only as a last resort, preferring to run swiftly and inconspicuously through the grass, almost like feathered voles. • This bird's common and scientific names reflect its broad North American distribution: "Savannah" refers to the city in Georgia, and *sandwichensis* is derived from Sandwich Bay in Alaska's Aleutian Islands.

ID: dark-mottled, brown upperparts; mostly white underparts; finely brown- or black-streaked breast, sides and flanks; possible dark breast spot; pale brown to white "jaw line"; often has buffy yellow lores; pale bill and legs. *In flight:* square-tipped, dark tail may have paler outer feathers.

Size: *L* 5–6 in; *W* 6½ in.

Habitat: agricultural fields (especially hay and alfalfa), moist sedge and grass meadows, pastures, beaches, bogs and fens.

Nesting: on the ground in a shallow scrape, well concealed by grass or a shrub; female weaves and lines an open cup nest using grass; female incubates 3–6 brown-marked, whitish to greenish or pale tan eggs for 10–13 days.

Feeding: gleans insects and seeds while walking or running along the ground; occasionally scratches.

Voice: high, thin *tsit* call. *Male:* song is a high-pitched, clear, buzzy *tea tea teeeeea today.*

Similar Species: *Vesper Sparrow* (p. 309): chestnut shoulder patch; white eye ring. *Lincoln's Sparrow* (p. 320): buff-washed breast; streaked undertail coverts; broad, gray "eyebrow." *Grasshopper Sparrow* (p. 313): unstreaked breast. *Song Sparrow* (p. 319): bolder central crown stripe; prominent, pale "eyebrow"; gray bill. *Baird's Sparrow* (p. 314): bolder crown streak; buffier face.

GRASSHOPPER SPARROW

Ammodramus savannarum

The Grasshopper Sparrow is named not for its diet but for the male's buzzy, insectlike song. During courtship flights, the male chases the female through the air, buzzing at a frequency that is usually inaudible to human ears. He sings two completely different courtship songs: one ends in a short trill and the other is a prolonged series of high trills that vary in pitch and speed. • These open-country birds prefer grassy expanses free of trees and shrubs. Wide, well-drained, grassy ditches occasionally attract nesting Grasshopper Sparrows, so mowing or harvesting these grassy margins early in the nesting season may be detrimental to these birds. Persuading local landowners and state governments to delay cutting until mid-August or September would benefit Grasshopper Sparrows. • The scientific name *Ammodramus* is Greek for "sand runner," and *savannarum* is Latin for "of the savanna," after this bird's grassy, open habitat.

ID: mottled brown upperparts with rusty, black and buffy markings; unstreaked, white underparts; buffy wash on breast, sides and flanks; flattened head profile; dark crown with pale central stripe; buffy "cheek"; beady, black eyes; pale legs. *In flight:* possible small, yellow patch on forewing edge.
Size: *L* 5–5½ in; *W* 7½ in.
Habitat: grasslands and grassy fields with minimal shrub or tree cover.
Nesting: in a shallow depression on the ground, usually concealed by grass; female builds a small cup nest of grass lined with rootlets, fine grass and hair; female incubates 4–5 creamy eggs, spotted with gray and reddish brown, for 11–13 days.

Feeding: gleans insects and seeds from the ground and grass; eats various insects, including grasshoppers.
Voice: indeterminate call. *Male:* first song is a high, faint, buzzy trill preceded by 1–3 high, thin, whistled notes: *tea-tea-tea zeeeeeeeeee;* other is *tea-sik-a-tsee sik-a-tsee.*
Similar Species: *Le Conte's Sparrow* (p. 316) and *Nelson's Sharp-tailed Sparrow* (p. 317): gray or dark streaking on breast, sides and flanks; buffy orange face; gray "cheek." *Henslow's Sparrow* (p. 315): more rust on upperparts; paler underparts; dark-streaked breast, sides and flanks; olive green face. *Baird's Sparrow* (p. 314): dark-streaked breast, sides and flanks; buffy yellow crown stripe and face.

BAIRD'S SPARROW

Ammodramus bairdii

Just when the form of this grassland sparrow drifts into focus through your binoculars, the bird frustratingly dives out of view from its perch. The male Baird's Sparrow will sing atop grass stems and low shrubs, but when he stops singing, he becomes almost impossible to find. • The Baird's Sparrow breeds in native grasslands, favoring lush areas over grazed shortgrass plains. It is seldom found during its migration to or from wintering grounds in north-central Mexico and adjacent parts of the U.S. • John James Audubon named this sparrow after Spencer Fullerton Baird (who went on to be instrumental in the development of modern ornithology), his then-young friend who was unable to join him on the 1843 expedition on which it was collected. If you think that this species is difficult to find and recognize even with today's aids to birding, consider that it took 30 years for a second ornithologist to "rediscover" Baird's Sparrow.

ID: dark brown upperparts with buffy feather edges; faint chestnut on wing coverts; whitish underparts; finely dark-streaked breast band and incomplete "necklace"; 2 black stripes border white throat; buffy nape and head; pale bill and legs. *In flight:* pale edges on brown tail.
Size: *L* 5 in; *W* 8–9 in.
Habitat: native grasslands and lightly grazed pastures with clumps of tall grass and short shrubs.

Nesting: occasionally semi-colonial; on the ground, often under bent grass or a small bush; cup nest woven with grass and other plant fibers is lined with fur and other fine materials; female incubates 4–5 chestnut-spotted, pale gray eggs for 11–12 days.
Feeding: gleans the ground, pecking and running through tall grass; eats mainly grass seeds but also other plant seeds and occasionally insects.
Voice: harsh *chip* call. *Male:* song is a tinkling, musical trill: *zip-zip-zip-zrrr-r-r-r.*
Similar Species: *Savannah Sparrow* (p. 312): grayer face and nape; often has yellowish lores. *Vesper Sparrow* (p. 309): bolder eye ring; white outer tail feathers; no "necklace" streaking. *Grasshopper Sparrow* (p. 313): unstreaked breast.

HENSLOW'S SPARROW

Ammodramus henslowii

The male Henslow's Sparrow is known for his unusual habit of singing at night. He is easier to observe by day as he throws back his streaky, greenish head while hurling his distinctive song from atop a tall blade of grass or a low shrub. • Without the male's vocal advertisements, the inconspicuous Henslow's Sparrow would be almost impossible to observe because this bird spends most of its time foraging alone along the ground. When disturbed, it may fly a short distance before dropping into cover, but it usually prefers to run through dense, concealing vegetation. Its habitat requirements are not well known and deserve further study. • John James Audubon named this sparrow after his friend John Stevens Henslow, a 19th-century British naturalist and one-time teacher of Charles Darwin.

ID: rust-tinged areas on upperparts; olive green on wings and nape; black streaking on back and wings; white underparts with dark streaking on buff breast, sides and flanks; flattened head profile; olive green central crown stripe and face; dark crown and "whisker" stripes; thick bill. *In flight:* sharp-pointed tail feathers.

Size: *L* 5–5½ in; *W* 6½ in.

Habitat: large, fallow or wild grassy fields and meadows with a matted ground layer of dead vegetation and scattered shrub or herb perches; often prefers moist areas.

Nesting: on the ground at the base of a grass clump or herbaceous plant; mostly the female builds an open cup nest of grass and weeds lined with fine grass and hair; female incubates 3–5 whitish to pale greenish eggs, spotted with gray and reddish brown, for about 11 days.

Feeding: gleans insects and seeds from the ground.

Voice: soft *tchip* call. *Male:* distinctive weak, liquidy, cricketlike *tse-lick* song is often given during rainy periods or at night.

Similar Species: *Other sparrows* (pp. 302–24): do not have olive green on wings, nape and head. *Grasshopper Sparrow* (p. 313): fainter streaking on breast and sides. *Savannah Sparrow* (p. 312): no buff on breast. *Le Conte's Sparrow* (p. 316): white edges on some upperpart feathers.

LE CONTE'S SPARROW

Ammodramus leconteii

L e Conte's Sparrows are difficult to find because of their remote breeding habitat, scattered distribution and secretive behavior. Like some of their close relatives, these sparrows prefer to scurry along the ground in thick cover, resorting to flight only for short distances before dropping out of sight again. • Even a singing male will typically choose a low, concealing perch from which to offer his gentle love ballads. A skilled birder may be able to follow this buzzy tune to its source to catch a fleeting glimpse of the singer before he dives into tall vegetation and disappears from view. • This bird's name honors John Le Conte, who is best remembered as one of America's preeminent 19th-century entomologists, but who was also interested in all areas of natural history.

ID: mottled, brown-and-black upperparts with some prominent white feather edges; buff-streaked back; buffy orange upper breast, sides, flanks and undertail coverts; dark streaking on sides and flanks, fainter on breast; white throat, lower breast and belly; black-bordered, pale central crown stripe; buffy orange face; gray "cheek"; black line behind eye; pale legs. *In flight:* sharp-pointed tail feathers.
Size: *L* 4½–5 in; *W* 6½ in.
Habitat: grassy meadows with dense vegetation, drier edges of wet sedge and grass meadows, willow and alder flats and forest openings.
Nesting: on or near the ground, concealed by tangled vegetation; female weaves an open cup nest of grass and rushes, lined with fine grass and hair and tied to standing plant stems; female incubates 3–5 grayish white eggs, spotted with gray and brown, for 12–13 days.
Feeding: gleans the ground and low vegetation for insects, spiders and seeds.
Voice: alarm call is a high-pitched whistle. *Male:* song is a weak, short, raspy, insect-like buzz: *t-t-t-zeeee zee* or *take-it ea-zeee*.
Similar Species: *Nelson's Sharp-tailed Sparrow* (p. 317): gray nape and central crown stripe; buffy throat. *Grasshopper Sparrow* (p. 313): unstreaked underparts; drabber face. *Henslow's Sparrow* (p. 315): olive green on wings, nape and head.

NELSON'S SHARP-TAILED SPARROW

Ammodramus nelsoni

If you're not prepared to get your feet wet, you probably won't find a Nelson's Sharp-tailed Sparrow. This relatively colorful sparrow will sometimes unexpectedly pop out of a soggy hiding place in its marshy habitat to perch completely exposed at a close distance. As with most sparrows, the best way to identify a Nelson's Sharp-tail is by sound—in this case, a single sharp note followed by a buzzy trill, which is a unique combination among prairie birds. • In the Nelson's Sharp-tailed Sparrow's very unusual breeding strategy, the males rove around the marsh mating with all available females. Both genders are promiscuous, and this sparrow does not establish pair bonds or territories. • Edward William Nelson was the chief of the U.S. Biological Survey and president of the American Ornithologists' Union in the early 20th century. His greatest contribution was the creation of the Migratory Bird Treaty, which is still in effect today. • This species was formerly grouped together with the Saltmarsh Sharp-tailed Sparrow (*A. caudacutus*) as a single species, the Sharp-tailed Sparrow.

ID: mostly brown upperparts with rusty wing areas and white back streaks; faintly chestnut-streaked, buffy orange underparts except for all-white lower breast and belly; gray nape; orangy face; gray "cheek"; light bill. *In flight:* sharp-pointed tail feathers.

Size: *L* 5–6 in; *W* 7 in.

Habitat: marshlands with tall emergent vegetation and shoreline vegetation.

Nesting: on the ground or low in upright grass or sedge stems; bulky, woven cup nest of dry grass and sedges is lined with fine materials; female incubates 3–5 chestnut-spotted, pale greenish to light turquoise eggs for 11 days.

Feeding: runs or walks along the ground gleaning ants, beetles, grasshoppers and often other invertebrates; also eats seeds.

Voice: soft *tick* call. *Male:* raspy *ts tse-sheeeee* song.

Similar Species: *Le Conte's Sparrow* (p. 316): buff-streaked back; dark-streaked nape. *Grasshopper Sparrow* (p. 313): unstreaked underparts; drabber face. *Savannah Sparrow* (p. 312): little or no orangy coloration in plumage. *Henslow's Sparrow* (p. 315): olive green on wings, nape and head.

FOX SPARROW

Passerella iliaca

Like the Eastern Towhee, the Fox Sparrow eagerly scratches out a living with both feet as it stirs up leaves and scrapes organic matter along the forest floor. This large sparrow's preference for impenetrable, brushy habitat makes it a difficult species to observe, even though its noisy foraging habits often reveal its whereabouts. • The male Fox Sparrow is generally agreed to be the best singer among the sparrows. The loud, whistled courtship songs are easily recognized and, to attentive listeners, can often be as moving as a loon's wail or a wolf's howl. Unfortunately for Great Plains birders, he sings only in his more northerly and westerly breeding areas and not while in migration or overwintering in our region. • Almost all birds in our area will be of the generally reddish brown eastern race that inspired taxonomists to name this species after the red fox. Any stray "Slate-coloreds" from farther west will have more gray on their upperparts and darker, more grayish brown streaking on their underparts.

ID: reddish brown wings and tail; streaked, gray-and-brown back; often shows thin, white wing bars; whitish underparts with heavy, reddish brown spotting and streaking that often converges into central breast spot; gray nape, crown stripe and "eyebrow"; reddish brown "cheek"; mostly white "jaw line"; stubby, conical, yellowish bill; pale legs. *In flight:* gray rump and brownish red tail.

Size: *L* 6½–7 in; *W* 10½ in.
Habitat: riparian thickets and brushy woodland clearings, edges and parklands.
Nesting: does not nest in the Great Plains.
Feeding: scratches the ground to uncover seeds, berries and invertebrates; visits backyard feeders in migration and winter.
Voice: calls include *chip* and *click* notes.
Similar Species: *Song Sparrow* (p. 319): generally darker, browner upperparts and underpart streaking; eye line is distinct from "cheek"; grayer bill. *Hermit Thrush* (p. 256): unstreaked, olive brown and reddish brown upperparts; blurry streaking on sides; thinner bill.

SONG SPARROW

Melospiza melodia

The Song Sparrow's heavily streaked, low-key plumage doesn't prepare you for the male's symphonic song. This well-named sparrow is renowned for the complexity, rhythm and emotion of its springtime rhapsodies, although some people will insist that the Fox Sparrow or the Lincoln's Sparrow carries the best tune. • Young male Song Sparrows and many other songbirds learn to sing by eavesdropping on mature males. By the time he is a few months old, a young male will have formed the basis for his own courtship tune. • Most songbirds are lucky if they can produce one brood per year, but, in some years, Song Sparrows in our region will successfully raise three broods. • The Song Sparrow has about 31 different subspecies, ranging from the pale desert birds to the larger and darker Alaskan forms.

ID: dark-mottled, brown upperparts, often with buff and chestnut tinges; heavy brown streaking on whitish to dingy brown underparts often converges into central breast spot; unstreaked belly; dark crown with pale central stripe; grayish face; dark eye line; whitish "jaw line"; dark "whisker" and "mustache" stripes. *In flight:* rounded tail tip.

Size: L 5½–7 in; W 8½ in.

Habitat: shrubby areas, often near water, including willow shrublands, thickets, forest openings and pastures.

Nesting: usually on the ground or low in a shrub or small tree; female builds an open cup nest of grass, weeds, leaves and bark shreds lined with finer materials; female incubates 3–5 heavily chestnut-spotted, greenish white eggs for 12–14 days.

Feeding: gleans the ground, shrubs and trees for cutworms, beetles, grasshoppers, ants, other invertebrates and seeds; also eats wild fruit; visits feeders.

Voice: short *tsip* and nasal *tchep* calls. *Male:* song consists of 1–4 bright, distinctive, introductory notes, such as *sweet, sweet, sweet,* a buzzy *towee* and a short, descending trill.

Similar Species: *Fox Sparrow* (p. 318): reddish brown upperparts and streaking, heavier on breast; "cheek" melds with eye line. *Lincoln's Sparrow* (p. 320): finely streaked throat and buff-washed breast. *Savannah Sparrow* (p. 312): finer breast streaking; less gray on face; often has yellow lores; notched, square-tipped tail.

LINCOLN'S SPARROW

Melospiza lincolnii

Radiating a certain beauty in its plumage that is greater than the sum of its feathers, the Lincoln's Sparrow can bring joy to the hearts of perceptive bird-ers. • Lincoln's Sparrows seem more timid than other sparrows. Males will sit openly on exposed perches and sing their bubbly, wrenlike songs, but when approached, they slip under nearby shrubs. When not singing their courtship songs, Lincoln's Sparrows remain well hidden in tall grass and dense, bushy growth. Their remote breeding grounds and secretive behavior conspire to keep this species one of the least-known sparrows. • If disturbed while sitting on her eggs, a female will run quietly through the grass like a mouse, hoping both she and the nest will be passed over. If the young have hatched, she will use her broken-wing distraction display to draw the intruder away. • Thomas Lincoln was a young companion of John James Audubon on his 1833 voyage to Labrador.

ID: mottled, grayish brown to reddish brown upperparts; finely dark-streaked, buffy breast band, sides and flanks; white belly and throat; dark, reddish "cap" with gray central stripe; gray "collar," face and "eyebrow"; dark line behind eye; buffy "jaw stripe"; very faint, white eye ring. *In flight:* rounded tail tip.
Size: *L* 5½ in; *W* 7½ in.
Habitat: *Breeding:* shrubby edges of bogs, swamps, beaver ponds and meadows; also in jack pine plains. *In migration:* brushy woodlands and shrubby fencerows.

Nesting: on the ground, often on soft moss or concealed beneath a shrub; female builds a well-hidden cup nest of grass and sedges lined with fine grass and hair; female incubates 4–5 pale green eggs with heavy, chestnut spotting for 11–14 days.
Feeding: scratches at the ground to expose invertebrates and seeds; occasionally visits feeders.
Voice: buzzy *zeee* and *tsup* calls. *Male:* musical song is a wrenlike mixture of buzzes, trills and warbled notes.
Similar Species: *Song Sparrow* (p. 319): heavier streaking on white or dingy brown breast. *Savannah Sparrow* (p. 312): often has whiter "eyebrow" and "jaw line" and yellow lores; yellower bill. *Swamp Sparrow* (p. 321): vaguer breast streaks; more contrast between head colors.

SWAMP SPARROW
Melospiza georgiana

Swamp Sparrows are well adapted to life near water. These wetland inhabitants skulk among the emergent vegetation of cattail marshes, foraging for a variety of invertebrates, including beetles, caterpillars, spiders, leafhoppers and flies. Like other sparrows, they are unable to swim, but that is no deterrent—many of their meals are snatched directly from the water's surface as they wade through the shallows. • The Swamp Sparrow must keep a lookout for daytime predators such as Northern Harriers, Great Blue Herons and large snakes. At night, the key to survival is finding a secluded, concealing perch that will keep it safe from raccoons, skunks and weasels. • Swamp Sparrows are most easily seen in spring as males sing their familiar trills from atop cattails or shoreline shrubs.

nonbreeding

ID: generally brownish upperparts; mostly reddish brown wings; dark streaking on back; vaguely streaked, dull gray breast and paler, unstreaked belly; gray "collar"; black stripes outline white throat and "jaw line"; gray face; dark line behind eye; dusky bill. *Breeding:* rusty "cap" (reddest on male) with gray central stripe; streaked, buff-washed sides and flanks. *Nonbreeding:* streaked, brown "cap"; more brownish sides.
Size: *L* 5–6 in; *W* 7½ in.
Habitat: cattail marshes, open wetlands, wet meadows and open hardwood riparian thickets.
Nesting: in emergent aquatic vegetation or shoreline bushes; female builds a cup nest, usually with a partial canopy and a side entrance, of coarse grass and marsh vegetation lined with fine grass; female incubates 4–5 pale green eggs, heavily marked with reddish brown, for 12–15 days.
Feeding: gleans insects from the ground, vegetation and the water's surface; takes seeds in late summer and fall.
Voice: harsh *chink* call. *Male:* song is a slow, sharp, metallic trill: *weet-weet-weet-weet.*
Similar Species: *Chipping Sparrow* (p. 305): breeding bird has uniformly gray underparts, white wing bars, bold white "eyebrow," full eye line. *American Tree Sparrow* (p. 304): white wing bars; dark central breast spot; yellow lower mandible. *Song Sparrow* (p. 319): heavily streaked underparts; no gray "collar." *Lincoln's Sparrow* (p. 320): fine breast and throat streaking; less contrasting crown stripe.

WHITE-THROATED SPARROW
Zonotrichia albicollis

The handsome White-throated Sparrow is easily identified by its bold, white throat and striped crown. One color morph has black and white stripes on the head, and the other has brown and tan stripes. White-striped males are more aggressive than tan-striped males, and tan-striped females are more nurturing than white-striped females. Each morph almost always breeds with the opposite color morph. • In migration, White-throated Sparrows can appear anywhere in our region in great abundance. Urban backyards dressed with brushy fence-line tangles and a bird feeder brimming with seeds can attract these delightful sparrows. • *Zonotrichia* means "hairlike," a reference to the striped heads of birds in this genus; *albicollis* is Latin for "white neck"—not quite accurate, because it is the bird's throat and not its neck that is white.

white-striped morph

ID: mottled brown upperparts; unstreaked gray underparts; white throat; striped, black-and-white or brown-and-tan head; gray "cheek"; yellow lores; black eye line; grayish bill. *In flight:* grayish brown tail.

Size: *L* 6½–7½ in; *W* 9 in.

Habitat: *Breeding:* semi-open conifer and mixed forests, especially in regenerating clearings and along shrubby forest edges. *In migration* and *winter:* woodlots, wooded parks and riparian brush.

Nesting: on or near the ground, often concealed by a low shrub or fallen log; female builds an open cup nest of grass, weeds, twigs and conifer needles lined with rootlets, fine grass and hair; female incubates 4–5 variably marked, greenish blue to pale blue eggs for 11–14 days.

Feeding: scratches the ground to expose invertebrates, seeds and berries; also gleans insects from vegetation and while in flight; eats seeds from feeders in winter.

Voice: sharp *chink* call. *Male:* variable song is a clear, distinct, whistled *Old Sam Peabody, Peabody, Peabody.*

Similar Species: *White-crowned Sparrow* (p. 324): gray "collar"; less distinctive throat; grayish or black lores; pinkish bill. *Swamp Sparrow* (p. 321): smaller; vaguely streaked, dull gray breast; less distinctive throat; chestnut-and-gray crown; grayish lores.

HARRIS'S SPARROW

Zonotrichia querula

Wintering Harris's Sparrows are very attractive, with warm brown or cinnamon-buff faces and variable amounts of black on the throat and upper breast. The size of the black "bib" is controlled by hormones and tends to increase with age. The larger a male's "bib," the greater his social dominance in winter flocks. Call notes and songs are used to maintain contact within each typically midsized, cohesive flock and also assist in determining status within the flock. • The nesting range of the Harris's Sparrow, in the muskeg of the Canadian Arctic, is restricted to more northerly lattitudes than other *Zonotrichia* sparrows. At the breeding grounds, each male's high, whistled song, practiced during winter, helps verify his status. • John James Audubon named this sparrow after Edward Harris, a friend and amateur naturalist, with whom he traveled up the Missouri River in 1843. The scientific name *querula*, which means "plaintive" in Latin, refers to the male's quavering, whistled song.

nonbreeding

ID: mottled, brown-and-black upperparts; white wing bars; white underparts; pinkish orange bill. *Breeding:* black streaks on sides and flanks; gray face; black crown, ear patch, throat and "bib." *Nonbreeding:* brownish sides and flanks; white flecks on black crown; brown face.

Size: *L* 7–7½ in; *W* 10½ in.

Habitat: brushy roadsides, shrubby vegetation, forest edges and riparian thickets.

Nesting: does not nest in the Great Plains.

Feeding: gleans the ground and vegetation for seeds, fresh buds, insects and berries; occasionally takes seeds at feeders.

Voice: *jeenk* or *zheenk* call; flocks in flight may give a rolling *chug-up chug-up. Male:* song is a series of 2–4 long, quavering whistles; each series may be at the same or a different pitch.

Similar Species: *House Sparrow* (p. 359): male has chestnut on wings and nape area, 1 bold, wing bar, white "cheek," black bill. *Lapland Longspur* (p. 327): breeding male has chestnut nape, white stripe curving down to shoulder from eye, black "cheek," yellow bill. *Chickadees* (pp. 232–33): smaller; plainer upperparts; fuller "cap"; white "cheek."

WHITE-CROWNED SPARROW
Zonotrichia leucophrys

Large, bold and smartly patterned, male White-crowned Sparrows brighten brushy expanses and suburban parks and gardens across much of the Great Plains with their cheeky song throughout much of winter. Flocks of White-crowns foraging on the ground will quickly ascend to the branches of nearby shrubbery when they sense an intruder's approach. • Migration, largely by night, is short and swift, as if this bird is in turn acutely aware of the short breeding period ahead and the need to find winter food. Although some populations on the Pacific Coast remain there year-round, birds seen on the Great Plains are entirely migratory. Research into this much-studied sparrow has given science tremendous insight into bird physiology, homing behavior and the geographic variability of song dialects. Several races of White-crowned Sparrow have been identified, but plumage differences are minor.

ID: brown back with black and chestnut accents; 2 narrow, white wing bars; unstreaked, gray underparts, lighter on belly; gray "collar" and face; black crown and line behind eye; bold, white, central crown stripe and broad "eyebrow"; orangy pink bill. *In flight:* brown rump and tail.
Size: *L* 5½–7 in; *W* 9½ in.
Habitat: woodlots, parkland edges, brushy tangles and riparian thickets, occasionally in open, weedy fields, lawns and roadway edges with juncos and other sparrows.
Nesting: does not nest in the Great Plains.
Feeding: scratches the ground to expose insects and seeds; also eats berries, buds and moss caps; visits feeders.
Voice: hard *pink* call. *Male:* song is a highly variable mix of bright whistles, slurs and churring trills.
Similar Species: *White-throated Sparrow* (p. 322): clearly defined, white throat; yellow lores; gray bill. *Golden-crowned Sparrow:* rare transient; bright golden yellow forecrown; dark upper mandible; no white "eyebrow."

DARK-EYED JUNCO
Junco hyemalis

Juncos usually congregate in backyards with feeders and sheltering conifers—such amenities are attracting more and more juncos to overwinter in urban areas. They rarely perch at feeders, preferring to snatch up seeds knocked to the ground by visitors such as chickadees, sparrows, nuthatches and jays. Juncos spend most of their time on the ground, and they are readily flushed from wooded trails and backyard feeders. As they seek cover in a nearby tree or shrub, their distinctive white outer tail feathers flash in alarm. • In 1973, the American Ornithologists' Union reclassified five junco species into a single species, the Dark-eyed Junco. They have similar habits and interbreed where their various ranges meet, but they differ in coloration. The wide-ranging "Slate-colored" subspecies described below is the most common junco here. Distinctively rufous-toned, dark-hooded "Oregon" birds are also likely, particularly in western areas. Breeding is restricted to small numbers of the "White-winged" race, marked by white wing bars and wider white tail edges, in South Dakota's Black Hills.

Slate-colored Junco

ID: occasionally 2 white wing bars; pale, yellowish to pinkish bill; pinkish legs; white outer tail feathers. *Male:* dark slate gray overall, except for white lower breast, belly and undertail coverts. *Female:* mostly brown rather than gray. *In flight:* dark, rounded wings with whitish linings; rounded tail.
Size: *L* 5½–7 in; *W* 9½ in.
Habitat: shrubby woodland borders; backyards with feeders.

Nesting: on the ground; female builds a usually concealed cup nest of twigs, bark shreds, grass and moss lined with fine grass and hair; female incubates 3–5 gray- and brown-marked, whitish to bluish eggs for 12–13 days.
Feeding: scratches the ground for invertebrates; also eats berries and seeds.
Voice: smacking *chip* call, often given in series. *Male:* song is a long, dry trill, like a Chipping Sparrow's, but more musical.
Similar Species: *Canyon Towhee* (p. 366): limited range; larger; dark central breast spot; rusty undertail coverts and "cap." *Eastern Towhee* (p. 301): larger; unlike "Oregon," has back and wings that match head; dark bill.

MCCOWN'S LONGSPUR

Calcarius mccownii

If you are in the northwestern Great Plains in summer, do yourself a favor and pull off onto a gravel road through the grasslands. On a good piece of native mixed-grass prairie, you might see a McCown's Longspur retreating from a fence post. As with so many other grassland species, the range of the McCown's Longspur has been shrinking as native grasslands have given way to cultivation. • The male McCown's Longspur delivers his tinkling song on the wing as he sails to the ground with tail fanned and wings held high. Although his soft voice does not dominate the morning chorus of prairie birds, his is a harmony that adds dimension to the musical feast. • Female McCown's Longspurs are persistent incubators, abandoning their nests only when they are practically stepped on. • John McCown was an American military officer posted in southern Texas, where he collected several birds, including this one.

breeding

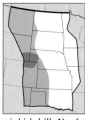

ID: *Breeding male:* mottled, brown-and-buff upperparts; rufous shoulder; light gray underparts and face; black "cap," "bib," "whisker" and robust bill. *Breeding female:* grayer and less bold overall; mostly pale pinkish bill. *Nonbreeding:* like breeding but drabber. *In flight:* white tail has dark tip and central stripe.

Size: *L* 6 in; *W* 11 in.

Habitat: shortgrass prairie, native grasslands, pastures and agricultural areas.

Nesting: on the ground, at the base of a clump of vegetation; cup nest is woven with coarse grass and lined with finer materials; female incubates 3–4 whitish, brown-and-lilac-marked eggs for up to 12 days.

Feeding: walks on the ground gleaning seeds and invertebrates, especially grasshoppers, beetles and moths; occasionally drinks at shallow ponds.

Voice: *poik* call. *Male:* song is a fast, twittering warble delivered on the wing.

Similar Species: *Chestnut-collared Longspur* (p. 329): usually has chestnut or pale chestnut nape; no rufous shoulder patch. *Smith's Longspur* (p. 328): buffy underparts. *Lapland Longspur* (p. 327): nonbreeding bird has chestnut nape. *Vesper Sparrow* (p. 309): dark-streaked upperparts; white eye ring and "jaw line." *House Sparrow* (p. 359): white wing bar; male has smaller "bib" and more chestnut on upperparts; female has less white on face.

LAPLAND LONGSPUR
Calcarius lapponicus

Throughout winter, Lapland Longspurs wheel about over the fields in large numbers. From day to day, their movements are largely unpredictable, but they typically appear wherever open fields offer an abundance of seeds or waste grain. Flocks of longspurs can be surprisingly inconspicuous until closely approached—anyone attempting a closer look at the flock will be awed by the sight of the birds suddenly erupting into the sky, flashing their white outer tail feathers.
• In fall, these birds arrive from their breeding grounds looking like mottled, brownish sparrows and retain their drab plumage throughout the winter months. When farmers work their fields in spring, lingering Lapland Longspurs have already molted into their bold breeding plumage, which they will wear through summer.
• The Lapland Longspur breeds in northern polar regions, including the northern Scandinavian area for which it is named.

nonbreeding

ID: *Breeding male:* brown upperparts marked with buff, white and black; white underparts, black-streaked on breast and sides; chestnut nape; broad, white stripe curving down to shoulder from eye (often buff-tinged behind eye); black crown, face and "bib"; yellowish bill. *Female:* like male, but rufous and black areas appear washed out; chestnut wing patch; lightly streaked, buff breast band; white throat and black "whisker." *Nonbreeding male:* resembles female; diffuse blackish breast coloration; pinkish bill. *In flight:* mostly gray underwings; white outer tail feathers.
Size: *L* 6½ in; *W* 11½ in.

Habitat: pastures, meadows and croplands.
Nesting: does not nest in the Great Plains.
Feeding: gleans the ground and snow for seeds and waste grain.
Voice: musical calls; flight calls include a rattled *tri-di-dit* and a descending *teew.*
Similar Species: *Chestnut-collared Longspur* (p. 329): breeding male has black belly and mostly buffy face; female and nonbreeding male are drabber overall. *McCown's Longspur* (p. 326): drabber, with little black in plumage. *Smith's Longspur* (p. 328): buffy underparts and neck markings. *Snow Bunting* (p. 330): white wing patches. *Harris's Sparrow* (p. 323): larger; grayish brown nape and face; orangy bill. *House Sparrow* (p. 359): breeding male has mostly chestnut wing with white bar and black bill.

SMITH'S LONGSPUR

Calcarius pictus

Smith's Longspurs are uncommon on the Great Plains during spring and fall migrations, and their passage is framed by the much larger movements of Lapland Longspurs. When birdwatchers start taking notice of Smith's Longspurs, they will likely be surprised at their numbers over frozen fields in winter and during spring migration. Although it takes patience, large flocks of Laplands should be checked thoroughly in spring for the presence of boldly colored male Smith's Longspurs. In fall, the two species look so similar that the exercise might prove too daunting for people hoping to maintain their sanity. • Smith's Longspurs often remain very still on the ground, and they can effectively disappear from view from one moment to the next. • John James Audubon named this bird in honor of his friend and subscriber, Gideon Smith.

nonbreeding

ID: brown upperparts with black, white and buff streaking; white shoulder (often concealed); buff underparts and "collar"; yellowish orange bill is dusky on top; dark-centered tail with white outer feathers. *Breeding male:* black crown; white-bordered, black "cheek" with central white patch. *Nonbreeding male, female* and *immature:* like breeding male, except dark areas are brownish, buffy areas are paler, breast shows brownish streaking, and white areas are buffy. *In flight:* medium gray underwing.

Size: *L* 6 in; *W* 11 in.

Habitat: patures, fields and airports.

Nesting: does not nest in the Great Plains.

Feeding: forages on the ground for waste grain and seeds; eats insects when available.

Voice: alarm call is a slow *tick tick tick*, like a watch.

Similar Species: *Other longspurs* (pp. 326–29): often show chestnut areas on wings or at napes; underparts are mostly white, black or gray, not buffy; either more or less white on tails; breeding males have different black areas on heads.

CHESTNUT-COLLARED LONGSPUR

Calcarius ornatus

In spring, in areas where the dry, flavorless smell of stale prairie dust hangs in the breeze, turn your ear for the tinkling song of the Chestnut-collared Longspur. The male Chestnut-collared Longspur is the most colorful of the grassland sparrows. Gaudily marked in comparison to the dull plumage typical of his neighbors, he can occasionally be seen in flight or atop a boulder, shrub or fence post that rises out of the dancing waves of grass. • The Chestnut-collared Longspur was one of the most abundant birds in the Great Plains before the plow arrived and altered the landscape. Now it is only found in areas that have escaped cultivation or where the natural forces of the grasslands have retaken once-plowed fields. • Longspurs are so named because they have an extremely long hind claw (the genus name, *Calcarius,* also refers to this feature). Presumably this elongated appendage is beneficial to their ground-focused lifestyle.

breeding

ID: *Breeding male:* mottled upperparts of brown, buff and white; black underparts except for white undertail coverts; yellowish throat; chestnut nape; black cap; white "eyebrow"; gray bill. *Female* and *nonbreeding male:* drabber than breeding male; paler chestnut or none at nape; light, brownish breast streaking; pale, often pinkish bill. *In flight:* pale gray underwing; white tail shows black "Y" from above.
Size: *L* 6 in; *W* 10 in.
Habitat: shortgrass prairie; does not usually tolerate tallgrass areas.

Nesting: in a depression or scrape, well concealed by grass; small cup nest woven with grass is lined with feathers and fur; female incubates 3–5 off-white eggs with various dark-colored markings for 10–13 days.
Feeding: gleans the ground for plant seeds and invertebrates.
Similar Species: breeding male is distinctive. *McCown's Longspur* (p. 326): drabber, with little black in plumage; hint of chestnut on wing; breeding male has blackish breast. *Smith's Longspur* (p. 328): buffy underparts and neck markings. *Lapland Longspur* (p. 327): chestnut on wing; dark-streaked sides; bolder facial markings. *Vesper Sparrow* (p. 309): bolder "jaw line" and eye ring; smaller, orangy bill; orangy legs; no "eyebrow." *Savannah Sparrow* (p. 312): striped crown; smaller bill; white outer tail feathers.

SNOW BUNTING

Plectrophenax nivalis

In early winter, when flocks of Snow Buntings descend on the Great Plains, their startling black-and-white plumage flashes in contrast to the snow-covered backdrop. It may seem strange that Snow Buntings are whiter in summer than in winter, but the darker winter plumage may help these birds absorb heat on clear, cold days. • Snow Buntings venture farther north than any other songbird in the world. A single individual, likely misguided and lost, was even recorded not far from the North Pole in May 1987. • In winter, Snow Buntings prefer expansive areas—including grain croplands, fields and pastures—where they scratch and peck at exposed seeds and grains. They will also ingest small grains of sand or gravel from roadsides as a source of minerals and to help digestion. • Snow Buntings are definitely cold-weather songbirds, often bathing in snow in early spring, and burrowing into it during bitter cold snaps to stay warm.

nonbreeding

ID: black-and-white wings and tail; white underparts. *Breeding male:* black back; all-white head and rump; black bill. *Breeding female:* streaky, brown-and-whitish back and crown; dark bill. *Nonbreeding male:* golden brown rump, back streaks, shoulder patch, crown and "cheek"; yellowish bill. *Nonbreeding female:* resembles male; larger patches and deeper hues of golden brown; blackish forecrown. *In flight:* otherwise white wings are black or gray on outer third and part of upper leading edge; dark triangle on upper side of white tail.

Size: *L* 6–7½ in; *W* 14 in.
Habitat: manured fields, feedlots, pastures, grassy meadows, lakeshores, roadsides and railroads.
Nesting: does not nest in the Great Plains.
Feeding: gleans the ground and snow for seeds and waste grain; takes insects when available.
Voice: whistled *tew* call.
Similar Species: *Longspurs* (pp. 326–29): female and nonbreeding male have much less white on wings, larger dark "cheek" patches and most have less white on underparts.

NORTHERN CARDINAL

Cardinalis cardinalis

A bird as beautiful as the Northern Cardinal rarely fails to capture our attention and admiration. It is often the first choice for calendars and Christmas cards. Most people can easily recognize this delightful year-round neighbor—which is attracted to backyards with feeders and sheltering trees and shrubs—even without the help of a bird field guide. • Northern Cardinals form one of the bird world's most faithful pair bonds. The male and female remain in close contact year-round, singing to one another through the seasons with soft, bubbly whistles. The female is known to sing while on the nest, possibly to inform her partner whether or not she and the young need food. The highly territorial male will challenge even his own reflection in a window or shiny hubcap! • The Northern Cardinal owes its name to the male's vivid red plumage, which resembles the red robes of Roman Catholic cardinals.

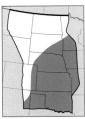

ID: *Male:* red overall; brownish wash on wing; pointed crest; black "mask" and throat; robust, conical, red bill. *Female:* brownish buff to buffy olive plumage, tinged red on wings, crest and tail; pale belly; blackish around eye and bill. *In flight:* bright red wing linings.

Size: *L* 7½–9 in; *W* 12 in.

Habitat: brushy thickets and shrubby tangles along forest and woodland edges; backyards and suburban and urban parks.

Nesting: in a dense shrub, thicket, vine tangle or low in a conifer; female builds a cup nest of twigs, bark shreds, weeds, grass, leaves and rootlets, lined with hair and fine grass; female incubates 3–4 whitish, often blue- or green-tinged eggs, marked with gray, brown and purple, for 12–13 days.

Feeding: gleans seeds, insects and berries from low shrubs or while hopping along the ground.

Voice: metallic *chip* call; song is a variable series of clear, bubbly, whistled notes: *what cheer! what cheer! birdie-birdie-birdie what cheer!*

Similar Species: *Summer Tanager* (p. 297) and *Scarlet Tanager* (p. 298): males are smaller with slight or no crest, no black on face or throat and smaller, paler bill.

ROSE-BREASTED GROSBEAK

Pheucticus ludovicianus

It is difficult to miss the boisterous, whistled tune of the Rose-breasted Grosbeak. This bird's easily recognized, hurried, robinlike song is one of the more common songs heard in our hardwood forests through spring and summer. Although the female does not have the magnificent colors of the male, she shares his talent for beautiful song. • Mating grosbeaks appear pleasantly affectionate toward each other, often touching bills during courtship and after absences. • Rose-breasted Grosbeaks usually build their nests low in a tree or tall shrub, but they typically forage high in the canopy, where they can be difficult to spot. Luckily for birders, the abundance of berries in fall often draws these birds to ground level. • The misleading species name, *ludovicianus*, is Latin for "from Louisiana," but this bird is only a migrant through Louisiana and other southern states.

♀

breeding

♂

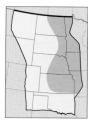

ID: mostly white underparts; robust, conical, pale bill. *Male:* black upperparts; small, white wing patches; red breast; black "hood." *Female:* brown upperparts; 2 white wing bars; buff-washed, brown-streaked breast and sides; thin crown stripe; dark face; bold, white "eyebrow." *In flight:* male has white "wrist" patches, red wing linings, white rump and black-centered, white-cornered tail; female has dull yellow wing linings and all-dark tail.
Size: *L* 7–8½ in; *W* 12½ in.
Habitat: hardwood and mixed forests.

Nesting: low in a tree or tall shrub, often near water; mostly the female builds a flimsy cup nest of twigs, bark strips, weeds, grass and leaves lined with rootlets and hair; pair incubates 3–5 pale, greenish blue eggs, spotted with reddish brown, for 13–14 days.
Feeding: gleans vegetation for insects, seeds, buds, berries and some other fruit; occasionally hover-gleans or catches flying insects on the wing; may also visit feeders.
Voice: distinctive squeak call; song is a long, melodious series of whistled notes, much like a fast version of a robin's song.
Similar Species: male is distinctive. *Black-headed Grosbeak* (p. 333): female and immature have less boldly streaked under-parts, more orangy buff on sides, breast and neck. *Purple Finch* (p. 352): female is smaller, has heavier streaking on under-parts and less bold facial features. *Sparrows* (pp. 302–24): smaller; smaller bills.

BLACK-HEADED GROSBEAK
Pheucticus melanocephalus

Almost any visit to hardwood woodlands in the western Great Plains in spring and summer will bring the apprentice birdwatcher into contact with the Black-headed Grosbeak. Often, one of the first discoveries is a treetop song resembling that of the American Robin coming from the throat of the impressive-looking male Black-headed Grosbeak. With extended bouts of complex, accented caroling, he advertises his territory from late April to early July. Meanwhile, the duller female forages and conducts all the household chores within dense foliage cover, betraying her presence and reassuring the male with frequent sharp, wood-pecker-like calls. • Characteristic of hardwood habitats, even in broken conifer forests, Black-headed Grosbeaks are sometimes found in campgrounds and picnic sites and will visit feeders in migration. • The scientific name *Pheucticus* is thought to be derived from the Greek *phyticos*, meaning "painted with cosmetics," referring to the male's apparent overindulgence with blush.

ID: robust, conical, grayish bill; darker upper mandible. *Male:* black upperparts; small, white wing patches; rusty orange rump, sides, breast and "collar"; white undertail coverts; yellow belly; black head. *Female:* brown upperparts; rusty buff wash on breast and lightly streaked flanks; dark face; off-white crown stripe and bold "eyebrow." *In flight:* yellow wing linings; male has white "wrist" patches and black-centered, white-cornered tail; female has all-dark tail.
Size: *L* 7–8 in; *W* 12 in.
Habitat: lowland forests and shrubby coulees.
Nesting: in a tall shrub or hardwood tree, often near water; female builds the loosely woven cup nest of twigs, lined with fine grass, in 3–4 days; pair incubates 3–5 chestnut-spotted, light turquoise eggs for 12–14 days.
Feeding: forages in the upper canopy for invertebrates and plant foods; occasionally visits feeders.
Voice: high *eek* call. *Male:* song is a long series of robinlike phrases without breaks.
Similar Species: male is distinctive. *Rose-breasted Grosbeak* (p. 332): female and immature have bold streaking across breast and paler bill. *Purple Finch* (p. 352): female is smaller, has heavier streaking on under-parts and less bold facial features. *Sparrows* (pp. 302–24): smaller; smaller bills.

BLUE GROSBEAK

Passerina caerulea

Oddly enough, male Blue Grosbeaks owe their spectacular spring plumage not to a fresh molt, but to feather wear. While they overwinter in Mexico and Central America, their brown feather tips slowly wear away, leaving the familiar blue color. • Blue Grosbeaks are very expressive during courtship—the tail-spreading, tail-flicking and crown-raising antics are a sure sign that nesting activities may soon be underway. • Pairs are found as far north as southern Wyoming and north-central South Dakota, wherever their preferred mix of oak–hickory forest, hardwood thickets and farmlands provides ideal nesting and feeding conditions. Further sightings can be expected as the Blue Grosbeak expands its range northward. Look carefully, though, for the rusty wing bars that distinguish it from the more common but smaller Indigo Bunting. In shaded conditions, Brown-headed Cowbirds may also look similar. • *Caerulea* is from the Latin for "blue," a description that fails to grasp this bird's true beauty.

ID: 2 rusty wing bars; stout, gray bill with darker upper mandible; habitually flicks tail. *Male:* royal blue plumage overall; darker wings; black around base of bill. *Female:* soft brown plumage overall; rump and shoulder can have blue hints; whitish throat. *In flight:* undulating flight; wing lining and rump match sides.
Size: *L* 6–7½ in; *W* 11–12 in.
Habitat: thick lowland brush; thickets, wooded margins or weedy fields near water; sewage ponds.
Nesting: in a shrub or low tree; cup nest woven with twigs, roots and grass is lined with finer materials, including paper and occasionally reptile skins; female incubates 2–5 light blue eggs for 11–12 days.
Feeding: gleans the ground by hopping around, taking insects and occasionally seeds; periodically gleans vegetation; rarely visits feeders.
Voice: *chink* call. *Male:* sweet, melodious, warbling song with rising and falling phrases.
Similar Species: *Lazuli Bunting* (p. 335): smaller; white or buffy wing bars; white belly and undertail coverts; smaller bill; male has chestnut breast band; female is cooler brown. *Indigo Bunting* (p. 336): smaller; smaller bill; male has faint or no wing bars; female has buffy wing bars and breast streaking. *Brown-headed Cowbird* (p. 348): female is larger with no wing bars and smaller bill.

LAZULI BUNTING

Passerina amoena

Lazuli Buntings do not demand much of their environment—a selection of song perches, a bit of low, shrubby cover and somewhere to hunt for insects is all they require. Lazuli Buntings make use of dry brushlands and woodland edges, often sharing their quarters with Black-headed Grosbeaks working the upper canopy. • Small flocks making their way northward in spring stop off at feeders and desert oases along the route, bringing a splash of color to their surroundings. From May to early July, the brightly colored male's crisp and varied songs punctuate the hot "siesta hours," when only a handful of other species regularly vocalize. Singing intensity diminishes as broods are fledged, and by late August most birds appear to have deserted their summer homes. Like their grosbeak cousins, Lazuli Buntings undergo a partial molt before they leave, completing their change of plumage at their wintering grounds.

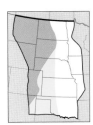

ID: stout, conical, pale to grayish bill. *Male:* turquoise blue rump, back and hood; dark wings with 2 bold, white bars; chestnut upper breast; white belly. *Female:* soft brown overall. *In flight:* whitish (male) or drab buff (female) wing linings; hints of blue on dark rump and tail.

Size: *L* 5–6 in; *W* 8–9 in.

Habitat: *Breeding:* expanses of low shrubs with elevated song perches, sagebrush, chaparral, forest edges and streamsides to 9000 ft. *In migration:* lowland areas, including foothill canyons.

Nesting: in an upright crotch low in a shrubby tangle; small, woven grass cup nest is lined with finer grass and hair; female incubates 3–5 bluish white eggs for 12 days.

Feeding: gleans the ground and low shrubs for grasshoppers, beetles, other insects and native seeds; visits feeders in some areas.

Voice: indeterminate calls. *Male:* song is a brief complex of whispering notes: *swip-swip-swip zu zu ee, see see sip see see.*

Similar Species: *Indigo Bunting* (p. 336): female has fainter wing bars, streaked breast. *Blue Grosbeak* (p. 334): female is larger and warmer brown, rusty wing bars, larger bill. *Western Bluebird* (p. 250) and *Eastern Bluebird* (p. 249): males are larger, have blue wings without bars, more extensive chestnut on breasts, slimmer bills.

INDIGO BUNTING

Passerina cyanea

I n the shadow of a towering tree, a male Indigo Bunting can look almost black. If possible, reposition yourself quickly so as to see the sun strike and enliven his rich shade of blue, which is rivaled only by the sky. • Raspberry thickets are a favored nest location for many Indigo Buntings. The dense, thorny stems protect the nestlings from many predators, and the berries provide convenient food. • In its clever and comical foraging strategy, the Indigo Bunting lands midway on a stem and then shuffles slowly toward the seed head, eventually bending it enough to give easy access. • Male Indigo Buntings learn their musical warble not from their fathers, but from neighboring males during their first spring. • Where ranges overlap, about 30 percent of Lazuli Buntings and Indigo Buntings hybridize, but the hybrids have reduced viability. Song switching and interspecific territories both occur in overlap zones.

breeding

ID: faint, rusty wing bars; stout, conical, gray bill. *Male:* blue overall; black on wings, lores and tail. *Female:* soft brown overall; brown-streaked breast; pale throat. *Nonbreeding male:* patchy blue and gray overall; whitish belly and undertail coverts.

Size: *L* 5½ in; *W* 8 in.

Habitat: prefers hardwood forest and woodland edges, regenerating forest clearings, shrubby or abandoned fields, orchards and hedgerows.

Nesting: usually in an upright fork of a small tree or shrub or within a vine tangle; female builds a cup nest of grass, leaves and bark strips lined with rootlets, hair and feathers; female incubates 3–4 rarely spotted, white to bluish eggs for 12–13 days.

Feeding: gleans low vegetation and the ground for insects, especially grasshoppers, beetles, weevils, flies and larvae; also eats the seeds of thistles, dandelions, goldenrods and other native plants.

Voice: quick *spit* call. *Male:* song consists of paired, warbled whistles: *fire-fire, where-where, here-here, see-it see-it.*

Similar Species: *Lazuli Bunting* (p. 335): female has bolder wing bars and unstreaked breast. *Blue Grosbeak* (p. 334): larger; rusty wing bars; larger bill; warmer-colored female has unstreaked breast. *Mountain Bluebird* (p. 251): male is larger, has all-blue wings and tail, slimmer bill. *Pinyon Jay* (p. 220): much larger; paler.

PAINTED BUNTING

Passerina ciris

The brilliantly colored male representatives of this species look like living fragments of precious rainbows, a characteristic more typical of birds found in the warm tropical forests of Central and South America. Fortunately for our senses, this bird only spends winters in its tropical home, traversing the Gulf of Mexico each spring to grace southern thickets and tangles with its colors and sweet songs. • The bright males and the more subdued greenish females are often seen migrating alongside pure blue Indigo Buntings, providing observers with a truly overwhelming feast of color. Once they have arrived on their breeding grounds, they tend to be rather secretive among the preferred shelter of dense foliage, making observation a difficult endeavor. • During the short breeding season, a singing male, who may have multiple mates, often finds himself caught in violent altercations over territory and breeding privileges.

ID: robust, conical, pale bill. *Male:* yellowish green back; darker wings and tail show reddish highlights; red underparts and rump; blue head; red eye ring. *Female:* yellowish green upperparts; pale yellow underparts and neck.

Size: L 5½ in; W 8–9 in.

Habitat: semi-open areas, including roadside thickets, hedgerows, woodland edges, clearings and undergrowth, townsite parks, gardens and brushlands.

Nesting: in a low tree, dense shrubbery or vines; female weaves various vegetative materials into an open cup lined with fine plant material and animal hair; female incubates 3–5 chestnut-spotted, whitish to grayish eggs and feeds the nestlings; male often takes over care of young if female re-nests.

Feeding: forages for seeds and insects on the ground or in low vegetation; occasionally eats berries and other fruits.

Voice: sharp *chip* call. *Male:* song is a sweet, clear series of warbling.

Similar Species: male is distinctive. *Warblers* (pp. 269–96): greenish birds have dull, olive green upperparts and finer bills.

337

DICKCISSEL

Spiza americana

Irruptive on the Great Plains, the Dickcissel may be common one year and absent the next. This "miniature meadowlark" has a special fondness for fields of alfalfa. • Arriving in suitable nesting habitat before the smaller females, breeding males bravely announce their presence with stuttering, trilled renditions of their name. The territorial males perch atop tall blades of grass, fence posts or rocks to scour their turf for signs of potential mates or rivals. Males of this polygynous species may mate with up to eight females in a single breeding season, without participating in nest-building or brooding. • Dickcissels eat mostly insects on their breeding grounds, but seeds and grain form the main part of their diet on their South American wintering grounds, making them unpopular with local farmers. Each year, large numbers of these birds are killed in efforts to reduce crop losses, which may partially explain the Dickcissel's pattern of absence and abundance in our region.

ID: brown upperparts; rufous shoulder patch; pale, grayish brown underparts; yellow-washed breast; whitish undertail coverts; gray head and nape; conical, gray bill; white "chin"; black "bib"; yellow wash on white "jaw-line" patch and "eyebrow." *Female:* duller than male; white throat; buffy "eyebrow." *In flight:* grayish underwing with brown-edged flight feathers.
Size: *L* 6–7 in; *W* 9½ in.
Habitat: abandoned fields dominated by forbs, weedy meadows, croplands, grasslands and grassy roadsides.

Nesting: on or near the ground; well concealed among tall, dense vegetation; female builds a bulky, open cup nest of grass, weed stems and leaves lined with rootlets, fine grass or hair; female incubates 4 pale blue eggs for 11–13 days.
Feeding: gleans insects and seeds from the ground and low vegetation.
Voice: buzzerlike *bzrrrrt* flight call. *Male:* song consists of 2–3 single notes followed by a trill, often paraphrased as *dick dick dick-cissel*.
Similar Species: *Eastern Meadowlark* (p. 341) and *Western Meadowlark* (p. 342): larger; more cryptic upperparts; yellow "chin"; black "necklace"; pointier bill. *American Goldfinch* (p. 357): female and nonbreeding birds have wing bars, smaller bills and no "eyebrow."

BOBOLINK
Dolichonyx oryzivorus

During the nesting season, male and female Bobolinks rarely interact with one another. For the most part, males perform aerial displays and sing their bubbly, tinkling songs from exposed grassy perches while the females carry out the nesting duties. Once the young have hatched, the males become less conspicuous, spending much of their time hunting along the ground for insects. • At first glimpse, the female Bobolink resembles a sparrow, but the male, with his plumage of buff, black and white, is colored like no other bird. • Bobolinks once benefited from increased agriculture, but modern practices, such as harvesting hay early in the season, now thwart their reproductive efforts. • Many people believe that the common name reflects the male's song. • The Bobolink winters entirely in the Southern Hemisphere, where it forms huge flocks.

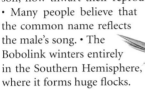

breeding

ID: *Breeding male:* generally black; buff nape; white back stripes and rump; black bill. *Breeding female:* buff brown overall; dark-streaked back, sides, flank and rump; pale "eyebrow"; dark eye line; pale central crown stripe with dark border; whitish throat; yellowish bill. *Nonbreeding:* similar to breeding female; richer golden buff on upperpart feather edges, underparts and face. *In flight:* wing linings match sides.
Size: *L* 6–8 in; *W* 11½ in.
Habitat: tall, grassy meadows and ditches, hay fields and some croplands.
Nesting: on the ground, usually in a hay field; well concealed in a shallow depression; female builds a cup nest of grass and weed stems lined with fine grass; female incubates 5–6 grayish to light reddish

brown eggs, heavily blotched with lavender and brown, for 11–13 days.
Feeding: gleans the ground and low vegetation for adult and larval invertebrates; also eats many seeds.
Voice: *pink* flight call. *Male:* song is a series of banjolike twangs: *bobolink bobolink spink spank spink*.
Similar Species: breeding male is distinctive. *Savannah Sparrow* (p. 312): smaller; dark breast streaking; often has yellow lores. *Vesper Sparrow* (p. 309): smaller; streaked breast; white outer tail feathers. *Grasshopper Sparrow* (p. 313): smaller; white belly; unstreaked sides and flanks.

RED-WINGED BLACKBIRD

Agelaius phoeniceus

To many birders, the definitive sound of spring is the voices of Red-winged Blackbirds staking out territory at the nearest wetlands. • A male's bright red shoulders and short, raspy song are his most important tools in the often intricate strategy he employs to defend his territory from rivals. A flashy and richly voiced male with a large and productive territory can attract several mates to his cattail kingdom. In field experiments, males whose red shoulders were painted black soon lost their territories to previously defeated rivals. • After the male has wooed the female, she weaves a nest amid the cattails. Her cryptic coloration allows her to blend in perfectly with the surroundings as she sits inconspicuously upon her nest. • *Agelaius* is a Greek word meaning "flocking," which accurately describes this bird's winter behavior—impressive flocks can sometimes be seen. The species name, *phoeniceus,* is a reference to the color red; the ancient Phoenicians introduced red dye to the Greeks.

Nesting: colonial; in cattails or shoreline bushes; female weaves an open cup nest of dried cattail leaves and grass lined with fine grass; female incubates 3–4 darkly marked, pale bluish green eggs for 10–12 days.
Feeding: gleans the ground for seeds, waste grain and invertebrates; also gleans vegetation for seeds, insects and berries; occasionally catches insects in flight; may visit feeders.
Voice: calls include a harsh *check* and a high *tseert*. *Male:* song is a loud, raspy *konk-a-ree* or *ogle-reeeee*. *Female:* may give a loud *che-che-che chee chee chee*.
Similar Species: male is distinctive when shoulder patch shows. *Brewer's Blackbird* (p. 345) and *Rusty Blackbird* (p. 344): females are more uniformly brown.

ID: *Male:* all black with large, red shoulder patch edged in yellow (occasionally concealed); black bill and legs. *Female:* chestnut-and-buff-mottled, brown upperparts; heavily streaked, pale underparts; light "jaw line" and "eyebrow." *In flight:* black (male) or brown (female) underwing.
Size: *L* 7–9½ in; *W* 13 in.
Habitat: cattail marshes, wet meadows and ditches, croplands and shoreline shrubs.

EASTERN MEADOWLARK

Sturnella magna

The voice of rural areas, the Eastern Meadowlark's trademark tune rings throughout spring from fence posts and powerlines, wherever grassy meadows and pastures are found. • The male uses his bright yellow underparts, V-shaped black "necklace" and white outer tail feathers to help attract mates. The female uses her similar plumage when a predator approaches too close to her nest as she explodes from the grass in a burst of flashing color. Most predators cannot resist chasing the moving target, and once the intruder has been led away from the nest, she simply folds away her white tail flags, exposes her camouflaged back and disappears into the grass without a trace. • Meadowlarks are not actually larks but members of the blackbird family, even though they don't seem to fit in color-wise. When the birds are seen in silhouette, the similarities become very apparent.

breeding

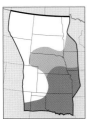

ID: *Breeding:* dark-mottled, brown upperparts; yellow underparts; broad, black breast band; dark-streaked, white sides and flanks; dark-bordered, pale central crown stripe; pale "eyebrow"; blackish eye line; yellow lores; long, sharp bill; pinkish legs; short, wide tail with white outer feathers. *Nonbreeding:* paler overall. *In flight:* drab, white-lined underwing.
Size: *L* 9–9½ in; *W* 14 in.
Habitat: grassy meadows and pastures; also in some croplands, weedy fields, grassy roadsides and old orchards.
Nesting: on the ground, in a depression or scrape; female weaves a domed grass nest with a side entrance into surrounding vegetation; female incubates 3–7 white eggs,

heavily spotted with brown and purple, for about 13–15 days.
Feeding: gleans grasshoppers, crickets, beetles and spiders from the ground and vegetation; probes soil for grubs and worms; also eats seeds.
Voice: rattling flight call and a high, buzzy *dzeart. Male:* song is a rich series of 2–8 melodic, clear, slurred whistles: *see-you at school-today* or *this is the year.*
Similar Species: *Western Meadowlark* (p. 342): paler upperparts, especially crown stripes and eye line; shorter streaks; yellow extends from throat onto lower "cheek"; different call and song. *Dickcissel* (p. 338): smaller; unstreaked sides and flanks; white throat; solid dark crown; conical bill.

WESTERN MEADOWLARK

Sturnella neglecta

One of the most abundant, widely distributed and popular birds in much of the U.S., the brightly colored Western Meadowlark is the state bird in six states, but it is rare in the East. In the early 19th century, members of the Lewis and Clark Expedition overlooked the Western Meadowlark, mistaking it for the very similar-looking Eastern Meadowlark, hence the scientific name *neglecta*. The best way for birders to distinguish one from the other is by the songs of the males: the Western Meadowlark's song is more constant, whereas the Eastern Meadowlark varies his song during bouts of singing.
• Please exercise extreme caution when you walk through meadowlark nesting habitat. The grassy domed nests are very difficult to locate and are so well concealed that you often accidentally crush them before you see them.
• Eastern Meadowlarks and Western Meadowlarks may occasionally interbreed where their ranges overlap, but the offspring are infertile.

breeding

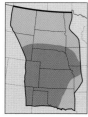

ID: *Breeding:* dark-mottled, brown upperparts; yellow underparts and lower "cheek"; broad, black breast band; dark-streaked, white sides and flanks; brown-bordered, pale central crown stripe; pale "eyebrow"; brown eye line; yellow lores; long, sharp bill; pinkish legs; short, wide tail with white outer feathers.
Nonbreeding: paler overall. *In flight:* drab, white-lined underwing.
Size: *L* 9–9½ in; *W* 14½ in.
Habitat: grassy meadows and pastures; also in some croplands, weedy fields and grassy roadsides.

Nesting: on the ground, in a depression or scrape; female weaves a concealed, domed grass nest with a side entrance into surrounding vegetation; female incubates 3–7 white eggs, heavily spotted with brown and purple, for about 13–15 days.
Feeding: gleans grasshoppers, crickets, beetles, other insects and spiders from the ground and vegetation; probes soil for grubs and worms; also eats seeds.
Voice: calls include a low, loud *chuck* or *chup*, a rattling flight call and a few clear, whistled notes. *Male:* song is a rich, melodic series of bubbly, flutelike notes.
Similar Species: *Eastern Meadowlark* (p. 341): darker upperparts, especially crown stripes and eye line; white lower "cheek"; different call and song. *Dickcissel* (p. 338): smaller; unstreaked sides and flanks; white throat; solid dark crown; conical bill.

YELLOW-HEADED BLACKBIRD

Xanthocephalus xanthocephalus

You might expect a bird as handsome as the male Yellow-headed Blackbird to have a song as splendid as his gold-and-black plumage, but a trip to a favored wetland will quickly reveal the shocking truth: when the male arches his golden head backward, his struggles produce only a painful, pathetic grinding noise. • A large cattail marsh is often highlighted by the presence of male Yellow-headed Blackbirds perched high atop the plants like candle flames. Yellow-heads often nest in small colonies of about 30 pairs. Where Yellow-headed Blackbirds occur together with Red-winged Blackbirds, the larger Yellow-heads dominate, commandeering the prime territory at the center of the wetland and pushing their red-winged competitors to the periphery, where the danger of predation is generally higher.

ID: *Male:* black body; white wing patches; yellow head and breast; black lores; black bill; long tail. *Female:* dusky brown overall; little white on wings; yellow breast, throat and "eyebrow"; hints of yellow on face. *In flight:* dark underwing and tail.
Size: *L* 8–11 in; *W* 15 in.
Habitat: deep, permanent marshes, sloughs, lakeshores and river impoundments where cattails dominate.
Nesting: loosely colonial; female weaves a bulky, deep basket of emergent aquatic plants lined with dry grass and other

vegetation into emergent vegetation over water; female incubates 4 pale green to grayish eggs, marked with gray or brown, for 11–13 days.
Feeding: gleans the ground for seeds, beetles, snails, waterbugs and dragonflies; also probes into cattail heads for larval invertebrates.
Voice: deep *krrt* or *ktuk* call; low quacks and liquidy clucks may be given during breeding season. *Male:* song is a strained, metallic, grating note followed by a descending buzz.
Similar Species: male is distinctive. *Rusty Blackbird* (p. 344) and *Brewer's Blackbird* (p. 345): females have brown breast and face.

343

RUSTY BLACKBIRD

Euphagus carolinus

The Rusty Blackbird owes its name to the rusty color of its fall plumage, but the name could just as well reflect the male's grating, squeaky song, which sounds very much like a rusty hinge. • Rusty Blackbirds spend their days foraging along the wooded edges of fields and wetlands and occasionally pick through the manure-laden ground of cattle feedlots. At day's end, when feeding is curtailed, most birds seek the shelter of trees and shrubs and the stalks of emergent marshland vegetation. • Generally less abundant and less aggressive than their relatives, Rusty Blackbirds usually avoid human-altered environments. In migration, they typically do not travel with grackles and other blackbirds, instead preferring to keep to themselves. • The most northerly breeding of our blackbirds, the Rusty Blackbird favors boggy areas from eastern Minnesota to northern New England and across Canada and Alaska for its nest sites.

nonbreeding

ID: yellow eyes; long, sharp, dark bill; dark legs and feet. *Breeding male:* black overall; subtle green gloss on body; subtle bluish or greenish gloss on head and breast. *Breeding female:* dark brown overall; without gloss. *Nonbreeding male:* rusty upperparts and head; rust-mottled underparts. *Nonbreeding female:* paler than male; buffy underparts; rusty "cheek." *In flight:* dark underwing.
Size: *L* 9 in; *W* 14 in.
Habitat: *Breeding:* treed bogs, fens, beaver ponds, wet meadows and the shrubby shorelines of lakes, rivers and swamps. *In migration:* marshes, open fields, feedlots and woodland edges near water.

Nesting: does not nest in the Great Plains.
Feeding: walks along shorelines gleaning waterbugs, beetles, dragonflies, snails, grasshoppers and occasionally small fish; also eats waste grain and seeds.
Voice: call is a harsh *chack*. *Male:* song is a squeaky, creaking *kushleeeh ksh-lay.*
Similar Species: *Brewer's Blackbird* (p. 345): breeding male's glossier, iridescent plumage often shows purple; female usually has dark eyes; no rusty highlights on nonbreeding birds. *Common Grackle* (p. 346): larger; brown overall with bronzy iridescence, except bluish on head and breast; longer bill; longer, keeled tail. *European Starling* (p. 264): speckled appearance; dark eyes; yellow bill on breeding bird; orangy pink legs.

BREWER'S BLACKBIRD

Euphagus cyanocephalus

Even in residential areas, the glossy-plumaged male Brewer's Blackbird can easily be seen strutting his stuff to impress the dowdy females. An iridescent quality is obvious as rainbows of reflected sunlight move along this bird's feather shafts. Its head jerking back and forth like a chicken's as it walks enhances the glossy effect and distinguishes the Brewer's from other blackbirds. • Urban development has benefited this blackbird, with agriculture and ranching providing foraging sites, landscaping affording sheltered nest locations and highways supplying a bounty of vehicle-struck insects. The Brewer's Blackbird exploits the "roadkill resource niche" better than any other songbird. • Unlike the more solitary Rusty Blackbird, the Brewer's Blackbird usually nests in colonies (up to 14 pairs). As fall approaches, the colonies join to form large migrating flocks. • John James Audubon named this bird after Thomas Mayo Brewer, a friend and prominent 19th-century oologist (a person who studies eggs).

ID: long, sharp, dark bill. *Male:* black overall with iridescent, bluish green body and purplish head; yellow eyes; nonbreeding male may show some faintly rusty feather edgings. *Female:* flat, brown plumage; usually dark eyes.
Size: *L* 8–10 in; *W* 15½ in.
Habitat: moist, grassy meadows and roadsides with nearby wetlands and patches of trees and shrubs.
Nesting: in small colonies; on the ground or in a shrub or small tree; female builds a bulky, open cup nest of twigs, grass and plant fibers lined with rootlets, fine grass

and hair; female incubates 4–6 brown-spotted, pale gray to greenish gray eggs for 12–14 days.
Feeding: walks along shorelines and open areas gleaning invertebrates and seeds.
Voice: metallic *chick* or *check* call. *Male:* song is a creaking, 2-note *k-shee.*
Similar Species: *Rusty Blackbird* (p. 344): breeding bird has longer, more slender bill; male has more subtle glossy greenish or bluish head; female has yellow eyes. *Common Grackle* (p. 346): larger; bronzy body; much longer, keeled tail. *Brown-headed Cowbird* (p. 348): shorter tail; stubbier, thicker bill; male has brown head and dark eyes; female has paler, streaked underparts and very pale throat. *European Starling* (p. 264): speckled appearance; dark eyes; yellow bill on breeding bird.

COMMON GRACKLE

Quiscalus quiscula

After slowly taking a deep breath to inflate his breast, causing his feathers to spike outward, usually while perched in a shrub, the male Common Grackle will close his eyes and emit a loud, strained *tssh-schleek*. Despite his lack of musical talent, this poor but spirited singer remains smug and proud, posing with his bill held high. • In rural areas in fall, large flocks of Common Grackles commonly forage for waste grain in open fields. Smaller bands occasionally venture into urban neighborhoods, where they assert their dominance at backyard feeders—even bullying Blue Jays will yield before these cocky, aggressive birds. • The long, heavy bill and lengthy, wedge-shaped tail, which trails behind in flight, easily distinguish the Common Grackle from the Rusty Blackbird and the Brewer's Blackbird. • At night, Common Grackles often roost with groups of European Starlings, Red-winged Blackbirds and even Brown-headed Cowbirds.

ID: yellow eyes; long, sturdy, dark bill; long, keeled tail. *Male:* dark, iridescent plumage; bronze back and sides; purple wings and tail; purplish blue breast and head. *Female:* smaller; duller; browner. *Immature:* dull brown overall; dark eyes.
Size: *L* 11–13½ in; *W* 17 in.
Habitat: wetlands, hedgerows, fields, wet meadows, riparian woodlands and along the edges of conifer forests and woodlands; shrubby urban and suburban parks and gardens.
Nesting: sometimes in small colonies; in dense tree or shrub branches or emergent vegetation; often near water; female builds a bulky, open cup nest of plant materials and mud lined with fine grass or feathers; female incubates 4–5 brown-blotched, pale blue eggs for 12–14 days.
Feeding: slowly struts along the ground, gleaning, snatching and probing for insects, earthworms, seeds, waste grain and fruit; also catches insects in flight and eats small vertebrates; may take some bird eggs.
Voice: quick, loud *swaaaack* or *chaack* call. *Male:* song is a series of harsh, strained notes ending with a metallic squeak: *tssh-schleek* or *gri-de-leeek*.
Similar Species: *Great-tailed Grackle* (p. 347): larger; bluish purple overall. *Rusty* (p. 344), *Brewer's* (p. 345) and *Red-winged* (p. 340) *blackbirds:* smaller; finer bill; shorter tail. *European Starling* (p. 264): speckled appearance; dark eyes; thin bill; short tail.

GREAT-TAILED GRACKLE
Quiscalus mexicanus

Sacrificing function for beauty, the male Great-tailed Grackle has a tail so long that it acts as a sail on windy days, continually pointing the bird into the wind. • Great-tailed Grackles are farmland feeders, devouring waste grain before heading into suburban areas at night, announcing their presence with squeaks and hoots in noisy gangs. These gangs, especially in winter, will bully other birds from feeders. • The largest of the three grackles in North America, the Great-tailed Grackle was formerly considered to be a subspecies of the Boat-tailed Grackle (*Q. major*) of the eastern and Gulf coasts, but the two differ in habitat choices and do not interbreed. • Since the 1960s, following the path of agriculture and urbanization, the Great-tailed Grackle population has been expanding to northern Nebraska, southeastern South Dakota and eastern Colorado. • In nesting colonies, females may steal nest material from each other, and both genders will stray from their mates, with females sometimes switching territories within a breeding season.

ID: *Male:* all-black body with bluish purple iridescence; yellow eyes; very long, wide tail. *Female:* grayish brown body, lighter below; light "eyebrow" on yellow eye; shorter tail.
Size: *Male: L* 18 in; *W* 23 in. *Female: L* 15 in; *W* 19 in.
Habitat: open to semi-open habitat; urban parks, farmland and wetlands.
Nesting: near water, in a tree or in cattails; tree nest is made of mud, moss and varied debris; wetland nest is made of cattails and thick vegetation; female incubates 3–4 light gray, speckled eggs for 13–14 days.
Feeding: largely on the ground; varied diet includes other birds' eggs, insects, fish and grains.
Voice: very verbal; ascending whistles, hoots and squeaks; noisy chattering in large groups, especially in winter. *Male:* screeches to proclaim his territory.
Similar Species: *Common Grackle* (p. 346): smaller; bronze back and sides; shorter wings and tail; female has darker head.

347

BROWN-HEADED COWBIRD

Molothrus ater

Other bird species probably translate the bubbling, liquidy *glug-ahl-whee* sung by male Brown-headed Cowbirds as "here comes trouble!" Historically, Brown-headed Cowbirds followed bison herds across the Great Plains—they now follow cattle—and their nomadic lifestyle made constructing and tending a nest impossible. Therefore, cowbirds engage in "nest parasitism," laying their eggs in the nests of other songbirds. Many parasitized songbirds do not recognize that the eggs are not theirs, incubating them and raising the cowbird young as their own. Cowbird chicks typically hatch first and develop much more quickly than their nestmates, which are pushed out of the nest or outcompeted for food. • The expansion of livestock farming, the fragmentation of forests and the expanding network of transportation corridors have significantly increased the range of the Brown-headed Cowbird. It now parasitizes more than 140 North American bird species, including some that probably had no contact with it before widespread human settlement.

ID: dark eyes; thick, conical bill; short, squared tail. *Male:* iridescent, greenish blue body plumage usually looks glossy black; dark brown head. *Female:* brown plumage overall; faint streaking on light brown underparts; pale throat.
Size: *L* 6–8 in; *W* 12 in.
Habitat: open agricultural and residential areas, including fields, woodland edges, roadsides, fence lines, landfills, campgrounds and areas near cattle.
Nesting: lays up to 40 whitish eggs, marked with gray and brown, annually in the nests of other birds, usually 1 per nest (larger numbers, up to 8 eggs per nest, are probably from several different cowbirds); eggs hatch after 10–13 days.
Feeding: gleans the ground for seeds, waste grain and invertebrates, especially grasshoppers, beetles and true bugs.
Voice: squeaky, high-pitched *seep, psee* and *wee-tse-tse* calls, often given in flight; also a fast, chipping *ch-ch-ch-ch-ch-ch*. *Male:* song is a high, liquidy gurgle: *glug-ahl-whee* or *bubbloozeee*.
Similar Species: *Rusty Blackbird* (p. 344) and *Brewer's Blackbird* (p. 345): yellow eyes (except female Brewer's); slimmer, longer bills; males have purplish to greenish heads; females' head color matches body; longer tails. *Common Grackle* (p. 346): much larger; larger bill; longer, keeled tail.

ORCHARD ORIOLE

Icterus spurius

Orchards may once have been favored haunts of this oriole, but because most commercial orchards are now typically heavily sprayed and manicured, it is unlikely that you will ever see this bird in such a locale. Instead, the Orchard Oriole is most commonly found in large shade trees that line roads, paths and streams. Smaller than all other North American orioles, the Orchard Oriole is one of only two oriole species commonly found in the eastern United States. • Orchard Orioles are best seen in spring, when eager males hop from branch to branch, singing their quick and musical courtship songs. They are among the first species to migrate following breeding and are usually gone by late August. • This oriole is a frequent victim of nest parasitism by the Brown-headed Cowbird. In some parts of its breeding range, over half of the Orchard Oriole's nests are parasitized by cowbirds.

Habitat: open woodlands, suburban parklands, forest edges, hedgerows and groves of shade trees.

Nesting: in the fork of a hardwood tree or shrub; female weaves a hanging pouch nest using grass and other fine plant fibers; female incubates 4–5 pale bluish white eggs, blotched with gray, brown and purple, for about 12–15 days.

Feeding: inspects trees and shrubs for insects and berries; probes flowers for nectar; may visit hummingbird feeders or take orange halves.

Voice: quick *chuck* call. *Male:* song is a loud, rapid, varied series of whistled notes.

Similar Species: *Baltimore Oriole* (p. 350): bolder wing markings; male has bright orange plumage; female has orange overtones. *Bullock's Oriole* (p. 351): male is mostly orange; female has mostly pale gray underparts. *Tanagers* (pp. 297–99): females and nonbreeding males have less crisp wing bars or none and thicker bills.

ID: *Male:* dark back and wings; wing has 1 reddish chestnut bar, 1 white bar and white feather edgings; reddish chestnut rump and underparts; black "hood" and tail. *Female:* dull olive upperparts; yellow to olive yellow underparts; 2 faint, white wing bars on each dusky gray wing. *In flight:* reddish chestnut (male) or mostly white (female) wing linings.

Size: *L* 6–7 in; *W* 9½ in.

BALTIMORE ORIOLE

Icterus galbula

A striking, Halloween-style, black-and-orange plumage that flickers like smoldering embers among our neighborhood treetops marks the male Baltimore Oriole. As if his brilliant plumage was not enough to secure our admiration, he also sings a rich, flutelike courtship song and will vocalize almost continuously until he finds a mate. • In the northern plains, the Baltimore Oriole has been documented as enlarging its breeding range westward at about 6 miles per year, taking territory away from the Bullock's Oriole, with which it often hybridizes. Meanwhile, in the south, the reverse appears to have been happening. • The city of Baltimore was first established as a colony by Irishman George Calvert, Baron Baltimore. Mark Catesby, one of America's first naturalists, chose this bird's name because the male's plumage mirrored the colors of the baron's coat of arms.

ID: *Male:* black back, wings, "hood" and central tail feathers; white wing bar and feather edgings; bright orange shoulder and underparts. *Female:* olive brown upperparts (darkest on head); dull yellowish orange underparts and rump; 2 white wing bars. *In flight:* wing linings, rump and outer tail feathers mostly match underparts.

Size: *L* 7–8 in; *W* 11½ in.

Habitat: hardwood and mixed forests, particularly riparian woodlands, natural openings, shorelines, roadsides, orchards, gardens and parklands.

Nesting: high in a hardwood tree, suspended from a branch; female builds a hanging pouch nest made of grass, bark shreds, rootlets, plant stems and grapevines lined with fine grass, rootlets, fur and occasionally string or fishing line; female incubates 4–5 darkly marked, grayish to bluish eggs for 12–14 days.

Feeding: gleans canopy vegetation and shrubs for caterpillars, beetles, wasps and other invertebrates; also eats some fruit and nectar; may visit hummingbird feeders or take orange halves.

Voice: 2-note *tea-too* call; rapid chatter. *Male:* ch-ch-ch-ch-ch song consists of slow, loud, clear whistles: *peter peter peter here peter.*

Similar Species: *Orchard Oriole* (p. 349): male has reddish chestnut underparts; female is olive yellow without orange overtones. *Tanagers* (pp. 297–99): females and nonbreeding males have less crisp wing bars or none and thicker bills.

BULLOCK'S ORIOLE

Icterus bullockii

Although common and widespread in much of the western Great Plains, the Bullock's Oriole goes unnoticed by most residents. The glowing orange, black and white of the male's plumage blends remarkably well with the sunlit and shadowed upper-canopy summer foliage where he spends much of his time. Finding the drab female is even more difficult. • The very elaborate hanging nests of orioles provide both shelter from the elements and protection from the eyes of predators. • The Bullock's Oriole clearly demonstrates the vagaries of avian nomenclature. It was considered a separate species for more than a century, and then it was lumped, as the Northern Oriole, with the Baltimore Oriole because of hybridization in areas of overlap. It is once again considered a separate species. • "Oriole" comes from the Latin *aureolus*, meaning "golden"—most North American orioles are largely yellow or orange.

ID: *Male:* black upperparts; large, white wing patch; bright orange underparts and face; black throat, cap and eye line. *Female:* olive gray upperparts; 2 white wing bars; pale gray underparts; dusky yellow upper breast; throat and face. *In flight:* wing linings match sides; rump and tail are orange (male; has black tip and center on tail) or yellowish gray (female).

Size: *L* 7–9 in; *W* 12 in.

Habitat: riparian hardwood forests, willow shrublands and urban areas.

Nesting: suspended from a high hardwood branch; pouch nest woven with fine plant fibers, hair, string and fishing line is lined with horsehair, plant down, fur and moss; female incubates 4–5 darkly marked, grayish to bluish eggs for 12–14 days.

Feeding: gleans canopy vegetation and shrubs for caterpillars, beetles, wasps and other invertebrates; also eats fruit and nectar; occasionally visits hummingbird feeders or takes orange halves.

Voice: call is a harsh, husky series of *check* notes. *Male:* song is an accented series of 6–8 whistled, rich and guttural notes.

Similar Species: *Baltimore Oriole* (p. 350): male has dark "hood"; female has yellowish orange underparts. *Black-headed Grosbeak* (p. 333): heavy, conical bill; male has mostly black head; female has dark face and whitish "eyebrow." *Tanagers* (pp. 297–99): females and nonbreeding males have mostly yellow underparts and thicker bills.

PURPLE FINCH

Carpodacus purpureus

A gentle nature and simple but stunning plumage endear the Purple Finch to many birdwatchers. The northeastern Great Plains offers plentiful opportunities to meet this charming finch, but its numbers decrease farther southward through its winter range. • The appealing courtship ritual of the Purple Finch begins with the male's liquid, warbling song bubbling through conifer boughs, announcing his presence to potential mates. Upon the arrival of an interested female, the colorful male dances lightly around her, beating his wings until he softly lifts into the air. • A flat, table-style feeder with nearby tree cover is sure to attract Purple Finches and may keep a small flock around over winter. • "Purple" *(purpureus)* is simply a false description—Roger Tory Peterson said it best when he described the male Purple Finch as "a sparrow dipped in raspberry juice."

forests, shrubby open areas and feeders with nearby tree cover.

Nesting: on a conifer branch, far from the trunk; female builds a cup nest of twigs, grass and rootlets lined with moss and hair; female incubates 4–5 dark-marked, pale greenish blue eggs for about 13 days.

Feeding: gleans the ground and vegetation for seeds, buds, berries and insects; readily visits table-style feeders.

Voice: single metallic *cheep* or *weet* call. *Male:* continuous, bubbly, warbling song.

Similar Species: *House Finch* (p. 353): squared tail; male has fewer red areas; female has plainer face. *Cassin's Finch* (p. 367): limited range; white eye ring; male has redder, plusher-looking crown; female has indistinct "eyebrow." *Common Redpoll* (p. 355): male has black "chin" and smaller bill. *Red Crossbill* (p. 354): male has crossed mandibles. *Pine Grosbeak* (p. 367): male is larger and brighter red.

ID: pale, unstreaked belly and undertail coverts; sturdy, pale to grayish bill. *Male:* streaked, red-and-brown back and flanks; raspberry red (occasionally yellow to salmon pink) breast, throat, nape and head; reddish brown "cheek." *Female:* streaked, brownish to olive upperparts; heavily dark-streaked white breast and sides; dark brown "jaw line" and "cheek"; white "eyebrow" and lower "cheek" stripe. *In flight:* red (male) or olive (female) rump; notched tail.

Size: *L* 5–6 in; *W* 10 in.

Habitat: *Breeding:* conifer and mixed forests. *In migration* and *winter:* various

HOUSE FINCH

Carpodacus mexicanus

Now common throughout the continental U.S. and southern Canada, the House Finch is native to western North America. It was brought eastward as an illegally captured cage bird known as "Hollywood Finch." In the early 1940s, New York pet shop owners released their birds to avoid prosecution and fines; the descendants of those birds are thought to have colonized the Great Plains. • Only the resourceful House Finch has been aggressive and stubborn enough to successfully outcompete the Eurasian House Sparrow. Both birds often build their messy nests among eaves, rafters, chimneys and other human-fashioned habitats, and both birds thrive on seeds. Like the House Sparrow, this finch has prospered in urban environments, and it is regularly found in natural settings only in the West. • The male House Finch's plumage varies from light yellow to bright red, but females will choose the reddest males as mates.

ID: streaked, brown upperparts; white flanks and undertail coverts heavily streaked with grayish brown. *Male:* bright red breast, throat, forecrown and "eyebrow"; brown "cap." *Female:* brown-streaked breast and throat; indistinct facial patterning. *In flight:* red (male) or grayish brown (female) rump; square tail.
Size: *L* 5–6 in; *W* 9½ in.
Habitat: cities, towns and agricultural areas.
Nesting: in a cavity, building, dense foliage (especially in evergreens and ornamental shrubs near buildings) or abandoned nest; mostly the female builds an open cup nest of grass, twigs, leaves, hair, feathers and other debris; female incubates 4–5 lavender- and black-dotted, pale blue eggs for 12–14 days.
Feeding: gleans vegetation and the ground for seeds; also takes berries, buds and some flower parts; often visits feeders.
Voice: sweet *cheer* flight call, often repeated. *Male:* song is a bright, disjointed, 3-second warble, often ending with a harsh *jeeer* or *wheer.*
Similar Species: *Purple Finch* (p. 352): notched tail; red on male extends to wings and flanks; female has white-bordered "cheek." *Cassin's Finch* (p. 367): limited range; white eye ring; male has plush, red crown; female has crisper streaking. *Common Redpoll* (p. 355): male has black "chin," smaller bill. *Red Crossbill* (p. 354): male has crossed mandibles. *Pine Grosbeak* (p. 367): male is larger, brighter red with unstreaked gray flanks.

RED CROSSBILL

Loxia curvirostra

Red Crossbills may breed at any time of year, including midwinter, if they discover a bumper crop of pine cones as they wander the forests, but their nomadic ways make them difficult to find, even in years of plenty. Winter is typically the time to see Red Crossbills, and in irruptive years, large flocks can appear as far south as Oklahoma. They regularly nest in Minnesota and the Black Hills of South Dakota—and often do so elsewhere as well—and are known to wander from their breeding areas. • The oddly shaped bill is adapted for prying open conifer cones. While holding the cone with one foot, the crossbill inserts its closed bill between the cone and scales and pries them apart by opening its bill. Once a cone is cracked, a crossbill uses its nimble tongue to extract the soft, energy-rich seeds hidden within. • The scientific name *curvirostra* is Latin for "curve billed."

grass, bark shreds and rootlets lined with finer materials; female incubates 3–4 pale bluish to greenish eggs, dotted with black and purple, for 12–18 days.

ID: bill has crossed tips. *Male:* dull orangy red to brick red plumage; dark wings and tail; always has color on throat. *Female:* olive gray to dusky yellow plumage; plain, dark wings. *In flight:* slightly notched tail.

Size: *L* 5–6½ in; *W* 11 in.

Habitat: favors red and white pines; also uses other pine and spruce–fir forests and plantations.

Nesting: high on a conifer's outer branch; female builds an open cup nest of twigs,

Feeding: eats primarily conifer seeds (especially pine); also eats buds, hardwood tree seeds and occasionally insects; often licks road salt or minerals in soil and along roadsides; rarely visits feeders.

Voice: distinctive *jip-jip* call, often given in flight. *Male:* song is a varied series of warbles, trills and chips (similar to other finches).

Similar Species: *White-winged Crossbill* (p. 367): 2 broad, white wing bars. *Pine Grosbeak* (p. 367): larger; white wing bars; stubby, conical bill. *House Finch* (p. 353) and *Purple Finch* (p. 352): males are lighter red overall with none on lower bellies, conical bills.

COMMON REDPOLL
Carduelis flammea

A predictably unpredictable winter visitor, the Common Redpoll is seen in varying numbers—it might appear in flocks of hundreds in the northern Great Plains or as a few individuals in the southern parts of the region. • Because redpolls are so small, they have only a small internal volume to produce and retain heat and a relatively large surface area from which heat can be lost. As a result, they are in constant danger of running out of fuel and dying of hypothermia in winter. Therefore, these birds must eat almost constantly, and they continually glean waste grain from bare fields or stock up on seed at winter feeders. Their focus on food helps make wintering redpolls remarkably fearless of humans. • Redpolls can endure lower temperatures than other small songbirds. They will sit with their highly insulative feathers fluffed out, trapping layers of warm, insulating air and keeping a circle of warmth around their bodies.

nonbreeding

ID: streaked, grayish brown upperparts, including rump; lightly streaked, whitish sides, flanks and undertail coverts; black "chin"; red forecrown; yellowish bill. *Male:* pinkish red breast (brightest in breeding plumage). *Female:* whitish to pale gray breast. *In flight:* notched tail.
Size: *L* 5 in; *W* 9 in.
Habitat: open fields, meadows, roadsides, utility rights-of-way, railroads, forest edges and backyards with feeders.

Nesting: does not nest in the Great Plains.
Feeding: gleans the ground, snow and vegetation in large flocks for seeds in winter; often visits feeders.
Voice: songs and calls are indistinguishable from the Hoary Redpoll's; calls are a soft *chit-chit-chit-chit* and a faint *swe-eet. Male:* song is a twittering series of trills.
Similar Species: *Hoary Redpoll:* generally paler and plumper overall; usually has faint, little or no streaking on sides, flanks, undertail coverts and rump; bill may look stubbier. *Pine Siskin* (p. 356): heavily streaked overall; yellow highlights on wings and tail; no red in plumage; no black "chin."

PINE SISKIN
Carduelis pinus

You can spend days, weeks or even months in pursuit of Pine Siskins, only to meet with frustration, aching feet and a sore, crimped neck. The Pine Siskins themselves also put in the miles, because their favored habitats are widely scattered across the Great Plains. The easiest way to meet them is to stock a backyard finch feeder with black niger seed and wait. If the feeder is in the right location, you can expect to be visited by Pine Siskins, particularly in winter. • Tight flocks of these gregarious birds are frequently heard before they are seen. With practice, a birder can identify them by their characteristic rising *zzzreeeee* calls and boisterous chatter alone. • Aside from occasional flashes of yellow, the Pine Siskin's wardrobe is drab and sparrowlike. But for people who get to know it, this bird reveals a gentle nature that radiates the playfulness and enthusiasm of a goldfinch.

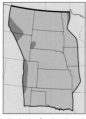

ID: dark, heavily pale-streaked upperparts; yellow highlights at base of tail feathers and on wings (easily seen in flight); dull wing bars; heavily dark-streaked, whitish underparts; indistinct facial pattern. *In flight:* slightly forked tail.
Size: *L* 4½–5½ in; *W* 9 in.
Habitat: conifer and mixed forests. *Breeding:* urban and rural ornamental and shade trees. *Winter:* forest edges, meadows, roadsides, agricultural fields and backyards with feeders.
Nesting: usually loosely colonial; typically at midlevel on an outer conifer branch; female builds a loose cup nest of twigs,

grass and rootlets lined with finer materials; female incubates 3–5 pale blue eggs with dark dots for about 13 days.
Feeding: gleans the ground and vegetation for seeds (especially thistle seeds), buds and some insects; attracted to road salts, mineral licks and ashes; regularly visits feeders.
Voice: buzzy, rising *zzzreeeee* call. *Male:* variable song is a bubbly mix of squeaky, raspy, metallic notes, sometimes resembling a jerky laugh.
Similar Species: *Common Redpoll* (p. 355) and *Hoary Redpoll:* no yellow on wings and tail; red forecrown. *Purple Finch* (p. 352) and *House Finch* (p. 353): females have no yellow on wings and tails, thicker bills. *Sparrows* (pp. 302–24): no yellow on wings and tails.

AMERICAN GOLDFINCH

Carduelis tristis

Bright and cheery in breeding plumage, American Goldfinches are commonly seen throughout summer and fall, but in drab winter plumage they may go unrecognized. As these birds flutter over parks and gardens in their distinctive, undulating style, it's hard to miss their jubilant calls. • Goldfinches nest in late summer and early fall. They seem to delight in perching upon thistle heads as they forage to feed their offspring, and it is a joy to observe a flock raining down to poke and prod dandelion heads. These birds can look quite comical as they step down on the stems to reach the seeds. A dandelion-covered lawn always seems a lot less weedy with a flock of glowing goldfinches hopping through it. • The scientific name *tristis*, Latin for "sad," referring to the voice, seems an unfair choice for such a pleasing and playful bird.

breeding

ID: *Breeding male:* bright yellow body; white wing bars, undertail coverts and tail base; black wings, tail and "cap" (extends onto forehead); orange bill. *Breeding female:* yellowish green upperparts and head; yellow throat and breast; orange bill. *Nonbreeding:* olive brown back and head; grayish brown underparts; brownish bill; yellow-tinged face and throat. *In flight:* white "wing pits"; forked tail.

Size: *L* 4½–5½ in; *W* 9 in.

Habitat: weedy fields, woodland edges, meadows, riparian areas, parks and gardens.

Nesting: in a fork in a hardwood shrub or tree (often hawthorn, serviceberry or sapling maple); female builds a compact cup nest of plant fibers, grass and spider silk lined with soft materials; female incubates 4–6 pale bluish eggs for about 12–14 days.

Feeding: gleans vegetation for seeds (primarily thistle, birch and alder), insects and berries; visits feeders.

Voice: calls include *po-ta-to-chip* or *per-chic-or-ee* (often delivered in flight) and a whistled *dear-me, see-me*. *Male:* song is a long, varied series of trills, twitters, warbles and hissing notes.

Similar Species: *Lesser Goldfinch* (p. 367): limited range; darker bill; male has dusky to black nape and back and larger white areas on wings and tail; female has less distinct wing bars. *Wilson's Warbler* (p. 294): olive upperparts; unbarred, olive wings; yellow forehead; thin, dark bill.

357

EVENING GROSBEAK

Coccothraustes vespertinus

One chilly winter day, a flock of Evening Grosbeaks descends unannounced upon your backyard bird feeder filled with sunflower seeds. You watch the stunning gold-and-black grosbeaks with delight, but you soon realize that these aesthetic blessings are also a financial curse—they will eat great quantities of expensive birdseed and then abruptly disappear in late winter. • In the southern plains, several years may pass with no Evening Grosbeaks sighted; then suddenly they are being reported everywhere. • The massive bill of this seed-eater is difficult to ignore. In French, *gros bec* means "large beak," and any seasoned bird bander will tell you that the Evening Grosbeak's bill can exert an incredible force per unit area— it may be the most powerful bill of any North American bird. • Both the common and scientific names (*vespertinus* is Latin for "of the evening") reflect the former belief that the Evening Grosbeak sang only in the evening.

ID: white-marked, black wings; massive, conical, pale bill. *Male:* dark brown of head gradually fades into golden yellow on belly and lower back; black crown; bright yellow "eyebrow" and forehead band. *Female:* grayish brown upper back and head; yellow-tinged shoulder and underparts; white undertail coverts. *In flight:* large, white patches on wings; female has white markings on black tail.

Size: *L* 7–8½ in; *W* 14 in.

Habitat: *Breeding:* conifer and mixed forests and woodlands; occasionally hardwood woodlands, suburban parks and orchards. *Winter:* various forests and woodlands; parks and gardens with feeders.

Nesting: on an outer limb in a conifer; female builds a flimsy cup nest of twigs lined with fine materials; female incubates 3–4 pale blue to bluish green eggs, blotched with purple, gray and brown, for 11–14 days.

Feeding: gleans the ground and vegetation for seeds, buds and berries; also eats insects and licks mineral-rich soil; visits feeders for sunflower seeds.

Voice: loud, sharp *clee-ip* and ringing *peeer* calls. *Male:* song is a wandering, halting warble.

Similar Species: *American Goldfinch* (p. 357): much smaller; smaller bill; smaller wing bars. *Orioles* (pp. 349–51): different head patterns; finer bills. *Tanagers* (pp. 297–99): less or no white on upperwings; smaller bills.

HOUSE SPARROW

Passer domesticus

The House Sparrow is the first bird that many of us meet and learn to recognize in our youth. Although this omnipresent backyard neighbor is one of our most abundant and conspicuous birds, few of us know much about it. • The House Sparrow was introduced to North America in the 1850s around Brooklyn, New York, to help control the insects that were damaging grain crops. This sparrow's diet is largely vegetarian, so its effect on crop pests to be minimal. Since then, this Eurasian sparrow has managed to colonize most human-altered environments on the continent, and it has benefited greatly from a close association with humans. Unfortunately for many native bird species, its aggressive behavior has helped it to usurp territory, especially in rural habitats. • Only distantly related to North American sparrows, the House Sparrow belongs to the family of Old World Sparrows or "Weaver Finches."

breeding

ID: *Breeding male:* dark, mottled upperparts; white wing bar; chestnut wing markings and nape; gray underparts; gray crown; light gray "cheek"; black "bib" and bill. *Nonbreeding male:* smaller black "bib"; pale bill. *Female:* dark-and-buff-streaked, brown upperparts; unstreaked, paler, grayish underparts; indistinct facial patterns; buffy "eyebrow"; pale bill. *In flight:* rounded wings and tail.
Size: *L* 5½–6½ in; *W* 9½ in.
Habitat: townsites, urban and suburban areas, farmyards and agricultural areas, railroad yards and other developed areas; avoids undeveloped and heavily wooded areas.

Nesting: often communal; in a human-made structure, ornamental shrubs or natural cavities; pair builds a large, dome-shaped nest of grass, twigs, plant fibers and litter, often lined with feathers; pair incubates 4–6 whitish, sometimes greenish eggs, dotted with gray and brown, for 10–13 days.
Feeding: gleans the ground and vegetation for seeds, insects and fruit; frequently visits feeders for seeds.
Voice: short *chill-up* call. *Male:* song is a plain, familiar *cheep-cheep-cheep-cheep.*
Similar Species: female is distinctively drab. *Harris's Sparrow* (p. 323): male has gray face, black "cap," pinkish orange bill. *Other sparrows* (pp. 302–24): often have streaking on breast and sides, stronger facial patterns or eye rings.

OCCASIONAL BIRD SPECIES

AMERICAN BLACK DUCK
Anas rubripes

Common but apparently declining in the eastern U.S., with spotty breeding records in North Dakota. Uncommon in winter in eastern Kansas and northeastern Oklahoma.

American Black Duck

GREATER SCAUP
Aythya marila

Winters in small numbers throughout the Great Plains. Use care when distinguishing this species from the similar Lesser Scaup.

GREATER SAGE-GROUSE
Centrocerus urophasianus

In the Great Plains, breeds in Wyoming and Montana. The Greater Sage-Grouse and the Gunnison Sage-Grouse (*C. minimus,* confined largely to west-central Colorado) were formerly lumped together as "Sage Grouse."

Greater Sage-Grouse

SPRUCE GROUSE
Falcipennis canadensis

The Spruce Grouse's breeding range touches northwestern Minnesota, but the species is much more common in dense spruce forest farther north.

RED-THROATED LOON
Gavia stellata

Casual through the Great Plains in migration. A few may linger in Oklahoma through winter.

Spruce Grouse

PACIFIC LOON
Gavia pacifica

Rare in winter and in migration between its arctic breeding grounds and Pacific Coast wintering grounds.

Pacific Loon

CLARK'S GREBE
Aechmophorus clarkii

Summer resident in portions of Colorado and Wyoming; rare in Montana, Kansas and Oklahoma. Similar to Western Grebe in appearance—compare head patterns.

Clark's Grebe

BLACK VULTURE
Coragyps atratus

Breeding resident in southeastern Oklahoma. Vagrants drift northward to Kansas, Nebraska and Iowa, and westward to the Texas panhandle.

WHOOPING CRANE
Grus americanus

Breeds in Wood Buffalo National Park in northern Alberta, Canada, and winters on the central Texas coast. May be seen in spring and fall, with luck, along the narrow migratory corridor. Recent attempts to reestablish populations within its historic range have had mixed results.

Whooping Crane

RUDDY TURNSTONE
Arenaria interpres

This shorebird breeds in the Arctic and is a rare to uncommon migrant through the Great Plains. In breeding plumage, the Ruddy Turnstone has bright orange legs, a black-and-white head and "bib" and a chestnut-and-black back. In nonbreeding plumage it retains the black "bib" and orange legs.

Ruddy Turnstone

SANDERLING
Calidris alba

Breeds in arctic Canada; winters on the Atlantic, Gulf and Pacific coasts. It is a rare to uncommon wanderer throughout the interior U.S. It has a bold, white wing stripe and is most often seen in its pale, white-and-gray winter plumage.

CASPIAN TERN
Sterna caspia

Uncommon migrant. Breeds largely in Canada's prairie provinces and winters on southern coasts.

Caspian Tern

EURASIAN COLLARED-DOVE
Streptopelia decaocto

Introduced species. Established in Texas, Oklahoma and Kansas, and expanding northward into Colorado, Nebraska and Wyoming.

MONK PARAKEET
Myiopsitta monachus

Introduced species. Most populations established in Texas and Oklahoma have failed because of natural pressures or human intervention.

Eurasian Collared-Dove

WESTERN SCREECH-OWL
Megascops kennicotti

Uncommon resident along the western margin of the Great Plains, including New Mexico, Colorado, the Oklahoma panhandle and extreme southwestern Kansas. Best distinguished from the Eastern Screech-Owl by voice.

BLACK-CHINNED HUMMINGBIRD
Archilochus alexandri

Breeds in Texas and Oklahoma panhandles, northeastern New Mexico and southeastern Colorado, and is an uncommon migrant in southwestern Kansas.

Western Screech-Owl

RUFOUS HUMMINGBIRD
Selasphorus rufus

Migrant in the southwestern Great Plains. Accidental in winter in the southern portion of the region, especially Oklahoma, usually at feeders.

GOLDEN-FRONTED WOODPECKER
Melanerpes aurifrons

Resident in the Texas panhandle and southwestern Oklahoma. Yellow on head and white rump differentiate it from the similar Red-bellied Woodpecker.

Golden-fronted Woodpecker

RED-NAPED SAPSUCKER
Sphyrapicus nuchalis

Uncommon resident in the Black Hills and marginally into eastern Wyoming. Rare migrant in western Great Plains.

AMERICAN THREE-TOED WOODPECKER
Picoides dorsalis

Uncommon resident in the Black Hills of South Dakota and in suitable habitat in north-central Colorado. Compare carefully with the Black-backed Woodpecker.

BLACK-BACKED WOODPECKER
Picoides arcticus

Rare resident in the Black Hills. Very similar in appearance to the American Three-toed Woodpecker.

Red-naped Sapsucker

DUSKY FLYCATCHER
Empidonax oberholseri

Nests in the Black Hills. Infrequent in eastern Wyoming and central Montana. Migrates along the western edge of the Great Plains.

CORDILLERAN FLYCATCHER
Empidonax occidentalis

Breeds along the western edge of the Great Plains from the Black Hills to southeastern Colorado and northeastern New Mexico. Rare migrant in the western Great Plains.

Dusky Flycatcher

VERMILION FLYCATCHER
Pyrocephalus rubinus

Uncommon (has nested) in western Oklahoma. More common in eastern New Mexico. Accidentals have been recorded to the north and east of there.

CASSIN'S KINGBIRD
Tyrannus vociferans

Breeds in New Mexico, Colorado and the Oklahoma panhandle and northward to Wyoming and Montana. Compare with the very similar Western Kingbird.

Vermilion Flycatcher

BLACK-CAPPED VIREO
Vireo atricapilla

Endangered. Uncommon breeder in suitable scrub oak–juniper habitat in central Texas and south-central Oklahoma.

PLUMBEOUS VIREO
Vireo plumbeus

Summer resident in southeastern Montana and eastern Wyoming; migrant through eastern Colorado, western Kansas and New Mexico. Until 1997 it was lumped with the very similar Blue-headed Vireo and the Cassin's Vireo *(V. cassinii)* as a single species, "Solitary Vireo."

Plumbeous Vireo

GRAY JAY
Perisoreus canadensis

Restricted to the Black Hills area of South Dakota and eastern Wyoming. May wander eastward onto the plains in winter.

FISH CROW
Corvus ossifragus

A common summer resident in eastern Oklahoma into Kansas and southern Missouri, following recent range expansion. Prefers forested areas near rivers and lakes. Best distinguished by its nasal *cah* or *ca-aah*.

Gray Jay

COMMON RAVEN
Corvus corax

Ranges from northeastern New Mexico and the Oklahoma panhandle northward through Colorado to Wyoming and Montana. Compare carefully to the similar Chihuahuan Raven.

Fish Crow

JUNIPER TITMOUSE
Baeolophus ridgwayi

Range in this area is restricted to southeastern Colorado, northeastern New Mexico and the Oklahoma panhandle. A plain, rather drab titmouse.

Juniper Titmouse

BLACK-CRESTED TITMOUSE
Baeolophus atricristatus

Range extends through the eastern Texas panhandle and into southwestern Oklahoma. The black crest normally distinguishes this bird from the Tufted Titmouse, but hybrids do occur.

PYGMY NUTHATCH
Sitta pygmaea

Pygmy Nuthatch

Uncommon breeder in southwestern South Dakota and parts of eastern Wyoming. Wanders southward and eastward to Kansas and northern Oklahoma in some winters.

BLUE-WINGED WARBLER
Vermivora pinus

Blue-winged Warbler

Breeds in extreme eastern Oklahoma and southern Missouri, with vagrants reported from most of the Great Plains. Primarily inhabits eastern hardwood forests. Hybridizes with the Golden-winged Warbler.

GOLDEN-WINGED WARBLER
Vermivora chrysoptera

Golden-winged Warbler

Usually seen as a migrant on its journey northward from South America. Breeds in northern Minnesota forests and into adjacent Canada. Hybridizes with the Blue-winged Warbler.

VIRGINIA'S WARBLER
Vermivora virginiae

Uncommon breeder in brushy habitat in northeastern New Mexico and southeastern Colorado but prefers dry montane areas farther west. Accidental in the Oklahoma panhandle and southwestern Kansas.

Virginia's Warbler

CAPE MAY WARBLER
Dendroica tigrina

Accidental through most of the Great Plains but a regular migrant in Minnesota and parts of Iowa en route to its largely Canadian summer range.

Cape May Warbler

CERULEAN WARBLER
Dendroica cerulea

Uncommon to rare breeder in central Missouri and eastern portions of Kansas and Oklahoma. Has declined in recent years.

WORM-EATING WARBLER
Helmitheros vermivorum

Rare breeder from extreme eastern Oklahoma and Kansas into Missouri, where it is slightly more common. Iowa also has a few nesting records.

Cerulean Warbler

SWAINSON'S WARBLER
Limnothlypis swainsonii

Rare breeder in southeastern Oklahoma; vagrant in extreme eastern Kansas.

MACGILLIVRAY'S WARBLER
Oporornis tolmiei

Breeds in eastern Wyoming and western South Dakota in suitable habitat. A migrant through Colorado, Kansas and New Mexico; accidental elsewhere.

Worm-eating Warbler

HOODED WARBLER
Wilsonia citrina

Rare summer resident in eastern portions of Oklahoma and Kansas and western Missouri. Accidental in the western plains.

GREEN-TAILED TOWHEE
Pipilo chlorurus

Breeding range extends from the western U.S. into southeastern Montana and Wyoming; transient through eastern Colorado, western Kansas and New Mexico. Accidental in the central and eastern Great Plains.

MacGillivray's Warbler

CANYON TOWHEE
Pipilo fuscus

Resident in the Oklahoma panhandle and adjacent areas of New Mexico and Colorado. Similar to, but plainer than, the Green-tailed Towhee.

Canyon Towhee

BLACK-THROATED SPARROW

Amphispiza bilineata

Resident in southeastern Colorado, northwestern New Mexico and adjoining areas in Oklahoma and Texas. Accidental in the central Great Plains.

GRAY-CROWNED ROSY-FINCH

Leucosticte tephrocotis

Winters on the plains of Montana, Wyoming and Colorado; accidental on the northern plains.

Black-throated Sparrow

PINE GROSBEAK

Pinicola enucleator

Winters in the northern plains but may wander in some years, with accidentals reported as far south as Oklahoma.

CASSIN'S FINCH

Carpodacus cassinii

Resident in the Black Hills, South Dakota. Rare in winter from South Dakota to western Oklahoma. Compare carefully to House Finch and Purple Finch.

Pine Grosbeak

WHITE-WINGED CROSSBILL

Loxia leucoptera

Winters anywhere from Montana to Minnesota and northern South Dakota; rarely to Iowa. Accidental winter visitor to the southern plains.

Cassin's Finch

LESSER GOLDFINCH

Carduelis psaltria

Breeds in southeastern Colorado and northeastern New Mexico, with some birds reaching southwestern Kansas and the Oklahoma and Texas panhandles. Mostly withdraws southward in winter.

White-winged Crossbill

SELECT REFERENCES

American Ornithologists' Union. 1998. *Check-list of North American Birds.* 7th ed. (and its supplements). American Ornithologists' Union, Washington, D.C.

Choate, E.A. 1985. *The Dictionary of American Bird Names.* Rev. ed. Harvard Common Press, Cambridge, MA.

Cox, Randall T. 1996. *Birder's Dictionary.* Falcon Publishing, Inc., Helena, MT.

Kaufman, K. 1996. *Lives of North American Birds.* Houghton Mifflin Co., Boston.

Kaufman, K. 2000. *Birds of North America.* Houghton Mifflin Co., New York.

National Geographic Society. 2002. *Field Guide to the Birds of North America.* 4th ed. National Geographic Society, Washington, D.C.

Poole, A. F. and Frank B. Gill, eds. 1992. *Birds of North America: Life Histories for the 21st Century.* The Birds of North America, Inc., Philadelphia, PA.

Sibley, D.A. 2000. *National Audubon Society: The Sibley Guide to Bird Life and Behavior.* Alfred A. Knopf, New York.

Sibley, D.A. 2000. *National Audubon Society: The Sibley Guide to Birds.* Alfred A. Knopf, New York.

Sibley, D.A. 2002. *Sibley's Birding Basics.* Alfred A. Knopf, New York.

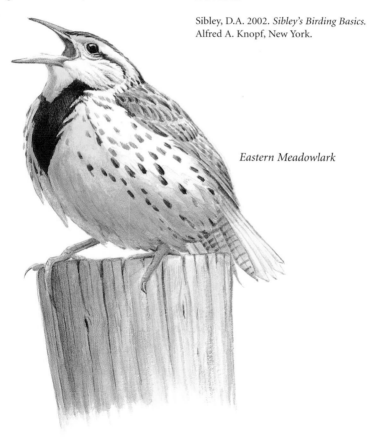

Eastern Meadowlark

GLOSSARY

avifauna: the community of birds found in a specific region or environment.

borrow pit: in construction, an area of land where materials have been excavated for use as fill at another site.

cavity nester: a bird that builds its nest in a tree hollow or nest box.

cere: bare skin joining the forehead and the base of the upper bill.

corvid: any member of the family Corvidae, including crows, jays, magpies and ravens.

cryptic plumage: a coloration pattern that helps to conceal the bird.

diagnostic: the distinguishing characteristics of a bird.

disjunct population: two groups of the same species found in widely separated regions.

diurnal: active primarily during the day.

extirpated: a species that no longer exists in the wild in a particular region but occurs elsewhere.

fecundity: fertility.

feral: a bird that is living in the wild but was once domesticated.

flush: a behavior in which frightened birds explode into flight in response to a disturbance.

forb: a herb other than grass.

gizzard shad: a freshwater fish from the herring family.

grub: to dig up from the roots.

hybridism: the mating of two species to produce an offspring, often infertile, with characteristics of both species.

irruptive: a sporadic, mass migration of birds into an unusual range.

lead: a small channel of water that runs between ice floes.

lek: a place where males gather to display for females in the spring.

lores: the area on a bird between its eye and upper bill.

mantle: the area that includes the back and uppersides of the wings.

mast: food that is high in fiber, including tree nuts, conifer seeds and acorns.

migrant trap: an oasis of vegetation that attracts large groups of migrating birds.

mixed-emergent marshes: a wetland with a mixed community of vegetation, including bulrushes, cattails, wild rice and water lilies.

morph: one of several alternate color phases displayed by a species; may change seasonally or from region to region.

neotropical: the biogeographic region that includes southern Mexico, Central and South America and the West Indies.

nominate subspecies: the subspecies for which the scientific species name and subspecies name are identical; for example, the lineatus subspecies of the Red-shouldered Hawk (*Buteo lineatus lineatus*).

obligate: a habitat, feeding style or other factor that is essential to the survival of a species.

peeps: small, similar-looking sandpipers of the *Calidris* genus.

pelagic: open ocean habitat far from land.

Phragmites: reeds found in the wetlands of temperate or tropical regions.

pigeon milk: not true milk; a nutritious secretion produced in the crop of members of the pigeon family that is fed to their young.

pishing: a repeated, sibilant sound made especially to attract birds.

polygynous: a mating strategy in which one male breeds with several females.

raft: a gathering of birds.

relict: the remaining small population of a species in a region where it is otherwise extirpated.

riparian: habitat along riverbanks.

riprap: a pile of rocks and concrete chunks used as a supporting wall on an embankment near water.

scapulars: feathers of the shoulder, seeming to join the wing and back.

sexual dimorphism: a difference in plumage, size or other characteristics between males and females of the same species.

silviculture: division of forestry that deals with the care and cultivation of forests.

speculum: a brightly colored patch on the wings of many dabbling ducks.

squeaking: making a sound to attract birds by loudly kissing the back of the hand, or by using a specially designed, squeaky bird call.

stage: to gather in one place during migration, usually when birds are flightless or partly flightless during molting.

stoop: a steep dive through the air, usually performed by birds of prey while foraging or during courtship displays.

successional woodlands: sequence of vegetation that grows after a major disturbance such as a fire.

swale: a low-lying, marshy tract of land.

tertials: innermost feathers under the wing.

understory: the shrub or thicket layer beneath a canopy of trees.

vent: the single opening for excretion of uric acid and other wastes and for sexual reproduction; also known as the "cloaca."

zygodactyl feet: feet that have two toes pointing forward and two pointing backward; found in osprey, owls and woodpeckers.

eyebrow/supercilium • crown • eye line • lore • wing bars • greater coverts • chin • rump • throat • tips of primary feathers • breast • tail feathers • flank • belly • undertail coverts • secondary feathers

CHECKLIST

The following checklist contains 457 birds that have been officially recorded in one or more states of the Great Plains. They are grouped by family and listed in taxonomic order in accordance with the A.O.U. *Check-list of North American Birds* (7th ed.) and its supplements (current to *The Forty-fifth Supplement*, 2004).

Casual and accidental species (those that are not seen on a yearly basis) are listed in *italics*. Any species that is regular anywhere in the Great Plains appears as regular. Introduced species are marked with (is). The following federal risk categories are noted (with information from the U.S. Fish and Wildlife Service Threatened and Endangered Species System database, current as of May 2004): believed extinct or extirpated (ex), endangered (en) and threatened (th). Because of space restrictions, the individual state status of each species is not given.

Waterfowl (Anatidae)
- [ ] *Black-bellied Whistling-Duck*
- [ ] *Fulvous Whistling-Duck*
- [ ] Greater White-fronted Goose
- [ ] Snow Goose
- [ ] Ross's Goose
- [ ] Cackling Goose
- [ ] Canada Goose
- [ ] *Brant*
- [ ] Trumpeter Swan
- [ ] Tundra Swan
- [ ] Wood Duck
- [ ] Gadwall
- [ ] *Eurasian Wigeon*
- [ ] American Wigeon
- [ ] American Black Duck
- [ ] Mallard
- [ ] Blue-winged Teal
- [ ] Cinnamon Teal
- [ ] Northern Shoveler
- [ ] Northern Pintail
- [ ] *Garganey*
- [ ] Green-winged Teal
- [ ] Canvasback
- [ ] Redhead
- [ ] Ring-necked Duck
- [ ] Greater Scaup
- [ ] Lesser Scaup
- [ ] *Harlequin Duck*
- [ ] Surf Scoter
- [ ] White-winged Scoter
- [ ] Black Scoter
- [ ] Long-tailed Duck
- [ ] Bufflehead
- [ ] Common Goldeneye
- [ ] *Barrow's Goldeneye*
- [ ] Hooded Merganser
- [ ] Common Merganser
- [ ] Red-breasted Merganser
- [ ] Ruddy Duck

Grouse & Allies (Phasianidae)
- [ ] Gray Partridge (is)
- [ ] Ring-necked Pheasant (is)
- [ ] Ruffed Grouse
- [ ] Greater Sage-Grouse
- [ ] Spruce Grouse
- [ ] Sharp-tailed Grouse
- [ ] Greater Prairie-Chicken
- [ ] Lesser Prairie-Chicken
- [ ] Wild Turkey

New World Quail (Odontophoridae)
- [ ] Scaled Quail
- [ ] Northern Bobwhite

Loons (Gaviidae)
- [ ] Red-throated Loon
- [ ] Pacific Loon
- [ ] Common Loon
- [ ] *Yellow-billed Loon*

Grebes (Podicipedidae)
- [ ] Pied-billed Grebe
- [ ] Horned Grebe
- [ ] Red-necked Grebe
- [ ] Eared Grebe
- [ ] Western Grebe
- [ ] Clark's Grebe

Pelicans (Pelecanidae)
- [ ] American White Pelican
- [ ] *Brown Pelican* (en)

Cormorants (Phalacrocoracidae)
- [ ] *Neotropic Cormorant*
- [ ] Double-crested Cormorant

Darters (Anhingidae)
- [ ] *Anhinga*

Frigatebirds (Fregatidae)
- [ ] *Magnificent Frigatebird*

Herons & Bitterns (Ardeidae)
- [ ] American Bittern
- [ ] Least Bittern
- [ ] Great Blue Heron
- [ ] Great Egret
- [ ] Snowy Egret
- [ ] Little Blue Heron
- [ ] *Tricolored Heron*
- [ ] Cattle Egret
- [ ] Green Heron
- [ ] Black-crowned Night-Heron
- [ ] Yellow-crowned Night-Heron

Ibis & Spoonbills (Threskiornithidae)
- [ ] *White Ibis*
- [ ] *Glossy Ibis*
- [ ] White-faced Ibis
- [ ] *Roseate Spoonbill*

Storks (Ciconiidae)
- [ ] *Wood Stork* (en)

Vultures (Cathartidae)
- [ ] Black Vulture
- [ ] Turkey Vulture

Kites, Hawks & Eagles (Accipetridae)
- [ ] Osprey
- [ ] *Swallow-tailed Kite*
- [ ] *White-tailed Kite*
- [ ] Mississippi Kite
- [ ] Bald Eagle (th)
- [ ] Northern Harrier
- [ ] Sharp-shinned Hawk
- [ ] Cooper's Hawk
- [ ] Northern Goshawk
- [ ] *Harris's Hawk*
- [ ] Red-shouldered Hawk
- [ ] Broad-winged Hawk
- [ ] Swainson's Hawk
- [ ] Red-tailed Hawk
- [ ] Ferruginous Hawk
- [ ] Rough-legged Hawk
- [ ] Golden Eagle

Caracaras & Falcons (Falconidae)
- [ ] *Crested Caracara*
- [ ] American Kestrel
- [ ] Merlin
- [ ] *Gyrfalcon*
- [ ] Peregrine Falcon
- [ ] Prairie Falcon

Rails, Gallinules & Coots (Rallidae)
- [ ] Yellow Rail
- [ ] Black Rail
- [ ] King Rail
- [ ] Virginia Rail
- [ ] Sora
- [ ] *Purple Gallinule*
- [ ] Common Moorhen
- [ ] American Coot

Cranes (Gruidae)
- [ ] Sandhill Crane
- [ ] Whooping Crane (en)

Plovers (Charadriidae)
- [ ] Black-bellied Plover
- [ ] American Golden-Plover
- [ ] Snowy Plover
- [ ] Semipalmated Plover
- [ ] Piping Plover (en, th)
- [ ] Killdeer
- [ ] Mountain Plover

Stilts & Avocets (Recurvirostridae)
- [ ] Black-necked Stilt
- [ ] American Avocet

Sandpipers & Allies (Scolopacidae)
- [ ] Greater Yellowlegs
- [ ] Lesser Yellowlegs
- [ ] Solitary Sandpiper
- [ ] Willet
- [ ] Spotted Sandpiper
- [ ] Upland Sandpiper
- [ ] *Eskimo Curlew* (en, possibly ex)
- [ ] Whimbrel
- [ ] Long-billed Curlew
- [ ] Hudsonian Godwit
- [ ] Marbled Godwit
- [ ] *Ruddy Turnstone*
- [ ] *Red Knot*
- [ ] Sanderling
- [ ] Semipalmated Sandpiper
- [ ] Western Sandpiper
- [ ] Least Sandpiper
- [ ] White-rumped Sandpiper
- [ ] Baird's Sandpiper
- [ ] Pectoral Sandpiper
- [ ] *Sharp-tailed Sandpiper*
- [ ] Dunlin
- [ ] *Curlew Sandpiper*
- [ ] Stilt Sandpiper
- [ ] Buff-breasted Sandpiper
- [ ] *Ruff*
- [ ] Short-billed Dowitcher
- [ ] Long-billed Dowitcher
- [ ] Wilson's Snipe
- [ ] American Woodcock
- [ ] Wilson's Phalarope
- [ ] Red-necked Phalarope
- [ ] *Red Phalarope*

Gulls & Allies (Laridae)
- [ ] *Pomarine Jaeger*
- [ ] *Parasitic Jaeger*
- [ ] *Long-tailed Jaeger*
- [ ] *Laughing Gull*
- [ ] Franklin's Gull
- [ ] *Little Gull*
- [ ] *Black-headed Gull*
- [ ] Bonaparte's Gull
- [ ] *Heermann's Gull*
- [ ] Ring-billed Gull

☐ California Gull
☐ Herring Gull
☐ *Thayer's Gull*
☐ *Iceland Gull*
☐ *Lesser Black-backed Gull*
☐ *Glaucous Gull*
☐ *Great Black-backed Gull*
☐ *Sabine's Gull*
☐ *Black-legged Kittiwake*
☐ *Ross's Gull*
☐ Caspian Tern
☐ Common Tern
☐ Forster's Tern
☐ Least Tern (en)
☐ Black Tern

Pigeons & Doves (Columbidae)
☐ Rock Pigeon (is)
☐ *Band-tailed Pigeon*
☐ Eurasian Collared-Dove (is)
☐ *White-winged Dove*
☐ Mourning Dove
☐ Passenger Pigeon (ex)
☐ *Inca Dove*
☐ *Common Ground-Dove*

Parrots (Psittacidae)
☐ Monk Parakeet (is)
☐ *Carolina Parakeet* (ex)

Cuckoos & Anis (Cuculidae)
☐ Black-billed Cuckoo
☐ Yellow-billed Cuckoo
☐ Greater Roadrunner
☐ *Groove-billed Ani*

Barn Owls (Tytonidae)
☐ Barn Owl

Owls (Strigidae)
☐ Western Screech-Owl
☐ Eastern Screech-Owl
☐ Snowy Owl

☐ *Northern Hawk Owl*
☐ Burrowing Owl
☐ Barred Owl
☐ *Great Gray Owl*
☐ Long-eared Owl
☐ Short-eared Owl
☐ *Boreal Owl*
☐ Northern Saw-whet Owl

Nightjars (Caprimulgidae)
☐ *Lesser Nighthawk*
☐ Common Nighthawk
☐ Common Poorwill
☐ Chuck-will's-widow
☐ Whip-poor-will

Swifts (Apodidae)
☐ Chimney Swift
☐ White-throated Swift

Hummingbirds (Trochilidae)
☐ *Green Violet-ear*
☐ *Magnificent Hummingbird*
☐ Ruby-throated Hummingbird
☐ Black-chinned Hummingbird
☐ *Anna's Hummingbird*
☐ *Calliope Hummingbird*
☐ *Broad-tailed Hummingbird*
☐ Rufous Hummingbird
☐ *Allen's Hummingbird*

Kingfishers (Alcedinidae)
☐ Belted Kingfisher

Woodpeckers (Picidae)
☐ Lewis's Woodpecker
☐ Red-headed Woodpecker
☐ *Acorn Woodpecker*

☐ Golden-fronted Woodpecker
☐ Red-bellied Woodpecker
☐ *Williamson's Sapsucker*
☐ Yellow-bellied Sapsucker
☐ Red-naped Sapsucker
☐ Ladder-backed Woodpecker
☐ Downy Woodpecker
☐ Hairy Woodpecker
☐ American Three-toed Woodpecker
☐ Black-backed Woodpecker
☐ Northern Flicker
☐ Pileated Woodpecker

Flycatchers (Tyrannidae)
☐ Olive-sided Flycatcher
☐ Western Wood-Pewee
☐ Eastern Wood-Pewee
☐ Yellow-bellied Flycatcher
☐ Acadian Flycatcher
☐ Alder Flycatcher
☐ Willow Flycatcher
☐ Least Flycatcher
☐ *Hammond's Flycatcher*
☐ Dusky Flycatcher
☐ Cordilleran Flycatcher
☐ Eastern Phoebe
☐ Say's Phoebe
☐ Vermilion Flycatcher
☐ Ash-throated Flycatcher
☐ Great Crested Flycatcher
☐ Cassin's Kingbird
☐ Western Kingbird
☐ Eastern Kingbird
☐ Scissor-tailed Flycatcher

Shrikes (Laniidae)
- [ ] Loggerhead Shrike
- [ ] Northern Shrike

Vireos (Vireonidae)
- [ ] White-eyed Vireo
- [ ] Bell's Vireo
- [ ] Black-capped Vireo (en)
- [ ] Yellow-throated Vireo
- [ ] Plumbeous Vireo
- [ ] *Cassin's Vireo*
- [ ] Blue-headed Vireo
- [ ] Warbling Vireo
- [ ] Philadelphia Vireo
- [ ] Red-eyed Vireo

Jays & Crows (Corvidae)
- [ ] Gray Jay
- [ ] *Steller's Jay*
- [ ] Blue Jay
- [ ] Western Scrub-Jay
- [ ] Pinyon Jay
- [ ] *Clark's Nutcracker*
- [ ] Black-billed Magpie
- [ ] American Crow
- [ ] Fish Crow
- [ ] Chihuahuan Raven
- [ ] Common Raven

Larks (Alaudidae)
- [ ] Horned Lark

Swallows (Hirundinidae)
- [ ] Purple Martin
- [ ] Tree Swallow
- [ ] Violet-green Swallow
- [ ] Northern Rough-winged Swallow
- [ ] Bank Swallow
- [ ] Cliff Swallow
- [ ] *Cave Swallow*
- [ ] Barn Swallow

Chickadees & Titmice (Paridae)
- [ ] Carolina Chickadee
- [ ] Black-capped Chickadee
- [ ] *Mountain Chickadee*
- [ ] *Boreal Chickadee*
- [ ] Juniper Titmouse
- [ ] Tufted Titmouse
- [ ] Black-crested Titmouse

Verdins (Remizidae)
- [ ] *Verdin*

Bushtits (Aegithalidae)
- [ ] *Bushtit*

Nuthatches (Sittidae)
- [ ] Red-breasted Nuthatch
- [ ] White-breasted Nuthatch
- [ ] Pygmy Nuthatch

Creepers (Certhiidae)
- [ ] Brown Creeper

Wrens (Troglodytidae)
- [ ] Rock Wren
- [ ] Canyon Wren
- [ ] Carolina Wren
- [ ] Bewick's Wren
- [ ] House Wren
- [ ] Winter Wren
- [ ] Sedge Wren
- [ ] Marsh Wren

Dippers (Cinclidae)
- [ ] *American Dipper*

Kinglets (Regulidae)
- [ ] Golden-crowned Kinglet
- [ ] Ruby-crowned Kinglet

Gnatcatchers (Sylviidae)
- [ ] Blue-gray Gnatcatcher

Thrushes (Turdidae)
- [ ] Eastern Bluebird
- [ ] Western Bluebird
- [ ] Mountain Bluebird
- [ ] Townsend's Solitaire
- [ ] Veery
- [ ] Gray-cheeked Thrush
- [ ] Swainson's Thrush
- [ ] Hermit Thrush
- [ ] Wood Thrush
- [ ] American Robin
- [ ] *Varied Thrush*

Mockingbirds & Thrashers (Mimidae)
- [ ] Gray Catbird
- [ ] Northern Mockingbird
- [ ] Sage Thrasher
- [ ] Brown Thrasher
- [ ] Curve-billed Thrasher

Starlings (Sturnidae)
- [ ] European Starling (is)

Pipits (Motacillidae)
- [ ] American Pipit
- [ ] Sprague's Pipit

Waxwings (Bombycillidae)
- [ ] Bohemian Waxwing
- [ ] Cedar Waxwing

Wood-warblers (Parulidae)
- [ ] Blue-winged Warbler
- [ ] Golden-winged Warbler
- [ ] Tennessee Warbler
- [ ] Orange-crowned Warbler
- [ ] Nashville Warbler
- [ ] Virginia's Warbler
- [ ] Northern Parula
- [ ] Yellow Warbler
- [ ] Chestnut-sided Warbler
- [ ] Magnolia Warbler
- [ ] Cape May Warbler

- [ ] *Black-throated Blue Warbler*
- [ ] Yellow-rumped Warbler
- [ ] *Black-throated Gray Warbler*
- [ ] Black-throated Green Warbler
- [ ] *Townsend's Warbler*
- [ ] *Hermit Warbler*
- [ ] Blackburnian Warbler
- [ ] Yellow-throated Warbler
- [ ] Pine Warbler
- [ ] Prairie Warbler
- [ ] Palm Warbler
- [ ] Bay-breasted Warbler
- [ ] Blackpoll Warbler
- [ ] Cerulean Warbler
- [ ] Black-and-white Warbler
- [ ] American Redstart
- [ ] Prothonotary Warbler
- [ ] Worm-eating Warbler
- [ ] Swainson's Warbler
- [ ] Ovenbird
- [ ] Northern Waterthrush
- [ ] Louisiana Waterthrush
- [ ] Kentucky Warbler
- [ ] *Connecticut Warbler*
- [ ] Mourning Warbler
- [ ] MacGillivray's Warbler
- [ ] Common Yellowthroat
- [ ] Hooded Warbler
- [ ] Wilson's Warbler
- [ ] Canada Warbler
- [ ] Yellow-breasted Chat

Tanagers (Thraupidae)
- [ ] Summer Tanager
- [ ] Scarlet Tanager
- [ ] Western Tanager

Sparrows & Allies (Emberizidae)
- [ ] Green-tailed Towhee
- [ ] Spotted Towhee
- [ ] Eastern Towhee
- [ ] Canyon Towhee
- [ ] Cassin's Sparrow
- [ ] Rufous-crowned Sparrow
- [ ] American Tree Sparrow
- [ ] Chipping Sparrow
- [ ] Clay-colored Sparrow
- [ ] Brewer's Sparrow
- [ ] Field Sparrow
- [ ] Vesper Sparrow
- [ ] Lark Sparrow
- [ ] Black-throated Sparrow
- [ ] *Sage Sparrow*
- [ ] Lark Bunting
- [ ] Savannah Sparrow
- [ ] Grasshopper Sparrow
- [ ] Baird's Sparrow
- [ ] Henslow's Sparrow
- [ ] Le Conte's Sparrow
- [ ] Nelson's Sharp-tailed Sparrow
- [ ] Fox Sparrow
- [ ] Song Sparrow
- [ ] Lincoln's Sparrow
- [ ] Swamp Sparrow
- [ ] White-throated Sparrow
- [ ] Harris's Sparrow
- [ ] White-crowned Sparrow
- [ ] Dark-eyed Junco
- [ ] McCown's Longspur
- [ ] Lapland Longspur
- [ ] Smith's Longspur
- [ ] Chestnut-collared Longspur
- [ ] Snow Bunting

Grosbeaks & Buntings (Cardinalidae)
- [ ] Northern Cardinal
- [ ] *Pyrrhuloxia*

- [ ] Rose-breasted Grosbeak
- [ ] Black-headed Grosbeak
- [ ] Blue Grosbeak
- [ ] Lazuli Bunting
- [ ] Indigo Bunting
- [ ] Painted Bunting
- [ ] Dickcissel

Blackbirds & Allies (Icteridae)
- [ ] Bobolink
- [ ] Red-winged Blackbird
- [ ] Eastern Meadowlark
- [ ] Western Meadowlark
- [ ] Yellow-headed Blackbird
- [ ] Rusty Blackbird
- [ ] Brewer's Blackbird
- [ ] Common Grackle
- [ ] Great-tailed Grackle
- [ ] Brown-headed Cowbird
- [ ] Orchard Oriole
- [ ] Bullock's Oriole
- [ ] Baltimore Oriole
- [ ] *Scott's Oriole*

Finches (Fringillidae)
- [ ] Gray-crowned Rosy-Finch
- [ ] Pine Grosbeak
- [ ] Purple Finch
- [ ] Cassin's Finch
- [ ] House Finch
- [ ] Red Crossbill
- [ ] White-winged Crossbill
- [ ] Common Redpoll
- [ ] *Hoary Redpoll*
- [ ] Pine Siskin
- [ ] Lesser Goldfinch
- [ ] American Goldfinch
- [ ] Evening Grosbeak

Old World Sparrows (Passeridae)
- [ ] House Sparrow (is)

INDEX OF SCIENTIFIC NAMES

This index references only the primary species accounts.

INDEX OF COMMON NAMES

Page numbers in **boldface** type refer to the primary, illustrated species accounts.

ABOUT THE AUTHORS

Bob Jennings began birding while still in graduate school, and his career as a naturalist and interpreter spanned over 30 years. He became the first director of the Oxley Nature Center and remained in that position for 25 years, until his retirement in 2002. Chasing birds took him from Attu Island in the Aleutians to Florida's Dry Tortugas, and from the Salton Sea to Nova Scotia, Canada. He edited two editions of *The Birds of Tulsa County, Oklahoma,* and wrote a book of essays, *From the Stump: Thoughts of a Naturalist.* The National Association for Interpretation (NAI) granted him the Master of Interpretation award in 1995 and named him a Fellow of the NAI, their highest honor, in 2004.

Ted T. Cable is a professor of Park Management and Conservation at Kansas State University. He has designed several nature parks and preserves and has consulted on conservation projects in more than 20 states and in Latin America and Africa. He is an author of more than 150 articles and presentations on conservation and five books, including *Commitments of the Heart: Odysseys in West African Conservation.* Both the U.S. Environmental Protection Agency and the U.S. Department of Agriculture have honored him for outstanding teaching in the field of environmental education. Like Bob Jennings, Dr. Cable has received the Master of Interpretation award and was named a Fellow of the NAI.

Roger Burrows has traveled North America extensively. While completing his BSc, he worked as a naturalist, interpretive planner and avifaunal consultant, and he has since worked as a bird identification workshop provider, avifaunal surveyor and naturalist on cruise ships. He has also coauthored a number of Lone Pine bird guides.